The Saint's Saints

Ancient Judaism & Early Christianity

Martin Hengel (Tübingen), Pieter W. van der Horst (Utrecht),
Martin Goodman (Oxford), Daniel R. Schwartz (Jerusalem),
Cilliers Breytenbach (Berlin), Friedrich Avemarie (Marburg),
Seth Schwartz (New York)

VOLUME LVIII

The Saint's Saints

Hagiography and Geography in Jerome

by

Susan Weingarten

BRILL
LEIDEN · BOSTON
2005

End Leaves: reproduction of map of the Holy Land after page 560 of Onomasticon urbium et locorum sacrae scripturae (1711)
Merton catalogue no. 95.EE.6(2)

This book is printed on acid-free paper.

Library of Congress Cataloging-in-Publication data

Weingarten, Susan.
  The saint's saints: hagiography and geography in Jerome/by Susan Weingarten.
    p. cm.—(Ancient Judaism & early Christianity, ISSN 0169-734X; v. 58)
  Includes bibliographical references (p. 000) and index.
  ISBN 90-04-14387-4 (alk. paper)
  1. Jerome, Saint, d. 419 or 20. 2. Christian hagiography. 3. Jerome, Saint, d. 419 or 20. Vita Pauli. 4. Paul, the Hermit, Saint, d. ca. 341. 5. Jerome, Saint, d. 419 or 20. Vita S. Hilarionis. 6. Hilary, Saint, Bishop of Poitiers, d. 367? 7. Jerome, Saint, d. 419 or 20. Vita Malchi monachi captivi. 8. Malchus, Saint. 9. Eusebius, of Caesarea, Bishop of Ceasarea, ca. 260–ca. 340. Onomasticon. 10. Bible—Geography. I. Title. II. Arbeiten zur Geschichte des antiken Judentums und des Urchistentums; Bd. 58. III. Series.

  BR65.J476W45 2005
  270.2'092—dc22

ISSN 0169-734X
ISBN 90 04 14387 4

PRINTED IN THE NETHERLANDS

For my father, who told me I would like Latin.

CONTENTS

ACKNOWLEDGEMENTS

This book has been many years in the making. It is now over ten years since I was examined on the *Life of Malchus* and accepted on to the straight track to a doctorate at Tel Aviv University. At that time I intended to see what evidence about the Holy Land in the fourth century could be found in Jerome's biblical commentaries, written as they were in Bethlehem. I found that there was less than I had expected, and that the commentaries were far less interesting than the '*Life of Malchus*' had been. So my plan changed. I still wanted to find what I could about Jerome's Holy Land, but I realised I needed some way of separating his *realia* from his rhetoric. I needed to analyse the way he wrote, and it seemed to me a good idea to start from his least realistic works, his saints' *Lives*, and to work from there. This book is the result.

Research for it has taken me to many libraries and to even more people. I could never have written it without the help of many librarians: Amira, Dolly, Jacqui, Sylvie, Yehudit, Zahava at Tel Aviv; Mary, Sahar and Sister Marianora at Tantur; Doris and Vicki in the Oriental Reading Room of the Bodleian, and others whose names I do not know in other Oxford libraries, at Göttingen and at Dumbarton Oaks. Libraries are also meeting places: I owe a great deal to my fellow MA and doctoral students with whom I spent many hours whispering in reading rooms and talking aloud in corridors and on staircases and even on occasion retiring to drink coffee together: Batya Dashti, Danny Goldenberg, Veronica Grimm, Tsiona Grossmark, Avi Laniado, Alla Stein, Perlina Varon, Uri Yiftach, and the late Aaron Sadeh. Above all Yuval Shahar, fellow student and good friend, to whom I owe the sub-title—and much more. And of course there are my fellow students in the virtual library of the aether, in particular Laura Holt and Andrew Jacobs, both of whom filled in many holes in my knowledge of late antique Christianity.

I am immensely grateful too to the scholars in Israel and abroad who gave me some of their time and shared their knowledge of Jerome: Peter Brown, Averil Cameron, Joshua Efron, Peter Garnsey, Nicholas de Lange, John Matthews, Ze'ev Rubin, David Satran. I am grateful too in another way to those who showed me what I did not want to do, Sally Humphreys and Aviad Kleinberg.

A long-standing debt I owe to my teachers over the years, beginning with Rabbi Arthur Kohn in Wallasey and Rabbi Irving Jacobs in Ilford who taught me at cheder, continuing with Mary M. Innes who taught me Latin at Woodford County High School and Elizabeth Mackenzie who showed me a scholarly approach to literature at Lady Margaret Hall, Oxford. So too my teachers at Tel Aviv: Raḥel Birnbaum and Rafi Freundlich for Latin and Greek; Moshe Fischer and Israel Roll who introduced me with enthusiasm to the archaeology of the classical world and Aharon Oppenheimer who painstakingly taught me the critical appraisal of Talmudic sources. More than all these, my doctoral supervisor Ben Isaac listened with patience, criticised constructively and showed me by example what scholarship should be.

Rewriting my thesis as a book has not been as easy as I expected. I am very grateful to the anonymous readers of my thesis for their comments, to Fergus Millar and Martin Goodman who also read the thesis and made helpful suggestions for turning it into a book and to Brill's reader who saved me from some of my own mistakes.

The map on the endpapers is reproduced from Jacob Bonfrere's edition of the *Onomasticon* (Amsterdam, 1711) by kind permission of the Warden and Fellows of Merton College, Oxford.

I have to thank my children, Neḥama, Miri, Bitya, Amos and Milca, for their forbearance: the phenomenon of a mother studying Christian religious literature was not easy to explain in their orthodox Jewish social context: they bore this cross well.

But there is nobody like Micky.

Tel Aviv, 2004

ABBREVIATIONS

Abbreviations of titles of journals follow the *Année Philologique*.
Abbreviations of ancient Greek and Latin authors follow L&S.
Abbreviations of books of the Bible follow *COD*.
Abbreviations of Jerome's works are noted under Texts.

ABD	D.N. Freedman *et al.* (eds) *Anchor Bible Dictionary* (NY etc., 1992)
ann.	annotations
ANRW	H. Temporini *et al.* (eds) *Aufstieg und Niedergang der römischen Welt* (Berlin, 1972–)
b.	*ben, bar* (Hebrew, Aramaic = son)
Blaise	A. Blaise *Dictionnaire latin-français des auteurs chrétiens* (Turnhout, 1954 repr. 1993)
BMC	Catalogue of coins in the British Museum
BT	Babylonian Talmud
CAH	Cambridge Ancient History
Cavallera	F. Cavallera *Saint Jérôme: sa vie et son oeuvre* (Louvain, 1922)
CC	Corpus Christianorum
CCSL	*Corpus Christianorum, Series Latina*
CETEDOC	Cetedoc library of Christian Latin texts on CD ROM: CLCLT-2 (Turnhout, 1994).
CIL	*Corpus Inscriptionum Latinarum*
Clavis G	M. Geerard *Clavis Patrum Graecorum* (Turnhout, 1983–7)
Clavis L	E. Dekkers *Clavis Patrum Latinorum* (Turnhout, 1961)
COD	Concise Oxford Dictionary, fifth edition, (Oxford, 1964)
com.	commentary
CSCO	*Corpus Scriptorum Christianorum Orientalium*
CSEL	*Corpus Scriptorum Ecclesiasticorum Latinorum*
CTh	*Codex Theodosianus*
DACL	F. Cabrol, C. Leclerq, H. Marrou *Dictionnaire d'archéologie chrétienne et de liturgie* (Paris, 1924–53)
EccR	Midrash Ecclesiastes Rabbah
ed(s)	editor(s)
ep.	*epistula*

esp.	especially
EstR	Midrash Esther Rabbah
GCS	*Die griechischen christlichen Schriftsteller der ersten drei Jahrhunderte*
GenR	Midrash Genesis Rabbah
Grützmacher	G. Grützmacher *Hieronymus: Eine biographische Studie* I–III (Berlin 1901, 1906, 1908, repr. Aalen, 1969)
Hagendahl	H. Hagendahl *Latin Fathers and the Classics* (Göteborg, 1958)
Hunt	E.D. Hunt *Holy Land Pilgrimage in the Later Roman Empire AD 312–460* (Oxford, 1982)
Intr.	introduction
JT	Jerusalem Talmud
Kelly	J.N.D. Kelly *Jerome: His Life, Writings and Controversies* (London, 1975)
LCL	Loeb Classical Library, (Harvard/London)
L&S	C.T. Lewis, C. Short *A Latin Dictionary* (Oxford, 1879 repr. 1993)
LIMC	Lexikon Iconographicum Mythologiae Classicae *(Zurich/Munich, 1981–)*
LRE	A.H.M. Jones *The Later Roman Empire 284–602* I–II (Oxford 1964, repr. 1990)
MGH	*Monumenta Germaniae Historiae*
MidPs	Midrash Psalms
NEAEHL	E. Stern *et al.* (eds) *The New Encyclopedia of Archaeological Excavations in the Holy Land* (Jerusalem, 1993)
Newman	H. Newman *Jerome and the Jews* (Ph.D., Jerusalem, 1997) (Hebrew with English summary)
OS	old series
N.T.	New Testament
PG	*Patrologia Graeca*
PL	*Patrologia Latina*
PLRE	A.H.M. Jones, J.R. Martindale, J. Morris *The Prosopography of the Later Roman Empire AD 260–395* I (Cambridge, 1971)
PRE	Pauly-Wissowa, *Realencyclopädie der classischen Altertumswissenschaft*
PTL	*PTL: a journal for descriptive poetics and theory of literature*
R.	Rabbi, Rav

RAC	T. Klausner *et al.* (eds.) *Reallexikon für Antike und Christentum* (Stuttgart, 1950–)
Rebenich	S. Rebenich *Hieronymus und sein Kreis: Prosopographische und Sozialgeschichtliche Untersuchungen* (Stuttgart, 1992)
repr.	reprinted
Roscher	W.H. Roscher *Ausfürliches Lexikon der griechischen und römischen Mythologie* (Leipzig, 1884–6; repr. Hildesheim, 1965)
RSbY	Rabbi Shimʿon bar Yohai
R.V.	Revised Version (of Bible)
SC	*Sources Chrétiennes*
SHA	*Scriptores Historiae Augustae*
SP	*Studia Patristica*
TIR	Y. Tsafrir, L. Di Segni, J. Green *Tabula Imperii Romani: Iudaea-Palaestina* (Jerusalem, 1994)
TLL	*Thesaurus linguae Latinae*
tr., trans.	translation
TRE	G. Krause, G. Müller *et al.* (eds) *Theologische Realenzyklopädie* (Berlin, 1976–)
v.	*vita*
Wilkinson	J. Wilkinson *Jerusalem Pilgrims before the Crusades* (Jerusalem, 1977)

INTRODUCTION

Jerome's Saints' *Lives*

In this book, I look at Jerome's saints' *Lives* as evidence of his world. The *Lives* are independent literary compositions—they are not dependent on books of the Bible, like his *Commentaries*, or on a particular recipient, like his *Letters*, or on an issue, like his polemic. In the *Lives* Jerome was free to present his world as he saw it, and as he would like it to be seen: they combine rhetoric with *realia*. I shall attempt to analyse his methods of writing in order to see how this is done and whether it is possible to disentangle the two. Jerome's saints' *Lives* comprise his *Lives* of Paul the hermit, of Hilarion, and of Malchus the captive monk. I shall also be looking at his letter to Eustochium, *ep.* 108, which was written as a life of his friend Paula, and has also been published as a saint's *Life*.[1] The *Life* of Paul heads Jerome's list of his own works in his *de viris illustribus*, and was written no later than 380 CE; the *Lives* of Hilarion and Malchus were written around 390–1, while the *Life* of Paula contained in *ep.* 108 was written after Paula's death in 404.[2] I shall analyse the texts of each of these works separately, to distinguish between the different levels of reality in Jerome's *Lives*.

Jerome's first hero, Paul the hermit, appears to be the least real. Jerome himself writes that many people doubted whether Paul ever existed. Such doubts persist to the present day. In considering the *vita Pauli*, I shall be looking at historical parallels to some of the details of the *Life*, as well as Jerome's use of his own experience, both actual and literary, to build layers of meaning and metaphor.

---

[1] See under Texts in Bibliography for details of the editions used here.

[2] Dates: Kelly pp. 60f. (*vita Pauli*); 170f. (*vita Malchi* and *vita Hilarionis*); 277f. (*ep.* 108). Kelly thinks both the *vita Malchi* and the *vita Hilarionis* were written in Bethlehem at about the same time, together with *de viris illustribus*, although he thinks the *vita Malchi* pre-dates the *vita Hilarionis*. However, his arguments against Cavallera's earlier dating mean that there is no longer any need to give precedence to the *vita Malchi*. Although Jerome places the *vita Hilarionis* after the *vita Malchi* in *de viris* cxxxv, he refers to the reception of the *vita Pauli* only in his preface to the *vita Hilarionis*, which would seem to indicate that the *vita Malchi* had not been written yet.

Here I shall be concerned with analysing the autobiographical elements in this *Life*, which deals with withdrawal from the world. The hero, Paul, asks three questions about the state of the world he has left behind him: what new roofs rise in the ancient cities, what power now rules the world, and who remains in the power of the demons? The answers to these questions are central to Jerome's agenda, as in all his saints' *Lives*, which deal with the acting out of the process of Christianisation. I shall also be considering here the question of whether Jerome used and Christianised Jewish aggadic sources about Rabbi Shim'on bar Yohai to build his own picture of the ascetic saint.

The longest of Jerome's saints' *Lives* is his *vita Hilarionis*. Jerome says he got all his information about this hero from his friend Epiphanius bishop of Salamis, who had known Hilarion and written a brief letter about him.[3] There are independent details of Hilarion's life and activities in Palestine from Sozomenus, who wrote around the middle of the fifth century.[4] Jerome's *Life* is about the saint and his relationship with society, and the process of Christianisation of the Roman empire. Thus it encompasses both Palestine, the Christian Holy Land where Christianity is beginning to win significant victories but where the process is far from complete, as well as the whole of the rest of the empire. Jerome is concerned both with the physical world and with the world of literature: I shall look here in some detail at his appropriation of the ancient novel and its conversion to Jerome's ascetic Christianity. I shall also look at the confrontation of the holy man with popular culture and pagan cults. This *Life* can be seen as a microcosm of the whole of the Roman world—both in terms of space and in terms of the social structure, the whole epitomised in a chariot race at the centre of the work.

Jerome tells us that he actually met the monk Malchus, the hero of the *vita Malchi*, in person, and heard his story from his own mouth.

---

[3] *vita Hilarionis* 1: *Epiphanius ... qui cum Hilarione plurimum versatus est, laudem ejus brevi epistula scripserit.*

[4] Sozomenus: *H.E.* 3, 14, 21 (*PG* 67, 1076). Date: Sozomène: *Histoire Ecclésiastique* I–II (*SC* 306, ed. G. Sabbah, Paris, 1983) 25–31. See on this B. Bitton-Ashkelony & A. Kofsky 'The monasticism of Gaza in the Byzantine period *Cathedra* 96 (2000, in Hebrew with English summary) 69f.

There seems little reason to doubt this, but the story has been written up as a new literary creation. The background is fourth century
Mesopotamia and I shall attempt to unravel Jerome's closely knit
fabric of reality, metaphor and stereotype using contemporary local
material from Ammianus and the Babylonian Talmud. We shall also
see how he makes use of both biblical and classical models to make
up his picture of the ascetic subjugation of sexuality, which once
again contains many autobiographical elements.

Finally Jerome's last saint's *Life, ep.* 108, was written as a *Life* of
Paula, who was undoubtedly his real friend and companion for many
years. It has long been used as a source of information about the
Holy Land in the fourth century.[5] However, it was clear to me even
on first reading that *ep.* 108 is a carefully contrived rhetorical product, and as such may not always be so reliable as evidence of the
realia of fourth century Palestine. Classical historians, including his
contemporary Ammianus, commonly included geographical *excursus*
in their works, and Jerome includes an account of the pilgrimage
he made together with Paula round the Holy Places. This *Life* deals
with yet another Christian appropriation, that of the Holy Land.
Jerome had already translated into Latin for western Christians the
book of the Holy Land as it was in ancient times, the Bible. Around
390 he had also set himself to translate the book of the new Christian
Holy Land, Eusebius' *Onomasticon*. Here he provides answers to the
question of the *vita Pauli*, what new roofs rise in ancient cities, for
he adds to the text details of all the new churches built since Eusebius
wrote. Comparison of his translation of the *Onomasticon* with the *Life*
of Paula, together with a close look at some of the vocabulary of
the text, will be used as an aid in disentangling his rhetoric from
his *realia*. The rhetorical elements will also be placed in context of
the various classical genre forms he uses in the letter: *consolatio, iter,
propempticon, encomium, epitaphium.*

There are clearly differences in the geographical settings of Jerome's

---

[5] See, for example, M. Avi-Yonah *Gazetteer of Roman Palestine* (Jerusalem, 1976);
TIR. Particularly noticeable is the tendency to extract the account of Paula's journey from its context and treat it as a document standing alone: A. Stewart, C.W.
Wilson (ed. and tr.) *The Pilgrimage of the Holy Paula by St. Jerome* (PPTS, London,
1887); F. Stummer *Monumenta historiam et geographiam Terrae Sanctae illustrantia* (Bonn,
1935); J. Wilkinson *Jerusalem Pilgrims before the Crusades* (Jerusalem, 1977); O. Limor
Holy Land Travels: Christian Pilgrims in Late Antiquity (Jerusalem, 1998, in Hebrew).

Lives. The *vita Pauli*, Jerome's first saint's *Life*, is set in the Egyptian desert which Jerome knew only by repute, and contains many symbolic, miraculous and mythological elements. The *vita Hilarionis* is set in Palestine where Jerome was living himself, and the *vita Malchi* is an account told to Jerome by its hero who experienced its Mesopotamian setting. The *vitae* of Hilarion and Malchus are both delicately poised between metaphor and reality, often flashing back and forth between the two. The *Life* of Paula brings us full circle. On the one hand, it is an account of the saint's actual life including the real journey which she took along the roads of Palestine in Jerome's company. But the other, divine world is there too and for Jerome and Paula it is arguably even more 'real.' Here the saint's journey is on two levels, both a spiritual and physical progress, culminating at Bethlehem, the site of the incarnation and birth of Jesus, as well as the life and death of Paula, and her spiritual rebirth. However, Jerome integrates *realia* in even the most rhetorical of his productions and rhetoric even in the most realistic. My analysis aims to see how he does this, and how it might to be possible to separate the two strands.

Jerome's *Lives* are the first hagiography written in Latin, following the success of the Greek *Life of Antony* attributed to Athanasius. As such, they were immensely popular, judging from the huge number of surviving manuscripts and large number of translations.[6] Jerome did not create his works *ex nihilo*, as it were. There was a long classical tradition of ancient biography,[7] as distinct from history and novel-writing.[8] Jerome himself also wrote brief biographies on the

---

[6] B. Lambert *Bibliotheca Hieronymi manuscripta* (Steenbrugge, 1969–1972).

[7] Cf. Plutarch: *Life of Alexander* i.2. Polybius: x.24. On ancient biography see e.g. A. Momigliano *The development of Greek biography* (Cambridge Mass./London, 1971 repr. 1993); F.B. Titchener 'Autobiography and the Hellenistic Age' in F.B. Titchener & R.F. Moorton, Jr. *The Eye Expanded: Life and the Arts in Greco-Roman Antiquity* (Berkeley etc., 1999) 155–163. B. Baldwin *Suetonius* (Amsterdam, 1983) has a useful summary of Latin biography: chapter 3, 'Biography at Rome.' Late antiquity: A. Momigliano 'Pagan and Christian historiography in the fourth century AD' in *id. Essays in ancient and modern historiography* (Oxford, 1947, repr. 1977) 107f. = *id.* (ed.) *The conflict between Paganism and Christianity in the fourth century* (Oxford, 1963) 79–99; R. Syme *Emperors and biography: Studies in the Historia Augusta* (Oxford, 1971); P. Cox *Biography in Late Antiquity: A Quest for the Holy Man* (Berkeley, 1983) esp. p. xiv, and now M.J. Edwards & S. Swain *Portraits: Biographical representation in the Greek and Latin literature of the Roman Empire* (Oxford, 1997).

[8] On ancient history as a literary enterprise, see especially A.J. Woodman *Rhetoric in Classical Historiography: Four Studies* (London etc., 1988); G.W. Bowersock *Fiction as*

model of the lost biographies of Suetonius—*de viris illustribus.*[9] Although the saints' *Lives* were intended, he says, specifically as Christian biographies, the criteria he uses to judge his Christian heroes are not their Christian acts or beliefs, but their classical style. Full-length classical biography dealt more with a man's life[10] as moral exemplar than with the acts that were left to history. It included panegyrical exaggerations of the hero's achievements or his faults and weaknesses, and idealised types of individuals, especially philosophers and kings. By the fourth century however, these classical lines were less clear, so that the author of the *Historia Augusta* included much strange, exotic and even ridiculous material in his *Lives* of the later Roman emperors.[11] Thus I shall be using these contemporary parallels when this can enlighten my discussion, like the work of the serious historian Ammianus Marcellinus. Thus I shall be looking at the moral purposes of each of Jerome's saints' *Lives* as well as Jerome's literary style and in particular his rhetorical methods and use of vocabulary. I shall also be looking at how far an autobiographical element is present in the saints' *Lives* and how it affects them.

Apart from his classical background, as a Christian author Jerome had before him the example of the Bible. By his time it had become common for Christians to read the Hebrew Bible as metaphorically pre-shadowing the New Testament, providing *typoi* which prefigured the heroes of the New Testament. Jerome discusses this in his *ep.* 53. These types had found their way into Christian literature too, and the lives of Christian heroes were often represented on biblical patterns. The Bible did not provide full enough details of the lives of its heroes to satisfy many readers: Jewish *aggadah* and Christian *acta* supplied this deficiency, and often underlined the moral of the story.[12]

History: Nero to Julian (Berkeley etc., 1994); J. Marincola *Authority and tradition in ancient historiography* (Cambridge, 1997).

[9] On Suetonius' lost illustrious men see A. Wallace-Hadrill *Suetonius: the Scholar and his Caesars* (London, 1983) 50f.

[10] I do not know of an ancient classical biography of a woman until the *Historia Augusta's Life of Zenobia*, no. 30 of the *Thirty Pretenders*, followed by Victoria (no. 31!), which are included as mockery—*ad ludibrium.*

[11] For the modern debate as to whether Jerome preceded the *Historia Augusta* or vice versa, see the convenient summary in N. Adkin 'The *Historia Augusta* and Jerome again' *Klio* 79 (1997) 459–467 with bibliography.

[12] See now on the *acta* as Christian novels: G. Huber-Rebenich 'Hagiographic fiction as entertainment' in H. Hofmann (ed.) *Latin fiction: The Latin novel in context* (London/NY 1999) 187–212 esp. 190–192.

Some of the heroes and heroines of the *acta* died a martyr's death; the *passiones* were accounts of the deaths of the early martyrs and were read in churches on the anniversaries of their deaths. Once the empire was Christianised and persecution of Christians ceased, the 'daily martyrdom' of the ascetic way of life was considered to be the successor to death as a martyr. Thus the *Lives* of ascetic saints can be seen (with hindsight) as a natural development of Christian literature.[13] The author of the *Life of Antony* had used both his Christian heritage and his classical one: there are even echoes of the Hellenistic novel to be heard in his *Life* and he writes of Antony's βίος and his πολιτεία like the writer of any classical biography. Jerome follows him in this when he writes of Hilarion's *conversatio vitaque*.[14] However, unlike a classical biography, the *Life* of Antony was to be a pattern of asceticism for monks: ἔστι γὰρ μοναχοῖς ἱκανὸς χαρακτὴρ πρὸς ἄσκησιν ὁ Ἀντωνίου βίος. This was clearly Jerome's primary source, as he writes himself, and this has been discussed by a number of scholars.[15] Biblical types are also an important part of his work: in his saints' *Lives* Jerome is sometimes overt about this—Paul is explicitly compared to Elijah, John the Baptist and Jesus, but other types are to be inferred by his reader. I shall be looking in particular at how some of these less explicit types dictate the presentation of his material in the first three *Lives*, and how the biblical 'type' of *ep.* 108 is the Holy Land itself. Analysis of the types can help distinguish between *realia* and rhetoric in his works.

I have already pointed out how Jerome appropriates parts of his world in the service of christianisation—the classical novel for example, or the Holy Land. This may be seen not only as a literary device but as polemic. Patricia Cox has written of ancient *Lives* 'not only as models for the perpetuation of particular philosophical schools, but also as polemics to be employed in furthering one tradition at the expense of others.'[16] Jerome was heavily involved in written

---

[13] Cf. E. Hendrikx 'Saint Jérôme en tant que hagiographe' *La Ciudad de Dios* 181 (1968) 662.

[14] *vH praef.*

[15] See A.A.R. Bastiaensen 'Jérôme hagiographe' *CC Hagiographies: International History of the Latin and Vernacular Hagiographical Literature in the West from its origins to 1550*, vol. I (Turnhout, 1994) 107f., with bibliography.

[16] P. Cox *op. cit.* n. 7 above.

polemics throughout his life. His saints' *Lives* also express his polemical presentation of Christian appropriation of various parts of the world around him. Thus I shall be considering whether Jerome made use of Jewish *aggadot* in the *vita Pauli* as a sub-text of anti-Jewish polemic. It has been claimed that in his other works Jerome does not engage in polemic against the pagan world.[17] In his saints' *Lives* at least, he makes use of Apuleius and Virgil for a confrontation with paganism in the *Lives* of Hilarion and Malchus, for the Christian appropriation of the classical literary heritage was most important to him. Regarding *ep.* 108, I shall be looking at his presentation of the christianisation of the Holy Land, using his translation and adaptation of Eusebius' *Onomasticon* as collateral evidence. Furthermore, I shall consider Jerome's geographical concepts in general against the background of recent discussions of ancient geography. There is little Christian geography before Jerome, for earlier Christians were more interested in the celestial rather than the terrestrial Holy Land. All this changed in the fourth century following Constantine. Finally, I shall look at the mixture of genres in which *ep.* 108 was written to see how far the genre forms could have influenced the contents of the letter, in particular the geographical excursus, the *iter* of Paula's pilgrimage, which it contains. Latin literature of the fourth century was characterised by a mixing of previously separate literary genres. I shall be looking at Jerome's writing to see the use he makes of different genre forms, and how this may affect the interpretation of what he writes as *realia* or rhetoric.

Before turning to the actual saints' *Lives*, however, I would like to look briefly at those details of Jerome's own life that are relevant to this book, since one of the subjects I will be treating is the autobiographical element in these biographies.

JEROME'S LIFE

'Jerome, son of Eusebius, of the town of Stridon which was overthrown by the Goths and was once at the border of Dalmatia and

---

[17] B. Bitton-Ashkelony *Pilgrimage: Perceptions and reactions in the patristic and monastic literature of the fourth–sixth centuries* (Ph.D. thesis, Jerusalem, 1995) (Hebrew with English summary).

Pannonia'[18] writes thus of himself in the last entry of his catalogue of Famous Men. His date of birth is disputed—either 331 or 347— and the site of his birthplace has not been identified.[19]

Education

Jerome presumably received his elementary education in Stridon, but was sent to Rome for his secondary education, rather than to one of the nearer provincial centres, such as Emona (present day Ljubljana) or the city of Aquileia.[20] At Rome he studied with the *grammaticus* Donatus, celebrated (and not just by Jerome) for his two grammar books and his commentaries on Virgil and Terence.[21] From Donatus he would ideally have learned what Quintilian calls '*orbis ille doctrinae quem Graeci* ἐγκύκλιον παιδείαν *vocant*,'[22] or, in Jerome's own words *liberal[ia] stud[ia]*,[23] including geometry, arithmetic, astronomy and music, but with Donatus as teacher the stress would naturally have been on grammar and classical literature. Sallust and Cicero will have been added to Virgil and Terence as the authors most studied, and it is these four who are most loved and quoted by Jerome throughout his life.[24] It is clear that Jerome did not study Greek to

---

[18] *De viris illustribus* cxxxv: *Hieronymus, natus patre Eusebio, oppido Stridonis, quod a Gothis eversum Dalmatiae quondam Pannoniaeque confinium fuit.*

[19] Date of birth: see Kelly, Appendix: the date of Jerome's birth p. 337f. and bibliography *ad loc*. The *oppidum* of Stridon has not been certainly identified archaeologically and is not mentioned at all elsewhere.

[20] For Roman education in general, see the classic study of H.I. Marrou *Histoire de l'éducation dans l'antiquité* (Paris, 1944), and now R. Kaster *Guardians of Language* Berkeley/LA/London 1988; W.V. Harris *Ancient Literacy* (Cambridge, Mass./London, 1989).

Jerome later shows many connections with Emona and Aquileia as well as other towns in the area (Kelly p. 4). For a convenient summary and bibliography see M. Buora, I.L. Plesnicar Gec *Aquileia Emona: Archeologia fra due regioni dalla preistoria al medioevo* (Udine, 1989).

[21] For the functions of the *grammaticus* see now Kaster *op. cit.* above. For Donatus *id.* p. 275f.

[22] Quintilian *Inst.* 1, 10, 1.

[23] *Com. in Hiez.* xl 5–13 (*CCSL* 75, 556f.; *PL* 25, 392): *Dum essem Romae puer et liberalibus studiis erudirer.*

[24] For Jerome's education see Kelly 10–17; for the Latin classics he quotes see A. Lübeck *Hieronymus quos noverit scriptores et ex quibus hauserit* (Leipzig, 1872); H. Hagendahl *Latin Fathers and the Classics* (Göteborg, 1958). Most work done since Hagendahl has added very little to the knowledge of Jerome's pagan Latin sources, as can be seen from titles such as Alan Cameron 'Echoes of Vergil in St Jerome's *Life of St Hilarion*' *Classical Philology* 63 (1968) 55–6, which provides four 'echoes.'

the same level as Latin, for Greek studies had declined considerably since the time of Cicero. How much Greek he learned, and when, has been the subject of debate. He may have gained a very elementary grounding in Rome, for Donatus used Greek technical terms. But unlike Latin pagan authors, whom he quotes often in his works, he does not quote any of the Greek pagan authors. Those he implies he has read he may have known in translation—or he may be exaggerating his knowledge. There is general agreement among scholars that he did not study Greek seriously until his stay in Antioch, and then he only read authors of interest to himself as a Christian ascetic.[25] This will be discussed in chapter 2.

After his secondary education with Donatus, Jerome would have continued in a Roman school of rhetoric.[26] He learned his lessons well: I shall discuss his very skilled use of the arts of rhetoric in his later prose writings, both letters and saint's *Lives*. It is clear that he received legal training, as he writes in *Com. in Gal.* 2,1 (*PL* 26, 408), and he shows considerable knowledge of Roman law and its settings and procedures.[27]

Life in Rome

Before his baptism, Jerome writes that he led a wild life as a young man in Rome, which made him feel guilty in later life. Scholars have cast doubt on this, seeing it as Jerome's usual tendency to exaggeration, or possibly the tendency of the newly religious to magnify their pre-conversion misdemeanours. Kelly thinks we should take Jerome at his word about his sexual adventures: 'in youth and young manhood he was strongly sexed', but is not so disposed to take his word about his schoolboy enjoyment of obscene literature, including 'Milesian tales', which, Kelly feels 'are not necessarily reminiscences of his own youthful experiences.'[28] The discussion of Jerome's use of

---

[25] This is the general scholarly consensus. For example F. Cavallera *Saint Jérôme: sa vie et son oeuvre* (Louvain, 1922): 'du grec il n'était alors plus sérieusement question dans l'enseignement occidental et en général on se contentait d'en apprendre les éléments'. See too the discussion of P. Courcelle *Late Latin Writers and their Greek Sources* (Eng. tr. Cambridge, Mass., 1969) 58–89.

[26] See Marrou *op. cit.*; Kelly 14–16 and now M. Gleason *Making Men: Sophists and Self-Presentation in Ancient Rome* (Princeton, 1995) esp. 103f.

[27] For Jerome's legal knowledge: G. Violardo *Il pensiero giuridico di san Girolamo* (Milan, 1937).

[28] Kelly 20–21. Jerome on Milesian tales: *Apol. contra Ruf.* i, 17 (*CCSL* 79, 17;

Apuleius in his *vita Hilarionis* in chapter 2 will point out that, on the contrary, there are many reasons for taking Jerome at his word about his reading, for he displays intimate acquaintance with the 'Milesian tales' of Apuleius.

However, Jerome came from a Christian family and some of his companions came from a similar background. Christianity eventually took a firmer hold of him than his wilder pursuits, and he decided to be baptised as a Christian[29]—a serious step, which many contemporary Christians preferred to postpone: Constantine, for example was not baptised until on his deathbed.

During his time as a student, Jerome records going with friends to visit the underground tombs of 'apostles and martyrs' in the catacombs of Rome. His graphic description, embellished with quotations from both Virgil and the Psalms, appears in his Commentary on Ezekiel written at the end of his life, but the boyhood memory is still vivid, of walking in darkness like that of Hell, pierced by rare beams of light.[30] The catacombs were refurbished by Jerome's patron Pope Damasus, who put up plaques with his own poetry. They were ornamented with paintings on walls and ceilings, and contained carved sarcophagi, with subjects including Daniel in the Lions' Den.[31] In chapter 1 there is a suggestion that traces of memories of some of these paintings may be found in Jerome's *vita Pauli*.

Trier and Aquileia

There is very little extant information for the years immediately following Jerome's student days in Rome. It is clear that he spent time at Trier near the 'semi-barbarian' banks of the Rhine.[32] Trier was at the time an imperial centre and it has been suggested that Jerome

---

PL 23, 412) *Quasi non cirratorum turba Milesiarum in scholis figmenta decantent.* Cf. *Com. in Es.* xii, *praef.* (*CCSL* 73a, 465; *PL* 24, 419).

[29] *epp.* 15,1; 16,2.

[30] *Com. in Hiez.* xl 5–13 (*CCSL* 75, 556–7; *PL* 25, 392).

[31] For a convenient summary on the catacombs, J. Stevenson *The Catacombs: Rediscovered monuments of early Christianity* (London, 1978). Daniel and lions p. 80 and pls. 41, 52. Note that pl. 52, where Daniel appears prominently in the centre of a ceiling, is taken from the catacomb of Peter and Marcellinus, which has an inscription by Damasus.

[32] *Rheni semibarbaras ripas* (*ep.* 3, 5). This is discussed below in chapter 2.2.1b.

had hopes of a career in the public service.[33] However it is clear that, on the contrary, fourth century Trier acted as incitement to an ascetic life and not only for Jerome, for his contemporary Augustine writes of the considerable influence of the arrival of a copy of the *vita Antonii*, attributed to Athanasius of Alexandria, on people in the city.[34]

After his stay at Trier Jerome seems to have spent time nearer home in the growing Christian centre of Aquileia, with its magnificent fourth century basilical church.[35] He certainly had connections in this area around the north of the Adriatic—in his birth-place at Stridon, as well as at Concordia and Emona.[36] Some scandal led to his leaving the area, but no details are available.[37] This was the first, but by no means the last time he was involved in bitter accusations and recriminations.

Antioch and Constantinople

Thus probably in 372 Jerome travelled to the East, via Asia Minor. It was at one time thought that he visited Jerusalem for the first time on this journey, but the consensus now is that he never went there at this time.[38] Jerome arrived in Antioch sometime around 373 and stayed in the city with the priest Evagrius, friend of Pope Damasus and translator of the *vita Antonii*. Presumably it was here that he

---

[33] See on this Kelly p. 29f. with bibliography ad loc.; Cavallera i, 17; Rebenich 32f.

[34] Augustine *Confessions* viii, 14–15. Cf. *ib.* viii, 29 (ed. J.J. O'Donnell [Oxford, 1992]) 94–5; 101; *PL* 32, 659).

[35] The huge church of Aquileia with its two mosaic floored basilical halls was built by Bishop Theodore in the first decades of the fourth century. See L. Marcuzzi, M. Zanette *Aquileia* (Aquileia, 1993).

[36] Jerome's *ep.* 10 to the aged Paul of Concordia accompanied a copy of his *Vita Pauli*. See below chapter 1. His *epp.* 1, 3, 5–14 and esp. 11 are addressed to nuns at Emona.

[37] Kelly 33–35.

[38] Cf. Cavallera, i, 87; Kelly p. 41 who cites *ep.* 5, 1 which shows him abandoning this project; Rebenich p. 85. C. Krumeich *Hieronymus und die christlichen Feminae clarissimae* (Bonn, 1993) 355f. twice has Jerome in Jerusalem in 372, but she seems to be relying here on the outdated chronology of *DACL* 14, 65–176 'Pèlerinages aux lieux saints' (Leclerq). Leclerq and other earlier scholars seem to have taken Jerome's statement in his preface to his translation of Didymus of Alexandria's *de Spiritu Sancto* (*PL* 23, 101): *Jerosolymam sum reversus* as relating to the earthly, rather than the heavenly Jerusalem. See on this chapter 3.1.1. The body in law—*postliminium*, below.

learned Greek, for he stayed for at least two years, partly he says, because of repeated bouts of illness. It may have been at this time that he had his famous dream, of being taken before a Judge and being accused of being a Ciceronian, not a Christian.[39] As a result he seems to have forsworn reading pagan literature for a time, until he came to terms with himself.[40] Antioch at this time was one of the great imperial centres, the residence of the eastern emperor Valens.[41] Nearby Daphne was famous—or notorious—for its plea- sure gardens and temple of Apollo, while Antioch itself had a magnificent imperial palace, a hippodrome and many theatres and bath houses. There was also a growing number of Christian churches but evidently the atmosphere in the city was such that some young Christians chose in contrast to devote themselves to an ascetic life. Between the years 372–8 John Chrysostom withdrew to the caves of Mount Silpius above the city to lead first a semi-communal, then a solitary monastic life.[42] Late in 374 or early in 375 Jerome too retreated from Antioch to the 'desert of Chalcis.' It was probably here that he wrote his *vita Pauli*, before he became disillusioned with his retreat.[43] This retreat has been much discussed recently, partic- ularly by Stefan Rebenich,[44] who develops the suggestion that Jerome did not live in a cave in the desert as is usually depicted in later art. Indeed, Jerome says he had his whole library there, and slaves

---

[39] *ep.* 22, 30.

[40] *ep.* 70. See on this H. Hagendahl *Latin Fathers and the Classics* (Göteborg, 1958) and chapter 2.1.7. below.

[41] For late antique Antioch see P. Petit *Libanius et la vie municipale à Antioche au IVe siècle après J.-C.* (Paris, 1955); G. Downey *A History of Antioch in Syria from Seleucus to the Arab Conquest* (Princeton, 1961); J.H.G.W. Liebeschuetz *Antioch: City and Imperial Administration in the Later Roman Empire* (Oxford, 1972); E. Will 'Antioche sur l'Oronte, métropole de l'Asie' *Syria* 74 (1997) 99–113.

[42] J.N.D. Kelly *Golden Mouth: The story of John Chrysostom, ascetic, preacher, bishop* (London, 1995) 24–35; Rebenich 52–75. Doubts have, however, been cast on this recently: W. Mayer 'What does it mean to say that John Chrysostom was a monk?' Paper presented at the Fourteenth International Conference on Patristic Studies, Oxford, August 2003.

[43] Both Kelly and Cavallera date this to after his return from the 'desert,' although Kelly admits that a 'reasonable case' could be made for dating it 'rather earlier.' Jerome's early letters from the 'desert' contain paradisial descriptions (e.g. *ep.* 14, 10) more like the *vita Pauli* than the disillusioned letters he wrote at the end of his stay (e.g. *ep.* 17, 2–3). It would seem to me more likely that he wrote this *Life* while he was still full of enthusiasm for withdrawing from the world. Further bibliography on the question of dating: chapter 1, introduction.

[44] Rebenich 85–98 and now *id. Jerome* (London, 2002).

to copy more books for him. Rebenich suggests a retreat to the country estate of Bishop Evagrius. It was here that Jerome says he met the old monk Malchus, whose life story he was to make into his *vita Malchi*. Whatever sort of desert Jerome lived in, he still burned with sexual fantasies.[45] He writes that he sought to suppress these by learning the 'panting' sounds of Hebrew from a converted Jewish monk.[46] However, he certainly did not get on with his other fellow monks, who denounced him as a heretic.[47] He suffered bitter disillusionment and returned to the city, where he was ordained as priest by Paulinus, bishop of one of the competing congregations of Antioch.

It is not known exactly when Jerome left Antioch for Constantinople, but he was certainly there when the major church Council was held in 381. The years just before the council are also the time when a new version of the *Apostolic Constitutions* was being made in Antioch. Jerome deals with some of the same issues as this document, as will be seen in chapter 2. Constantinople, the new Rome, impressed Jerome, who adds many notes about it to his translation of Eusebius' *Chronicle* about the city. Jerome never mentions the church Council, which resulted in a defeat for the supporters of the bishop Paulinus, but he was certainly influenced by its second head, Gregory of Nazianzus. His Greek was good enough by this time for him to begin making major translations, not only of the brief notes of Eusebius, but also the homilies of Origen. In 382 he returned to Rome with Paulinus and Epiphanius, bishop of Salamis in Cyprus.

Rome

Jerome stayed on in Rome to become the secretary and friend of Pope Damasus, and even entertained hopes of being his successor,[48] though it is not clear how realistic his hopes were.[49] Damasus—so

---

[45] *ep.* 125, 12.
[46] *Loc. cit.*
[47] *epp.* 15–17.
[48] *epp.* 45, 3 and 123, 9 (*CSEL* 54, 325; *ib.* 56, 82).
[49] Nautin has suggested that Jerome re-wrote his relationship with Damasus after the Pope's death, creating the appearance of a greater closeness than had really been the case. See P. Nautin, 'Le premier échange épistulaire entre Jérôme et Damase: Lettres réelles ou fictives?' *Freiburger Zeitschrift für Philosophie und Theologie*, 30, (1983) 331–444 and the same author's article *s.v.* Hieronymus in the *TRE*, but see now Rebenich 145f.

Jerome tells us—was not slow in using Jerome's remarkable gift for languages: he ordered translations of various Greek texts and encouraged him to revise the Latin translation of the Bible, based on the Greek text, beginning with the Gospels. Jerome was also to revise the translation of the Hebrew Bible, based on the Septuagint. The Septuagint, so-called because seventy separate translators under Ptolemy had miraculously come to an identical Greek text, was regarded as a divine provision for Christians of a Bible which was no longer dependent on the Jews for the Hebrew text.[50] Jerome very soon realised that there were many problems with the Septuagint translation as opposed to what he called the *Hebraica veritas*. Both Hayward and Kamesar date this realisation to these years in Rome,[51] where Jerome writes that he surreptitiously borrowed books from a synagogue to copy, although it was not till some years later that he set about his translation.

During his time in Rome Jerome also became spiritual mentor to a group of noble ladies who were apparently attracted by his asceticism. With Paula and Marcella he even studied the Bible in Hebrew. But the situation changed on the death in 384 of Blesilla, another of this circle, who had mortified herself with repeated fasting encouraged by Jerome, and finally died. Damasus died shortly after and his successor Siricius was no friend to Jerome. Churchmen who disapproved of excessive emphasis on asceticism spoke against Jerome, or in his own words *senatus Pharisaeorum conclamavit*[52]—the reference to the condemnation of Jesus is clear, and it is certain Jerome felt himself crucified and forced to flee Rome. Some of his group of ladies continued to support him, however, including Paula and Eustochium, the mother and sister of the dead Blesilla. They too left Rome, though not together with Jerome.

The East

Having left Rome separately, Jerome appears to have met up again with Paula and her daughter Eustochium in the east, probably in

---

[50] See on this Augustine *ep.* 28 = Jerome *ep.* 56. Jerome himself cast doubts on the miraculous aspects of the story: *Praef. in Pentateucho* (Weber, p. 3).
[51] Kamesar 41f.; Hayward 10f.
[52] *In Did. Praef.* (*PL* 23, 101f.); cf. *Apol. contra Ruf.* 3, 21–22 (*CCSL* 79, 92–3; *PL* 23, 472–3).

Cyprus or Antioch.[53] From Antioch they travelled together by land to the holy places of Palestine. Jerome has left an account of this journey in his *ep.* 108, his epitaph on Paula, which will be discussed in detail in chapter 4.

Paula and Jerome went on to visit Egypt, including the monks in the desert of Nitria.[54] Derwas Chitty points out that Nitria is on the edge of the desert, and was then easily accessible from Alexandria by river.[55] Jerome was later to translate the *Rule* of Pachomius,[56] the Egyptian founder of coenobitic monasticism[57] in the first half of the fourth century, but there is no evidence that he actually visited the Pachomian communities some 400 miles further down the Nile. He did, however, spend time in the great imperial and Christian centre of Alexandria, where he met the blind scholar Didymus, whose work on the Holy Spirit was to be one of the first works Jerome translated after he left Egypt and arrived in Bethlehem.

In Bethlehem, Paula's money was used to build them two monasteries, for men and for women, where they lived until their deaths. Two of Jerome's first works written in Bethlehem were the *Lives* of Hilarion and Malchus. He also began to write commentaries on biblical books, as well as his translation and revision of Eusebius' *Onomasticon*. Around 390 he finally began to translate the Hebrew Bible into Latin directly from the Hebrew text. This translation, together with his revision of the Gospels from the Greek, was to form the basis of the Vulgate, the Latin version of the Bible most widely used in the west.[58]

Scholars used to assume that Jerome travelled extensively in Palestine, but Wilkinson has pointed out that there is no evidence that he travelled much after settling finally in Bethlehem.[59] However,

[53] *ep.* 108, 6ff., (*CSEL* 55, 310ff.) and see Kelly, 116–117.
[54] D. Chitty *The Desert a City* (Oxford, 1966 repr., NY, no date).
[55] Chitty *op. cit.* p. 12.
[56] *Regulae S. Pachomii translatio Latinae* (*PL* 23, 61f.) See on this A. de Vogüé *Histoire littéraire du mouvement monastique dans l'Antiquité: Première partie: Le monachisme latin **** Sulpice Sévère et Paulin de Nole (393–409); Jérôme, homéliste et traducteur des 'Pachomiana.'* (Paris, 1997).
[57] On coenobitic monasticism, see Chitty 20f.; Jerome *ep.* 22, 34–5 (*CSEL* 54, 196–7).
[58] On the Vulgate, see C. Brown Tkacz '*Labor tam utilis*: the creation of the Vulgate' *VChr* 50 (1996) 42–72.
[59] J. Wilkinson 'L'apport de Saint Jérôme à la topographie' *RB* 81 (1974) 245f.

Jerome does write of visiting his Jewish teacher in Lydda, and going to the library at Caesarea.[60] Bethlehem is also only six miles from Jerusalem, and was intimately connected with it by the processions of the liturgy.[61] Jerome was often involved in violent controversy with the Christians of Jerusalem, particularly Bishop John, who even excommunicated him for a time at the end of the 390's, as well as with his erstwhile friend Rufinus.[62] Jerome outlived both Paula and Eustochium. He died in 420 and was buried near them in the Church of the Nativity in Bethlehem.[63]

---

[60] Kelly p. 135.

[61] Egeria: 39, 1; 42 (ed. A. Franceschini & R. Weber, *CCSL* 175) 83–4. Kelly p. 133 points out, however, that Jerome in Bethlehem celebrated the nativity on the Latin date of December 25th, while Jerusalem and much of the East preferred January 6th. Cf. Jerome's Christmas Homily (*CCSL* 78, 527).

[62] Cf. *Contra Iohannem* 42 (*CCSL* 79A, 79–80; *PL* 23, 393). For accounts of Jerome's controversies see Kelly and Rebenich, as well as I. Opelt *Hieronymus' Streitschriften* (Heidelberg, 1973); E. Clark *The Origenist Controversy* (Princeton, 1992).

[63] See chapter 2 for accounts of the subsequent transfer of his relics.

CHAPTER ONE

THE *VITA PAULI*:
THE HOLY MAN IN THE WILDERNESS:
DID JEROME APPROPRIATE JEWISH *AGGADAH*?

INTRODUCTION

Jerome's holy man in the wilderness

The *vita Pauli* is Jerome's first attempt at creating a holy man, and the first written for a Latin speaking audience.[1] There had been *Lives* of martyrs before, but not *Lives* of ascetic saints in Latin. Jerome prefaces his saint's *Life* with the accounts of two martyrdoms, and then moves on to the new account of the ascetic saint. The saint is depicted in terms of types taken from the Hebrew Bible and the New Testament,[2] and I shall suggest that Jerome may well have constructed his Christian saint's *Life* in full knowledge of the body of Jewish *aggadah* about the ascetic Rabbi Shim'on bar Yohai. Jerome appears to create his Christian spirituality by contrast with the material Jewish world.

This first attempt of Jerome's at a saint's *Life* was written very close to the time when he himself attempted to retreat from the world around him, and withdraw to the desert. Paul also withdraws from the world, far more successfully than Jerome: the *vita Pauli* is an idealised picture of the monk in the wilderness. It is particularly remarkable for its stark contrasts of setting, settings which, as we shall see, are in themselves metaphors for the spiritual struggles of

---

[1] On the Christian holy man in late antiquity, see the classic study of Peter Brown 'The Rise and Function of the Holy Man in Late Antiquity' *JRS* 61 (1971) 80–101, now revised in (*id*) *Authority and the sacred: Aspects of the Christianisation of the Roman World* (Cambridge, 1995): chapter 3 'Arbiters of the Holy: the Christian holy man in late antiquity' 57–78. The *Journal of Early Christian Studies* 6 (Fall, 1998) is completely devoted to a re-assessment of Brown's Holy Man. See now also: J. Howard-Johnston & P.A. Hayward (eds.) *The Cult of Saints in Late Antiquity and the Middle Ages: Essays on the Contribution of Peter Brown* (Oxford, 1999).

[2] For a discussion of Jerome's typology, see chapter 3.2.1 below.

the ascetic life, but also contain material based on Jerome's contemporary world of Late Antiquity.

From the Middle Ages onwards, St. Jerome in his cave in the desert, accompanied by a lion,[3] was a very popular subject of paintings. This is probably partly due to a confusion of St. Jerome with St. Gerasimus.[4] However, the saint with a lion or lions plays an important part here in the *vita Pauli* and there is another lion (or rather lioness) which plays an important part in Jerome's later *vita Malchi*.[5] Jerome took care to use his own literary creations to construct a literary *persona* for himself: we shall see how he writes himself into the *vita Pauli* as the holy man of the desert *par excellence*.[6]

Chronology

The *vita Pauli*, the *Life of Paul, the first hermit*, is chronologically the first of Jerome's saints' *Lives*. It heads Jerome's list of his own writings with which he ends his catalogue of *Famous Men*.[7] It appears to have been written after Jerome's first visit to Antioch, either act-

---

[3] For a charming, but ultimately unconvincing suggestion about holy men and tame lions, see N. Ševčenko 'The Hermit as Stranger in the Desert' in D.C. Smythe (ed.) *Strangers to Themselves: the Byzantine Outsider* (Aldershot etc., 2000) 75–86.

[4] The story of Gerasimus and the lion, which also took place in Palestine, is told by Johannes Moschus: *Pratum Spirituale* 107 (*PG* 87(3), 2965–70; *PL* 74, 172–4). See Kelly, 333 with bibliography *ad loc.*; E.F. Rice *Saint Jerome in the Renaissance* (Baltimore/London, 1985) 37–45; A. Vauchez 'Iconographie et histoire de la spiritualité: À propos d'un ouvrage récent (D. Russo *Saint Jérôme en Italie)' Le Moyen Age* 95 (1989) 142–144.

[5] It has been suggested that Jerome's lions may owe something to the *Apocryphal Acts of the Apostles*, and in particular to the baptized lion in the *acta* of Paul and Thecla: T. Adamik 'The influence of the apocryphal Acts on Jerome's Lives of Saints' in J.N. Bremmer (ed.) *The Apocryphal Acts of John* (Kampen, 1995) 171–182, but the other parallels brought there are less convincing. Jerome himself called the story of Paul, Thecla and the baptized lion 'apocryphal.' *(de vir. ill. 7): Igitur* Περιόδους Pauli et Theclae *et totam baptizati leonis fabulam inter scripturas apocryphas computemus.* Wall paintings of Paul, Thecla and Thecla's mother (with unfortunately only the heads preserved) have recently been found in an underground cave at Ephesos: R. Pillinger 'Neue Entdeckungen in der sogenannten Paulusgrotte von Ephesos' *Mitteilungen zur Christlichen Archäologie* 6 (2000) 16–29.

[6] For Jerome's creation of a literary persona for himself, M. Vessey 'Jerome's Origen: The Making of a Christian Literary Persona' *Studia Patristica* 28 (1993) 135f. and cf. C. Favez 'Saint Jérôme peint par lui-meme' *Latomus* 16 (1957) 655f.; *ib.* 17 (1958) 81–96; 303–316. Both these articles relate to his letters and prefaces only. For Jerome in the *vita Pauli* see below esp. 1.5: Jerome's literary methods.

[7] *de viris illustribus.* cxxxv.

ually during his time in the 'desert of Chalcis' or shortly after he had left there and returned to Antioch once more, in other words, some time between 375 and around 380.[8] Jerome wrote his *vita Pauli* following the success of the *vita Antonii*, attributed to Athanasius.[9] The *vita Pauli* was extremely successful: there are hundreds of extant manuscripts.[10]

Historicity

Jerome begins the *vita Pauli* with the claim that Antony was not the first of the monks, but that Paul preceded him. Whether Paul himself actually existed, or whether he is merely a distillation of a number of stories about hermits, is a difficult question to resolve.[11] There is no evidence for Paul's existence outside Jerome, and ever since the first appearance of the work there have been suggestions that he is entirely Jerome's invention. However, Jerome angrily refuted

---

[8] Kelly 60f. See too J.H.D. Scourfield 'Jerome, Antioch and the Desert: a Note on Chronology' *JThS* 37 (1986) 117f.; Rebenich 76n., 331, 86; A. de Vogüé 'La "Vita Pauli" de saint Jérôme et sa datation; Examen d'un passage-clé (ch. 6)' in G.J.M. Bartelink. A. Hilhorst, C.N. Kneepkens (eds.) *Eulogia: Mélanges offerts à Anton A.R. Bastiaensen à l'occasion de son soixante-cinquième anniversaire* (Instrumenta Patristica 24, Hague, 1991) 395–406; A.A.R. Bastiaensen 'Jérôme hagiographe' *CC Hagiographies: International History of the Latin and Vernacular Hagiographical Literature in the West from its origins to 1550*, vol. I (Turnhout, 1994) 106 and now B. Degórski 'Un Nuovo indizio per la Datazione della Vita S. Pauli di Girolamo?' *Studia Patristica* 33 (1997) 302f. The scholarly debate on whether the *vita Pauli* was written during or after Jerome's stay in the 'desert of Chalcis,' has concentrated mainly on different manuscript readings. As noted above in the introduction, Jerome's early letters from the 'desert' contain paradisial descriptions more like the *vita Pauli* than the disillusioned letters he wrote at the end of his stay, and it thus seems to me more likely that he wrote this *Life* while he was still full of enthusiasm for withdrawing from the world. For the problem of the 'desert of Chalcis,' see n. 45 below.

[9] There is considerable scholarly debate as to whether Athanasius was author of the *vita Antonii*, or merely its redactor. For discussion and bibliography see now: G.J.M. Bartelink *Athanase d'Alexandrie: Vie d'Antoine* (*SC* 400, Paris, 1994) 27–35.

[10] H.C. Jameson 'The Greek Version of Jerome's Life of Malchus' *TAPA* 69 (1938) 411, writes that there are over 900 extant manuscripts of Jerome's *Vitae Patrum Eremitorum* (the *vita Pauli*, *vita Hilarionis* and the *vita Malchi*) including translations into Greek, Syriac 'and most of the vernaculars of modern Europe.' For a list of the manuscripts of the *vita Pauli* and their dates see B. Lambert *Bibliotheca Hieronymiana Manuscripta: la tradition manuscrite des oeuvres de saint Jérôme* vol. II (Steenbrugge 1969) sect. 261, pp. 459–480.

[11] For a summary of the scholarly debate on whether Paul existed or not, see Bastiaensen *op. cit.* n. 8 above.

such contemporary attacks and Kelly points out that he appears convinced of the historicity of his own character.[12] Philip Rousseau also
notes that the 'account of Antony's dream [in the *vita Pauli*], for
example—that someone more perfect than himself lived further within
the desert—rings absolutely true . . . it was typical of many anxieties
expressed in other sources by Egyptian ascetics.'[13] David Brakke has
written of the *vita Antonii* that:

> the entire *Life* . . . is the bishop's programmatic statement on the exem-
> plary ascetic, not a reliable report on the life and teaching of the his-
> torical Antony.[14]

This may equally be applied to Jerome and his *vita Pauli*. I have not
found another case where Jerome invents *ex nihilo*, although he manip-
ulates and embroiders his material often.[15] Here he seems to have
taken a story which he himself believed in, on which to base his literary creation. We shall see below that there were hermits who
retired to live alone in the Egyptian and Syrian deserts, so Jerome
could also have combined a number of different traditions to flesh
out his figure. The *vita Pauli* is a complex construction, where Jerome
uses material from his own experience, both actual and literary, to
build different layers of meaning and metaphor.

---

[12] Kelly, 61. For a suggestion that Jerome took his material for the *vita Pauli*
from the *vita Onuphrii [Peregrinatio Paphnutii]* see Alison Goddard Elliot *Roads to Paradise*
(Hanover and London, 1987) 58, 164, 204, based on E. Amélineau 'Voyage d'un
moine égyptien dans le désert' *Recueil de travaux rélatifs à la philologie et à l'archéologie
égyptiennes et assyriennes* 6 (1884) 166–94 (*non vidi*) who dates a Coptic manuscript to
'the mid-fourth century.' The latest editor of the *vita Onuphrii*, T. Vivian *Histories of
the Monks of Upper Egypt and the Life of Onnophrius* (Kalamazoo, 1993) tends to place
it at the end of the fourth century (p. 49). However, there is no evidence that the
vita Onuphrii was extant in Greek or Latin at this time. See the further discussion
below in 1.2.2.
[13] P. Rousseau *Ascetics, Authority and the Church in the age of Jerome and Cassian* (Oxford,
1978) 134. A. de Vogüé *Histoire littéraire du mouvement monastique dans l'Antiquité: Première
partie: Le monachisme latin * de la mort d'Antoine à la fin du séjour de Jérôme à Rome
(356–385)* (Paris, 1991) 165, provides a list of parallels, adding that all these seem
to be subsequent to Jerome 'et l'on peut se demander si [Jérôme] n'est pas l'ori-
gine du thème.'
[14] D. Brakke '"Outside the places, within the truth": Athanasius of Alexandria
and the location of the holy' in D. Frankfurter (ed.) *Pilgrimage and Holy Space in Late
Antique Egypt* (Leiden etc., 1998) 445f. and esp. p. 453.
[15] Jerome is suspected of re-writing his relationship with Pope Damasus after the
latter's death: P. Nautin 'Le premier échange épistolaire entre Jérôme et Damase:
lettres réelles au fictives?' *Freiburger Zeitschrift für Philosophie und Theologie* 30 (1983)
331f. *Contra:* Rebenich, 145. See also M. Vessey 'Jerome's Origen: The Making of
a Christian Literary Persona' *Studia Patristica* 28 (1993) 135f.

SUMMARY OF THE *VITA PAULI*

The *vita* begins with two particularly nasty martyrdoms. The first tells of a Christian burned on plates of red-hot metal and then smeared with honey and stung, while the second martyr is tempted by a prostitute in a beautiful garden and bites out his own tongue, conquering lust with pain. Jerome then turns to the story of Paul, of Thebes in Egypt, who goes into hiding at the time of the persecution of Christians. When his brother-in-law threatens to betray him to the authorities, he flees to the desert far from humankind, going to live an ascetic life in an underground forgers' cave with a hidden spring and palm tree. Here he subsists for many years on water and dates, supplemented by bread brought by a raven. Jerome tells us that Antony himself had believed that he was the first and only monk, but a divine revelation brings him to go and seek out Paul. Antony goes through the desert to look for Paul and is shown the way by a satyr, a centaur and a she-wolf. When he finds him, Paul asks him three questions about the state of mankind: are there new buildings in the ancient cities, what power now rules the world, and are there any people left whose minds are controlled by demons? They eat a miraculously doubled portion of bread together and then Paul sends Antony home to bring the cloak given him by Athanasius to bury him in. Antony goes back to his own monastery to tell his two disciples what he has seen, and when he returns Paul is already dead in a posture of prayer. He wraps the body in the cloak and buries him with the help of two lions, taking Paul's palm-leaf tunic. Jerome ends by bidding his reader remember him, Jerome, who would prefer Paul's tunic to the purple robes of kings.

JEROME'S PROGRAMMATIC INTRODUCTION TO THE *VITA PAULI*: THE LETTER TO PAUL OF CONCORDIA

The *vita Pauli* has no formal preface, but we do have the letter Jerome wrote to the aged Paul of Concordia when sending him the *vita*.[16] Here he requests Paul to send him commentaries on the words

---

[16] *ep.* 10, 3. *Misimus interim tibi, id est Paulo seni, Paulum seniorem, in quo propter simpliciores quosque multum in deiciendo sermone laboravimus.* On the relationship between *ep.* 10 and the *vita Pauli*, see de Vogüé (*op. cit.* n. 8) pp. 396; 405–6.

of God, which are pure words, as silver tried in a furnace of earth: *eloquia Domini eloquia casta, argentum igne examinatum terrae* (Ps. 11:7[12:6]). In exchange, says Jerome, he will send to him, the aged Paul, the story of a still older Paul, where he, Jerome, has laboured to bring down his style to the level of the common people:

> *in quo propter simpliciores quosque multum in deiciendo sermone laborauimus.*

However, he says, with polite disclaimer, *nescio quomodo*, even if we fill a jar with water it still keeps something of the smell of the wine that was stored in it originally.[17] I shall discuss below whether this really tells us something of Jerome's audience,[18] as well as the question of Jerome's style, and its intimate relation to spirituality.[19] Jerome promises to ship Paul further oriental merchandise if he likes the story.[20]

1.1. THE SPIRITUAL WORLD OF THE *VITA PAULI*: MARTYRS AND ASCETICS

1.1.1. *The two martyr accounts—'the crowns of roses and violets'*

The *vita Pauli* begins with two martyr accounts, which are unconnected with the story of Paul and Antony. Jerome tells us elsewhere of his own trials in the desert, and it would seem that the function of these episodes is to externalise and make concrete the spiritual struggles of the monk in the desert as he strives to overcome his fleshly temptations.[21] Thus the first martyrdom is by red-hot metal—the burning desert—and by stinging flies, attracted to honey which is smeared over the martyr. There is an incident in Apuleius similar to Jerome's account, a similarity which was first noted by Rosweyde

---

[17] *sed nescio quomodo, etiam si aqua plena sit, tamen eundem odorem lagoena seruat, quo dum rudis esset inbuta est.* Cf. Horace *ep.* i, 2, 69–70.

[18] Below, 1.3: 'Classical learning and Jerome's audience.'

[19] Below, 1.5.2: Style.'

[20] *ep.* 10, 3: *alia condita quae cum plurimis orientalibus mercibus ad te . . . nauigabunt.* For discussion of the significance of this oriental merchandise, see below: 1.4.2: Jerome's use of aggadic material; 1.3: Classical learning and Jerome's audience.

[21] *ep.* 22, 7. The stings here, as suits this highly rhetorical and exaggerated passage, come from scorpions rather than mere flies, but this suits a passage where Jerome can describe himself as black as an Ethiopian.

and has been discussed by Bauer.[22] We shall see below in chapter 2 how Jerome made considerable use of Apuleius in the *vita Hilarionis*. The second martyr account has the martyr bound on a feather bed in a shady garden with trickling water, and fondled by a prostitute. He bites off his own tongue to prevent his shameful response to his temptress.[23] This is reminiscent of the martyrdom of Romanus who had his tongue cut out in Antioch, where Jerome had just been staying.[24] There are two homilies by John Chrysostom on the martyrdom of Romanus, which dwell on the spiritual significance of the cutting out of his tongue, and the subsequent miraculous restoration of his speech.[25] Even though these particular homilies post-date Jerome's stay in Antioch, they seem to have been delivered on the saint's day, which implies public recognition and celebration of this saint. Antioch, of course, was next to the notorious gardens of Daphne,[26] with its Castalian spring and oracle of Apollo, which was silenced by the presence of the remains of another Antiochene martyr, Babylas. The removal of these remains by Julian had caused riots only a dozen years (361–2) before Jerome arrived (374–5).[27] Thus it is not surprising that Jerome sites this martyrdom in a garden of

---

[22] Rosweyde's commentary to the *vita Pauli* is to be found in *PL* 73, 109; J.B. Bauer 'Novellistisches bei Hieronymus' *Wiener Studien* 74 (1961) 130f. Both note the parallel to Apuleius *Met.* viii 22. The *Passio Sancti Mammetis* 20, edited by H. Delehaye from a 10th century ms. in *AB* 58 (1940) 140, tells of Mammas who was smeared with honey and bound to a tree swarming with ants. A lion freed him and licked the honey off him. This Passion is undated.

[23] See on this T. Urbainczyk *Theodoret of Cyrrhus* (Ann Arbor, 2002), p. 49: 'For sexual temptation one should always try Jerome first, whose life of Paul of Thebes is astonishing even for him.' Urbainczyk then goes on to quote in full Jerome's description of the second martyr's temptation (*V. Pauli* 3).

[24] Eusebius *de mart. Pal.* 2 (*PG* 20, 1464f.). A. de Vogüé (*op. cit.* n. 8 above) 157f. gives a long list of other possible precedents to this martyrdom, but does not mention Romanus.

[25] John Chrysostom: *in S. Roman. mart.*, *PG* 50, 605–618 and see H. Delehaye 'S. Romain, martyr d'Antioche' *AB* 50 (1932) 241f.

[26] On Daphne as a notorious resort of licentious behaviour in the fourth century see e.g. *SHA: Avidius Cassius* v, 5; *Severus Alexander* liv, 7, and comments in B. Isaac 'Orientals and Jews in the Historia Augusta: Fourth-Century Prejudice and Stereotypes' *The Jews in the Hellenistic-Roman World: Studies in Memory of Menahem Stern* (ed. I. Gafni, A. Oppenheimer, D.R. Schwartz, Jerusalem, 1996) 101*–118* = *id. The Near East under Roman Rule: Selected Papers* (Leiden/NY/Köln, 1998) 268–283.

[27] See G. Downey *A History of Antioch in Syria* (Princeton, 1961) 387f. Jerome relates to Daphne and its spring in *Com. in Hiez.* xiv xlvii 15/17 (*CCSL* 75,723; *PL* 25,499).

temptations with a spring. The allusion to Cicero should also be noted: he too had written of a man suffering pain and thirst in a beautiful garden with the sound of running water.[28] In Jerome's account he thus externalises the temptations, rather than the afflictions of the monk, who must long for such a garden of sweet flowers and running water in the arid wilderness. The real nature of the stream, however, is shown by the fact that it flowed in coils—*serperet*—which immediately reminds us of the *serpens*, the tempter in the Garden of Eden. The feather couch is contrasted with the stony ground Jerome tells us he slept on, and comes complete with a harlot such as he tells us he fantasied, to his agonised shame.[29] The biting out of the martyr's tongue is perhaps a metaphor for Jerome's famous ab-negation of pagan literature following his dream condemnation as a 'Ciceronian, not a Christian.'[30] For Jerome, who went to the desert together with his whole library, abnegation of the classical pagan works which formed so large a component of his education must have seemed like biting off his own tongue.

1.1.2. *Asceticism as the successor of martyrdom—'the crown of lilies'*

When the persecution of Christians by the Roman authorities ceased, martyrdom was succeeded by asceticism.[31] Jerome himself writes to Eustochium of Paula, his long-time companion whose monastery was next to his in Bethlehem:

---

[28] Cicero: *Tusc.* v xxvi; cf. discussion of misery and being put on rack with rela-tion to lust: *ib.* iii xiii; *ib.* v xxxiii: discussion of pleasure and pain. The third cen-tury *Passio Sanctorum Mariani et Iacobi* (ed. Franchi de Cavalieri *Studi e testi* (1900) 47f.) also sets the vision of the martyrdom in a *locus amoenus* with green trees and a spring of water, but here the setting symbolises the paradise which the martyrs will achieve: they drink from the spring in words taken from Ps. 42:1–2, a verse often found illustrated in church decoration in late antiquity: cf. P.A. Underwood 'The Fountain of Life' *DOP* 5 (1950) 43f.

[29] Bauer (*op. cit.* above n. 22) discusses this episode where the martyr is placed on a feather bed *plumis lectum* and fondled by a prostitute, and rejects Erasmus' sug-gestion of Apuleius as a possible additional influence on this as well as on the pre-vious martyrdom, preferring Petronius. While I would accept Bauer's suggestion of Petronius as the main source for this episode, it may still be that Apuleius was an additional source, for a *lectus* with feathers *plumea . . . tumidus* which presaged shame-ful exposure with a *scelest[a] pollut[a]que femin[a]* is to be found in *Met.* x 34.

[30] *ep.* 22, 30.

[31] On this see: R.A. Markus *The End of Ancient Christianity* (Cambridge, 1990) 70–72.

Eustochium. . . . mater tua longo martyrio coronata est. Non solum effusio san-
guinis in confessione reputatur, sed deuotae quoque mentis seruitus cotidianum mar-
tyrium est. Illa corona de rosis et uiolis plectitur, ista de liliis.[32]

Jerome's two martyr accounts in the *vita Pauli* are now followed by
the account of the life of Paul, the ascetic, who is thus part of a
trilogy, although of a different nature from the two anonymous martyrdoms. Here, as suits the ascetic life, description is pared down to
a bare minimum. The glaring light of the desert is succeeded by the
darkness of Paul's cave, with its paradisial palm tree and spring.[33]
The desert is inhabited by semi-barbaric creatures who have, however, heard of the glory of Christ.[34] Paul's paradisial cave is very
similar to the habitation of Antony in the earlier *vita Antonii* and
Jerome's own later *vita Hilarionis*. In contrast to the desert and cave,
Jerome pictures Antony recalling the wickedness of men in cities, in
particular Alexandria. Paul's three brief questions summon up the
whole state of man in his day and in Jerome's.

Paul, educated in both Greek and Egyptian literature, flees from
persecution to the desert, then chooses to stay and live the life of
an ascetic, alone.[35] Thus he gives up both the possibility of speaking to other men, and reading what they have written, as fore-
shadowed in the second martyrdom where we saw the martyr bite
out his own tongue. Paul's act of abnegation is greater than the
unlettered Antony's: he had more to lose.[36]

---

[32] *ep.* 108, 31: Tr. 'Eustochium . . . your mother was crowned after a long martyrdom. It is not only the spilling of blood which is reckoned as a profession [of
Christian faith], but the immaculate service of a devoted mind is a daily martyrdom. The first is a crown woven of roses and violets, the second is a crown of
lilies.' For Jerome's long relationship with Paula and her daughter Eustochium, see
above, Introduction: Jerome's Life: Rome.

[33] For a suggestive account of the symbolism and ambiguities of caves as contexts, see R. Buxton *Imaginary Greece* (Cambridge, 1994).

[34] On these animals see now: R. Wisnieski '*Bestiae Christum loquuntur* ou des habitants du désert et de la ville dans la *Vita Pauli* de saint Jérôme' *Augustinianum* 40
(2000) 105–144.

[35] For a similar phenomenon at a later period, cf.: Evelyne Patlagean 'Ancient
Byzantine hagiography and social history' in S. Wilson (ed.) *Saints and their Cults:
Studies in Religion, Sociology, Folklore and History* (Cambridge, 1983, repr. 1987) 103.

[36] See P. Leclerc 'Antoine et Paul: métamorphose d'un héros' in *Jérôme entre
l'Occident et l'Orient* (ed. Y.-M. Duval, Paris, 1988) 257–265.

1.2. The Material World

1.2.1. *Jerome's 'vivid imagination'*

We noted above the doubts that have been cast on the historicity
of Jerome's hero. Several scholars have also proposed that some of
the more lurid details in his saints' *Lives* have their origin in Jerome's
vivid imagination. Having quoted Gibbon's cynical statement on
Jerome's saints' *Lives*: 'the only defect in these pleasing compositions
is the want of truth and common sense,'[37] Syme writes ironically of
Jerome producing 'a piece of corroborative invention of superior
quality, worthy of the *H[istoria] A[ugusta]* at its best.'[38] He then cites
the episode from the *vita Pauli* about the clandestine forgers' mint
going back to the days of Antonius and Cleopatra. 'Fabulous exploits,'
Syme says, 'appeal to the vulgar and credulous whatever be their
persuasions in cult and religion.' A whole book has indeed been written on 'St. Jerome as a Satirist', but while citing the same passage
of Gibbon, Wiesen, the author, still includes the saints' *Lives* under
the heading of historical works, and the only 'satire' he notes in the
vita Pauli is the attack on luxury in the final section, which he sees
as a Christian version of the Stoic tradition.[39] When we analyse
Jerome's literary methods and style in detail, we shall see that the
very episode of the illegal mint, which may seem like incredible or
satirical writing to a modern audience, had a very specific literary
function within the story, spelt out by Jerome in his introductory
letter. Nor is it due entirely to Jerome's invention—like many of the
vivid details in the saints' *Lives*, we will be tracing its literary and
historical sources or parallels. Syme was nearer to getting at the
quality of Jerome's writing when he quoted Hagendahl: Jerome is a
'thorough-paced compiler and plagiarist,'[40] although this too, in my
opinion, is too negative a judgement for the artist who re-fashioned
material taken from many different sources to produce a new literary form, the first Latin saints' *Lives*.

---

[37] E. Gibbon *The History of the Decline and Fall of the Roman Empire* IV, xxxvii (ed.
O. Smeaton, London/NY, 1910, repr. 1913) p. 5, n. 4.
[38] R. Syme *Ammianus and the Historia Augusta* (Oxford, 1968) 82–3.
[39] D. Wiesen *St. Jerome as a Satirist* (Ithaca/NY, 1964) 46–49.
[40] Syme *loc. cit.* p. 81.

1.2.2. *Contrasting settings*

2a. *Egyptian or Syrian?*

We shall turn now to look at Jerome's picture of the origins of monasticism in the *vita*. I noted above that Jerome appears to be convinced himself of the existence of Paul, whom he presents as the precursor of monasticism in Egypt. In his *vita Hilarionis* he presents Hilarion as the first to bring monasticism from Egypt to Syria.[41] His works were to be so effective that eventually Syrian monks believed this account of their origins themselves. However, Voöbus has suggested that this is not the true picture and that Syrian monasticism was autochthonous—it arose independently of Egyptian monasticism under influences from the east such as Manichaeism, hence the stress on lone prayer and extremes of ascetic practice.[42] But westerners such as Jerome had a tendency to see cultural influences as coming from the West to the East, rather than the other way. In early letters Jerome notes the speech of the monks he met in Syria as 'semi-barbaric', and eventually totally rejects their extremes of ascetic practices after his disillusionment with the desert.[43] However, at the time he wrote the *vita Pauli*, Jerome's only experience of the Egyptian desert was purely literary, deriving from the *vita Antonii*, recently translated anew by his patron Evagrius. Although Elliot has suggested that Jerome may have had a source in the Coptic *Vita Onuphrii*, which was dated by Amélineau to the mid-fourth century, she herself admits that the evidence is weak. There is no evidence of a Greek or Latin translation until later, although Jerome could have heard the story orally from refugee Egyptian monks.[44] But he did

---

[41] On relations between Egyptian and Palestinian monasticism, including a discussion of Jerome's own experience see S. Rubenson 'The Egyptian relations of early Palestinian monasticism' in A. O'Mahoney *et al. The Christian Heritage in the Holy Land* (London, 1995) 35–46.

[42] A. Voöbus *A History of Asceticism in the Syrian Orient* (Louvain, 1958) I, 138f., 'The trend which underlies his (*sc.* Theodoret's) information goes from Orient to West, not from West to East.' Cf. S. Brock 'Early Syrian Asceticism' *Numen* 20 (1973) p. 1f. esp. p. 3. *Contra*: Kelly 47 and bibliography *ad loc.*

[43] *ep* 7, 2 for the *barbarus semi-sermo* as opposed to his cultured western contacts during his first idealistic time in the desert (see below chapter 2.2.1b: 'Elusa *semibarbarum* oppidum' for a discussion of this phrase in the context of the *vita Hilarionis*); *ep.* 17, 2–3 for his disillusionment.

[44] Alison Goddard Elliot *Roads to Paradise: Reading the Lives of the Early Saints* (Hanover and London, 1987). *Contra*: P. Peeters' review of F.M.E. Pereia *Vida de santo Abunafre: AB* 25 (1906) 203–4. The *Vita Onuphrii* or *Peregrinatio Paphnutii* con-

have actual experience of the 'desert of Chalcis'[45] *qu[ae] iuxta Syriam Saracenis iungitur*,[46] and he uses this in the *vita Pauli* in his descriptions of the Egyptian desert. He cites the legendary feats of asceticism of the Syrian monks, at least one of which is paralleled in Theodoret, as will be seen below.

Caves joined by tunnels to form underground hideouts for refugees from taxes and persecution are very commonly found in Syria-Palaestina. Jerome knew that they served as refuges for Jews during both the First Revolt [the Jewish War] against the Romans and the Bar Kokhba Revolt:

> *ad Vespasiani Adrianique haec referunt tempora . . . sed in tantam habitatores Iudaeae uenisse formidinem, ut et ipsi cum coniugibus et liberis, auro et argento quae sibi auxilio fore aestimabant, in foueas terrae demersi sint et profundissima antra sectati.*[47]

---

tains various accounts of searches for hermits living in caves in the desert next to a spring and palm tree. Two of the hermits are covered with long hair, an attribute that Jerome denies for Paul: *Nonnulli et haec et alia prout uoluntas tulit, iactitant: subterraneo specu crinitum calcaneo tenus hominems, et multa . . . incredibilia fingentes. Quorum quia impudens mendacium fuit . . .* There is an episode where four loaves of bread suddenly become five when another traveller arrives, which Elliot (p. 58) compares to Paul's half-loaf of bread which is miraculously doubled when Antony arrives. Elliot also suggests that the incident of the burial by lions, which is only found in a sixteenth-century version of the life of Onuphrius, was an original detail which dropped out of the extant early versions, presumably after being borrowed by Jerome. However, she herself can only present this as a 'tenuous' conclusion (pp. 164; 204). The latest edition of the *Vita Onuphrii*, T. Vivian *Histories of the Monks of Upper Egypt and the Life of Onnophrius* (Kalamazoo, 1993), provides no further information on Latin versions, except for a reference to D.S. Chauler 'Saint Onuphre' *Les Cahiers Coptes* 5 (1954) 3–15, which I have not seen.

[45] The exact nature of Jerome's own experience of the desert has been questioned by S. Rebenich: *Hieronymus und sein Kreis: Prosopographische und Sozialgeschichtliche Untersuchungen* (Stuttgart 1992). While earlier scholars assumed that he lived 'probably in a cave in the rocks' (thus Kelly), Rebenich thinks that the recorded presence of his library, copyists, Jewish teacher etc., and his constant intercourse with Evagrius points to a somewhat less secluded site, probably a cottage on Evagrius' estate near Chalcis, an area of semi-desert. However, this does not deny the contacts he mentions with other monks in the vicinity. Rebenich has added further evidence to back up his convincing claim in his subsequent book *Jerome* (London, 2002).

[46] Cf. *ep.* 7, 1: *Euagrio transmittente in ea ad me heremi parte delatae sunt, quae inter Syros ac Sarracenos uastum limitem ducit*; cf. *vita Malchi* 4.

[47] *Com. in Es.* I, ii, 15 (*CCSL 73*, 36; *PL* 24, 49). For archaeological evidence of cave complexes used as hideouts in Judaea and Galilee see now: M. Fischer, B. Isaac & I. Roll *Roman roads in Judaea II: The Jaffa-Jerusalem roads* (Oxford, 1996) Part III, Appendix II: Y. Shahar and Y. Tepper: 'Subterranean Hideouts' 274f. Cf. Ammianus xxviii, 2 on the bandits called 'Maratocupreni,' whose name contains the elements 'cave' and 'village,' as has been pointed out by J. Matthews, *The Roman Empire of Ammianus Marcellinus* (London, 1989) 402 and n. 46.

Such caves are often found in connection with cisterns like the one Jerome tells us another monk lived in. Jerome's learned note on the Syriac word *Gubba*, meaning cistern, is repeated in the history of the monk Macedonius, nicknamed Gubba, mentioned by Theodoret of Cyr who wrote a generation after Jerome.[48] Macedonius Gubba lived on Mount Silpius just to the east of Antioch, for nearly seventy years (c. 350–420). For half of this period he lived in a cistern, so both Theodoret and Jerome seem to have been using the same local material. Theodoret adds that his family visited Gubba regularly, and that he himself was born as a result of Gubba's intervention. Gubba was purely Syriac-speaking, to the extent that he did not understand what had happened when he was ordained priest. The Greek-speaking and writing Theodoret notes that his own first language was Syriac, also.[49] I have already mentioned Jerome's difficulties in communicating with the Syriac-speaking monks around him in the 'desert of Chalcis' with their 'semi-barbaric' speech.[50] Theodoret also adds other material which is paralleled by John Chrysostom, so that he does not seem to have merely copied his material from Jerome.[51] A number of monks seem to have lived around Mount Silpius, and Chrysostom himself is also reported to have withdrawn there in 375, about the same time that Jerome went from Antioch to the 'desert of Chalcis.'[52]

Paul bolts his door against unwelcome visitors, a detail which surprised de Vogüé.[53] However, some of the monks depicted by Theodoret

---

[48] See Theodoret de Cyr *Histoire des moines de Syrie* I ed P. Canivet, A. Leroy-Molinghen (Paris, 1977, *Sources Chrétiennes* 234) ch. 3; Theodoret of Cyrrhus *A History of the Monks of Syria* ed. and tr. R.M. Price (Kalamazoo, 1985) 100f. For Gubba in Theodoret and the *vita Pauli*, see B. Degórski *op. cit.* n. 8 above.

[49] See discussion of the languages of the monks by P. Canivet *Le monachisme syrien selon Théodoret de Cyr* (Paris, 1977) 236f.

[50] *ep.* 7, 2. See below chapter 2.2.1b for a discussion of Jerome's use of 'semi-barbaric'.

[51] Canivet *op. cit.* n. 49 above.

[52] On Chrysostom see J.N.D. Kelly *Golden Mouth: The story of John Chrysostom—ascetic, preacher, bishop* (London, 1995) Chapter 3: Retreat to the Mountains, 24f. On monks in the desert, cf. CTh. (dated 390) 16, 3 telling monks to go to the desert. However, modern scholars are beginning to cast doubt on Chrysostom's withdrawal from the world also: W. Mayer 'What does it mean to say that John Chrysostom was a monk?' Paper presented at the Fourteenth International Conference on Patristic Studies, Oxford, August 2003.

[53] A. de Vogüé (*op. cit.* n. 13 above) 168 notes the parallels to *vita Antonii* 48, 2 and Matthew 7:7 but misses Luke 11:5–10, where a man comes after a journey and at first the door is closed against him.

lived in cells or caves with a walled courtyard in front. This courtyard was entered by a gate and was the place where the monk
received his visitors, or, if they were women, refused to receive them.[54]
Theodoret even notes (*HR* 12) that the monk Zeno had *no* bars on
the gate at the entrance to the tomb where he lived on Mt. Silpius.
This would imply that bars were a norm, while the *vita* of Jerome's
friend and mentor, Epiphanius of Salamis, describes him living in
an isolated cell with a door and bolt.[55] Paul's cave and courtyard
were reached by an underground tunnel. Archaeological finds of
stone doors with bolts and hinges have been made in some underground hideouts in Palaestina.[56] The monastery of Chariton at Pharan
in the Judaean desert made use of a cave, identified archaeologically
as a Jewish hideout dating back to the First Revolt against the
Romans. Chariton turned this into a cave-church which was dedicated in the days of Macarius, bishop of Jerusalem 314–333.[57] The
vita Charitonis writes that Chariton took over a cave which had been
used as a robbers' den for his church, which is reminiscent of Paul's
re-use of a forgers' cave.

Antioch was a city with an imperial mint, as was Trier where

[54] Theodoret *HR* 8. See Canivet (*op. cit.* n. 49) 211.
[55] *vita Epiphanii*, 20. See C. Rapp *The vita of Epiphanius of Salamis—an historical and literary study* (DPhil., Oxford, 1991) 113.
[56] A. Kloner & Y. Tepper *The Hiding Complexes in the Judean Shephela* (Tel Aviv 1987, in Hebrew) 55f.: discussion of locking devices; p. 167, pl. 70: Horvat Naqiq; p. 234: Horvat Shem Tov. Chariton's cave church exhibits 'hinge sockets and signs of a locking device' in its threshold: Y. Hirschfeld *The Judean Desert Monasteries in the Byzantine Period* (New Haven and London, 1992) 121; cf. p. 163 and n. 19.
[57] Pharan has been identified with Pheretae of Josephus *BJ* iv, 509f. See: Y. Hirschfeld '*Life of Chariton* in the light of archaeological research' in V.L. Wimbush (ed.) *Ascetic Behavior in Greco-Roman Antiquity* (Minneapolis 1990) 426f., and cf. the annotated translation of the pre-Metaphrastic *Vita Charitonis* by Leah Di Segni in the same volume 393–421. Jerome never mentions the monasteries founded by Chariton not far from Bethlehem, nor his successor Euthymius, but there are a number of similarities between the *Vita Charitonis* and the *vita Pauli*. Since the pre-Metaphrastic *Vita Charitonis* was probably written in the second half of the fifth century, it could simply be that its author was influenced by Jerome, but it is also possible that both were drawing on common local traditions about early monasticism in Syria and Palaestina. Chariton's takeover of a cave that had served as a robbers' den and his conversion of this into a church is stressed even in the later Greek version of the *Vita*: S. Metaphrastes *Vita S. Charitonis* (*PG* 115, 908): τὸ γὰρ τῶν λῃστῶν τουτὶ σπήλαιον ἐκκλησίαν Θεοῦ παρ' αὐτοῦ γενόμενον ὄψει just as Paul takes over the abandoned mint and uses it as a place in which to pray. Chariton also, when old age confines him alone to his cave, has a divinely provided stream to drink from.

Jerome had stayed earlier. Illegal mints have been found around Trier,[58] and there were laws which forbade people to shelter runaway coin makers.[59] The author of the contemporary *Historia Augusta* notes the Isaurian brigand leader Trebellianus, who lived in difficult mountain terrain, as having struck his own coins, and writes that forged coins of the pretender Victoria were extant in his time among the Treviri (who lived around Trier). The *Historia Augusta* is notoriously unreliable but does sometimes preserve corroborative contemporary information.[60] It is possible, then, that illegal mints existed in the vicinity of more than one imperial mint, and that Jerome knew of their reputed presence in caves around Antioch. I shall discuss below the spiritual and metaphorical function of the illegal mint in Jerome's saint's *Life*. Meanwhile I shall just note how the reference to the time 'when Antonius was joined with Cleopatra' not only serves to convert the setting to an Egyptian one, but stresses the contrast between the chaste Christian Antony and the licentious pagan hero.

2b. *The paradisial cave*

The spring in Paul's cave, too, unlike the stream in the garden of temptation which flowed in coils—*serperet*, is described as *lucidissimum*, reminiscent of the heavenly light of Luke 11:34–36. Paul's cave is described as being not far from the foot of a mountain: *montem, ad cuius radices haud grandis spelunca*, inside which was a spring whose waters were swallowed up by the earth: *fontem lucidissimum . . . cuius riuum tantummodo foras statim eadem, quae genuerat, terra sorbebat*. The description of this spring is very similar to the description of the spring at Beth Zur in southern Palestine, which Jerome added to his translation of Eusebius' *Onomasticon* (*On.* 52,1 and 53,1) years later.[61] Eusebius only writes that ἔνθα καὶ πηγὴ ἀπὸ ὄρους ἐξιοῦσα whereas

---

[58] E.M. Wightman *Roman Trier and the Treveri* (London, 1970) 197.

[59] See A.H.M. Jones *The Later Roman Empire* (Oxford 1964 repr. 1990) p. 436 and bibliography *ad. loc.* And note J.H.W.G. Liebeschuetz *Antioch: City and Imperial Administration in the Later Roman Empire* (Oxford, 1972) 58: 'we may wonder through what private business some *monetarii* had gained their indisputably curial fortunes.'

[60] Trebellianus: *SHA: TT* 26; Victoria and the Treviri: *ib.* 31. For the unreliability of the *Historia Augusta* see e.g. R. Syme *The Historia Augusta: A call of clarity* (Bonn, 1971).

[61] For a full discussion of Jerome's additions to Eusebius' *Onomasticon* and their significance, see chapter 4.5 below.

Jerome writes *iuxta quem fons ad radices montis ebulliens ab eadem, in qua gignitur, sorbetur humo.* I noted above that Jerome's contemporaries cast doubt on the existence of his hero Paul. Jerome later inserted references to Paul in various of his works, apparently to familiarise his audience with this otherwise unknown figure.[62] It may be that the insertion of a description of Paul's spring into the *Onomasticon* served a similar function—a sort of retroactive alibi for its existence.

As with the martyr accounts above, Jerome also uses these concrete details to express spiritual concepts. In the description of Paul's underground cave where he lived for many years on spring water and dates from a palm tree, Jerome no doubt wished to allude to the palm trees that are traditionally present in Paradise, and to the description of the paradisial abode of Antony, while according to Ps. 91[92] the just man will flourish like a palm tree.[63] However, he makes it more real to his audience by combining various local elements in his description.

1.2.3. *The* vita Pauli *and the visual arts*

3a. *New roofs in ancient cities*
Jerome generally exhibits little evidence of interest in the visual arts, except to condemn excess magnificence in churches—he objected to the crib of Jesus at Bethlehem being covered in silver rather than plain pottery. His relationship to places seen tends to be through literature rather than landscape, both biblical and classical. The straits of Messina are Scylla and Charybdis, just as the Holy Land is the site of the events of the Bible.[64] But it has been remarked that in his descriptions of Rome in his *Chronicon* he is more interested in

---

[62] E.g. *Chron.* 356 CE: *Antonius monachus CV aetatis anno in heremo moritur, solitus multis ad se uenientibus de Paulo quodam Thebaeo mirae beatitudinis uiro referre, cuius nos exitum breui libello explicuimus.* Cf *epp.* 22,36; 58,5; 108,6; *vita Hilarionis,* prol.

[63] Ps. 91[92]:13 *iustus ut palma florebit* in both the versions. In *vita Pauli* 11 Paul talks of his expectation of receiving the *corona iustitiae.* For Antony's paradisial abode, see *vita Antonii* 12, 3–5. Cf. Jerome *Tractatus de psalmo* I (*CCSL* 78, pp. 7–8) which associates the just man with paradise, the river and tree of life in Rev. 22:1, and discusses the injunction to meditate on the law day and night.

[64] Scylla and Charybdis: *adv. Ruf.* 22 (*CCSL* 79, 93; *PL* 23, 473): *ueni Regium in Scyllaeo litore paululum steti, ubi veteres didici fabulas, et praecipitem pellacis Vlixi cursum, et sirenarum cantica, et insatiabilem Charybdis uoraginem.* For Jerome and the Holy Land, see chapter 4.

the monumental buildings than, say, Eutropius.[65] Paul's first question indeed reflects this:

'Tell me ... if new roofs be risen in the ancient cities.'[66] Jerome
is aware of the new churches built from the time of Constantine. In
his translation of Eusebius' *Onomasticon* he adds to the text details of
the churches built in Palestine since Eusebius' time. Years later, in
his *ep.* 120, 8,[67] in his discussion of the status of Jerusalem as a holy
city or not, he contrasts the ruins of the Temple where the Jews
mourn with the triumphantly rebuilt Christian city where 'the crowd
of believers in Christ see new roofs of churches arising daily'—*in
Christum turba credentium noua cotidie uideat ecclesiae tecta consurgere.* The
words he uses here for Jerusalem's new churches are the same as
Paul's: *tecta, nova, consurgere.* The new Christian churches symbolise
by their architectural presence the Christian appropriation of the
urban landscape of the great cities of the empire,[68] and, in particular, the Christianisation of what had been Jewish Jerusalem.[69] Thus
in this first attempt at a saint's *Life,* when he was looking for material for vivid descriptions, Jerome did not exclude the visual arts. I
have already noted the tendency towards concretization of the spiritual or abstract in the martyr accounts and the description of the
illegal mint: this would seem to be yet another aspect of this tendency—what Averil Cameron has described as the 'figural side of
Christian discourse.'[70]

[65] R.W. Burgess 'Jerome and the *Kaisergeschichte*' *Historia* 44 (1995) 357f. and see
now S. Rebenich 'Asceticism, Orthodoxy and Patronage: Jerome in Constantinople'
SP 33 (1997) 358f. on Jerome's additions to his translation of Eusebius' Chronicon.
[66] *v. Pauli* 10: *An in antiquis urbibus noua tecta consurgant?*
[67] Kelly does not discuss this letter, but it is dated by Cavallera and Labourt *ad
loc.* to 407. See now B. Biton-Ashkelony *Pilgrimage: perceptions and reactions in the patristic and monastic literature of the fourth-sixth centuries* (Ph.D. thesis, Jerusalem, 1995, in
Hebrew) 92f., who includes *ep.* 120 in the context of a discussion of attitudes to
Jerusalem; cf. Newman 172.
[68] For this phenomenon see the discussion by Hunt mentioning Rome, Alexandria,
Antioch and Constantinople: *CAH* 13, 251 and bibliography *ad loc.*
[69] On this see O. Irs[h]ai *Jewish-Christian polemics around the Jerusalem church in the
fourth century: historical perspectives (in the light of patristic and rabbinical literature)*: (Ph.D.
thesis, Jerusalem, 1993, in Hebrew).
[70] Averil Cameron *Christianity and the Rhetoric of Empire: The development of Christian
discourse* (Berkeley, 1991) 50, and cf. pp. 13; 59; 63. Cameron sees the widespread
use of metaphor in Christian language as inevitably leading to the use of symbols
in Christian art.

3b. *The saving centaur*

On his journey to Paul, Antony meets a centaur, who, surprisingly, is both Christian and benign.[71] When centaurs appear elsewhere in Christian literature it is in a pagan context, as in the *vita Antonii*, where the onocentaur is demonic.[72] They do not appear in art which is certainly Christian before the Middle Ages.[73] However, in the late Roman town of Sepphoris [Diocaesarea] in Galilee there is a mosaic dated by its excavators to the fifth century which shows a rearing centaur with the inscription ΘΕΟΣ ΒΟΗΘΟΣ—God the Saviour or the saving god.[74] Jerome's centaur appears following Antony's declaration that he believes that God will show him His servant as He promised:

Credo in Deo meo quod seruum suum, quem mihi promisit, ostendet (v. Pauli 7). It is interesting that these two saving centaurs with their relation to one God appear so close in time and place.[75]

3c. *The* vita Pauli, *the Roman catacombs and the book of Daniel*

Jerome's depiction of Paul, dead in a position of prayer, with two lions (*vita Pauli* 16), is extremely reminiscent of early Christian iconog-

---

[71] For an interesting discussion of how Jerome converts pagan animals and monsters to Christianity see now: R. Wisnieski '*Bestiae Christum loquuntur* ou des habitants du désert et de la ville dans la *Vita Pauli* de saint Jérôme' *Augustinianum* 40 (2000) 105–144.

[72] *Vita Antonii* 53, 1–3.

[73] J. Kollwitz *et al.* (eds.) *Lexikon der Christlichen Ikonographie* II, (Rome etc., 1970) 504f. s.v. Kentaur. There is a mosaic of Orpheus found in Jerusalem which shows both a centaur and a satyr. The mosaic was in a building where there was another, unconnected mosaic with a cross: H. Vincent 'Une mosaïque byzantine à Jérusalem' *Revue Biblique* 10 (1901) 436–444; *id.* 'La mosaïque d'Orphée' 11 (1902) 100–103. H. Vincent and M. Avi-Yonah, 'Mosaic pavements in Palestine' *QDAP* 2 (1933) no. 133 pp. 172–3 with bibliography *ad loc.*, think this is a Christian mosaic, but A. Ovadiah, S. Mucznik 'Orpheus from Jerusalem—Pagan or Christian image?' *Jerusalem Cathedra* I (ed. L.I. Levine, Jerusalem, 1981) 152–166 have argued that it was originally pagan and only later appropriated by Christians. Estimates of dating range from the second to the seventh centuries (Ovadiah and Mucznik, *op. cit.* 165–6).

[74] E. Netzer, Z. Weiss *Zippori* (Jerusalem, 1995) 50. The mosaic comes from the 'House of the Nile Mosaic', which contains other mosaics with pagan subjects: the Festival of the Nile, and two mosaics featuring amazons: *op. cit.* 44–52. For ΘΕΟΣ ΒΟΗΘΟΣ in Jewish, Christian and Samaritan contexts, see L. Di Segni 'Εἷς θεός in Palestinian inscriptions' *SCI* (1994) 94–115.

[75] See also: P. Cox Miller 'Jerome's Centaur: A Hyper-icon of the Desert' *JECS* 4 (1996) 209–233 which stresses the position of the classical centaur between the civilised and the wild.

raphy of the prophet Daniel in the lions' den. In early Christian art, Daniel is often depicted as *orans*, in the praying position, with hands outstretched and upturned to heaven.[76] In his discussion of Constantine's Christian embellishment of Constantinople, Eusebius writes of gilded bronze statues of Daniel and the lions.[77] The triad of Daniel accompanied by two lions was extremely popular in third and fourth century frescoes in the catacombs of Rome,[78] for Daniel, like Paul, was seen as a type of Christ.[79] There is a graphic description by Jerome himself of how, in his youth, he used to visit the catacombs in Rome on Sunday afternoons,[80] and how the intense underground darkness was pierced from time to time by shafts of light:

> *Dum essem Romae puer . . . crebroque cryptas ingredi . . . raro desuper lumen admissum horrorem temperet tenebrarum.*

Jerome seems to have remembered paintings of Daniel from this time when he came to paint his verbal picture of Paul, dead in his

---

[76] Most of the depictions of Daniel show him standing with raised hands, but at least one late antique medallion shows him kneeling with raised hands like Paul: *DACL s.v.* Daniel (Leclerq) 4,1 p. 221f., pl. 3590.

[77] *Vita Constantini* iii, 49. Averil Cameron and S.G. Hall in their edition of *Eusebius: Life of Constantine* (Oxford, 1999) 298 suggest that Eusebius may here be putting a Christian interpretation on pagan statues of a man with lions.

[78] Above *DACL* art. cit. See e.g. J. Stevenson *The Catacombs: Rediscovered monuments of early Christianity* (London 1978) pl. 52. *DACL* has no less than 39 examples from the Roman catacombs alone, and the subject was also popular on sarcophagi cf. E.S. Malbon *The sarcophagus of Junius Bassus* (Princeton, 1990). Daniel was also popular in other parts of the empire: for an attempt to relate the iconography with that of the Christian martyrs: J.W. Salomonson *Voluptatem spectandi non perdat sed mutet: Observations sur l'iconographie du martyre en Afrique Romaine* (Amsterdam/Oxford/NY, 1979). There is also an example of Daniel and the lions from a Christian tomb in Palestine, although Jerome, of course, had not yet been here at the time he wrote the *vita Pauli*: G. Foerster 'Lohamei Haghétaot: Tombe Byzantine' *RB* 78 (1971) p. 586 and plate.

[79] Daniel was also seen as the type of the just man, following his reversal of the false judgement in the story of Susanna (Vulgate: Dan. 13): as noted above, Paul expects to be awarded the *corona justitiae* on his ascent to heaven. Daniel is also miraculously provided with a meal by the Lord when in the lions' den according to Bel and the Dragon (Vulgate: Dan. 14:36): *Danihel tolle prandium quod misit tibi Deus*: cf. *v. Pauli* 10: *inquit Paulus, Dominus nobis prandium misit.*

[80] *Com. in Hiez.* xii 40, 5–13 (*CCSL* 75, 556; *PL* 25,392). It should be noted that in this passage Jerome quotes from Virgil's description of the fall of Troy: *horror ubique animos, simul ipsa silentia terrent*, which comes from Book II of the Aeneid (l. 755), shortly after the passage quoted by Jerome in the *vita Pauli* (Aen. II 650), when Antony arrives at Paul's cave, discussed above, which may show that he connected them in his mind.

underground cave, then buried by two lions. Jerome's patron, Pope Damasus, took a great interest in the Roman catacombs, and wrote verses which were engraved on plaques placed on their walls.[81] Further support for the supposition that Jerome was thinking of catacomb paintings of Daniel here is to be found in the fact that, in the introduction to his translation of the biblical book of Daniel, when describing his struggles with the language of this book, Jerome uses a simile of light from above piercing dark underground space: *quasi per cryptam ambulans rarum desuper lumen aspicere.*[82] The vocabulary: *cryptam, rarum desuper lumen*, is almost identical to that of his description of the catacombs quoted above. Jerome is using the description he had once applied to the catacombs as an image of his problems in translating the book of Daniel. Thus Daniel and the catacombs are clearly associated in his mind.

There is a further association between Daniel and the *vita Pauli*. In Jerome's first letter, which is about the attempt to execute an innocent Christian woman at Vercelli, Jerome compares his heroine to Shadrach, Meshach and Abednego, the 'Three Children in the Fiery Furnace,' to Susannah and the Elders, and to Daniel in the Lions' den. All these came from the Vulgate Daniel[83] and its additions, and all these were popular in catacomb art too, but there is a further connection. Both Daniel's lions in Jerome's letter, and the lions in the *vita Pauli* which run up to Antony, are described as having wagging tails: *adulantibus caudis* (*v.Pauli* 16). The biblical description of the incident only relates to the lions' jaws, but a number of the catacomb paintings do show Daniel between lions with long up-curved tails.[84]

Thus there are a number of connections between Jerome's reading of the book of Daniel, the Roman catacombs and the *vita Pauli*, so that we can presume that the catacomb pictures of Daniel in the

---

[81] C. Pietri *Roma Christiana* I (Rome, 1976) 575f. 'La mission chrétienne à Rome de Damase à Sixte.'

[82] *Prol. in Danihele propheta* (ed. Weber, 1341) and see: I. Opelt 'San Girolamo e suoi maestri ebrei' *Augustinianum* 28 (1988) 327–338 esp p. 331, n. 14.

[83] Three Children: Dan. 3: 12–97 (Vulgate); Susannah: Dan. 13 (Vulgate); Lions' Den: Dan. 6:16–24.

[84] E.g. J. Stevenson *The Catacombs: Rediscovered monuments of early Christianity* (London, 1978) pl. 52 (catacomb of Peter and Marcellinus); A. Grabar *Christian Iconography: A Study of its Origins* (Princeton, 1968) pl. 26 (catacomb of Vigna Massimo).

lions' den were the source for Jerome's verbal tableau of Paul and
the lions.[85]

One of Jerome's strengths as writer lies in his vivid word-pictures,
which have sometimes been attributed to his vivid imagination. Here
we have seen how he used his real experiences of the natural world
as well as the art and architecture he saw around him. We shall
turn now to look at his use of classical material in his work.

1.3. Jerome's Classical and Christian Worlds

Classical learning and Jerome's audience

We have looked at Jerome's use of the material world around him
in creating the *vita Pauli*. We turn now to see how he makes use of
Classical literature in constructing his story, making it comprehens-
ible and more familiar to various potential Latin audiences, both
educated and less educated. Thus he uses classical material on various different levels, so that his work will be available to different
sorts of people.

The journey from Antony's monastery takes three days and during
it he meets a trio of beasts. The hippocentaur and the satyr form
a pair of mythological beings who point the way to Paul for Antony.[86]
Miller has noted the centaur's special status as being both extremely
civilised, like Chiron, and extremely barbaric, as in centauromachias,[87]
but both civilisation and barbarism are now converted to the mission of Christianity—the centaur, appearing after Antony's *credo*,

---

[85] Prudentius has a passage in his *Peristephanon* 11, 153–70 evoking a subterranean
catacomb, which has been compared to the passage in Jerome's *Commentary on Ezekiel*
for the feeling of horror which it evokes: M.A. Malamud *A Poetics of Transformation:
Prudentius and classical mythology* (Ithaca/London, 1989) 108–110. M. Roberts *Poetry
and the Cult of the Martyrs: The Liber Peristephanon of Prudentius* (Ann Arbor, 1993) 148f.
Both cite the Ph.D. thesis of A.R. Springer *Prudentius, pilgrim and poet. The Catacombs
as inspiration for the Liber Cathemerinon* (Wisconsin, 1984, *non vidi*) which they say argues
that the decoration of the Roman catacombs may have been influential on Prudentius'
poetry. In his *Peristephanon* xi Prudentius describes the martyrdom of Hippolytus,
then continues with a description of his underground martyrium in the Roman
catacombs and the painting of the martyrdom on its wall.

[86] For an extensive discussion of Jerome's satyr: P.B. Harvey, Jr. 'Saints and
Satyrs: Jerome the scholar at work' *Athenaeum* 86 (1998) 35–56.

[87] P. Cox Miller 'Jerome's Centaur: A Hyper-icon of the Desert' *JECS* 4 (1996)
209–233 Cf. Augustine *de Civ. Dei* xviii 13 (*PL* 41, 570).

gnashes its teeth but points out the right way. We have already seen
that Jerome mentions the monks of Syria earlier in the *vita*, and that
in his letters he relates how he found it very difficult to communicate with them in their semi-barbaric Syriac speech—is there a satirical allusion to these Syrian monks in these semi-barbaric beasts with
whom Antony finds it so difficult to communicate? The satyr, famous
for his participation in wild Dionysaic sex orgies, now speaks of God
and salvation. On speaking to the satyr, Antony is said to rejoice
for Christ's glory and the fall of Satan. For those who may not have
been familiar with classical mythology Jerome adds explanations and
even provides evidence for sceptics.

Antony would not have reached Paul without the help of a third
and rather different beast, a she-wolf. A non-urban audience would
have seen in this the miraculous conversion of an every-day threat
to divine aid.[88] A Roman audience should have picked up an allusion to the legendary she-wolf which fostered Romulus and Remus,
and now comes in answer to Antony's prayer to Christ.

When Antony finally reaches Paul's threshold, the recluse refuses
at first to let him in. Jerome quotes two lines from Virgil here.[89]
Paul Harvey[90] sees such quotations as an intrusion of Jerome's eru-
dition and love of displaying his learning, while de Vogüé[91] sees these
lines in particular as simply serving to relieve the tension of the

---

[88] On the traditional theme of miraculous guides in saints' *Lives* see: A. Goddard
Elliot *Roads to Paradise* (Hanover and London, 1987) 116f. Elliot curiously omits the
satyr from her discussion of Antony's encounters in the desert. Perhaps this is
another of the small flaws in this excellent book caused by the author's untimely
death: cf. G. Gould's review of Elliot *JThS* (1989) 627–31.

[89] These are not the only direct quotations in the *vita Pauli*, for there are other
allusions or references which perform the function of reminding a classically educated audience of similar situations, and hence underlining the point Jerome wants
to make: cf. e.g. *vita Pauli* 4, where Paul's brother-in-law betrays him for gold, where
Jerome quotes *Aeneid* III 56–7 where Polydorus' foster father kills him for gold. This
allusion, interestingly, is also cited as a rhetorical question. The passage, which deals
with religious persecutions, ends with another classical allusion, to Florus III, 5, 7
(I, 40, 7) where Mithridates murders Roman citizens and violates religious shrines.
For allusions or references, and their important function in Roman literature and
especially in Virgil, see R.F. Thomas 'Virgil's *Georgics* and the Art of Reference'
HSCP 90 (1986) esp. 172, n. 8.

[90] Paul B. Harvey Jr. *Jerome, Life of Paul the First Hermit: Introduction and Translation*
in V.L. Wimbush (ed.) *Ascetic Behavior in Greco-Roman Antiquity: A Sourcebook* (Minneapolis,
1990) 357f.

[91] A. de Vogüé (*op. cit.* n. 13 above) 169.

moment. But we can discover other functions for these lines. First, they add a note of familiar high culture for a Roman audience which would otherwise perhaps have felt progressively alienated by the strange wild setting—and would most certainly have been ignorant of Jewish aggadic material.[92] Secondly, the Virgilian context from which they are taken adds yet another layer of allusive meaning to the situation for this audience. The first line:

> And so he stood pleading and fixed there

> *Talia perstabat memorans, fixusque manebat*

is taken from Aeneid II, 650, and refers to the situation where Anchises, the father of Aeneas, at first refuses to listen to his son's entreaties to leave Troy. Antony and his quest are thus given a heroic dimension by the allusion to Rome's greatest hero, but Paul has become his respected father and predecessor, who at first refuses to listen to his request. The next line:

> To him the hero answered, in few words

> *Atque huic responsum paucis ita reddidit heros*

is taken from Aeneid VI, 672, and refers to Aeneas' quest for Anchises—in the Underworld. Aeneas, having passed through the darkness of Hades with its tortures, arrives at Elysium, where he is told that the souls of the blessed have no fixed abode. Antony, who has come through darkness in search of Paul, will find him in his earthly paradise, but this is no fixed abode—he is one of the Blessed who will reach the heavenly paradise.[93] Thus Jerome provides a network of allusions which form a familiar undertext for the classically educated, as well as an extra level of meaning.[94]

---

[92] See Leclerc (*op. cit.* n. 36 above) 262–3.

[93] See also A. Kleinberg *Fra Ginepro's Leg of Pork: Christian Saint's Stories and Their Cultural Role (sic)* (Tel Aviv, 2000, in Hebrew) 193.

[94] On the literary allusion as 'a device for the simultaneous activation of two texts' see Z. Ben Porat 'The Poetics of Literary Allusion' *PTL* 1 (1976) 105–128. See now: S. Hinds *Allusion and Intertext: dynamics of appropriation in Roman poetry* (Cambridge, 1998) for the latest (1990's) scholarly debate on this subject. While many of Jerome's audience could have been expected to recognise a Virgilian hexameter, only a small group of the most highly literate would have been aware of its context, but Hinds, like Thomas before him (n. 89 *supra*) shows that the habit of reference was both widespread and deeply rooted in classical Latin literature.

This classical background, then, would have been familiar to an intended lettered audience in Rome, an audience which belonged to the class which could afford to dress in silk and gold, and drink from jewelled cups. From the fact that he upbraids these so strongly we can infer that Jerome's work was at least partly intended for those who had just given up such luxuries, for he stresses the rewards such abnegation would bring. These would include such circles as those of Asella, Paula or Marcella at Rome, with whom he was later very involved. Indeed, Jerome uses the same images of jewelled cups and silk in a letter to Paula herself written years later when he was back in Rome, saying she should leave these very luxuries for others, for [the Christian's] delight is to meditate on the law of the Lord day and night (Ps. 1:2).[95] Rebenich thinks that 'it is obvious that the "Life of Paul the First Hermit" was addressed to a public of educated Christians who were themselves interested in the ascetic movement', while Averil Cameron writes that 'Jerome still resolutely fixed his attention on the upper class.'[96] It is noteworthy in this context to remember that one of the ways in which Paul is better than Antony is in his education. One of the most common charges thrown at his enemies by Libanius, Jerome's pagan contemporary in Antioch, was that of illiteracy.[97] By making Paul literate, and then having him abnegate his literacy, Jerome is answering charges of cultured pagans about illiterate monks.[98]

However, Jerome also intended his work for an even wider audience. In his letter to Paul of Concordia, he writes that he sought to lower his style for a less cultured audience: *propter simpliciores*.[99] In

---

[95] *ep.* 30, 13: *habeant sibi ceteras suas opes, gemma bibant serico niteant . . . nostrae deliciae sint in lege Domini meditari die ac nocte.* The letter then continues with further imagery reminiscent of the incidents of the locked door and the bread in the *vita Pauli: pulsare ianuam non patentem, panes trinitas accipere.* This derives ultimately from Luke 11:5–10 as I have noted above (n. 53).

[96] S. Rebenich 'Asceticism, Orthodoxy and Patronage: Jerome in Constantinople' *Studia Patristica* 33 (1997) 369; Averil Cameron *Christianity and the Rhetoric of Empire* (Berkeley, 1991) 186.

[97] J.H.W.G. Liebeschuetz *Antioch: City and Imperial Administration in the Later Roman Empire* (Oxford, 1972) 33; 234.

[98] Cf. Patlagean (*op. cit.* n. 35 above) 103: 'Hagiographical accounts are always built—if only to repudiate them—on the values of those milieux where poverty is alien.'

[99] See also the discussion below under 'Style.' Biblical commentary from Origen on had also been written on two levels, the literal meaning for the *simpliciores*, and the spiritual meaning for the *perfecti.* See on this M. Simonetti *Biblical Interpretation*

fact, the *vita Pauli* is deliberately written on more than one level. Although Jerome cites Virgil, this does not necessarily demand the very highest level of Roman culture, for knowledge of Virgil was extremely widespread—documents citing the poet have been found as far apart as Hadrian's Wall and Masada,[100] while Orosius, who visited Jerome in Bethlehem,[101] says that Virgil was 'burned into his memory' as early as primary school.[102] But Jerome does not demand even this level of culture from his audience.[103] Even though he cites Virgil, it is not necessary for his audience to know the poet to be able to understand the story line of the *vita*: the citations simply add extra depth to the web of allusions he has woven. Jerome actually discusses two-level writing in one of his letters, where he says that the holy Scriptures themselves are written on different levels, for both learned and unlearned: *in una eademque sententia aliter doctus, aliter audiret indoctus.*[104] We have seen, too, how Jerome explains the monsters of classical mythology for those of his audience to whom they were not familiar. The *vita Pauli* was written in Latin, so that originally it was presumably largely aimed at a western audience, for whom the descriptions of the desert would have seemed exotic.[105] Jerome is aware of the attractions of material from the Orient to a western audience—in his preface to *Hebrew Questions on Genesis*, he

---

in the Early Church: An Historical Introduction to Patristic Exegesis (Edinburgh, 1994, tr. J.A. Hughes) 43.

[100] For Virgil on Hadrian's Wall see A.K. Bowman, J.D. Thomas *The Vindolanda Writing-Tablets (Tabulae Vindolandenses II)* (London, 1994) 65f., Tablet no. 118; for Virgil at Masada, see H.M. Cotton, J. Geiger *Masada* II: *The Yigal Yadin Excavations 1963–1965: Final Reports: The Latin and Greek Documents* (Jerusalem, 1989) 31f., Document no. 721.

[101] Kelly 317–21.

[102] Orosius: *adv. paganos* 1.18.1: Aeneas' labours *ludi litterarii disciplina nostrae quoque memoriae inustum est.* Krauss (*op. cit.* n. 94) writes that 'Jerome's Hebrew tutor even quotes Virgil', referring to the *Praef. in Daniel* (ed. Weber, 1341): *Verum, adhortante me Hebraeo et illud mihi sua lingua crebrius ingerente "Labor omnia vicit inprobus" (Georg.* 1, 146). However, it is unclear what is the force of *sua lingua* here. It would seem unlikely that there was an extant translation of Virgil into Hebrew or Aramaic. It would also seem unlikely that a Hebrew or Aramaic speaker who knew Virgil in Latin would translate him into his own language, even for the purpose of instructing Jerome in Hebrew. What would seem most likely is that there was some sort of saying in Hebrew or Aramaic to this effect which Jerome translated into Virgilian Latin for his Latin speaking audience.

[103] Cf. A. de Vogüé (*op. cit.* n. 8) 151–2.

[104] *ep.* 53, 10.

[105] *QHG, praef.*

compares this work to expensive and exotic spices, brought by sea only to connoisseurs, and, as noted above, his letter to Paul of Concordia which accompanied the *vita Pauli* similarly compares the *vita* to rare oriental wares. Perhaps it was this very oriental material, now local rather than exotic, which led to the *vita Pauli*'s becoming popular with a non-Roman audience, for it was quickly translated not only into Greek but into Coptic, Syriac and Ethiopic as well.[106] The Preface to its predecessor, the *vita Antonii*, had addressed itself to monks as an example to be emulated. The Protestant scholar Grützmacher suggests that the erotic content made the *vita Pauli* especially popular in the eyes of monks.[107] We know from Augustine that martyr accounts were read aloud to church congregations, so it is possible that the *vita Pauli*, beginning with its two martyrdoms, was aimed at such an audience too.[108]

Turning now to look at possible connections between the *vita Pauli* and Jewish *aggadot*, it is impossible to say here whether the allusions to *aggadot* might point to an audience with Jewish connections, like the converted Jew who was Jerome's teacher. They are so well hidden as to make us suspect the opposite may be the case, and that Jerome was here just writing to define for himself the boundaries between Judaism and Christianity.

1.4. THE *VITA PAULI* AND THE *AGGADOT* ABOUT RABBI SHIM'ON BAR YOHAI: JEROME'S CHRISTIANISATION OF JEWISH SOURCES[109]

1.4.1. *Jews and Christians in the Holy Land: who influenced whom? The state of the debate*

Recently scholars have turned renewed attention to the question of contacts between Jews and Christians in the Holy Land in the fourth

---

[106] Kelly 60.

[107] Grützmacher I, 161–3. 'Diese Erzahlungen waren mit den elementen antiker Erotik getrankt und boten den Monchen Ersatz fur die sinnlichen Genusse, die sie aufgegeben hatten. Gerade in dieser pikanten Erbaulichkeit zeigt sich Hieronymus als Meister in der Vita Pauli.' Cf. A. de Vogüé (*op. cit.* n. 8 above) 156: 'tout moine hanté de fantasmes sexuels peut s'y reconnaître'.

[108] For a discussion of this point, noting that the liturgical calendar eventually celebrates 'des martyrs manqués', including the saint's days of all Jerome's saints see Bastiaensen (*op. cit.* n. 8 above) 97f.

[109] I am grateful to my friend and colleague Dr Yuval Shahar for discussion of many of the points in this section.

century, and to possible mutual influences. Daniel Boyarin has suggested that there may have been little to distinguish between Jews and Christians in the early centuries, and that Judaism and Christianity were two ends of a 'continuum where one hardly would know where one stopped and the other began.'[110] Both presumably drew on the same common pool of material and folklore. From the fourth century, however, there are attempts on both sides to differentiate themselves from the other, attempts which Boyarin feels do not always succeed. Boyarin takes the discourse of martyrdom as an example of where rabbinic Judaism and orthodox Christianity met and attempted to 'invent themselves as separate identities.'[111] In other areas too, rather than Christianity being seen as a daughter religion of Judaism, and influenced by her, by the fourth century Judaism was reacting, often violently, to Christianity.

Boyarin further notes that while there are isolated 'legends of the sages' with scattered episodes and various pieces of evidence on the lives of the talmudic sages, there are no extended biographies or hagiographies in any of the Talmudic texts. He suggests, however, that the groups of stories about particular rabbis can be taken together as a kind of sign or emblem, and that they represent the rabbis' marking out of the differences between themselves and the Christians. Christian hagiography of their holy men began in the fourth century, but the rabbis did not respond at length in kind, although they may have responded to isolated aspects.[112] This seems to me unlikely. In my opinion, Jerome in his *vita Pauli* is making a sustained and careful picture of the Christian holy man in contradistinction to the existing traditions about the Jewish Rabbi Shim'on bar Yohai [RSbY].

In the *vita Pauli* Jerome appears to be engaging with some of the same subjects that were of concern to the redactors of Jewish texts. Up to now, Boyarin has suggested, the stories of martyrdom to be found in both Jewish and Christian sources suggest competition between them: 'whose martyrdom is this anyway?' he titles his chapter. Christians generally had chosen martyrdom rather than escape, while Jews had often taken the opposite path. Now both RSbY and Jerome's

---

[110] D. Boyarin *Dying for God: Martyrdom and the making of Christianity and Judaism* (Stanford, 1999) p. 9.

[111] *Op. cit.* p. 20.

[112] *Op. cit.* p. 32f.

hero choose to escape: Jerome indeed writes that martyrdom has now given way to asceticism. Certainly in his own fourth century there are almost no opportunities for martyrdom anymore with the newly Christian empire. If up to now Judaism and Christianity have been fuzzy at the edges with unclear distinctions, Jerome here seems to be sharpening distinctions and making clear boundaries. I shall suggest that Jerome is now competing with the Jews for the figure of the ascetic holy man and clearly defining the Christian version.

Seth Schwartz has also tackled the subject of Jewish and Christian self-identification in his interesting and provocative reinterpretation of the evidence in *Imperialism and Jewish Society, 200 BCE to 640 CE*. He too sees a turning point in the fourth century, when, he thinks, because the Christians took over imperial power they must have influenced the Jews: he identifies a decline in Judaism in the second and third centuries followed by a 're-Judaizing' of the Jews by the Christian state.[113] Thus, in his opinion, cases where we can identify treatment of common themes in Jewish and Christian literature will have been the result of Christian statement followed by Jewish reaction. Schwartz is, of course, correct in suggesting that it is more likely that influences would diffuse from a centre of authority downwards. However, although Christians now held imperial power and hence temporal authority, they had long regarded Judaism as the source of the original divine authority, albeit now supplanted by Christianity. Because of this attitude, Christian sources consistently relate back to *typoi* from the Hebrew Bible, as we shall see later in the discussion of the *vita Malchi*. Similarly, early Christian art has far more scenes from the Hebrew Bible than from the New Testament, and early pilgrims visit more sites from the Hebrew Bible than sites connected with the New Testament.[114] By the fourth century, with the Christianisation of the empire, Christians are intent on demonstrating the overthrow and reversal of this source of authority and hence their superiority over Judaism, as well as paganism, at every opportunity. Jerome was, of course, deeply involved in the debate

---

[113] S. Schwartz *Imperialism and Jewish Society, 200 BCE to 640 CE* (Princeton, 2001) 180–202.

[114] Even Paula and Jerome, in spite of all Jerome's attempts to Christianise Jewish sites, saw 51 sites from the Hebrew Bible as opposed to 33 New Testament or newly Christianised sites.

about the status of Judaism and the Hebrew language. We shall discuss in chapter 2 Jerome's creation of Hilarion as an authority figure to rival the Roman *dux* and Jewish patriarch.

Now it is time to look at the parallels between Jerome's holy man, Paul of Thebes, and the Jewish holy man, Rabbi Shim'on bar Yohai, and ask whether it is possible to identify the direction of the borrowing, Jerome taking from Jewish sources or vice versa, or whether in the end it is only possible to speak of a common folklore tradition.

1.4.2. *Jerome's use of aggadic material*

Just as it was noted above that at least one of his martyr accounts seems to use local Antiochene tradition, so Paul's cave is reminiscent of another Syro-Palestinian tradition, the body of *aggadot* or traditions about Rabbi Shim'on bar Yohai [RSbY]. Rabbi Shim'on was a Jewish sage who lived in Palestine in the second century, and the Talmudic literature preserves many local traditions about him.[115] Like Jerome's Paul, RSbY is also said to have hidden from his Roman persecutors in a cave, living on spring water and dates (or carobs) for thirteen years.[116] Could Jerome have known these traditions? Jerome writes that he had contact with a monk who had converted from Judaism and began to learn Hebrew at the time when he was in the 'desert of Chalcis,' and that he later made considerable use of *aggadot* and *midrashim* in his biblical commentaries and especially in his *Hebrew Questions on Genesis*.[117] There are hundreds of

---

[115] Rabbi Shim'on bar Yohai is unusual among the rabbis of his generation in that he is portrayed as a combination of different types of Jewish holy man—learned sage, miracle worker, *saddiq* (righteous man) and *hasid* (pious man). For a full discussion of these terms and their application to Rabbi Shim'on see B.-Z. Rosenfeld 'R. Simeon b. Yohai: wonder worker and magician: scholar, *saddiq* and *hasid*' *REJ* 158 (1999) 349–384 esp. 369–375.

[116] I presented some of this material at the 13th International Conference on Patristics in Oxford in 1999 under the title: 'The hermit and the rabbi: Jerome's *vita Pauli* and the midrashim on Rabbi Shim'on bar Yohai.' See also A. Kleinberg *Fra Ginepros Leg of Pork: Christian Saint's Stories and Their Cultural Role (sic)* (Tel Aviv, 2000, in Hebrew) 190.

[117] Hebrew in the desert: *ep*. 125, 12. The classic source for Jerome's use of Jewish sources is S. Krauss 'The Jews in the works of the Church Fathers, vi: Jerome' *Jewish Quarterly Review* (1894) 225f. esp. Sect. 13, 'Jerome's Jewish traditions'. For more recent bibliography see J. Braverman *Jerome's Commentary on Daniel: A Study of comparative Jewish and Christian interpretations of the Hebrew Bible* (Washington, 1978); A. Kamesar *Jerome, Greek Scholarship and the Hebrew Bible* (Oxford 1992) esp.

examples of cases in his works where he cites '*hebraei*' as a source
for information about the meaning of a text, geographical identifications
etc. Most of these references to Jewish traditions are very brief indeed,
rarely more than a line or two long. We saw above that he uses
the metaphor of 'oriental merchandise' for the written material he
sends to Paul of Concordia. He uses this same image, of a ship laden
with oriental wares, to refer to material taken from Jewish sources,
which is only appreciated by the cognoscenti, in his preface to his
*Hebrew Questions on Genesis: peregrinae merces tantum volentibus navigent: bal-
samum, piper et poma palmarum rustici non emant.*[118] This may, then, be
a hint that here too he is referring to material taken from Jewish
sources.

Among the few rabbis Jerome names in his works is 'Symeon',
noted in *ep.* 121 together with Barachibas and Helles [Rabbi 'Aqiva
and Hillel]. As Rabbi Shim'on bar Yohai is cited in the Mishnah
over 300 times simply as 'Rabbi Shim'on,' it is most probable that
Jerome too is referring here to Rabbi Shim'on bar Yohai, and that
he was thus acquainted with some of the traditions about this rabbi.[119]
Jerome also knew that Jews hid from the Romans in caves during
the time of the Hadrianic persecutions.[120]

If Jerome did indeed use Jewish material about RSbY to build

---

p. 66; C.T.R. Hayward *Saint Jerome's Hebrew Questions on Genesis* (Oxford, 1995) esp.
p. 18f. and discussion of midrashic sources 19f.

[118] Hayward in his commentary notes that these are all exotic oriental products.
It may be further noted that balsam and dates were well-known products of the
Holy Land: balsam came from 'Ein Gedi which was also the source of the famous
Jericho date (*poma palmorum*). (For a discussion of the sources on balsam and dates:
M. Fischer, M. Gichon, O. Tal *'En Boqeq: excavations in an oasis on the Dead Sea* II:
[Mainz, 2000] balsam: 94–5; 120–123; dates: 95–6; 123–6). Pepper, on the other
hand, was imported from India at this period. Jewish traders in pepper are known
from a later period (cf. A. Oppenheimer 'Jews in International Trade with China
in Antiquity' in *Sino-Judaica: Jews and Chinese in Historical Dialogue, An International
Colloquium, Nanjing, 1996*, [Tel Aviv, 1999]): the inclusion by Jerome of pepper in
an image which is a metaphor for Jewish learning may suggest Jewish involvement
in the Indian pepper trade as early as the fourth century.

[119] *ep.* 121, 10: *[Judaei]solent respondere et dicere: Barachibas et Symeon et Helles, magistri nostri, tradiderunt nobis....* On R. Shim'on bar Yohai as just Rabbi Shim'on
300 times in Mishnah: G. Stemberger *Introduction to the Talmud and Midrash* (tr.
M. Bockmuel, Edinburgh, 1996²) 76. Newman 161 also thinks this identification is
probable. Newman further notes 169f. that Jerome's discussion of Jewish fasting
customs in his commentary on Zechariah viii 18–19 (*CCSL* 76A, 820–821; *PL* 25,
1546f.) is very close to the opinion of Rabbi Shim'on bar Yohai as quoted in the
Tosefta.

[120] Cf. 1.2.2a and n. 47 above (*Com. in Es.* I, ii. 15 (*CCSL* 73, 36; *PL* 24, 51).

his Christian hero, this would have been after his very first close contact with Jews, and in reaction to his first real acquaintance with Judaism. Obviously at this stage Jerome did not have an extensive knowledge of written Jewish sources, but Jewish *midrash* is based on oral tradition. At this time we know that Jerome was personally struggling to come to terms with the ascetic life, and even distracting himself from sexual fantasies by concentrating on the difficulties of learning Hebrew from the converted Jew who taught him during his stay in the 'desert of Chalcis.'[121] It could be that he had heard from his teacher then of the famous Jewish holy man whose different form of asceticism would have been of particular interest to both of them: I noted above that there is debate as to whether Paul actually existed, or whether Jerome invented him, or combined a number of traditions about Christian holy men to create his saint. If he was using a tradition with very few details (or, as many have suspected, none at all), he will have needed other material to flesh out his picture of Paul. The Jewish material on Rabbi Shim'on bar Yohai would have filled this gap neatly. But it is likely to have raised many questions in Jerome's mind as to the nature of asceticism, Jewish or Christian. So we should not be surprised that he appears to have used the writing of his first saint's *Life* as an opportunity to draw for himself the boundaries between Jewish and Christian asceticism, and to build his ascetic saint, as it were on the shoulders of the Jewish rabbi, showing where his ascetic Christianity differs from and surpasses Judaism.

It is true that stories about a holy man hiding in a cave are widespread, from the biblical Elijah to the stories of Egyptian monks written up by Jerome's friend (and later enemy) Rufinus. There are even Greek parallels as well, and I shall discuss a possible Latin source below.[122] However, in the case of the *vita Pauli* and the aggadic

---

[121] *ep.* 22, 7.
[122] Cf. K. Cooper 'A saint in exile: Thecla at Rome and Meriamlik' *Hagiographica* 2 (1995) 7: 'The religious literature of the Roman empire was riddled with a superfluity of caves and caverns as oracular grottoes, as hiding places for messianic revealers in flight from Roman authorities, as birth-places for the messianic sons of righteous women'. For a discussion of the *topos* of the holy man in the cave in Christian sources see Alison Goddard Elliot *Roads to Paradise* (Hanover and London, 1987) and cf. E. Benz 'Die heilige Höhle in der alten Christenheit und in der östlich-orthodoxen Kirche' *Eranos Jahrbuch* 22 (1953) 365–432; for Jewish and Greek

material about R Shim'on bar Yohai, the parallels are not merely general, but extend also to specific details, even details that have no function in the plot of the *vita*. Modern literary theory on literary borrowing proposes that in clearly related works details in one work which are not functional point to borrowing from the other work where they are functional. This would therefore imply that Jerome borrowed them from aggadic sources where they are functional. I shall discuss this critical point about the direction of the borrowing shortly.

When comparing different Talmudic sources, it is usual to compare the different redactions very closely, looking for similarities and divergences in language and structure. Jerome wrote in Latin and the talmudic material is in Hebrew and Aramaic, so that a very close comparison is generally very difficult. However, in spite of this, there are a number of surprising similarities of wording and structure between Jerome and the *aggadah*.

1.4.3. *Did Jerome know the original version of the* aggadah?

The *aggadah* about R Shim'on bar Yohai in the cave is to be found in a number of talmudic sources. The different versions found in the sources reflect earlier oral traditions. It is not easy to trace the development from oral source to written tradition, but we can analyse the literary and narrative components of these traditions and their inter-relationships. The versions found in the Jerusalem Talmud and Genesis Rabbah were both redacted very close to Jerome's time. Other Palestinian versions of this episode include Esther Rabbah, Ecclesiastes Rabbah, Pesiqta deRav Kahana and Midrash Tehillim, all of which are later in their dates of editing but include earlier material.[123] There is also a somewhat different version of the episode

---

parallels see L.I. Levine 'R Shim'on bar Yohai and the Purification of Tiberias: History and Tradition' *HUCA* 49 (1978) 160 (Jewish); 181f. (Greek). For a general discussion of problems of rabbinic biography see G. Stemberger (*op. cit.* n. 119 above) 59–62, who notes that 'the potential cross-links between biographical narratives in rabbinic texts and Christian hagiography merit closer examination.'

[123] Jerusalem Talmud Shevi'it ix, 38d; Genesis Rabbah lxxix, 6 (Theodor-Albeck edition, 941–945); Esther Rabbah iii, 7; Ecclesiastes Rabbah x, 8; Pesiqta de-Rav Kahana Beshalah 16–17 (Mandelbaum edition, 191–194; Pisqa 11 Braude and Kapstein 216–7); Midrash Tehillim xvii, 13. For dating of these see Stemberger *op. cit. supra* n. 119.

in the Babylonian Talmud, Shabbat 33b–34a. It is no longer fashionable among scholars to look for the 'original' version of a talmudic text. However, as we shall attempt to demonstrate below, Jerome seems to have been acquainted with details from both Palestinian and Babylonian versions of the *aggadah*. The Babylonian Talmud had, of course, not yet been written in Jerome's time. Thus, if my argument is accepted, it would appear that we cannot but conclude that the later Babylonian version was using earlier material that has not survived in our extant Palestinian sources, and that Jerome knew this 'original' version. It may be relevant here that the 'desert of Chalcis' is physically situated between Palestine and Babylonia.

Further support for the suggestion that Jerome knew an 'original' version of the Babylonian Talmud has now appeared in an article by Matthew Kraus.[124] Kraus examined Jerome's Commentary on Ecclesiastes, begun in Rome and finished in Bethlehem at the end of the 380's. Ginzberg had shown long ago that Jerome made use of Jewish traditions in this commentary,[125] but Kraus identifies a further tradition not brought by Ginzberg, that he claims Jerome owed to his Jewish informant and which he calls the 'old-age allegory.' Kraus demonstrates that similar details to Jerome's allegory about old age have been preserved in the Babylonian Talmud. He writes 'the presence of this Jewish tradition [sc. in Jerome] has major implications. Since the old-age allegory has been preserved in the Babylonian Talmud and not in the Palestinian midrashim, the Babylonian Talmud is thus proven to contain Palestinian aggadic material with a late fourth-century provenance.'[126] While I would not be prepared to go as far as Kraus in drawing conclusions about the Palestinian material in the Babylonian Talmud (the *vita Pauli*, unlike the Commentary on Ecclesiastes, was not written in Palestine) it is clear that he has come to the same conclusion about Jerome's use of Talmudic material in a different work. Jerome does seem to have been acquainted with an earlier version of material that is not extant in the Palestinian Talmud but has been preserved in the Babylonian Talmud.

---

[124] M. Kraus 'Jews, Pagans and Christians in dialogue: Jerome on Ecclesiastes 12:1–7' *HUCA* 70/71 (1999–2000) 183–231.

[125] L. Ginzberg 'Die Haggada bei den Kirchenvätern: V Der Kommentar des Hieronymus zu Kohelet' in *Abhandlung zur Erinnerung an Hirsch Perez Chajes* (Wien, 1933) 22–50, *non vidi*.

[126] Kraus, *op. cit.* n. 124 above, p. 184.

3a. The Jerusalem Talmud [JT] and other Palestinian versions
The Jerusalem Talmud's version of the *aggadah* on Rabbi Shim'on
bar Yohai goes as follows:

> R Shim'on bar Yohai hid for thirteen years in a cave of *terumah* carobs
> until his body became covered with rusty sores. At the end of thir-
> teen years he said: 'Perhaps I shall go out and see what is happening
> in the world.' He went out and sat at the mouth of the cave and saw
> a hunter tracking birds and spreading his net. He [R Shim'on] heard
> a heavenly voice [*bat qol*] say 'you are dismissed' [*dimus*] and the bird
> escaped.[127] R Shim'on said 'Without [the decree of] heaven even a
> bird does not perish, so much more a man.' When he saw that things
> had quietened down, he said: 'Let us go down and warm up in the
> public baths of Tiberias'. He said 'We ought to do something [for
> them], as our fathers of old have done, [as it is written in Gen. 33:18]
> *And he* [Jacob] *was gracious to* [lit. encamped before] *the city*—they estab-
> lished duty-free markets and sold [goods] in the market'. He said: 'Let
> us purify Tiberias' and he took lupines, sliced and scattered them, and
> wherever there was a corpse, it would float and rise up to the surface.
> A Samaritan seeing him said: 'Let me go and ridicule this old Jew'.
> He took a corpse, went and buried it in a place that he [RSbY] had
> purified. He then came to R Shim'on bar Yohai and said to him:
> 'Have you not purified that place? Nonetheless I can produce [a corpse]
> from there'. R Shim'on bar Yohai perceiving through the Holy Spirit
> that he had placed one there, said: 'I decree that those above shall
> descend [*i.e.* the Samaritan shall die] and those below [the corpse]
> shall arise. And thus it happened.[128]

The other Palestinian versions of this *aggadah* are very similar. One
difference is that the other versions do not present R Shim'on as
being alone in his cave, but accompanied by his son, R El'azar.
Both Midrash Ecclesiastes Rabbah [EccR] and Midrash Esther
Rabbah [EstR] add that RSbY lived on dates as well as carobs.
Otherwise differences are mainly in the order of presentation of

---

[127] You are dismissed: דימוס. MidGenR 79 (ed. Theodor-Albeck 941–5) adds 'you
are convicted אקולפס; it remained trapped.' Theodor-Albeck has a long discussion
of this passage bringing all the parallel Talmudic texts and variant readings, but
does not mention the parallel with the passage from the Gospels (below, sect 4b),
nor is this discussed by L.I. Levine in his article on this aggadah: 'R Shim'on bar
Yohai and the Purification of Tiberias: History and Tradition' *HUCA* 49 (1978)
143–85. It is however noted by Ofrah Me'ir in her article, which has a most careful and enlightening discussion of RSbY in the cave in Jewish sources: 'The story
of Rabbi Shim'on ben Yohai in the cave' *'Alei Siah* 26 (1989, in Hebrew) 145–60.
[128] JT Shevi'it ix, 1, 38d. (Tr. Levine, adapted).

events—the explanation of the verse in Genesis about Jacob insti-
tuting markets for the city of Shechem is the introductory event in
Midrash Genesis Rabbah [GenR], as might be expected in a midrash
on the book of Genesis.[129] The two late midrashim, EstR and Midrash
Psalms [MidPs] begin with the persecutions and the rusty sores
suffered by R Shim'on.

3b. *The Babylonian Talmud [BT] version*
The version in the Babylonian Talmud is rather different:

> Rabbi Judah and Rabbi Yose and Rabbi Shim'on [bar Yohai] were
> sitting and Judah b. Gerim was sitting beside them. R. Judah opened
> and said: 'How pleasant are the acts of this nation. They established
> markets. They established bathhouses. They established bridges.
> R. Yose was silent. R Shim'on answered and said: 'Everything they
> established, they established only for their own needs: they established
> markets—to place prostitutes there; bathhouses—to pamper themselves;
> bridges—to take tolls.' Judah b Gerim went and retold their words
> and it became known to the [sc.Roman] government. They said: Judah
> who praised—let him be praised. Yose who was silent—let him be
> exiled to Sepphoris. Shim'on who disparaged—let him be killed.[130]
> . . . He and his son went and hid themselves in the *bet ha-midrash*,
> [and] his wife brought him bread and a jug of water and they dined.
> When the decree became more severe he said to his son: 'Women are
> of unstable temperament: she may be put to torture and expose us.'
> So they went and hid in a cave. A miracle occurred, and a carob-
> tree and a spring of water were created for them. They would strip
> their clothes and sit up to their necks in sand. The whole day they
> studied; when it was time for prayers they dressed, covered themselves,
> prayed and then took off their clothes again, so they should not wear
> out. Then Elijah came and stood at the entrance to the cave and said
> 'Who will tell Bar Yohai that the emperor is dead and his decree
> annulled? So they emerged and saw a man ploughing and sowing. He
> said 'They forsake life eternal and engage in life temporal!' Whatever

---

[129] For Jewish sources dealing with this verse, see A. Shinan, Y. Zakovitz *And
Jacob came 'Shalem': Gen. 33:18–20 in the Bible, the old versions and the ancient Jewish literature* (Jerusalem, 1984, in Hebrew). That Jerome knew some Jewish sources on
this verse is clear from *QHG ad loc.: Tradunt Hebraei quod claudicantis femur Iacob ibi
conualerit et sanutum sit, propterea eandem ciuitatem [sc. Sychem] curati et perfecti uocabulum
consecutam.*

[130] Tr. of this paragraph: J.L. Rubenstein *Talmudic Stories: narrative art, composition
and culture* (Baltimore, 1999) 106, adapted. See on this Y. Ben Shalom: 'Rabbi Judah
bar Ilai's attitude towards Rome' *Zion* 49 (1984, in Hebrew) 9–24; Rubenstein
op. cit. pp. 110–111.

they cast their eyes upon was immediately burnt up. A heavenly voice [*bat qol*] came forth and said to them: 'Have you come out to destroy My world? Go back to your cave!' So they returned and dwelt there twelve months, saying: 'The punishment of the wicked in Gehenna is [limited to] twelve months.' A heavenly voice [*bat qol*] come forth and said: 'Go forth from your cave!' They emerged: wherever R El'azar wounded, R Shim'on healed. He said to him: 'My son, you and I are sufficient for the world!'. On the eve of the Sabbath before sunset they saw an old man holding two bunches of myrtle and running at twilight. 'What are those for?' they asked him. 'They are in honour of the Sabbath' he replied. 'But one should be enough for you?' 'One is for *Remember* and one for *Observe.*'[131] He said to his son: 'See how dear the commandments are to Israel'. At that their minds were set at ease.

R Pinhas ben Ya'ir, his son-in-law, heard and went out to meet him. He took him to the baths and massaged his flesh. Seeing the clefts in his body he wept and the tears streamed from his eyes. 'Woe is me that I see you in such a state!' he said. 'Happy are you that you see me in such a state' he replied, 'for if you did not see me in such a state, you would not find me thus [learned]'. For originally, when RSbY raised a difficulty, R Pinhas b. Ya'ir would give him a dozen answers, whereas subsequently when R Pinhas b Ya'ir raised a difficulty, RSbY would give him two dozen answers.

'Since a miracle has occurred', he said, 'let me go and amend something, for it is written *and Jacob came whole [to the city of Shechem]*', which Rav interpreted: bodily whole, financially whole, and whole in his learning. *And he was gracious to the city*: Rav said 'He instituted coinage for them'.... Is there anything that requires amending? he asked. They said to him: 'There is a place which may be impure and priests have the trouble of going round it.' He said: 'Does anyone know that there was a presumption of purity here?' A certain old man replied: 'Here Ben Zakkai cut down lupines of *terumah*.' So he did likewise. Wherever it [the ground] was hard he declared it clean, while wherever it was loose he marked it out. Said a certain old man: 'Bar Yohai has purified a cemetery!' [The source ends with RSbY's critic dying at his glance.]

1.4.4. *The* vita Pauli *and the* aggadah *compared*

Jerome's *vita Pauli* has points in common with both the Palestinian and the Babylonian versions of the episode of Rabbi Shim'on bar Yohai. I would like to suggest that other parts of the *vita* seem to

---

[131] The reference here is to the two versions of the fourth of the Ten Commandments in Exodus 20:8 and Deuteronomy 5:12 respectively.

have been written in full knowledge of the Jewish *aggadah*, but in deliberate contradiction to it, to express the superiority of Christianity over rabbinic Judaism. As already noted in the introduction, Patricia Cox in her book *Biography in Late Antiquity* has underlined the tendency of biographies of Christian holy men in Late Antiquity to be written 'as polemics to be employed in furthering one tradition at the expense of others.'[132] Jerome was to be a polemicist in various causes throughout his life.[133] It would not be surprising if this tendency were visible from one of the very earliest of his works.

If we take the line followed by Boyarin and Schwartz noted above, suggesting that much Jewish literature in late antiquity was written in reaction to Christian writing, it might be proposed that the legends about Rabbi Shim'on bar Yohai were based on the *vita Pauli*, and written in reaction to it, setting up a Jewish ascetic hero in deliberate contradistinction to the growing popularity of the Christian saint. However, the similarity of verbal phrases is such that this would assume the somewhat unlikely scenario of literate Jews reading the *vita*, presumably in Syriac or Greek translation, and then writing the Aramaic and Hebrew *aggadot* about Rabbi Shim'on in response. This is a somewhat less likely scene than Jerome reading the *aggadot*, or hearing them from the converted Jew whom we know was his Hebrew teacher and who could have served as the channel of communication. I shall show later by a mainly literary, rather than historical, analysis which was the more likely direction of the borrowing. To begin with, let us look at the structural parallels, followed by the theological parallels, before presenting a close reading of the linguistic and narrative parallels.

4a. *Structural parallels*

Flight from persecution   After the two martyr accounts at the opening of the *vita Pauli*, the story of Paul himself begins, presenting Paul as no mere illiterate peasant but a well-born, highly educated young

---

[132] P. Cox *Biography in Late Antiquity: A Quest for the Holy Man* (Berkeley, 1983) p. xiv, and see now P. Cox Miller 'Strategies of representation in collective biography: constructing the subject as holy' in T. Hägg, P. Rousseau *Greek Biography and Panegyric in Late Antiquity* (Berkeley etc., 2000) 222; 228.

[133] See the discussion of Jerome's polemics in chapter 2.2.1b: Authority figures in late antique Palestine.

man, a fit counterpart to the learned rabbi. Paul hides from persecuting
Roman emperors in a distant villa (v. Pauli 4). However, fearing that
a family member would betray him, he flees further to a cave. This
two-stage flight from the civilised to the cave is similar to the episode
in the Babylonian Talmud, where RSbY also hides first in his bet
ha-midrash, then later, fearing his faithful wife will betray him under
torture, flees to a cave.[134] He too is fleeing from persecuting Romans—
as is also noted in EccR, EstR, MidPs and implied in JT, which
adds later 'when things had quietened down.'

In parallel to the account of RSbY's fear of betrayal by his wife,
we find Paul, an ascetic Christian who is himself unmarried, but
fears betrayal through marriage—his sister's wicked husband who is
motivated, Jerome tells us, by lust for gold. R. Shim'on fears inad-
vertent betrayal by his wife, because of the innate weakness of women:
Paul fears betrayal by his brother-in-law because of a different weakness—the wicked lust for gold. Here Jerome improves on his source
in his literary composition. Woman's weakness has no other part to
play in the aggadah, but the abnegation of worldly goods, and money
in particular is an integral part of Jerome's ascetic agenda, and will
be noted again below when we discuss the illegal mint in the cave.
Thus in both cases the motive behind the second flight is fear of
betrayal by a family member.

The cave refuge   Both RSbY and Paul, then, take refuge in a cave
in all versions of the story, although it is only in the JT version that
RSbY is alone—the other versions of the aggadah have him accompanied by his son, R El'azar. In most of the accounts of RSbY he
lives on carobs, although, as noted above, some of the Palestinian
versions have both carobs and dates. The Babylonian account has
a carob-tree and a spring of water created for him by a miracle.
Similarly, Paul finds a date-palm and spring in his cave 'as if God
himself had provided it.'[135] R Shim'on lives in his cave for 13 years:

---

[134] For a discussion of the two-stage flight from the civilised to the wild, see J.L.
Rubenstein *Talmudic Stories: narrative art, composition and culture* (Baltimore, 1999) 111–113.
Rubenstein provides an excellent redaction analysis of the BT and JT versions of
the *aggadah*, building on the work of Levine and Me'ir (above, n. 127).

[135] *quasi quod a Deo sibi offeretur: vita Pauli*, 6. cf. *vita Antonii* 50, 1. Both would seem
to derive ultimately from Matthew 6:31–33: the palm tree provides Paul's clothing
too (v. Pauli loc. cit.).

Paul surpasses him: he lives in his until he reaches the age of 113.[136]

It was not uncommon in antiquity for people fleeing persecution to seek refuge in caves—to take a few examples from many, Apuleius and Ammianus both mention bandits in caves;[137] rebel groups in caves are to be found in Josephus. Jews certainly took refuge in caves during the Bar Kokhba revolt of 135–137 CE, and it is indeed possible that the historical RSbY, who was a pupil of Rabbi 'Aqiva, one of the great supporters of the revolt against the Romans, was also forced to take hiding then.[138] I have already noted the local phenomenon of Christian seekers after a solitary ascetic life around this time, such as John Chrysostom and Chariton. Although most surviving literary references are later, we also cannot exclude the possible existence of a local folk-lore of holy men in caves.[139] But there are also similarities in the circumstantial details here, in the palm-tree and spring of water, as well as the play on the length of time each hero spent in his cave.

4b. *Parallel theological statements*

Providence and the bird in aggadah, *gospel and Jerome*   When RSbY goes to the mouth of his cave to look out at the world, in the JT version, he sees a hunter trapping birds. A heavenly voice (*bat qol*) decrees the bird should be let free, and it escapes. The *aggadah* actually uses the Aramaic form of a Latin term taken from Roman law proceedings, *dimus*, as a metaphor for Divine providence judging the world. Seeing this RSbY declares:

'Without [the decree of] heaven even a bird does not perish, so much more a man'. If RSbY trusts in Divine providence, he will go

---

[136] See Levine on the number 13: 'R Shim'on bar Yohai and the Purification of Tiberias: History and Tradition' *HUCA* 49 (1978) 160. The BT has RSbY live in his cave for 12 years and a further 12 months. Antony had attained the age of 106: J.R. Curran *Pagan city and Christian capital: Rome in the fourth century* (Oxford, 2000) p. 269.

[137] Apuleius *Metamorphoses* iv, 23; vi, 25; Ammianus *loc. cit.* n. 47 above: the Maratocupreni in Syria; Josephus *BJ* i, 304: brigands and their families in Arbel caves.

[138] See on this: O. Bar *Rabbi Simeon bar Yochai and his role in public affairs* (Ph.D., Tel Aviv, 2002, Hebrew with English summary) pp. 81–4.

[139] Rubenstein (above, n. 130) 340 notes that although caves figure in many rabbinic miracle stories, the figure of a sage hiding in a cave is unparalleled.

free once more like the bird. The metaphor is then realised in the aggadic material—the persecution abates and RSbY leaves for Tiberias. A very similar statement occurs near the end of the *vita Pauli*.[140] Paul dies and his body is found by Antony. Two lions arrive, and Antony is at first afraid, until he puts his trust in God. The lions bury Paul, then come to Antony for his blessing, at which he declares:

> Lord, without whose command no leaf lights from the tree, nor a single sparrow falls upon the ground, grant unto these even as Thou knowest.[141]

Jerome, however has a specific bird here, a sparrow, so that the words of Antony recall the similar statement in the Gospel of Matthew:

> Are not two sparrows sold for a farthing? and one of them shall not fall on the ground without your Father.[142]

Even the fall or escape of a small bird is subject to Divine providence, as Antony says, having renewed his trust in Heaven, like RSbY.

In his preface to his commentary on Matthew, Jerome writes that the Gospel of Matthew was originally written in Hebrew for Christian converts.[143] We noted above that he often used rabbinic *aggadot* and

---

[140] *vita Pauli* 16.

[141] *v Pauli* 16: *Domine, sine cuius nutu nec folium arboris defluit, nec unus passerum ad terram cadit, da illis sicut tu scis.* Tr. H. Waddell *The Desert Fathers* (London, 1936 repr. 1987), adapted. I have, except where noted, preferred Helen Waddell's beautiful translation which while not always accurate to the letter, preserves more than any other the spirit of the text. See Jerome *ep.* 57, 5. Cf. also Amos 3:4–8, with both a bird which falls into a trap and a roaring lion.

[142] Mat. 10:29: *nonne duo passeres asse veneunt et unus ex illis non cadet super terram sine Patre vestro.* The version in Luke 12:6 *nonne quinque passeres veneunt dipundio et unus ex illis non est in oblivione coram Deo* is closer in wording to the midrash, but further from Jerome's version in the *vita Pauli*. On the resemblances between the midrash and the Gospel see: H.L. Strack, P. Billerbeck *Das Evangelium nach Matthaus erlautert aus Talmud und Midrasch* (München 1969⁵), 582f.; C.G. Montefiore *Rabbinic Literature and Gospel Teachings* (1930 repr. NY 1970) 229. For the theological aspects: J.G. Cook 'The Sparrow's Fall in Mt. 10: 29b' *Zeitschrift für die Neutestamentliche Wissenschaft und die Kunde der älteren Kirche* 79 (1988) 138f. with bibliography *ad loc.*; D.J. Weaver *Matthew's Missionary Discourse* (Sheffield, 1990) 207f. with bibliography. I am grateful to Dr Weaver for discussion of this verse.

[143] *Com. in Mat. Praef.* (*CCSL* 77, 2; *PL* 26, 18). I will not enter here the problematic question of Jerome's claims about a Hebrew original for the gospel of Matthew (see Kelly, 65), but maybe his insistence on this owed something to his recognition that there were Jewish parallels to some of the material in the gospel.

midrashim to clarify points in his commentaries on the Old Testament books. For example, he mentions learning about Rabbi 'Aqiva's interpretation of a passage from Ecclesiastes in his commentary on this book.[144] In his commentary on Isaiah, Jerome tells us that Jews could even help explain a passage in Matthew which Christians could not understand.[145] In the *vita Pauli* he appears to have noticed the parallel between *aggadah* and Gospel centuries before Strack and Billerbeck. He does not, however, mention this parallel in the commentary on Matthew, written years later than the *vita Pauli*, in 398. This was a work completed in considerable haste and thus, in Kelly's eyes at least, often perfunctory in its discussion of the text.[146] Jerome very often repeats himself, and the same idea, quotation or metaphor will reappear many times in different works. We cannot know why this is not the case here, whether it was because the commentary was written in such haste, or whether Jerome felt his Christian audience would not take kindly to the use of Jewish rabbinic sources in the interpretation of the Christian Gospel, as opposed to the Hebrew book of Genesis, where he did publish Jewish commentaries. The passage from Matthew noted in his commentary on Isaiah mentioned above is a philological, not a midrashic interpretation.

To return to the *vita Pauli*: functionally it looks as if Jerome has here converted the Jewish *aggadah* to the words of Jesus.[147] Jerome, for all his close contacts with Jews and wide use of Jewish material, clearly defines the boundaries between the religions.

4c. *Verbal parallels*

Rust   After his stay in the cave RSbY suffers from 'rust' [חלודה, חלד *haluda, heled*] i.e. sores on his body, in almost all the Palestinian versions. In MidEstR and MidPs this is presented as a prime example

---

[144] *Com. in Eccl.* iv, 13–16 (*CCSL* 72, 288; *PL* 23, 1048–9): *Hebraeus meus, cuius saepe facio mentionem, cum Ecclesiasten mecum legeret, haec Baracchibam, quem unum uel maxime admirantur, super praesenti loco tradidisse testatus est.*

[145] *Illud quod in evangelio Matthaei omnes quaerunt ecclesiastici, et non inveniunt ubi scriptum est 'quoniam Nazaraeus vocabitur', eruditi Hebraeorum de hoc loco assumptum putant.* (*Com. in Es.* iv, 11:1–3 [*CCSL* 73, 147; *PL* 24, 144]). In Matthew 2:23 Jesus is described as the 'Nazirite' as it says in the prophets, which Jerome explains through the Hebrew '*neser*' (*flos*) of the passage in Isaiah 11:1 he is discussing.

[146] Kelly 222f.

[147] For another example of Jerome's 'christianisation' of a midrash, see A. Kamesar *Jerome, Greek Scholarship and the Hebrew Bible* (Oxford 1992) 66.

of the sufferings undergone by the righteous man. In MidPs, in fact, the key word that the whole *midrash* comes to interpret is *heled*, rust. In BT the word used is not 'rust' but 'clefts.' In JT, PdeRK and GenR this rust (like the clefts in BT) is the reason for RSbY to leave his cave and go to the baths in Tiberias, the next link in the development of the story-line. Thus the rust is functional in all the aggadic material.

Rust is also mentioned in the *vita Pauli*. Here the hero arrives in his cave to finds that it had once been used as an illegal mint by forgers, 'in the time when Antonius loved Cleopatra.' The forgers' tools are still around, and they are covered with rust: *scabrae . . . incudes et mallei* which is translated by both Harvey and Ewald as 'rusty' forges or anvils, and mallets.[148] *Scaber* is indeed used metaphorically to mean scaly, rusty, (cf. *scabra robigo pilorum* Virgil *Georgics* 1, 495) but is more usually used, according to Lewis and Short's dictionary, of roughness and diseases of the skin. Jerome uses it in this sense in the *vita Hilarionis*, where Hilarion begins to suffer from skin ailments as a result of his ascetic diet,[149] but he does not use *scaber* in the sense of 'rust' anywhere else in his writings. Thus, in describing the forgers' instruments in the *vita Pauli*, Jerome may well have had in mind the 'rusty sores' [חלודה, *haluda*] of RSbY. There is no need for the rust on the instruments in the Paul's cave except as a picturesque detail: it is not connected functionally to the development of the plot or to the moral message of the *vita Pauli*. In contradistinction, the rust in the *aggadot* has the important function of providing the narrative reason for changing place.

It is unlikely that the presence of rust in both these narratives is merely coincidental: rust is not something that naturally comes to

---

[148] Waddell translates 'chisels'. She is obviously using the text of Rosweyde in *PL* 73,111 which was emended by him to *scalprae*, as he explains: *nempe exprimit tria praecipua cudendae monetae instrumenta ibidem inventa*. However *scabrae* is the version given in all the manuscripts cited in R. [= B.] Degórski *Edizione critica della 'Vita Sancti Pauli primi eremitae' di Girolamo* (Roma, 1987) 90. It is also the *lectio difficilior*, and thus more likely to be correct.

[149] *vita Hilarionis* 11: *totum corpus impetigine et pumicea quadam scabredine contrahi*. Cf. also Jerome's letter to Heliodorus about life in the desert *ep.* 14, 10: *scabra sine balneis adtrahitur cutis?* Here he replies to his own rhetorical question, saying that he who has washed in Christ need never wash again: *sed qui in Christo semel lotus est, non illi necesse est iterum lavare*. Jerome's Christian ascetic, unlike RSbY, has no need for the baths of Tiberias.

mind when thinking of holy men in caves. If, then, as we suggest, Jerome took it from the *aggadah*, it can be seen as indicative of the direction of the borrowing: the fact that it is functional to the plot of the *aggadah* and not functional in Jerome shows that it is more likely to have been Jerome taking from the Jewish tradition, rather than the other way round.[150]

Dimus *and* spicula   In the episode of the bird trapped by the hunter in the Jerusalem Talmud, the Heavenly Voice proclaims that the bird may be released, using the strange word '*dimus*,' which I have translated 'you are dismissed.' Midrash Esther Rabbah and Pesikta de-Rabbi Kahana expand on this here, with an episode where another bird is *not* allowed to escape, and the word used by the Heavenly Voice is '*spicula*.' These are not original Aramaic words, like the rest of the text in which they appear. They would seem to be loan words from Latin, the legal language even in the Greek-speaking east of the Roman empire. '*Dimus*' appears to come from the Latin '*dismissus*,' dismissed. '*Spicula*' which is used to mean 'you are condemned to death' is slightly more problematic, but probably comes from *specula*, a back-formation of '*speculator*,' an executioner, according to Sperber's dictionary of Greek and Latin legal terms in rabbinic literature.[151]

Within the text of the JT version there seems to be an intratextual play on the word *dimus*: a few lines below the mention of *dimus*, we have *dimision*, the public baths. As for the term *spicula*, Sperber writes that this is on other occasions confused with the Talmudic term *spiciria* which Sperber considers to be related to the Latin for a cave *specus* or *spelunca*. Could there also be another play on words within the text here, where a word which could also mean 'cave' appears in this narrative of the rabbi in his cave?

In the *vita Pauli*, as we have just seen, Jerome picks up the incident of the hunter and the bird, and in particular the theological lesson which is drawn from it, so that the statement of Rabbi Shim'on on Divine providence:

---

[150] I am grateful to Tova Cohen, professor of Jewish Literature, for a discussion of literary borrowing.

[151] D. Sperber *A Dictionary of Greek and Latin Legal Terms in Rabbinic Literature* (Ramat Gan, 1984) 131–2.

> Without [the decree of] heaven even a bird does not perish, so much
> more a man

is turned by him into Antony's prayer

> Lord, without Whom not. . . . . a single sparrow falls upon the ground,
> grant unto these even as Thou knowest

I wish to propose here that Jerome has appropriated not only the
theology of this episode of the bird, but also its vocabulary, in particular the use of the Roman legal word *dismissus*. It should not sur-
prise us that Jerome should be sensitive to a Latin legal term, for
he tells us with pride that he had a full Roman legal training in
Rome in his youth. However, he does not use *dismissus* of the bird,
but of Antony himself: Antony is sent away by Paul to fetch him a
cloak to bury him in, and during the journey back he has a vision
of Paul in heaven. Realising Paul has died he cries '*Cur me dimittis?*':
'why did you dismiss me?' And a few lines later he enters the '*spelunca*'
the cave where he will find Paul's dead body, reminding us of the
aggadic '*spicula*.' This might all of course be coincidence: these words
are not uncommon in Latin, but the fact that both are used in the
aggadic episode which Jerome seems to have used in constructing
his *vita* allows us to think that he also picked up these legal terms
and Christianised them: Antony sees Paul's death in his *spelunca* as
desirable, not a doom of execution, *spicula*, for in it he has achieved
eternal life, while he, Antony, is dismissed *dimittis* to mere earthly
life, which unlike the bird he does not see as escape (*dimus*).

   I noted above that it is probable that Jerome's acquaintance with
aggadah and *midrash* was with an oral rather than a written tradition.
In this case it might therefore be argued that it is unlikely that there
would then be specific words appearing in both the written version
of the *aggadah* and in Jerome—it would be unlikely for both our written tradition and the tradition Jerome knew to have preserved just
those words. However, as already noted, these are not just any words
in the text: 'rust' was actually the key word in some versions of the
aggadah on which the whole of the rabbinic exposition was hung,
and it was important to the narrative development in others. *Dimus*
and *spicula* are Latin words in an Aramaic context, and with legal
connotations as well: Jerome, with his legal training, may well have
noticed them particularly and kept them in mind while writing.

4d. *Narrative parallels*

What is happening in the world outside?   After years of solitude, both
heroes are naturally curious about the world outside and take steps
to find out what is happening there. Both Paul and Rabbi Shim'on
move to the entrance of their respective caves at a turning point in
the narratives, and stand on the border between cave and outside
world. In the Palestinian version of his story, R Shim'on goes to
look outside, saying 'perhaps I shall go out and see what is happening in the world.' Similarly, when Antony finally comes to visit
Paul in his cave after many years of solitude, Paul asks him questions about the state of mankind, the cities and what power now
rules the world:

> *narra mihi . . . ut sese habeat hominum genus. An in antiquis urbibus noua tecta*
> *consurgant: quo mundus regatur imperio.*[152]

Paul's first question about the state of the world is about new buildings in ancient cities. We saw above that the first part of the *aggadah*
about RSbY in the Babylonian Talmud version also deals with building in cities: R Judah b. Il'ai is quoted as praising the Roman building works—the markets, the bathhouses and the bridges. At this
point RSbY can only condemn—markets, he says were just places
for prostitutes, bathhouses were for pampering and bridges for extract-
ing taxes. But by the end of the episode, after he has been returned
to his cave as punishment for trying to apply his excess asceticism
to the whole community, he himself is taken to the bathhouse in
Tiberias to be healed and in his gratitude he comes to a new assessment: markets, coinage and bathhouses are part of 'being gracious
to the city,' they are facilities for the benefit of the whole community.

  Paul, who has withdrawn permanently from the world, is not concerned about bathhouses, markets and bridges. The new buildings
he is interested in could only be the churches now rising in place
of pagan temples, and Jerome could rely on his audience to be familiar with this from their everyday experience. If we as modern readers have any doubts on the matter we have only to look at Jerome's
ep. 120, 8, where he writes about the status of Jerusalem: 'the crowd

---

[152] *v. Pauli* 10.

of believers in Christ see the new roofs of the church arising daily'—
in Christum turba credentium noua cotidie uideat ecclesiae tecta consurgere.[153]
The words he uses for Jerusalem's new churches are the same as
Paul's: *tecta, noua, consurgere*. Here the new churches thronged with
Christians are contrasted to 'miserable Israel mourning the ruins of
her Temple with bared arms'—*miserabilis Israhel ruinas templi nudatis
plangat lacertis*. In other words, Jerome re-uses this picture in the context of a description of the Christian takeover of what had been the
centre of Judaism, its Temple. Having started with the *vita Pauli*, the
image has become part of his mental concept of the Christian victory over Judaism.

To return to the comparison of the *vita Pauli* and the *aggadah*: Rabbi
Shim'on actually prepares to leave his cave, and goes to stand at
the entrance. Jerome's hero also stands at the entrance to his cave
and refuses at first to let his visitor enter—not only is he not prepared to go out, but he does not want anything material from the
outside to invade his inner world. He is not prepared to look out—
he merely asks for a report on the state of the world. Once again,
Jerome portrays his Paul as ascetically superior to the rabbi who
actually goes out to look at the world, and eventually returns to it.
In the BT version, Elijah the Prophet stands outside Rabbi Shim'on's
cave and asks rhetorically 'Who will tell Bar Yohai that the Emperor
is dead and his decree annulled?' This question becomes the answer
to Rabbi Shim'on's wish to know what is happening in the world.
It lets him know that he can now leave his cave, and he does so.
It thus functions as a link in the narrative progression. In the *vita
Pauli*, one of the questions Paul asks of Antony is 'What power now
rules the world?' This too has the force of a rhetorical question, but
it remains unanswered in the text of the *vita*, and does not lead to
any progress in the narrative. For Jerome's audience, however, it
points to the fact that the persecutions have ceased and there is now
a Christian emperor, so that Paul could have left his cave had he
wanted to. It is noteworthy that in both the *aggadah* and in Jerome
the questions of the hero about the state of the world and the ruling powers are quoted as direct speech.

---

[153] *ep.* 120 is dated by Cavallera and Labourt to 407.

Paul's other two questions are not relevant to the rabbi, and are indeed anachronistic as concerns of the third-century Christian hermit, but Jerome uses them to underline the progress of the fourth-century Christianisation of the Roman empire, and Christianity's concern for conversion. Paul asks what new buildings are arising in ancient cities, a question clearly aimed at pointing out to Jerome's fourth-century audience how the new churches of Constantine and his successors are taking over the urban landscape of the empire.[154] RSbY, as we saw, on leaving his cave, asked how he can help the people of Tiberias materially, just as the patriarch Jacob had helped Shechem with markets and money. In contrast to this, Paul asks about the spiritual welfare of the world, without any intent to intervene—are there people who are still in the power of the demons? Jerome presents his ascetic Christian as concerned, but not active, about the spiritual enlightenment and salvation of the pagan world. The Jewish rabbi, on the other hand, shows active concern with the material world.

Both the *aggadah* and Jerome quote their heroes asking about the world outside, after their long stay in the cave. I am not aware that this sort of question is asked by any other ascetic hero. In both cases, further questions are asked about the ruling Roman power, with Elijah's rhetorical question informing Rabbi Shim'on of the situation, and Paul asking Antony what power now rules the world. Even if the content of these questions may be considered coincidental, or natural given the circumstances, the fact that they are presented structurally in the same way, as spoken questions, suggests that Jerome was familiar with the aggadic material. Once again, as we saw with the rust above, the rhetorical question of the *aggadah* about Roman power functions as a link in the narrative, leading to the next stage of RSbY leaving his cave. In Jerome's *vita* the unanswered question has no narrative function, suggesting once more that the direction of borrowing was from the *aggadah* rather than *vice versa*. But while there is no narrative function to the question, it does have an important function in Jerome's Christian agenda, by pointing out to his

---

[154] Churches at Rome, e.g.: *ep.* 107. In his translation of Eusebius' *Onomasticon* of biblical sites in the Holy Land (see chapter 4) Jerome took care to add details of new churches at Bethel, Arboc, Sychar and Bethany. The Jerusalem churches in *ep.* 120 have just been noted.

audience the progress in Christianisation of the world outside the
cave.

The weeping heir   After he leaves his cave in the BT version, RSbY
meets his former pupil and son-in-law, Rabbi Pinhas b. Yair, who
weeps to see the state he is in and is corrected by the rabbi, who
tells him how he is in a far better state spiritually than before—he
is far more learned. Similarly Antony, Paul's spiritual successor and
heir, weeps when he finds Paul dead. But Paul has died in an attitude of prayer—he too is in a better spiritual state than before, and
once again Jerome contrasts the Christian importance of prayer with
the Jewish stress on learning.

Of course tears from the hero's spiritual heir are a natural reaction
to his death or ill-health, in both cases. However, I would argue
that this is yet another of the many small similarities in the material which lead me to think that Jerome knew the *aggadah* and used
it as his source for the *vita Pauli*.

Contact with the Divine   Both *aggadah* and *vita* relate contact with
the Divine, through messengers and through more direct means.
Elijah the Prophet, who announces to Rabbi Shim'on that the emperor
is dead, is traditionally a divinely-sent messenger. In the *vita Pauli* it
is not Paul himself but Antony who meets messengers who show
him the way and tell him of Jesus: the satyr, the centaur and the
she-wolf. And there is more direct contact: Rabbi Shim'on is sent
back to his cave by a *bat qol*, a heavenly voice, in the BT and he
watches the *bat qol* proclaim the release of the bird in the JT. Antony
is first told of Paul in a divinely inspired revelation, and later he
has a vision of Paul in heaven, among the angels and apostles.

The raven, the bread and Elijah the prophet   We have just seen how
Elijah the prophet appears in the *aggadah* with the function of a
divinely-sent messenger who informs Rabbi Shim'on that it is now
safe for him to leave his cave.[155] Elijah is also alluded to in the *vita*

---

[155] Elijah is associated with Rabbi Shim'on bar Yohai in other traditions in the
Babylonian Talmud, one of which seems to imply that RSbY's cave became a holy
place after his death. For a discussion of this and other sources on RSbY see

Pauli: Paul is explicitly compared to him, which is only to be expected, perhaps, as the obvious biblical precedent. Jerome has told us in his preface that Elijah is one of Paul's archetypes, and this prophet is referred to several times in the *vita*, especially as he also had to flee from persecution by the ruler and lived for some time in a cave (I Kings 19:9).[156] But Jerome also includes a more deliberate reference to the prophet, which underlines the parallels and contrasts between his picture of Christian asceticism and its Jewish precursors. Apart from his dates and water, Paul has other food sent by Heaven— a raven comes every day to bring him half a loaf of bread, but once Antony arrives the raven brings double rations, a whole loaf.[157] The raven bringing bread is an allusion to I Kings 17:6, where ravens bring bread and meat to the prophet Elijah at the brook of Cherith. Paul's asceticism thus surpasses that of Elijah, for Paul does not eat meat. Jerome here 'demonstrates simultaneously the relevance of Hebrew scriptures to the Christian life, and the superiority of the new dispensation to the old.'[158] And here too Jerome's ascetic hero

---

Rosenfeld *op. cit.* n. 115 above. O. Bar *op. cit.* n. 138 above notes another midrash where Elijah and another rabbi, Joshua ben Levi stand outside the mouth of RSbY's burial cave discussing the coming of the messiah, and Bar notes that five of the mss of this midrash have 'the mouth of the garden of Eden' instead of the mouth of RSbY's cave.

[156] Elijah in the *vita Pauli*: named: 1; 13; implied: 10–11 (fed by ravens); 17 (transfer of clothes to heir).

[157] The *aggadah* about RSbY in BT Shabbat is part of a discussion about the mishnah which deals with the three reasons why women die in childbirth: for not observing the laws of sexual separation and abstinence, for not separating the holy part of the dough for baking bread, and for not lighting the Sabbath lamp (Mishnah Shabbat ii, 6. See on this Rubenstein (above, n. 130) 135). Jerome's hero is, of course, completely abstinent from all sex. It is possible that there is an allusion to this mishnah about the separation of the dough, in this episode where the raven comes every day to bring Paul half a loaf of bread, but once Antony arrives the raven brings double rations, a whole loaf. Antony and Paul struggle as to who should eat first, each trying to out-do the other in self-abnegation. They eventually decide that they will each take hold of the loaf and pull it in two between them. Jerome's saints are not concerned with what he would have seen as unimportant minutiae of Jewish practical laws, but rise above this in their competitive asceticism. This may have been why Jerome included this episode, where the incongruously humorous aspects have embarrassed scholars who failed to see a purpose in it (see below chapter 4.4.1c on humour in fourth and fifth century Latin writing). The doubled rations could also be an allusion to the mishnah which deals with the Sabbath, for Jews eat two loaves of bread at the Sabbath meal in memory of the doubled ration of manna that was miraculously provided for the Children of Israel in the desert.

[158] The quotation is taken from D. Krueger 'Typological Figuration in Theodoret

is shown to be ascetically better than his predecessor—Elijah's ravens brought bread and meat, but Paul lives only on bread (apart from his dates and water).

4e. *Negations*

We have looked so far at places where Jerome appears to be competing with the *aggadah* for the same ground, particularly the figure of the ascetic saint and the description of his flight from persecution. However by the fourth century Christianity was concerned to mark its differences from the Judaism of the Talmudic sources and there are a number of instances where, rather than similarities between the *vita* and the *aggadot*, we find that Jerome is displaying an attitude diametrically opposite to that of the Talmudic sources. I would like to suggest here that this shows that he was aware of the rabbinic attitude, and determined to oppose it—that these passages were written in deliberate opposition to the Jewish position.

Money and material possessions   Both heroes live without material possessions in their caves, but their general attitude is different. In the Babylonian Talmud the verse from Genesis 33:18: '*and Jacob came whole [to the city of Shechem]*,' is interpreted by Rav: 'bodily whole, financially whole, and whole in his learning.' Rav was a third century *amora* who travelled between Palestine and Babylonia, and thus may even have been responsible for the transfer of the whole *aggadah*. Rav continues and explains: '*And he [Jacob] was gracious to the city*' as meaning that Jacob instituted coinage for the city. In the *vita Pauli* Jerome is concerned to present a very different attitude to money, which seems to have been written in complete and deliberate negation of the attitude of the *aggadah*. At the beginning of the *vita*, money leads to evil. It was already noted above how Paul was nearly betrayed to the persecuting authorities by his brother-in-law who coveted his inheritance:

> What wilt thou not drive mortal hearts to do
> O thou dread thirst for gold?[159]

---

of Cyrrhus' *Religious History* and the Art of Postbiblical Narrative' *Journal of Early Christian Studies* 5 (1997) 410. Krueger was referring to Theodoret, but the observation is just as true of Jerome's use of typology here and elsewhere.
[159] *Verum quid pectora humana non cogit auri sacra fames?* Cf. Virgil *Aeneid* 3, 56–7.

Later in the *vita*, money is associated with sin and falsehood. On arrival in his cave Paul finds the abandoned instruments of forgers in an illegal mint. I have already noted how this may well reflect experience of Jerome's Syro-Palestinian material world, but functionally it also serves to stress Jerome's Christian asceticism against the Jewish concern with the world of every-day life, where coins represented commendable progress in a society that had begun with barter.[160] For the illegal mint brings us back to Jerome's introduction to the *vita Pauli* in his letter to Paul of Concordia. Here Jerome talked of the pure refined silver of the words of God, quoting Psalm 11:7.[161] The illegal mint with its base coins is the concrete opposite of this, but Paul will turn this infernal cave into heaven through the seven-times purified words of God—his only occupation there is described as *orationibus*—prayers.[162] The words of God are pure words—*eloquia casta*: as noted above, the reference to the time when Antony was joined with Cleopatra stresses the contrast between the chaste Christian Antony, Paul's successor, and the licentious pagan hero.

It is unlikely that the two references to mints are simple coincidence. As in the case of the rust, mints are the not the first association which comes to mind when thinking of holy men in caves (although, as already noted, illegal mints did exist in caves in antiquity). In both cases the mints present the world-view of the authors. The *aggadah* presents RSbY leaving his cave to benefit society on the model of the patriarch Jacob who instituted coinage. Jerome, in contrast, presents Paul who has fled real gold, and who now takes over from the forgers of counterfeit money to spend his time with the true refined silver of the pure words of God. I would thus suggest that not only was Jerome acquainted with this part of the *aggadah*, but that he deliberately took it over and negated it, to present his ascetic world view in opposition to that of the Jewish tradition.

---

[160] Cf. D. Brakke *Athanasius and the politics of asceticism* (Oxford, 1995) 226f., who sees the asceticism of the *vita Antonii* as 'withdrawal from the world: renunciation of sex, food and wealth'.

[161] Cf. also *Apol. Contra Ruf.* i, 16 (*CCSL* 79, *PL* 23, 409–410) where Jerome bids his prudent reader behave like a good banker and reject false coin in chosing translations of the Bible, and see on this C. Estin 'S. Jérôme; de la traduction inspirée à la traduction relativiste' *RB* 88 (1981) 199–215.

[162] *Oratio* means 'prayer' in ecclesiastical Latin and is used as such in the Vulgate, but its primary meaning of 'speech' or 'discourse' (perhaps with the Deity) cannot be far from the author's mind.

The material versus the spiritual   There is tension between the temporal and the spiritual world present in both *vita* and *aggadah*. But
the resolutions are opposite. After twelve years in the cave, Rabbi
Shim'on returns to the world he had retreated from. The necessity
for this return is underlined in the BT version, where the process
of leaving the cave is conducted in two stages, like the process of
entering it.[163] When RSbY first leaves, he sees a man ploughing and
sowing and exclaims 'They forsake life eternal and engage in life
temporal!' Whatever he puts eyes upon is then immediately burnt
up. Then a heavenly voice *bat qol* says: 'Have you come out to
destroy My world? Go back to your cave!' He returns to the cave
for another year (the length of time that the wicked are punished
in *gehinnom*) and eventually comes out. At this point he finds an old
man engaged in taking *hadassim* [myrtles] for the Sabbath, one for
each commandment:

> He said to his son: 'See how dear the commandments are to Israel'.
> At that their minds were set at ease.

Withdrawal from everyday life, according to the BT, leads to destruction: even RSbY must live in the everyday world, which is sustained
by observance of the commandments by the whole Jewish community. In contrast, Paul never leaves his cave until he dies and achieves
eternal life. He may have fled to his cave because of persecution,
but once in it, having turned his back on day to day life, he carries on living his spiritual life there in total asceticism, even refusing at first to let in the monk Antony. . . . *coelestem uitam ageret in
terris*.[164] This way of life is presented by Jerome as a Christian ideal.
The continuation of the Jewish *aggadah* with the account of RSbY's
visit to Tiberias shows a concern for money and material goods as
beneficial to society—we mentioned above how RSbY's actions were
seen as an illustration of the biblical passage about Jacob's bene-
faction to Shechem, where he set up markets and instituted coinage.
(Rabbi Shim'on is also noted in another place in the Jerusalem

---

[163] See the excellent discussion of this by Rubenstein (above, n. 130) 113–116.
Rubenstein underlines the fact that the whole of this episode and its message are
not present in the JT version.
[164] *vita Pauli* 7: He lived the life of heaven upon earth.

Talmud as having once miraculously filled a valley with coins).[165] In contrast, by taking up the image of bodily rust and transferring it to the tools of the illegal forgers, Jerome has linked these episodes, and he now rises to heights of satire of the rich and their possessions, as opposed to Paul, who had nothing material:

> Let me ask those who know not their own patrimony, who clothe their homes with marble, who string on a single thread the cost of villas, what did this naked old man lack?

he asks rhetorically.[166] Paul has achieved eternal life through an asceticism which Jerome appears to present as a deliberate opposite of his reading of the *aggadah*.

Gehenna   The different attitudes of *aggadah* and *vita* to the temporal and the spiritual are underlined by the different uses they make of *gehenna* as punishment for the wicked. When Rabbi Shim'on is sent back to his cave as a punishment for over-valuing life spiritual as opposed to life temporal, after twelve months he says: 'the sentence for the wicked in *gehinnom* is twelve months,' after which the Heavenly Voice allows him to come out. In contrast, in the *vita Pauli*, Paul, Jerome tells us, leads a 'heavenly life on earth.' And at the end of the *vita* Jerome addresses his readers, telling them that 'paradise awaits this poor old man, while *gehenna* will take you golden people.' Once again Jerome's hero as presented is far above the Jewish rabbi—Rabbi Shim'on has himself had to suffer punishment as long as the wicked undergo in *gehinnom*: Paul in contrast goes straight to paradise and only Jerome's materialistic readers, he warns, will have to suffer *gehenna*.

It is my contention that this has been written as a deliberate negation of the actions of the Jewish rabbi, who is taught by the Heavenly Voice that he cannot avoid life temporal, but must leave the spiritual life of his cave and come out and live among human beings. And he does indeed concern himself actively with their material needs. In my view, Jerome is here conducting a hidden dialogue

---

[165] JT Berakhot 13d: R. Hezekiah said in the name of R. Jeremiah: R. Shim'on is quoted as saying: 'Valley, valley, be filled with gold dinars,' and it was filled.

[166] *vita Pauli* 17 tr. Harvey (adapted).

with the Judaism of the *aggadah*. The satire of the rich and materialistic would have been clear to Jerome's contemporary readers, as
would the eventual reward of life eternal.[167] It is more difficult, however, to know whether any of these readers would have picked up
Jerome's hidden dialogue with Judaism. Jerome may have been using
this to define the Christian position for himself.

Intervention versus non-intervention   There is a further contrast between
the Jewish attitude to the material world and Jerome's Christian
asceticism. We have seen how Rabbi Shim'on, on leaving his cave,
makes use of the facilities of the city—the healing hot baths of
Tiberias. In return, he asks how he can help the people of Tiberias
materially, just as the patriarch Jacob had helped Shechem with
markets and money. He is prepared to intervene actively to promote
the material welfare of the community, and in particular the city,
and he actually does so. The Jewish rabbi sees his function as help-
ing the city's inhabitants, and correcting the problems of society.[168]
In contrast to this, Jerome presents his Paul merely asking about the
spiritual welfare of the world, without any intent to intervene—'Are
there people who are still in the power of the demons?' he asks
Antony, and no answer is supplied. Antony himself is opposed to
the city, and its corrupt life, where the power of the demons is
strong. He cries 'woe' on Alexandria, but from the desert, not from
anywhere where his cries may be heard.[169] Jerome's ascetic heroes'
withdrawal from the world is absolute, not temporary like the rabbi's.[170]

Corpses   The *aggadot* about RSbY in his cave continue after his
release to describe his visit to Tiberias, where he purified the town
by identifying the places where corpses had been buried, according
to the Jerusalem Talmud version, causing the corpses to float up to
the surface of the ground.[171] Following this, a Samaritan who wished

---

[167] 1.3: Classical learning and Jerome's audience.

[168] See Rosenfeld (*op. cit.* n. 115 above) 369.

[169] The Antony of the *vita Antonii* had visited Alexandria: cf. D. Brakke *Athanasius and the politics of asceticism* (Oxford, 1995) 204f.

[170] We shall see a similar refusal by the Christian holy man to act as economic mediator in the *vita Hilarionis* 18. See on this P. Rousseau *Ascetics, Authority and the Church in the age of Jerome and Cassian* (Oxford, 1978) 137–8, and R. Kirschner 'The Vocation of Holiness in Late Antiquity' *VChr* 38 (1984) 117, contrasting Jewish and Christian holy men and their practices.

[171] On the miraculous actions of RSbY see the discussion in Rosenfeld *op. cit.* n. 115 above.

to mock RSbY planted a corpse in a place which had been previously purified and challenged the rabbi, as it says in JT:

> Rabbi Shim'on bar Yohai perceiving through the Holy Spirit that he had placed one [corpse] there, said: 'I decree that those above shall descend [i.e. the Samaritan shall die] and those below [the corpse] shall arise'. And thus it happened.[172]

Jerome's *vita Pauli* is also much concerned with a corpse and its burial: Antony does not manage to bury Paul by himself and has to get help from two lions. Of course Christian tradition attributed no impurity to corpses—quite the opposite: the holy man in his grave was seen as a conduit to heaven.[173] Elsewhere, in his commentary on Psalms, Jerome contrasts the Jews who regards corpses as impure *inmund[um]* with the Christians who take literally the verse (Ps. 115[117]) *pretiosa in conspectu Domini mors sanctorum eius.*[174] In the *vita Pauli*, Jerome provides a Christian version of the statement of the rabbi, that the living shall die and the dead arise, for Paul who was alive dies, but his death is merely a passage to eternal life—Antony has a vision of him in the company of Jesus in heaven.

This parallel is not a very close one: there is rather a long way from the corpse rising to the surface and the scoffer dying, to Paul dying and passing to life eternal. However, in the context of a number of different sorts of parallels, it seems possible to include this too, even if the evidence is not as strong as some of the rest, as it appears to be yet another instance of Jerome's Christianising of the Jewish *aggadah*.

Prayers and learning   Paul's only occupation during his ninety-seven years in his cave is described as *oration[es]*—prayers. Jerome stresses Paul's background and learning in both Greek and Egyptian literature—his time spent only in prayer is not due to illiteracy, but is a voluntary abnegation of learning.[175] In contrast, RSbY spends all his

---

[172] JT Shevi'it ix, 1, 38d. (Tr. Levine, adapted).
[173] Peter Brown *The Cult of the Saints* (Chicago, 1981).
[174] *CCSL* 72, 244.
[175] E. Coleiro 'St. Jerome's Lives of the Hermits' *VChr* 11 (1956) 171 writes that 'the study of the Scriptures . . . is one of the occupations of [Jerome's] heroes' but while he produces evidence from the *v. Hilarionis* and *v. Malchi*, when it comes to the *v. Pauli* he can only say weakly that 'Paul's language echoes Scriptural quotations.'

time in the cave learning *Torah*, according to BT. He only stops briefly to pray—if at all, for another tradition in the Babylonian Talmud notes him as not even stopping to pray when he was involved in studying the *Torah*. This is not the way *haverim* [scholars] should behave, according to R. Johanan, it is only for special people like RSbY 'whose study was their profession.'[176] His learning is thereby greatly increased—before his time in the cave, his son-in-law could give him a dozen answers to each problem he raised; afterwards he could give two dozen answers to each problem his son-in-law raised.

In Jewish tradition, learning *Torah* is paramount: Jerome would appear to differentiate his hero from this attitude by stressing in contrast the primacy of prayer. It may seem natural that the Christian holy man is involved only in prayer. But Jerome has stressed that he was learned in different kinds of literature, and he could have spent time in his cave reading the Bible. Paul's deliberate abnegation of any sort of learning stands in total contrast to Rabbi Shim'on: Christians have no need for learning the *Torah* or Jewish *halakhah*.

1.4.5. *Historical note*

Up to now I have related to the traditions about Rabbi Shim'on bar Yohai as literary creations, like Jerome's *vita*. However, the basic historical elements of the Talmudic traditions are also relevant to this discussion. It is clear that the presentation of RSbY in the Talmudic traditions is in keeping with the known historical picture. Rabbi Shim'on was the pupil of and successor to the famous martyr Rabbi 'Aqiva (we might note here that the *Life of Paul* begins with two martyrdoms, with Jerome commenting that asceticism is the successor to martyrdom) and he is shown as hiding from the real persecution by the Romans. The portrayal of RSbY as coming from Judaea, and being forced to move to Galilee following the failure of the Bar Kokhba revolt and the subsequent Roman persecutions is also in accord with the general historical picture of this time,

---

[176] BT Shabbat 11a: It was taught: If *haverim* [scholars] are engaged in studying, they must break off for the reading of the *shem'a* [prayer], but not for [sc. ordinary] prayer. R. Johanan said: This was taught only of such as R. Shim'on b. Yohai and his companions, whose study was their profession; but we must break off both for the reading of the *shem'a* and for prayer. [Tr. Soncino, adapted]

of the movement of the Jewish population from Judaea to Galilee. Finally, the account of RSbY purifying Tiberias, whether or not it was a historical event, shows the need of the new centre of the Jewish leadership institutions in the city to make use of the important figure of the rabbi to stress the purification of the site at Tiberias. All these elements are an organic part of the Galilean Talmudic ethos of the second and third centuries CE. It is thus most unlikely that these traditions crystallised at the end of the fourth century as a reaction to Jerome's creation of a Christian holy man. From the point of view of the Jerusalem Talmud, this is actually impossible, for there are no sages or historical traces in this work which can be dated later than the sixth decade of the fourth century. Thus the historical elements in the traditions about RSbY appear to have pre-dated Jerome.

1.4.6. *The* vita Pauli *and the* aggadah: *Text and sub-text*

Jerome was to make very wide use of Jewish *aggadot* and *midrashim* in his later works, especially in his Bible commentaries. Newman has catalogued over 350 cases where Jerome says openly that he is using Jewish *midrash* and *aggadah*.[177] Hayward, who notes parallels even where Jerome does *not* specify that he is using Jewish material, has noted over 100 parallels to Midrash Genesis Rabbah alone.[178] However, most of these references are very short indeed, rarely more than a line or two long. If my case for Jerome's use of the *aggadot* about Rabbi Shim'on bar Yohai in the *vita Pauli* is accepted, then it would appear that he is relating, at length and repeatedly, to a considerable body of aggadic material on this subject. I do not know of another case where he makes similar use of aggadic material all connected to one subject. Jerome often quotes Jewish *midrash* and *aggadah* to agree with it or to disagree, but he does not elsewhere appear to enter into such a sustained dialogue with this material. However, this was his first attempt at a saint's *Life*, and there is no reason to reject the possibility that this was a trial attempt. The next chapter, however, will show how the *vita Hilarionis* appears to enter into a

---

[177] Newman, esp. ch. 4 'Jerome's Jewish sources'; ch. 6 'The *midrash* in Jerome's writings' includes a catalogue of the places where Jerome uses *midrash* which is attributed by him to the Jews.

[178] C.T.R. Hayward *Saint Jerome's Hebrew Questions on Genesis* (Oxford, 1995) 259–60.

dialogue with different outside material, this time using a pagan novel as sub-text. In writing his saints' *Lives* Jerome was creating Latin hagiography for the first time; I suggest here that he began this process through a hidden polemical dialogue with Jewish and pagan literature, working out for himself the Christian point of view as opposed to the Jewish and pagan ones. It is clear that both the *midrash* and the *vita* can be seen as competing for ownership of the same material. But the significance is very different for both sides. The ascetic saint is far more important to Jerome his creator than to the rabbis of the Talmud, for whom Rabbi Shim'on represents only one of many possibilities of rabbinic models.

I would like to return once more to consider the possibility that the *aggadot* about RSbY were written as a response to Jerome, as part of Jewish response to Christian religious hegemony, somewhat as Boyarin[179] claims that the themes of Christian martyrdom were recycled back into Talmudic texts as ways of grasping the deaths of Jews persecuted under Hadrian in the second century. We have here, on the one hand, Rabbi Shim'on bar Yohai, a Jewish figure who actually existed. On the other hand there is Paul the hermit, whose very existence is doubtful, who has been written up by Jerome as a literary creation. It is theoretically possible that the rabbis of the Talmud read local translations in Greek or Syriac of Jerome's popular saint's *Life* or heard oral versions of it, although oral transmission of the *Life* would seem less likely in view of the presence of close verbal parallels noted above. It is much more likely that Jerome learned the traditions of RSbY from the converted Jew whom we know was his teacher—especially as he specifically mentions a Rabbi Shim'on by name elsewhere—and used these traditions to build his picture of his ascetic saint. Not all the evidence I have brought to make my case is of equal weight. Sometimes there are only hints, and in other cases it is possible to argue that Jerome may have had other sources—a common pool of generic material, for example, or a biblical origin. But I should like to propose that the sum total of a number of different pieces of evidence, even if some of them are incomplete and insufficient, adds up to more than the constituent parts, and the result is a convincing picture of knowledge of and use

---

[179] Boyarin *op. cit.* (n. 110 above) 118.

by Jerome of *aggadah* in presenting his picture of Paul the hermit. The parallels with and negations of Jewish material are such that it is possible to see Jerome's *vita Pauli* as being written as a hidden polemical dialogue with the traditions on R. Shim'on bar Yohai. Thus, in my opinion, we have here a convincing picture of Jerome borrowing from Talmudic sources and converting them to his Christian agenda.

1.5. Jerome's Literary Methods: The *vita Pauli* and the Creation of a New Christian Genre

Turning now to analyse Jerome's literary methods, we shall see how an analysis of his careful structuring of the *vita Pauli*, together with his rhetorical style shows us how Jerome builds himself in to the structure of his saint's *Life*, so that the *Life of Paul the hermit* is used as a preparation for the *Life* of Saint Jerome.

1.5.1. *Structure*

In her sensitive analysis of the *vita Pauli*, Alison Goddard Elliot has shown how this work differs from other *vitae*, both earlier and later, in its structure.[180] It is, she points out, the only one to use a 'purely chronological order of narration', and its logical structure 'more closely resembles historical writing than romance.' She suggests that it is an example of a traditional form re-worked by 'a well-educated, sophisticated theologian.' This analysis is paralleled by Averil Cameron, who notes the 'mixture of apparent simplicity and actual sophistication.'[181] In her discussion, Elliot describes the structure of the *vita Pauli* as 'bi-partite', as does Adalbert de Vogüé in his literary history of monasticism.[182] De Vogüé sees the *vita* as consisting of a series of pairs, of people and actions. Thus there are two persecuting emperors, two martyrdoms, two disciples of Antony, two mythological beasts, two predecessors to Paul—Elijah and John the Baptist—leading up to the pair of Paul and Antony. Paul is also buried by two lions.

---

[180] Alison Goddard Elliot *Roads to Paradise* (Hanover and London, 1987) 72.
[181] Averil Cameron *Christianity and the Rhetoric of Empire: The development of Christian discourse* (Berkeley, 1991) 113.
[182] A. de Vogüé (*op. cit.* n. 8 above) 154: 'Tout, dans cette *Vie*, va par deux.'

However, it seems to me that Jerome is more subtle than this, and
that what we have here are triads, not pairs, more suited to a
Christian work, for three is the number of the Trinity. The third
member of the triad sometimes differs and is often transcendent, but
it is certainly clearly connected to the other two, emotionally, devel-
opmentally or visually.[183] The protagonists shift constantly throughout the *vita* to form varying groups of three. To the two notorious
persecuting emperors, Decius and Valerian, Jerome adds the ultimate 'cunning enemy' Satan, who destroys souls, not bodies. He
adds Antony, a third and greater figure, to form a triad with his
disciples Amathus and Macarius. Later Jerome returns to the figures
of Elijah and John and adds Paul himself as a third, transcending
even them: in Antony's words:

> I have seen Elijah, I have seen John in the desert, I have seen Paul
> in paradise.[184]

All three are Paul and he himself has made a heaven on earth by
his ascetic way of life. Thus there are satanic and heavenly triads
as well as human and superhuman ones. To complete this picture,
Jerome adds a triad of bestial and mythological creatures, the centaur, the satyr and the she-wolf, as well as a triad of beasts and
man, Paul and the two lions. These are succeeded by Antony and
the two lions, while there is a line of succession for the cloak which
passes from Athanasius to Antony and finally to Paul. But it is not
until the final paragraph that the dominant pair of Antony and Paul
finally receives the ultimate completion of their triad. Paul's one
material possession was the tunic he made for himself from palm-
leaves, which Antony takes, having wrapped him in Athanasius' cloak,
'lest the pious heir should receive none of the goods of the ines-

---

[183] Cf. M. Granek, M.A. Weingarten, 'The Third Party in General Practice
Consultations' *Scandinavian Journal of Primary Health Care* 14 (1996) 66–70.
[184] *v. Pauli* 13: *Vidi Eliam, uidi Ioannem in deserto, et uere in paradiso Paulum vidi.* de
Vogüé notes the reminiscence of 2 Cor. 12:4 where the apostle Paul talks of the
man *raptus . . . in paradiso.* Jerome incidentally describes himself as *raptus in spiritu*
when he dreams of himself being brought before the heavenly tribunal in *ep.* 22,
30, to be accused of being a Ciceronian, rather than a Christian. For a sensitive
discussion of the visual aspect in this statement, see G. Frank *The Memory of the Eyes:
Pilgrims to Living Saints in Christian Late Antiquity* (Univ of California, 2000) Ch. 3. I
am grateful to Professor Frank for letting me see a pre-publication copy of her
enlightening comments on the *vita Pauli.*

tate.'[185] And, 'if God grant it', this is the one possession that Jerome himself would aspire to, rather than the purple robes of kings. Jerome, in the guise of a humble prayer, has set himself up to be the true ascetic successor to Paul and Antony, the third who completes the final triad.[186] He has written himself into his saint's *Life*.

1.5.2. *Style*

Jerome himself gives us a pointer to the style of the *vita*, when he says, in his letter to Paul of Concordia, that he has laboured greatly to lower his style:

multum in deiciendo sermone laboravimus

for the benefit of the less cultured—*propter simpliciores*. However, he says, 'I don't know how'—*nescio quomodo*—even if we fill a jar with water it still keeps something of the smell of the wine that was stored in it originally.[187] '*Nescio quomodo*' is, in fact, Jerome at his most disingenuous, for the apparently simple story is built with considerable skill, with different layers of allusive depth for different parts of his audience. He includes learned notes which explain what a centaur is, for a non-classical audience, and the meaning of a Syriac word for a non-local audience. Classical allusions abound, but while it is not necessary to be able to identify these for an understanding of the story line, they add extra meaning for those who can recognise them. Spiritual conflict is expressed in concrete examples, and a vivid series of pictured scenes, some perhaps based on contemporary art, makes the action easy to comprehend. However, *deicio* was a technical term, used to describe the *sermo humilis*[188] that Christian writers had turned from an embarrassment into a glory. Classical writers had used language to correspond to the subject matter—high, intermediate or low—but for a Christian writer such distinctions in subject

---

[185] *v. Pauli* 16: *ne quid pius heres ex intestati bonis non possideret.*

[186] Leclerc (*op. cit.* n. 36 above) 'Il est bien possible que ce Paul ait un peu les traits d'un autre romain cultivé qui avait tenté l'expérience de la solitude à Chalcis: Jerome lui-même.'

[187] Cf. Horace *ep.* i, 2, 69–70.

[188] This analysis owes much to the discussion of *sermo humilis* in Erich Auerbach *Literary Language and its Public in Late Latin Antiquity and in the Middle Ages* (tr. Princeton 1965). For Jerome himself on simple style see his *Praef.* to *Com in Galat.* III (*PL* 26, 399–401).

matter were no longer valid. The simplest objects, if connected with God's plan, were worthy of the highest language. Furthermore, debasement was in itself a virtue, for Jesus had debased himself to come among men. So the struggle between Paul and Antony as to who should give the other precedence in breaking bread is paradoxical in its nature, who should exceed in humility? And in order to underline this, Jerome writes it in rhetorical terms: carefully balanced isocola.

> *Paulus more cogebat hospitii, Antonius iure refellebat aetatis.*[189]

But the juxtaposition of the incongruous is a recipe for humour, and modern commentators have felt uncomfortable with this scene.[190] Jerome is more successful for a modern audience in the rhetoric of Antony's speech:

> *Qui bestias suscipis, hominem cur repellis?*[191]

with its balanced phrases, or the self-debasing

> *Vae mihi peccatori, qui falsum monachi nomen fero*[192]

which so shockingly repeats the form of his outburst against the sinful city:

> *Vae tibi, Alexandria, quae pro Deo portenta ueneraris.*[193]

And it is Antony's rhetoric which brings us Paul transcendent, in a series of phrases which accumulate to a climax:

> *Vidi Eliam, uidi Ioannem in deserto et uere in paradiso Paulum uidi.*[194]

---

[189] *v. Pauli* 11.

[190] See de Vogüé (*op. cit.* n. 8 above) *ad loc.*; Leclerc sees a general tendency to make Antony a comic figure (*op. cit.* n. 36 above) 262; cf. A.J. Festugière 'Lieux communs littéraires et thèmes de folk-lore dans l'hagiographie primitive' *Wiener Studien* 73 (1960) 142–5 for the motif of the contest for the greatest humility in the *Historia Monachorum*. We might also note that it is this scene only from the life of Antony that was chosen by the German artist known as Grünwald for his altar piece at Isenheim, which is otherwise typified by terrible suffering. This scene, derided as 'insipid' by G.G. Harpham *The Ascetic Imperative in Culture and Criticism* (Chicago, 1987) was presumably chosen deliberately by the artist to display the quintessence of ascetic abnegation.

[191] *v. Pauli* 9.

[192] *v. Pauli* 13.

[193] *v. Pauli* 8. Rubenstein (above, n. 130) 117 notes the use of balanced phrasing in the BT version of the aggadah on R Shim'on bar Yohai.

[194] *v. Pauli* 13.

The most important elements are here underlined by alliteration—
uidi is used for Elijah and John but becomes *uere uidi* for Paul in
paradise.

But it is the final paragraphs [17 and 18] that rise to the heights
of rhetoric: Jerome shows how the lack of possessions far outweighs
the possession of great wealth, that the lowly has become the sublime. And to show this paradox, he shows the sublimity of the lowly,
using the highest flights of rhetoric. The passage is based on antitheses—the old naked man without possessions is set against houses
dressed with marble and the price of a mansion strung on a thread.
As if we are looking at a painting, Jerome then focusses in on detail:
the rich drinking from jewels and the cupped hands that sufficed
Paul.[195] The antitheses gather force, expressed in almost identical
form with *paradisus* once more underlined by alliteration:

> *illi pauperculo paradisus patet, uos auratos gehenna suscipiet.*[196]

Throughout the passage great play is made with the words signifying clothing—*uestiunt/uestem/uestiti/uestibus*—in antithetical contexts:
uestem Christi is opposed to *uestiti sericis* and *auratis uestibus*. Section 17
ends with a series of rhetorical questions rising to an ironic climax:

> *An cadauera diuitum nisi in serico putrescere nesciunt?*
>
> Is it because the corpses of the rich know not how to decay unless
> clothed in silk?

After this climax Jerome drops to what now seems truly *sermo humilis*,
asking his reader to remember him, the sinner, in his prayers:

> *Obsecro, quicumque haec legis, ut Hieronymi peccatoris memineris.*[197]

The person of the verb has changed here too. In his rhetoric Jerome
has moved from the totally impersonal to a personal appeal to each
reader:

---

[195] For a discussion of the use of these tiny, brilliant patches of description in
Late Antiquity, see M. Roberts *The Jeweled Style: Poetry and poetics in Late Antiquity*
(Ithaca/London, 1989), 53; 116–7. Roberts is writing of poetry and the visual arts,
but much of what he says can be applied to prose as well.
[196] *v. Pauli* 17.
[197] *v. Pauli* 18.

> *Libet in fine opusculi eos interrogare, qui sua patrimonia ignorant, qui domos mar-moribus vestiunt . . .*

From the impersonal *libet* and the third person plural *eos, qui* he changes to the more personal second person plural *vos* to make his upbraiding of the rich more immediate:

> *Vos gemma bibitis . . . vos in tunicis aurum texitis . . . vos auratos gehenna suscipiet.*

Finally in the last paragraph [18] he turns to appeal personally to each individual reader, using the second person singular:

> *Obsecro, quicumque haec legis, ut Hieronymi peccatoris memineris.*

This is emotionally very affecting, and inclines the reader to take Jerome's protestations on their face value, without reflecting on the way he has manipulated them:

> [Jerome], who, if the Lord gave him the choice, would rather have the tunic of Paul with his merits, than the purple of Kings with their thrones.[198]

The final juxtaposition of Paul's palm-leaf tunic with the imperial purple sums up the play on *uestis* throughout the preceding paragraph. Jerome, under guise of renouncing almost all, has taken to himself the place of Paul as the leading holy man of the desert.

Thus the *vita Pauli* has laid the foundations for a new Christian genre, the Latin saint's *Life*. Paul is an idealised holy man, predecessor of Antony and of Jerome himself. Jerome here has drawn on a combination of Christian and classical sources together with his own experience of retiring from the world to the desert. He has also appropriated Jewish *aggadah* here, and converted it to his own Christian agenda.

---

[198] *v. Pauli* 18: *cui si Dominus optionem daret, multo magis eligeret tunicam Pauli cum meritis eius quam regum purpuras cum regnis suis* tr. Helen Waddell *The Desert Fathers* (London, 1936).

CHAPTER TWO

THE *VITA HILARIONIS*: THE CHRISTIANISATION
OF THE ROMAN WORLD

INTRODUCTION

In the previous chapter we saw Jerome's foundation of a new Christian
genre: the saint's *Life*. We saw how he used a combination of his
Christian and classical sources together with his own experience to
form this new genre. We also proposed that he appropriated Jewish
aggadic material on the holy man and converted it to his own
Christian agenda. Jerome's Paul was an idealised holy man who
retired from the world, to the desert. This was a way of life that
Jerome himself had tried and rejected. So now in the *Life* of Hilarion
he shows us a saint who once again tries to retire from the world,
but Hilarion is unsuccessful in this. And, in Chitty's words, the world
breaks in.[1] Thus here, in the longest of his saints' *Lives*, Jerome comes
to deal with the saint and his relationship with late antique Roman
society, and the developing process of the Christianisation of the
Roman empire. The *vita Hilarionis* encompasses both Palestine, the
Christian Holy Land, as well as the whole of the rest of the empire.
Jerome shows his readers how the Christian must conquer pagan
Roman society from within, and come to terms with all aspects of
power and popular culture. Jewish *midrash* is scarcely relevant here.
This *Life* includes the Christian appropriation of the most popular
and threatening form of Classical literature—the ancient novel.[2] In
this chapter, then, I shall be looking at Jerome's use of the ancient

---

[1] D.J. Chitty *The Desert a City: an introduction to the study of Egyptian and Palestinian monasticism under the Christian empire* (Oxford, 1966) 46f.

[2] On the appropriation of the pagan novel by Christian hagiographic literature, described as 'elements of entertainment literature . . . put to the service of Christian doctrine,' see now G. Huber-Rebenich 'Hagiographic fiction as entertainment' in H. Hofmann (ed.) *Latin fiction: The Latin novel in context* (London/NY 1999) 187–212, citation: p. 190. Huber-Rebenich discusses the *Recognitiones* of Jerome's friend and later rival, Rufinus and Jerome's own *vita Pauli* and *vita Malchi*, only mentioning the *vita Hilarionis* in passing.

novel and its conversion to his ascetic Christianity. I shall also look
at the confrontation of the holy man with popular culture and pagan
cults. I shall attempt to show that this *Life* can be seen as a microcosm of the whole of the Roman world—both in terms of space and
in terms of the social structure, the whole epitomised in the chariot
race at its centre.

No-one seems to have noticed that in writing the *vita Hilarionis*
Jerome made considerable use of Apuleius' pornographic novel,
Metamorphoses or *the Golden Ass*. In view of the significance of this
discovery, I will be giving close attention to the various parallels
between the two texts.[3] Consequently, some of the general discussion of the relationship between monk and society in Part 2.2 of the
chapter has been anticipated in the discussion of Jerome's use of
Apuleius in Part 2.1.

Summary of the vita Hilarionis

The hero of the *vita Hilarionis*, Jerome tells us, was an avowed ascetic,
the first to bring monasticism to Palestine. Hilarion was influenced
by Antony, the first of Egyptian monks (or as Jerome would have
it, the second, for Jerome's *vita Pauli* had been written to demonstrate that Paul preceded Antony). Hilarion returns from Egypt to
settle near Gaza not far from where he was born, and struggles with
the demons of temptation. He begins to perform various miracles
and is too successful for his own comfort—he would have preferred
a solitary life but attracts crowds of both monks and converts. A
chariot race at Gaza ends in Christian victory over the local god,
Marnas: a visit to Elusa results in the transfer of the allegiance of
the local Saracens from Venus/Lucifer to Jesus. His successes are
resented by many pagans and he is forced to flee, his monastery is
destroyed, and he wanders around the Mediterranean in a vain
search for solitude, his miracles always betraying him. Even after his
death his body is fought over by rival communities in Cyprus and
Palestine.

---

[3] For a brief preliminary version of this comparison: S. Weingarten 'Jerome and
the *Golden Ass*' *Studia Patristica* 33 (1997) 383f.

2.1. The Literary World of the *vita Hilarionis*: Jerome's Appropriation of Apuleius' *Golden Ass*

Introduction

Some scholars have pointed out superficial similarities in structure and landscape between Jerome's saints' *Lives* and between Hellenistic novels and *Lives* of pagan holy men, but it is now generally agreed that Jerome, who learned his Greek as an adult for the purpose of reading the Bible and Christian commentators such as Origen, shows no acquaintance with classic Greek literature and indeed is most unlikely to have read anything other than sacred texts in Greek.[4] Latin, on the other hand, was probably his native language, and certainly the language of his secular education and of his early recreational reading. Jerome himself records that he read 'Milesian fables' in his youth at Rome.[5] This could just mean obscene tales in general, as Kelly seems to have understood, but it is also possible that Jerome is here referring specifically to Apuleius, who calls his work a Milesian tale in the preface to the *Golden Ass*, as well as in the body of the work (*Met.* iv 32).[6] Christians were undoubtedly acquainted with obscene literature; some, such as Ausonius, even wrote some themselves.[7]

---

[4] As noted above in the discussion of the *vita Pauli*, Jerome was influenced by the *vita Antonii*. This in turn was influenced by such works as the Greek *Life* of Pythagoras and Philostratus' *Life of Apollonius of Tyana*. The classic study is R. Reitzenstein *Hellenistische Wundererzählungen* (Leipzig, 1906, repr. Darmstadt, 1963); see now G.J.M. Bartelink *Athanase d'Alexandrie: Vie d'Antoine* (Paris, 1994: *SC* 400) 47f. Jerome mentions Apollonius in *ep.* 53,1,4 (*CSEL* 54, 444–5) but he does not appear to make use of his *Life* in the *vita Hilarionis*.

[5] *Apol. contra Ruf.* I, 17 (*CCSL* 79,17; *PL* 23,412): *quasi non cirratorum turba Milesiarum in scholis figmenta decantent, et Testamentum Suis Bessorum cachinno membra concutiat; Com. in Es.* xii, *praef.* (*CCSL* 73A, 465; *PL* 24, 419): *nullus tam imperitus scriptor est qui lectorem non inveniat similem sui: multoque pars maior est Milesias fabellas revolventium, quam Platonis libros. In altero ludus et oblectatio est....* See Kelly, p. 20. For the *Testamentum Suis* or *Testamentum Porcelli*, see now http://www.fh-augsburg.de/~harsch/tst_intr.html.

[6] 'Milesian tales' were so called after the works of Aristides of Miletus (c100 BCE), latinised by Cornelius Sisenna (cf. Ovid *Tristia* 2, 413–4; 443–4). The *Historia Augusta*, which is contemporary with Jerome, refers to Apuleius' Milesian writings: *Milesias Punicas Apulei sui et ludicra litteraria* (*Clodius Albinus* xii 12).

[7] Some of Ausonius' *Epigrammata* are not even translated in the Loeb edition. Hagith Sivan *Ausonius of Bordeaux: Genesis of a Gallic aristocracy* (London/NY, 1993) describes the existence of such literature as a 'breath of fresh air,' but does not attempt a further analysis of the phenomenon.

In 1615, Rosweyde noted in his commentary on the *Vitae Patrum*[8]
that an anonymous martyrdom at the beginning of Jerome's *vita Pauli*
had a parallel in Apuleius' *Metamorphoses* or *Golden Ass*. J.B. Bauer[9]
also discusses this episode of the martyr smeared with honey, then
stung and eaten by insects, which is paralleled by Apuleius *Met.* viii
22.[10] However, neither of the two scholars who have dealt in considerable detail with Jerome's classical sources, Lübeck and Hagendahl,
have noted any other use made by Jerome of Apuleius.[11] Both these
scholars, it should be noted, concentrate on very close verbal parallels or actual quotations. De Vogüé, in his literary history of monasticism, noted one isolated use of an image from Apuleius' *Florida* in
Jerome's *vita Malchi*,[12] while Coleiro[13] has pointed out vague general
similarities between Jerome's fictionalised saints' *Lives* and Apuleius'
Golden Ass, but does not note any close parallels, nor does von
Albrecht,[14] although the latter does point out that the first person
narrative in the *vita Malchi* is reminiscent of Apuleius. In chapter 3,
I shall discuss Jerome's use of the legal term *postliminium* as a metaphor
in his *vita Malchi*, and Apuleius' similar use of this term.

It is thus somewhat surprising to find on close reading of Jerome's
vita Hilarionis together with the *Golden Ass* rather more parallels than
might have been expected, given this scholarly silence on the subject.
Jerome indeed appears to have had the *Golden Ass* very much in

---

[8] *Vitae Patrum* (*PL* 73, 109). Rosweyde cites the *Golden Ass* under the title '*Milesia*.'

[9] J.B. Bauer 'Novellistisches bei Hieronymus' *Wiener Studien* 74 (1961) 130f.

[10] Bauer also notes that Erasmus suggested Apuleius as a source for the next
anonymous martyrdom too, in his commentary on the *vita Pauli*. However, Bauer
does not give an exact reference nor say which edition of Erasmus he used, and I
was unable to find this comment.

[11] A. Lübeck *Hieronymus quos noverit scriptores et ex quibus hauserit* (Leipzig, 1872);
H. Hagendahl *Latin Fathers and the Classics* (Göteborg, 1958). These are quite exhaus-
tive studies, which do indeed only leave Alan Cameron 'Echoes of Vergil in St
Jerome's *Life of St Hilarion*' *Classical Philology* 63 (1968) 55–6.

[12] A. de Vogüé, *Histoire littéraire du mouvement monastique dans l'Antiquité: Première partie: Le monachisme latin: de l'itinéraire d'Égérie à l'éloge funèbre de Népotien (384–396)* (Paris,
1993).

[13] E. Coleiro 'St Jerome's Lives of the Hermits' *VChr* 11 (1957) 171–72: 'Jerome's
romance has echoes of both Virgil and Apuleius.' Coleiro continues: 'the particular element of romance which connects Jerome with Apuleius and his own Age is
the use of the weird' but he then goes on only to cite 'weird' episodes from Jerome,
and does not mention Apuleius again.

[14] M. von Albrecht, *A History of Roman Literature from Livius Andronicus to Boethius*
vol. II (Leiden/N.Y./Köln, 1997, rev. G. Schmeling and the author) 1650.

mind while writing the *vita Hilarionis*. In a paper on the 'poetics of literary allusion,' Ziva Ben Porat has written of how allusions in one text to another text are a way of activating both texts at the same time.[15] Thus the text on the page and the other text referred to both become active simultaneously in the mind of the reader. This intertextuality is achieved by allusions, shared images and also by deliberate reversals. Allusions to Apuleius' *Golden Ass* will be seen here to serve Jerome's purpose of appropriating the literary form of the ancient novel in order to create a new Christian genre of hagiography written in Latin.

Let us now turn to look more closely at the parallels between Jerome's *Life of Hilarion* and Apuleius' *Golden Ass*.

2.1.1. *Functional parallels*

1a. *Blurring of borders between fact and fiction*
Apuleius' *Golden Ass* purports to be the autobiography of Lucius, a Greek, who was attracted to the magic arts, and turned himself into an ass by mistake. After a long series of comic adventures, some of them frankly pornographic in nature, during which Lucius wanders all over Greece searching for some roses to eat and thereby turn himself back to a man again, he is saved by the intervention of the goddess Isis, whose faithful acolyte he becomes. Many readers of Apuleius must have found it hard to separate his realistic detail from his fiction.[16] Even Augustine[17] was unsure whether the metamorphosis had really occurred or not, and Apuleius was later charged in court with witchcraft. Similarly, Jerome's saints' *Lives*, including the *vita Hilarionis* in particular, have given rise to considerable scholarly debate as to whether they are based on fact or purely fictional.[18] Ancient

---

[15] Z. Ben Porat 'The Poetics of Literary Allusion' *PTL* 1 (1976) 105–128.

[16] On this see A. Laird 'Fiction, bewitchment and story worlds: The implications of claims to truth in Apuleius' in C. Gill, T.P. Wiseman (eds) *Lies and Fiction in the Ancient World* (Exeter, 1993) 147f.

[17] See *de civ. Dei* 18,18. A. Momigliano 'Ancient Biography and the study of religion in the Roman Empire' *Annali della scuola normale superiore di Pisa* 16 (1986) 25f. = *ib. On Pagans, Jews and Christians* (Middleton, 1987) 159f. notes that Lactantius (*Div. Inst.* 5.3.21) puts Apuleius together with pagan thaumaturges such as Apollonius of Tyana. On a possible revival of interest in Apuleius and Apollonius as philosophers in the fourth century, see N. Horsfall 'Apuleius, Apollonius of Tyana, Bibliomancy: some neglected dating criteria' in G. Bonamente & G. Paci (eds.) *Historiae Augustae Colloquium Maceratense* (Bari, 1995) 169–177.

[18] This debate is well summed up by A.A.R. Bastiaensen 'Jérôme hagiographe'

biography in general was a genre which was seen as belonging to
the borders between fact and fiction,[19] but these two works are exceptional in their perceived ambiguity.

1b. *General similarities of background*
Apart from the unclear borders between fact and fiction in both
these works, there are various immediately obvious general similarities—both contain more vivid details of everyday life, particularly
of the lower social classes, than is usual in Roman imperial literature. This has been noted as a feature of saints' *Lives* by Evelyne
Patlagean, and as a feature of the *Golden Ass* by Fergus Millar.[20] We
find details about *lictores* and *duumviri* and the effect of *munera* on local
people, not to mention the retinues of rich ladies and their slaves,
seen from below, as it were. Both works have vivid pictures of
different aspects of popular shows in amphitheatre and circus, and
both Lucius the ass and the holy man Hilarion attract crowds of
voluble and volatile onlookers. Both works appear to be similar in
structure at first glance: loosely strung together stories of geographical wanderings, which on closer inspection are actually knitted
together with rather more sophisticated artistry. Apuleius uses the
device of a story within a story used to such effect by a previous
writer of *Metamorphoses*—the poet Ovid—while Jerome uses Biblical
quotations and the motif of chariots to lend unity to his work,[21] and
Hilarion ends where he began, in Palestine.

1c. *Interest in languages*
It is not usual to find sensitivity to language problems in classical
authors.[22] However, another point of resemblance between Jerome
and Apuleius is their interest in languages as both a means of com-

---

*CC Hagiographies: International History of the Latin and Vernacular Hagiographical Literature
in the West from its origins to 1550*, vol. I (Turnhout, 1994) 97f.

[19] On ancient biography see Introduction.

[20] E. Patlagean 'Ancient Byzantine hagiography and social history' in *Saints and
their Cults: Studies in Religion, Sociology, Folklore and History* ed. S. Wilson (Cambridge,
1983, repr. 1987); F. Millar 'The World of the *Golden Ass*' *JRS* 71 (1981) 63f.

[21] For the use of the chariot motif, and its pagan and Christian connections, see
below.

[22] This is less true of Christian authors—see Marcus Diaconus *vita Porphyrii* 68
where a divine voice speaks Greek through a seven year old child: ὁ παῖς εἶπεν τῇ
ἑλληνικῇ διαλέκτῳ, whereas before he had spoken only Syriac τῇ Σύρων φωνῇ.

munication, and sometimes an obstacle to communication. Apuleius in the *Golden Ass* tells a story of a Roman soldier *miles e legione* who talks to a Greek speaking countryman in Latin and inevitably is not understood (*Met.* ix 39). Apuleius uses this misunderstanding to comic effect, and the soldier is forced to communicate in Greek. On another occasion Apuleius makes a pun on the name of Apollo, the Milesian god, who

> *quamquam Graecus et Ionicus, propter Milesiae conditorem sic Latina sorte respondit* (*Met.* iv 32).

In the *vita Hilarionis* (22) there is an incident where a much higher ranking army officer, a *candidatus Constantii imperatoris*,[23] who is possessed by a demon, comes to Gaza to be exorcised by Hilarion. Hilarion speaks to him in Syriac:

> *videres de ore barbaro, et qui Francam tantum et Latinam linguam noverat, Syra ad purum verba resonare. . . . et ut interpretes eius intelligerent qui Graecum tantum et Latinam linguam noverant, Graece quoque eum interrogavit.*[24]

After the marvel of the Frank (or his demon) who spoke Syriac, he too, like the soldier in Apuleius, is forced to give a translation into Greek. Jerome also uses the incident for comic effect—the demon is forced to translate his words into Greek—so that the officer's *translators* could understand! Jerome seems here to be satirising the upper classes of the Roman empire for whom the only languages which counted were Latin and Greek, neither of which were of use in this encounter in rural Palestine. The Christian Hilarion, in contrast, can speak Syriac, the local language of the people—and of the demons.

Another surprising speaker of Syriac in the *vita Hilarionis* (23) is a Bactrian camel *enormis magnitudinis*, also possessed by a devil. There is another parallel here to the *Golden Ass*: Lucius, the man inside the ass, is on one occasion given a large amount of barley and hay, enough for a Bactrian camel—*camelo Bactrinae sufficiens* (*Met.* vii 14). Lucius as an ass never manages to speak, so that here Hilarion goes one better in managing to communicate with the demon in the camel.

---

[23] For the *candidatus Constantii* see the appendix of occupations.
[24] Tr. From a barbarian mouth, and one which only knew Frankish and Latin, purely Syrian words came out . . . and so that his interpreters could understand, for they knew only Greek and Latin, he also questioned him in Greek.

1d. *Parallel functionaries*

Other small details of everyday urban life in antiquity are similarly
present in both Apuleius and Jerome. Lucius is arrested by *lictores
duo de iusso magistratuum* (*Met.* iii 2) while Hilarion is sought by *Gazenses
cum lictoribus praefecti* (*vita Hilarionis* 33) on order of the Emperor Julian,
not a mere magistrate. Unlike Lucius, he manages to evade his pursuers. Similarly Apuleius (*Met.* iv 9) relates an episode of Chryseros,
a rich banker who tries to avoid performance of public duties: *metu
officiorum ac munerum publicorum magnis artibus magnam dissimulabat opu-
lentiam*. Jerome relates the story of Italicus, *oppidi municeps Christianus*
who bred horses and asked Hilarion's help in a horse race against
an avowed pagan worshipper of Marnas. When Hilarion asked why
he did not do something better with his money, he answered that
this was an unavoidable public duty: *functionem esse publicam; et hoc se
non tam velle, quam cogi: nec posse hominem Christianum uti magicis artibus . . .*
In Roman society it was part of the public function of the city
officials to contribute money for the city services, as both Apuleius
and Jerome make clear.[25] With Hilarion's help, the horses of Christ
beat the horses of Marnas, but the Christian local functionary is also
seen as triumphing over the pagans in not avoiding his duty or using
magicis artibus. Jerome seems here to be alluding to Apuleius' *magnis
artibus*, but he has developed them into the magic arts forbidden to
a Christian.

1e. *Circus and amphitheatre*

Metamorphoses x contains an account of how Lucius, the man inside
the ass, is brought to the local amphitheatre, where games (*munera*)
are about to be held. Lucius is brought there in a procession—*pom-
patico*.[26] Apuleius then describes the performance of a mime of the

---

[25] City functionaries' contributions to paying for services in general: *LRE* 732;
for games in particular *ib.* 736. For attempts by people to evade public functions
in late antique Palestine cf. Jerusalem Talmud Mo'ed Qatan ii,1b and parallels:
'Rabbi Yohanan said: If they mention you in connection with the *boule*, make the
Jordan your boundary [i.e. flee the country]. R Yohanan said: [People] appeal to
get permission to be exempted from [serving on] the *boule*.' Rabbi Yohanan was a
third century rabbi in Galilee: see on this: G. Stemberger *Jews and Christians in the
Holy Land: Palestine in the fourth century* (tr. R. Tuschling, Edinburgh, 2000) 30f.

[26] On the *pompa circensis* with its pagan gods, satire and transvestism see M.W.
Gleason 'Festive satire: Julian's *Misopogon* and the new year at Antioch' *JRS* 76
(1986) 106f.

Judgement of Paris, dwelling on the charms of Venus, *nudo et intecto corpore*, as if on her way to a wedding feast. Venus is finally swallowed up by a gaping *terrae uorago* (*Met.* x 34). Lucius as ass is to be shown having intercourse in public with a depraved woman, and wishes he could be dead rather than polluted by her—sentiments that the monk Hilarion can be supposed to approve equally. Lucius is also fearful of being attacked and eaten by wild animals. He manages to escape and finds refuge in a *mollissimo harenae gremio* just as the sun is about to set—Apuleius uses the image of the sun in his chariot: *ultimam diei metam curriculum solis deflexerat*.

When we first meet Hilarion he is described as one who, believing in Lord Jesus, was not pleased by *circi furoribus . . . arenae sanguine . . . theatri luxuria* (*vH* 2). However, when Jerome describes Hilarion's temptations in the desert they are all of these spectacles—the Gaza sands *litus quod Palaestinae Aegyptoque praetenditur . . . molle arenis* (*vH* 19),[27] which remind us of Lucius' soft sandy shore, become the arena of the amphitheatre and the circus. Hilarion is tempted, Jerome says, by processions (*pomp[ae]*) he has never experienced (*vH* 5)—he is in an amphitheatre in spirit. Thus he hears the sounds of wild animals which are reminiscent of the *uenationes* Lucius feared, and then a procession, *pompa*, consisting of a *rhed[a] ferventibus equis* is sent to distract him from praying, reminding us of the beginning and end of *Met.* x with its procession and then the sun's chariot racing round the circus. On Hilarion's calling on Jesus, the chariot is swallowed up by a *hiatu terrae*—like the *terrae uorago* which swallowed up Venus in the amphitheatre where Lucius found himself. Following this Hilarion is tempted by naked women and by lavish feasts—Apuleius' suggestive descriptions of the nude Venus include a reference to a wedding feast. Jerome also uses other vocabulary (*palaestrita, agitator*) connected to circus and amphitheatre.

Jerome later takes up the chariot race in the circus and develops it to become a major episode in *Life of Hilarion*, which will be dealt with in detail below.

1f. *Forbidden burials*
Jerome further develops Hilarion's spiritual amphitheatre by adding one element which does not belong to *Met.* x: a gladiatorial contest

---

[27] Cf. also *arenis mollibus* (*vH* 22); *in arenis* [var. *in terra*] (*vH* 18); *baculo arenas discutiens* (*vH* 30).

enacted by demons to distract the saint from his psalms, where an apparently dying man begs him for burial: *gladiatorum pugna spectaculum praebuit: et unus quasi interfectus et ante pedes eius corruens sepulturam rogavit.* This, however, is reminiscent of *Met.* vi 18, Apuleius' story of Psyche. Here Psyche herself is warned not to take account of distractions on her journey, not even a dead man begging for burial while she is in Charon's boat crossing the Styx: *nec setius tibi pigrum fluentum transmeanti quidam supernatans senex mortuus putris adtollens manus orabit ut eum intra nauigium trahas; nec tu tamen inlicita adflectare pietate.* The similarity between these two stories of forbidden distractions, both of which concentrate on a dying or dead man begging for burial is clear. The warning to Psyche: *nec tu tamen inlicita adflectare pietas,* could just as well be addressed to Hilarion.

2.1.2. *Verbal and visual parallels*

2a. *A shared joke*

Over and above these similar aspects there are further striking parallels between these works, both verbal and visual.

In the *vita Hilarionis* 12 there is a story of thieves who set out to search for Hilarion. Having searched for him all night they find him at daybreak and ask jokingly (*quasi per jocum*) what he would do if robbers arrived.[28] He replies that a naked man does not fear robbers: *Nudus latrones non timet.* When they point out that he may be killed, he agrees that this is a possibility but that he is not afraid because he is ready to die.[29]

A very similar story is to be found in Apuleius (*Met.* i 15).[30] Here a man is preparing to leave an inn before daybreak. The porter protests that it is too early:

> Don't you know the roads are infested with robbers (*latronibus*)? Even if you have a crime on your conscience and are eager to die, I am not such a blockhead as to die for you.

---

[28] *A vespere usque ad solis ortum discurrentes. Porro claro luce . . . quasi per jocum: Quid, inquiunt, faceres si latrones ad te venirent?*

[29] *Certe, ajunt occidi potes. Possum, inquit, possum: et ideo latrones non timeo, quia mori paratus sum.*

[30] *Tu, inquit, ignoras latronibus infestari uias, qui hoc noctis iter incipis? Nam etsi tu alicuius facinoris tibi conscius scilicet mori cupis, non cucurbitae caput non habemus ut pro te moriamur. Non longe, inquam, lux abest.*

The traveller protests that it is nearly daybreak and anyway,

> What can robbers take from the very poorest? Or don't you know,
> idiot, that a naked man (*nudum*) can't be stripped even by ten wrestlers?[31]

The similarities between the stories are many. Both take place at or
near daybreak, in both the hero is asked if he does not fear '*latrones.*'
In both cases he replies that a man who is '*nudus*' need have no
fear of being robbed, and in both cases this is presented as a joke,
quasi per jocum, as Jerome writes. However, for Apuleius, the idea
that the protagonist might not fear death is presented as ridiculous.
Jerome transforms the ridiculous into a transcendent statement of
Hilarion's Christian faith. He, like Apuleius, uses jokes to point his
satire.

2b. *Shared vocabulary*

Having noted that Apuleius enlivens his description by the parallel
image of the naked man who cannot be stripped even by ten pro-
fessional wrestlers—*palaestritis*, we find that Jerome picks up this
unusual Greek word and uses it later in *vH* 18 where Orion, *vir primarius et ditissimus Ailae*, is possessed by a legion of devils.[32] When he
seizes Hilarion, the crowd fear for the latter's safety, but Hilarion
bids them be quiet and leave him to deal with his *palaestritam*, whom
he overcomes. Apuleius' nude man could not be despoiled by ten
wrestlers—Hilarion, who models himself on Jesus, is a match for a
whole legion of devils.

2c. *The grotesque*

Both Jerome and Apuleius appear to share a non-classical interest
in the grotesque and the extreme. Lucius suffers extremes of punishment just as Hilarion indulges in extremes of asceticism. Lucius
as an ass is unmercifully beaten just as Hilarion as an ass is ridden
and flagellated by the Devil. Apuleius has a particularly grotesque
description of a man called Thelyphron whose nose *nasum* and ears
aures are cut off by evil spirits when he is bewitched while watching

---

[31] *Et praeterea quid uiatori de summa pauperie latrones auferre possunt? An ignoras, inepte,
nudum nec a decem palaestritis despoliari posse?*

[32] K.C. Gutwein *Third Palestine: A regional study in Byzantine urbanization* (Washington,
1981) cites this as evidence for the *Legio X Fretensis* at Aila [present-day Eilat on
the Red Sea], but it is clearly an allusion to Mark 5:2–9; Luke 8:27–31.

a corpse.[33] This is paralleled in the *vita Hilarionis* by Messicas (or Marsitas), who was afflicted by a demon which caused him to bite off the nose *nasum* and ears *aures* of many people.[34] It should be noted here that Messicas was noted as carrying large amounts of grain: *quindecim frumenti modios diu longeque portaret.* The associations with the ass are then made explicit: Jerome describes him as surpassing an ass in endurance: *hanc haberet palmam fortitudinis suae, si asinos vinceret.*

2.1.3. *Shared images*

3a. *Roses and thorns*

At the beginning of the *vita Hilarionis* (2) Hilarion is described as *rosa, ut dicitur, de spinis floruit.* Although Jerome cites this as a commonplace, and a similar sentiment is indeed found in different words in Jerome's contemporary Ammianus (xvi,8,4), the combination of roses and thorns is not in fact common in the surviving Latin literature.[35] The crown of the martyr was traditionally seen as a crown of roses,[36] and this image is used by Jerome himself elsewhere.[37] But roses together with thorns appear several times as a key image in the *Golden Ass.*[38] Lucius, the hero-turned-ass, knows that he must eat roses

---

[33] *Met* ii, 20: *iniecta manu nasum prehendo, sequitur; ib.* 30: *aures pertracto deruunt.*

[34] *vita Hilarionis* 17: *multorum nasum et aures morsibus amputaverat.*

[35] Canticles 2:2, כשושנה בין החוחים, which in modern Hebrew would refer to a 'rose among thorns,' is translated by the Vulgate as lily, not rose: *sicut liliam inter spinas* and the LXX also has κρίνον = lily, and cf. Jerome *ep.* 22,19 on Canticles 2:1: *lilium convallium.* A search of the Cetedoc CD ROM database revealed no roses together with thorns before the fourth century in patristic Latin literature, when there are only two occurrences in Ambrose and three in Maximin of Turin. Jerome himself mentions this combination on four occasions, e.g. *ep.* 22,20. See also P. Winter 'Der literarische Charakter der Vita beati Hilarionis des Hieronymus' in *Zur Gedächtnisfeier für den Senator Philipp Ferdinand Adolf Just* (Zittau, 1904) p. 5, n. 2.

[36] For example cf. the 3rd century *Passio Sanctorum Mariani et Iacobi* (ed. Franchi de Cavalieri, *Studi e testi* (1900) 47f.) which includes a wreath of roses for the martyr (11) and a vision of a *locus amoenus* (6). The martyrdom itself takes place in a natural amphitheatre: *spectaculo* (11).

[37] *ep.* 108,31: *Eustochium. . . . mater tua longo martyrio coronata est. Non solum effusio sanguinis in confessione reputatur, sed deuotae quoque mentis seruitus cotidianum martyrium est. Illa corona de rosis et uiolis plectitur, ista de liliis.*: Tr. 'Eustochium . . . your mother was crowned after a long martyrdom. It is not only the spilling of blood which is reckoned as a profession [of Christian faith], but the immaculate service of a devoted mind is a daily martyrdom. The first is a crown woven of roses and violets, the second is a crown of lilies.'

[38] M. von Albrecht *op. cit. supra* 1455, notes the important function of roses in the *Golden Ass,* and their mystic and erotic significance.

in order to be saved from his fate as an ass: he begins to see roses even where they do not exist:

> *iam enim loco proximus non illas rosas teneras et amoenas, madidas diuini roris et nectaris, quas rubi felices, beatae spinae generant . . . (Met.* iv, 2).

Later Lucius hopes for deliverance now that spring was come (*Met.* x 29):

> *dirrupto spineo tegmine spirantes cinnameos odores promicarent rosae.*

Another time he sees roses but refrains from eating them:

> *Mihi inopinatum salutem Iuppiter ille tribuit . . . . . hortulum quendam prospexi satis amoenum, in quo praeter ceteras gratas herbulas rosae uirgines matutino rore florebant* (*Met.* iii, 29).

He is offered salvation, as he thinks, from Jupiter, but it is too dangerous to take advantage of it, so

> *tunc igitur a rosis et quidem necessario temperaui.*

Note here the siting of the roses in a '*hortulum amoenum*' and that Lucius refrains from eating for fear of being killed:

> *ne . . . exitium inter manus . . . offenderem.*

Finally it is not Jupiter but Isis (who tells us she is called, among other things, *Paphiam Venerem* by the people of Cyprus) who saves Lucius when her priest gives him a wreath of roses:

> *coronam, quae rosis amoenis intexta fulgurabat (Met.* xi 13).

3b. *The goddess Venus/Isis*
The appearance of Venus/Isis in *Met.* xi is by no means Venus' only appearance in Apuleius' erotic work—she appears in other contexts too, persecuting the beautiful young girl Psyche who fell in love with Love himself:

> *sic ignara Psyche sponte in Amoris incidit amorem (Met.* v 23)

as well as in the mime of the Judgement of Paris which is part of the spectacle in the amphitheatre, where she is eventually swallowed up together with the scenery by a marvellous piece of stage machinery (*Met.* x 34).

Venus appears in the *vita Hilarionis* (25) also. She is the goddess worshipped by the Saracens of Elusa as Lucifer. Hilarion is known to the Saracens, for he has exorcised many demons from them, and on this occasion he persuades them of their error, so that they agree to convert to Christianity. Hilarion plans a church for them and marks their priest, *ut erat coronatus* with the sign of the cross. This is not Hilarion's only victory over Venus and her arts, although she is not again mentioned by name. A Christian virgin is seduced by *magicis artibus*, which include *portentosas figuras in aeris Cyprii lamina*—and forced against her will into a passion for a young man. Cyprus is traditionally associated with the goddess Venus (like Apuleius' Paphian Venus already encountered above). The demon *proditor castitatis* whom Hilarion exorcises from the girl says his colleague is the demon of love (*vita Hilarionis* 21), just as Venus is associated with Cupid. Hilarion's final home is on Cyprus itself, in the ruins of Paphos (*vita Hilarionis* 42–3). Thus Jerome reminds us of the city's past as the home of Venus, now vanquished and not even to be mentioned by name:

> Thus he entered Paphos, the noble city of Cyprus in the songs of the poets .... which now shows in the remains of its ruins how great it was formerly.[39]

The triumph over Venus is not, however, complete, for there still remain for Hilarion some demons to struggle with in her 'very ancient temple.'

2.1.4. *Paradise versus Hades*

The *vita Hilarionis* includes a description of Hilarion's visit to the *habitaculum* where Antony, the father of monasticism, had lived:

> *Saxeus et sublimis mons per mille circiter passus ad radices suas aquas exprimit, quarum alias arenae ebibunt, aliae ad inferiora delapsae, paulatim rivum efficiunt; super quem ex utraque ripa palmae innumerabiles multum loco et amoenitatis et commodi tribuunt . . . hic, aiebant, psallere, hic orare, hic operari, hic fessus residere solitus erat . . . hanc piscinam ad irrigandum hortulum multo sudore fabricatus est . . . . . praeterea in sublimi montis vertice, quasi per cochleam ascendentibus, et arduo valde nisu . . . cellulae visebantur. (vita Hilarionis 31)*

---

[39] *[Hilarion] ingressus ergo Paphum, urbem Cypri nobilem carminibus poetarum, . . . nunc ruinarum tantum vestigiis quid olim fuerit, ostendit.* Venus on Paphos is mentioned e.g. by Virgil *Aeneid* x, 51 *celsa . . . Paphus,* cf. Hilarion's final home high in the mountains (*vita Hilarionis* 43) See the discussion of Venus at Elusa and Paphos in 2.2.2b below.

Tr. There was a sublime and rocky mountain for about a mile. At its roots there gushed forth water, some of which was absorbed by the sands, while the rest fell deeper, little by little forming a river. Innumerable palm-trees over it on either bank gave much delight and ease to the place ... Here, they said, he would sing psalms, here he would pray, here work, here he would rest when he was tired.... He sweated to make this fish pond for watering his garden ... Apart from this, at the top of the sublime mountain, ascending by a most difficult climb in a sort of spiral, there were cells ...

Various commentators have noted that this description, while similar to that found in the *vita Antonii* which Jerome certainly knew, adds various details—Antony's palm trees have multiplied greatly, for example. Since Jerome had not had time on his short visit to Egypt to actually visit Antony's cell, these details must come from another source or be products of Jerome's imagination.[40] The possible missing sources here are the book of Ezekiel with its vision of the Heavenly Temple, and the book of Revelation. In Ezekiel 47:1–6 the waters fall from the different sides of the Temple to form a river, where there are many trees on either bank (*ib.* v.7)

in ripa torrentis ligna multa nimis ex utraque parte;

in Revelation (22:1–2) the river proceeds from the throne of God and the Lamb and the tree of life is on either side of the river:

ex utraque parte fluminis lignum vitae.

By multiplying the trees by the stream Jerome has turned the place where Antony lived into an image of the earthly paradise. Other words add to this impression, such as *amoenitas*—Paradise was traditionally *locus amoenus*. So too the vocabulary of the garden, *hortulum*, and the work in it—*operari*—Adam was placed in Paradise *ut operaretur* (Gen. 2:15). Later Jerome describes the last home of Hilarion in very similar terms (*vita Hilarionis* 43):

inter secretos asperosque montes, ex quo vix reptando manibus genubasque posset ascendi ....contemplatus quidem est terribilem valde et remotum locum, arboribus

---

[40] de Vogüé (*op. cit.* n. 12 above) 216 'Cette transformation de l'ermitage antonien est-elle autre chose qu'une fantaisie inspirée par la *Vita Antoninii*? Sans exclure que Jerome tienne quelques renseignements des disciples d'Hilarion, ni qu'il ait vu ces lieux lui-même ou éntendu parler d'eux par des pèlerins, on peut se demander s'il n'a pas simplement excercé son imagination sur le récit très sobre d'Athanase.'

hinc inde circumdatum, habentem etiam aquas de supercilio collis irrigans, et hor-
tulum peramoenum et pomaria plurima quorum fructum numquam in cibo sump-
sit: sed et antiquissimi juxta templi ruinam ex quo ... tam innumerabilium per
noctes et dies daemonum voces resonabant ... propter asperitatem difficultatemque
loci ... aut nullus aut rarus ad se vel posset vel auderet ascendere.

Tr. Amongst secret and rough mountains, which could only be ascended
by crawling on hands and knees ... he saw, however, that the exceed-
ingly terrible and remote place was surrounded on all sides by trees
and was even watered by streams from the summit of the hill. There
was a most delightful garden, and many fruit trees, but he never took
the fruit for food. Next to this was the ruin of a very ancient temple
from which ... resounded the voices of innumerable demons night and
day ... Because of the roughness and difficulty of the place ... no-
one (or almost no-one) could ascend or dared to.

Antony lived in an earthly Paradise, so too Hilarion. However,
Hilarion, unlike Antony and Adam, does not work in his *hortulum*
peramoenum, nor does he eat the fruit of the trees—he does not com-
mit the sin which led to the Fall. What is more, he fights with
demons. If Antony is a type of Adam,[41] Hilarion surpasses him: he
is the type of Jesus.

As we have noted, *locus amoenus* is a common-place for Paradise,
but the term *hortulum [per]amoenum* I have found only in Apuleius (see
above). In the *hortulum amoenum* of *Met.* iii 29, as noted earlier, Lucius
refrains from eating the roses for fear of death. In the *hortulum per-*
amoenum in the *vita Hilarionis*, Hilarion refrains from eating the fruit
of the trees of Paradise, by eating which Adam and Eve had became
subject to expulsion and death.

Ewald has noted a few words similar to Sallust[42] in Jerome's
description of Antony's and Hilarion's homes, but there are more
convincing similarities to Apuleius' description of the entrance to
Hades:

---

[41] On monks who have left the cities for the caves and mountains as engaged
in the work of Adam before the Fall, cf. John Chrysostom *Hom. in Mat.* 68,3 (*PG*
58, 643): ἔργον δὲ αὐτοῖς ὅπερ ἦν καὶ τῷ Ἀδαμ παρὰ τὴν ἀρχὴν καὶ πρὸ τῆς
ἁμαρτίας

[42] The resemblances to Sallust noted by Ewald are very slight, in comparison
with the similarities to Apuleius. She quotes Catilina 59.2: *planities erat inter sinistros*
montis et ab dextra rupe aspera quae loca et nationes ob calciem aut asperitatem, item solitudines
minus frequentata sunt; Jugurtha 17.2: *quae loca et nationes ob calorem aut asperitatem, item*
solitudines minus frequentata sunt.

Uidesne insistentem celsissimae illi rupi montis ardui uerticem, de quo fontis atri fuscae defluunt undae proxumaeque conceptaculo uallis inclusae Stygias inrigant paludes . . . uidet . . . saxum immani magnitudine procerum et inaccessa salebritate lubricum mediis e faucibus lapidis fontes horridos euomebat, qui . . . delapsi . . . proxumam conuallem latenter incidebant. dextra laeuaque cautibus cauatis proserpunt . . . saeui dracones . . . iamque et ipsae semet muniebant uocales aquae, nam et . . . 'caue' et 'fuge' . . . clamant. (Met. vi 13–14).

Tr. Do you see the lowering peak of the high mountain with its difficult cliff from which flow down the dark waves of a black spring, which are enclosed in the basin of the nearby valley and water the marshes of the river Styx and feed the raucous stream of Cocytus? . . . She saw . . . a high slippery rock of huge size, inaccessible because of its ruggedness, which vomited out horrid fountains from its stone jaws which fell . . . and ran down secretly into the next valley. On the right and left on the hollow rocks crept terrible serpents . . . And now even the vocal waters were defending themselves, crying '. . . Beware! Fly! You will die . . .'

This description has various pictures and vocabulary shared with Jerome's descriptions of the paradisial homes of Antony and Hilarion. Both speak of a high and almost inaccessible mountain peak *celsissimae illi rupi montis ardui verticem* in Apuleius, *sublimi montis vertice . . . arduo valde nisu* in Jerome (*vita Hilarionis* 31) and both tell of the *difficultas* of the ascent (Apuleius *loc. cit.* 14; Jerome *op. cit* 43); *vix posset ascendi* (Jerome *ib.* 43) and *inaccessa* (Apuleius *loc. cit.* 13). In both streams of water flow down from the rock and join to form a river which is described as *delaps[ae]* (Apuleius *loc. cit.* 14; Jerome *ib.* 31). Here the verbal resemblances end, but the descriptions are still so alike as to give the impression that Jerome's paradise is a deliberate *reversal* of Apuleius' Hades—the waters of Styx flow underground and form marshes, while those of Jerome's descriptions form pools of fish, and water fertile paradisial gardens. On either side of the rivers of Jerome we have noted fruitful trees, the *lignum vitae* of Revelation. This would appear to be in direct opposition to the river of Apuleius where on either side there are terrible serpents, *saevi dracones*. Serpents have no power in the paradise of Jerome, where Hilarion refrains from eating from the trees. Finally the *innumerabilium . . . daemonum voces* which Hilarion hears from the ruined temple nearby (*vH* 43) may be a reminiscence of the *vocales aquae* of the Styx, which attempt to frighten Psyche, as the demons contend with Hilarion.

2.1.5. *Biographical notes*

The *Golden Ass* purports to be autobiographical. While this may seem to modern readers a transparent literary device, I have already pointed out that the late antique audience was not so sure. Augustine appears to have kept an open mind on the subject, writing of it as a work which may or may not be true, and warning against those who see Apuleius as a magician whose powers surpass Christ.[43] Presumably at least some of Apuleius' audience must have believed in the truth of his conversion into an ass, as a result of the use of magical arts. Apuleius' *Apology* makes it clear that a friend called Pontianus introduced Apuleius to his mother Pudentilla, a rich widow, whom Apuleius married. Later the son died and the rest of the family took Apuleius to court on a charge of seducing the widow by witchcraft, a serious charge. Apuleius was acquitted, but forced to leave town. *Met.* x, which Jerome uses extensively in the *vita Hilarionis*, contains a diatribe against corrupt judges who have convicted the innocent, even the learned and wise, throughout history.[44]

Jerome, too, was associated with a rich widow, Paula, who eventually used her money to build two monasteries where they ended their lives living side by side, in chastity. After Paula's child Blesilla died as a result of repeated fasting encouraged by Jerome, charges were brought against Jerome *infamiam falsi criminis inportarunt* (*ep.* 45, 6), presumably about his relations with Paula, and there was some sort of enquiry by what Jerome calls the senate of the Pharisees, *Pharisaeorum senatus*, which would seem to have been some sort of ecclesiastical body. As a result of this, a judgment was passed on Jerome (Jerome: *Apol.* iii 21). He appears to have been acquitted but forced to leave Rome.[45] Anderson has noted the parallel between Jerome's relationship with Paula, and Apuleius' relationship with Pudentilla.[46] It is possible that Jerome's conscious or unconscious identification with

---

[43] Augustine *ep.* 136 (*PL* 33). On Apuleius and magic see http://ccat.sas.upenn.edu/jod/apuleius.

[44] R.G. Summers, 'Roman Justice and Apuleius' Metamorphoses' *TAPA* 101 (1970) 511–31, sees the whole of Apuleius' work as a subtle indictment of the administration of criminal justice in the Roman provinces.

[45] See Kelly 113–114 for a convincing reconstruction of the events from the fragmentary evidence.

[46] G. Anderson *Sage, saint and sophist: Holy men and their associates in the Early Roman empire* (London/NY 1994) 117.

Apuleius because of their similar experiences forms part of his motivation for using Apuleius in the *vita Hilarionis*. Jerome identifies similarly, this time openly, with the dramatist Terence (and Virgil and Cicero) attacked by his detractors, in the preface to his *Hebrew Questions on Genesis*.[47]

2.1.6. *The Christian ass*

The *vita Hilarionis* contains various sorts of references to asses. *Asinus* and its diminutive *asellus* were commonly used by both pagan and Christian Roman writers as a metaphor for human beings who were 'stupid, lazy, obstinate, vile and deserving of whipping.'[48] Jerome also uses the ass elsewhere as a metaphor for the bestial aspects of man.[49]

For Christians, the ass was also closely associated with Jesus. The Entry to Jerusalem with Jesus riding an ass was a popular subject of early Christian art, especially on sarcophagi at Rome, and there are many depictions of the ass and ox next to the infant Jesus in his manger at Bethlehem.[50] Apart from these, it is clear that the subject of the ass itself was of particular but mysterious significance in early Christian art, as the ass also appears in catacomb art and on gold glass and amulets. There seems to be no consensus on its meaning, although there are some anti-Christian texts which refer to Christians as worshipping an ass.[51] Tertullian tells of a Jewish gladiator

---

[47] Identification with Terence: see discussion by Hayward in commentary *ad loc.* C.T.R. Hayward *Saint Jerome's Hebrew Questions on Genesis* (Oxford 1995).

[48] *TLL sv asinus* II quoting among others Plautus, Terence, Quintillian, Jerome, Eucherius and Isidore. Eucherius notes as metaphorical uses of *asinus* both *corpus humanum* and *populus gentium*. Both may come from Jerome, whom Eucherius knew (see chapter 4 on Jerome's *ep.* 129) for Jerome explains the foal of the ass used by Jesus in his Entry to Jerusalem as metaphor for the gentiles in his *Com. in Mat.* iii, 21,5 (*CCSL* 77, 183; *PL* 26, 147). Cf. *Com. in Es.* x, 32, 20 (*CCSL* 73A, Adriaen, 410; *PL* 24, 362).

[49] E.g. *Com. in Es.* vi, 20 (14,1) 712 (Gryson) = vi, 14, 1 235 (*CCSL* 73, Adriaen; *PL* 24, 215). However, there are well over a hundred references to asses in Jerome's work, and it is beyond the scope of this book to analyse them all.

[50] Entry to Jerusalem: T.F. Mathews *The Clash of Gods: A reinterpretation of Early Christian Art* (Princeton, 1999²) 27f., citing 28 sarcophagi at Rome alone; ass and crib: *ib.* 48.

[51] Qv *RAC s.v.* Esel: Christlich (I. Opelt); *DACL s.v.* Âne (H. Leclerq). The dubious evidence for early Christian ass-worship (cf. Tacitus Hist. 5, 3) is discussed by Mathews, *op. cit.* above, 45f. Mathews' work has come in for a great deal of scholarly criticism, but not on the subject of the importance of the ass in early Christian art.

who taunted the Christians with a representation of a figure in a toga with ass's ears inscribed *Deus Christianorum* ὀνοκοίτης.[52] The meaning of the word ὀνοκοίτης/*onocoetes* has been debated; the first element undoubtedly refers to an ass.[53] The various interpretations of the second element discussed by Opelt and Leclerq are not relevant here, but Leclerq immediately associates it with Apuleius (*Met.* ix, 14) and the depraved woman who wanted to have sexual intercourse with Lucius the ass. If this was Leclerq's immediate association, it is possible it was Jerome's also, and that for him the ass had both divine and forbidden sexual connotations. Jerome certainly knew Tertullian's works well and used them often.[54]

The various sorts of references to asses in the *vita Hilarionis* serve to link it closely by allusion to Apuleius' *Golden Ass*. Lucius, the hero of the *Golden Ass*, is a man who is turned into an ass. He is often beaten and reviled,[55] but still has human feelings and aspirations. He objects to being forced to eat non-human food like barley, *hordeum*.[56] He also objects to being forced to have sexual intercourse with a depraved woman.[57] Most particularly, he wishes to escape from his status as an ass and become human once more. Hilarion, the hero of Jerome's *vita*, is also explicitly personally identified with an ass. Here the ass is a metaphor for the bestial aspects of the human body, which the Christian hero must subdue. Tempted by the devil with seductive images Hilarion even addresses himself as an ass: *Ego, inquit, aselle, faciam ut non calcitre: nec te hordeo alam, sed paleis. Fame te conficiam et siti . . .* (*vita Hilarionis* 5). Like Lucius, Hilarion too wishes to escape from his body's material needs and desires, which are the same as the bodily needs and desires of an ass. Later in the *vita*, the Devil, in the form of a circus *agitator*, leaps onto Hilarion's back, flogs him and tauntingly offers him barley *hordeum* to eat (*vH* 8).[58]

---

[52] Tertullian *ad Nationes* i, 14 (*PL* 1, 579). Cf. *id. Apol.* 16,12.

[53] Qv Opelt and Leclerq *loc. cit.* above: Âne: Calumnie de l'onolatrie.

[54] *E.g. epp.* 5, 2, 2; 58, 10, 1. Cf. Kelly 33; 64; 108. N. Adkin 'Tertullian's de praescriptione haereticorum and Jerome's Libellus de virginitate servanda (Epist. 22)' *Eirene* 30 (1994) 103–107 and further bibliography *ad loc.*

[55] *Met.* iii; 27; iv, 4; viii, 30; ix, 15 etc.

[56] *Met.* vii, 14.

[57] *Met.* ix, 14.

[58] This use of *asellus* to describe the human body undergoing flagellation can be paralleled in Jerome's Christian contemporary and correspondent, Paulinus of Nola, who writes (*Carmen* 24, 617): *sit fortis anima mortificans asinum suum.*

Apart from this metaphorical use of the ass in the *vita Hilarionis*, Jerome also introduces a real ass. This, too, carries both allusions to Apuleius as well as Christian undertones. Jerome depicts Aristaenete, the wife of the future praetorian prefect, as forgetting all matronly processional—*oblita matronalis pompae*, so that her husband could scarcely manage to persuade her even to ride on an ass: *ut asello sedens pergeret* (*vH* 14). In his *ep.* 108 Jerome also relates something very similar of his companion, the noble lady Paula, on her pilgrimage to the Holy Places.[59] The relationship between Hilarion and Aristaenete, while clearly based on the biblical holy man Elisha and the rich Shunamite woman[60] has several other parallels to the relationship between Jerome and Paula. Aristaenete is a rich *matrona* of a higher social status than Hilarion, but recognises in him her spiritual superior. Jerome depicts the relationship between himself and Paula similarly. For both Aristaenete and Paula their humility despite their status is expressed in their choosing to ride only on an ass. Asses in antiquity were a common mode of transport, but presumably those who could afford it preferred horses or carriages.[61] It was seen as a mark of Jesus' humility that he entered Jerusalem riding on a lowly ass. Thus both Aristaenete and Paula are displaying expressly Christian humility in riding on an ass.

Apuleius also writes of a virgin called Charite (later also called a *matrona*) who flees from captivity on the back of Lucius the ass.[62] He even describes a painting of this episode. Later Charite is described as riding in triumph on an ass—*virginem asino triumphantem*—in a procession described as a *pomp[a]*. Christian commentators in the past have made much of this description, immediately relating it both to the Virgin Mary and her flight to Egypt riding on an ass, and also to Jesus' Entry to Jerusalem riding an ass. Some have even tried to use this episode to demonstrate Apuleius' attitude to Christianity.[63]

---

[59] Jerome *ep.* 108, 7: . . . *femina nobilis, quae prius eunuchorum manibus portabatur, asello sedens profecta est.*

[60] II Kings 4:8f. esp. 22 (for the ass).

[61] L. Casson *Travel in the Ancient World* (Baltimore/London, 1974, repr. 1994) 176f.

[62] *Met.* vi, 29: *Asino uectore uirgo regia fugiens captiuitatem.*

[63] See L. Hermann 'L'âne d'or et le christianisme' *Latomus* 12 (1953) 188f.; *contra* V. Hunink 'Apuleius, Pudentilla and Christianity' *VChr* 54 (2000) 80–94. For a suggestion that Apuleius may have been using Christian sources: D. Shanzer, '*Asino vectore virgo regia fugiens captivitatem*: Apuleius and the Tradition of the Protoevangelium Jacobi' *ZPE* 84 (1990) 221–229.

Without entering into the discussion about Apuleius and Christianity, it would be reasonable for Jerome too to have noticed this description. Thus in the *vita Hilarionis* his description of Aristaenete riding an ass uses the words *matronalis pompae* and although he has changed Charite's *asinus* to an *asellus* this would seem to be an allusion to Apuleius' virgin as well as to Jesus and Mary.

As already noted, Jesus' Entry to Jerusalem riding an ass was popular in early Christian art. Mathews has suggested that these depictions of the Entry to Jerusalem are deliberately contrasted to imperial images of *adventus*. He quotes Zechariah to illustrate this and notes that this prophet is cited in the Gospel.[64] Jerome has a commentary on this very same passage from Zechariah in his *Com. in Zach.* (II, ix, 9–10):

> *Exsulta satis, filia Sion; iubila, filia Hierusalem. Ecce rex tuus ueniet tibi, iustus et saluator, ipse pauper et ascendens super asinam, et super pullum filium asinae. Et disperdam quadrigam ex Ephraim, et equum de Hierusalem, et dissipabatur arcus belli et loquetur pacem gentibus. . . .*

> Tr. RV: Rejoice greatly, O daughter of Zion; shout, O daughter of Jerusalem: behold, thy King cometh unto thee: he is just, and having salvation; lowly, and riding upon an ass and upon a colt, the foal of an ass.
>
> And I will cut off the chariot from Ephraim, and the horse from Jerusalem, and the battle bow shall be cut off: and he shall speak peace unto the heathen . . .

The biblical image here is of the heavenly King on an ass bringing peace, as opposed to the chariots of war.

Jerome comments (*loc. cit.*)

> *de his quadrigis et curribus legimus: 'hi in curribus et hi in equis, nos autem in nomine Domini Dei nostri inuocabimus'* (Ps. 19,8–9).

The horses and chariots of war—even the chariots of Pharoah—he continues, will be brought into the service of God:

> *transferuntur in Domini seruitutem.*

Jerome makes much use of chariots in the *vita Hilarionis*, citing Ps. 19,8–9 here too, as well as mentioning the chariots of Pharoah. This will be discussed further below in Part 2 of this chapter.

---

[64] Zech. 9:9–10; Matthew 1:21.

To return to the *vita Hilarionis*, there is yet another connection to an ass. On leaving Rome, Kelly notes, '[Jerome's] last act, before the ship weighed anchor, was to dictate a long letter of protest and self defence to Asella.'[65] Asella was another of the circle of noble women associated with Jerome at Rome. There is a manuscript tradition that the *vita Hilarionis* itself was sent to Asella.[66] The dedication to Asella, if genuine, would show that when writing the *vita Hilarionis* Jerome was thinking of the woman whose name means 'little ass' (used as a term of endearment)[67] to whom he justified himself after the trauma of his judgment and expulsion. There are, as already noted, a number of parallels with Apuleius' charges and trial, which could well have resulted in Jerome's identifying personally with Apuleius, whether consciously or not.

2.1.7. *The* Golden Ass *and Jerome's attitude to profane literature*

Jerome long felt immense guilt at reading profane literature—he tells Eustochium of the dream where he was accused of being a Ciceronian, not a Christian, and then flogged on order of the Judge (*ep.* 22), which led him to forswear such reading for many years.[68] He was unable to keep to this however, and eventually[69] argued that he was justified in taking what was good from pagan writers and leaving the rest: had not Moses, the prophets and Paul all used pagan literature? Origen and Augustine, using the same argument, cite as their justification the passage in Exodus where the Israelites despoil the Egyptians of their gold and silver.[70] Jerome, however, aware of the power of sexual temptations, cites as his justification for using pagan literature the passage from Deuteronomy 21:10–13 where the

---

[65] Kelly 114.

[66] This tradition is found in some late MSS from the 9th and 12th centuries, but de Vogüé (*op. cit.* n. 12 above) 181 notes that there is no reason to doubt that it is a genuine tradition.

[67] See *RAC s.v.* Esel (I. Opelt). There is a letter from Augustus using *asellus* as a term of endearment. This sort of use can be paralleled by modern Israeli mothers who use the word for a cockroach as a term of endearment for their babies.

[68] This has been the consensus of scholarly opinion: see Hagendahl p. 318f. For a somewhat different emphasis see now N. Adkin 'Jerome's use of Scripture before and after his dream' *Illinois Classical Studies* 20 (1995) 183–90.

[69] Kelly, 41–44 dates the dream around 374, and *ep.* 70 'more than twenty years later.'

[70] Origen: *ep. ad Gregorium [Thaumaturgium]* (*PG* 11, 88–92); Augustine *de doctrina* 2, 60.

Israelites are allowed to take in a beautiful woman captured from the enemy provided they first shave her head and cut her nails (*ep.* 70).[71]

Jerome, then, consciously or unconsciously identifying with Apuleius, had the *Golden Ass* in mind when writing his *vita Hilarionis*. As I have shown, almost every episode in the *vita Hilarionis* is used to show how Hilarion in his militant Christianity far surpasses his pagan rivals; for this purpose, episodes in the *Golden Ass* appear to have been used to show how Hilarion can go one better. Even the description of the entrance to Hades is reversed to become a description of an earthly Paradise. In his commentary on Zechariah, Jerome was to stress the coming of Jesus as saviour on an ass, taking over from the chariots of war, which are transferred to the service of the Lord.[72] The bawdy and indecent *Golden Ass* was used by Jerome as a sort of basic antithesis for his *vita Hilarionis*—the beautiful pagan captive has been shorn and converted to Jerome's ascetic Christianity.

2.1.8. *A Latin, not a Hellenistic novel*

I noted above that it has been suggested that Jerome's saints' *Lives* owe much to the Hellenistic novel.[73] Scholars have pointed out similarities in structure and landscape between Jerome's saints' *Lives*, and between Hellenistic novels and *Lives* of pagan holy men. On the other hand, it is also generally agreed that Jerome, who learned his Greek as an adult for the purpose of reading the Bible and Christian commentators such as Origen, shows no acquaintance with classic Greek literature and indeed is most unlikely to have read anything other than sacred texts in Greek. It is now possible to reconcile this apparent contradiction. In the *vita Hilarionis* Jerome made considerable use of Apuleius' Latin work, which he read in his wilder youth.

---

[71] *ep.* 70, 2, 5 (*CSEL* 54, 702). Cf. *ep.* 52, 2 with a reversal of this image: Scripture is like the young maiden Abishag who is brought to warm and revive the ageing King David, who represents pagan literature *gentilis litteratura*. (I Kings 1:1–4; and see P. Rousseau *Ascetics, authority and the church in the age of Jerome and Cassian* (Oxford, 1978) 127; Kelly, 191. Rousseau thinks Kelly misunderstands Jerome, but he does not allow for the multivalence of Jerome's imagery.

[72] Kelly, 290–1 dates the *Com. in Zach.* to 406, but writes that 'there are hints that he had been engaged on them, perhaps preparing initial drafts, for years.'

[73] Above: The literary world of the *vita Hilarionis*: Jerome's use of Apuleius' *Golden Ass*.

Thus the similarities with the Hellenistic novel do indeed exist, but at one remove—via Apuleius, who based himself on the Greek work *Metamorphoses*, of which only an abridgement (entitled *Lucius, or the Ass*) survives.[74]

To sum up this first part of the chapter. In the *vita Hilarionis* the hero, Hilarion, compares himself to an ass, with the devil riding his back. Jerome has taken the central event of Apuleius' bawdy and pornographic novel, the conversion of the hero to an ass, and used it as a metaphor for his Christian hero. He has appropriated the popular pagan novel (complete with its jokes) for his Christian agenda. This appropriation is in turn a metaphor for the process of the Christianisation of the Roman Empire described in this *Life*. We shall now turn to look at this process in more detail in part 2 of this chapter, which deals with the Roman context of the *vita Hilarionis*.

2.2. THE ROMAN CONTEXT OF THE *VITA HILARIONIS*

Introduction

Jerome's *vita Hilarionis* entailed the Christian appropriation of the most popular, and the most threatening, of classical literature— the ancient novel. I have shown the relationship to the *Golden Ass* in the *vita Hilarionis*, as Jerome sought to conquer pagan Roman society from within. But having tried and failed to withdraw from society himself, Jerome was not oblivious to the world outside. Part 2 of this chapter will consider the *vita Hilarionis* as Jerome's portrayal of the relationship of the holy man to the whole Roman world in late antiquity.[75] I will start with a consideration of the holy man and his relationship to Roman society, both in its social and geographical aspects, from the most powerful figures in the social order, the bishops and *duces*, to the urban and rural poor, with a particular emphasis on the geography of language—a subject of great interest to the translator of the Vulgate. Following this, the focus will turn to the conflict with paganism, and Jerome's use of classical and biblical

---

[74] J.J. Winkler *Auctor and Actor: a Narratological reading of Apuleius's* The Golden Ass (Berkeley/LA/Oxford, 1985, repr. 1991) 6–7; 252f.

[75] On the holy man in late antiquity the classic work is Peter Brown, 'The Rise and Function of the Holy Man in Late Antiquity' *JRS* 61 (1971) 80–101. See Chapter 1, n. 1 above.

models to spell this out, with the emotional peak in the image taken from everyday life, the chariot race. The third and final section of part 2 will deal with Jerome's relationship to sacred geography in its fourth-century guise—the rise and development of Christian holy sites.

2.2.1. *The holy man and Roman society*

1a. *The holy man, his social context and the geographical setting*

Most extant information about Hilarion comes from Jerome. However, there is a little further independent information to be found in Sozomenus, who lived in the Gaza area somewhat later.[76] It is generally accepted now that Hilarion did actually exist, that he was born around 290 and died in 371.[77] During this time the pagan Roman empire became increasingly Christian under Constantine and his successors, and briefly pagan again under Julian between 361–3, before reverting to Christianity. Jerome wrote the *vita Hilarionis* in the last decade of the fourth century, in the early 390's.[78] In the first part he shows Hilarion as a holy man so withdrawn from the outside world that even the accession of Constantine is not noted as affecting him. However, he is drawn back into contact with people again (albeit undesired), and in particular he is affected by the events of the rule of the emperor Julian the Apostate, which Jerome himself must have experienced in his youth.[79]

Jerome gives his account authenticity by writing that Epiphanius,

---

[76] Sozomenus *HE* iii, 14, 21f.; v, 15. And see Sozomène *Histoire Ecclésiastique* III–IV ed. G. Sabbah, tr. A.-J. Festugière (*SC* 418, Paris, 1996) and notes *ad loc.* Some of Sozomenus' information may, of course, derive from Jerome, but he reports family connections in the area and adds some material that is not to be found in the *vita Hilarionis*.

[77] For discussion and bibliography see: A.A.R. Bastiaensen 'Jérôme hagiographe' *CC Hagiographies: International History of the Latin and Vernacular Hagiographical Literature in the West from its origins to 1550*, vol. I (Turnhout, 1994) 97f. and now B. Bitton-Ashkelony & A. Kofsky 'The monasticism of Gaza in the Byzantine period *Cathedra* 96 (2000, in Hebrew) 69f. esp. pp. 73–4, where the authors come down on the side of a 'historical kernel' in the *vH*.

[78] Cavallera dates the *vita Hilarionis* to the years between 389 and 392. Kelly places it 'almost certainly' later than the *vita Malchi*, which he dates to 390/1. It is mentioned among Jerome's own works in *de viris illustribus* which is no later than 393. For arguments for placing the *vita Hilarionis* before the *vita Malchi*, see Introduction, note 2.

[79] See on this Kelly, 337–9.

whom he knew well, had met Hilarion and heard his story. In the *vita Hilarionis* Jerome also distinguishes between different periods, although it is not always possible to be certain how far he distinguishes between events occurring in his own time at the end of the fourth century, and the time of his hero, at its beginning.

Jerome presents Hilarion as the first Palestinian monk, so that it is inevitable that many of his social contacts are with the pagan world. Jerome shows him as a holy man, sometimes convincing pagans by his true miracles, as opposed to their false pagan magic. At other times he comes into conflict with pagans. Here Hilarion is not totally successful: there are occasions when he emerges victorious, but others when he refuses to act, or simply leaves the arena: Christianity has not yet conquered the whole Roman world. Hilarion also acts as intercessor and moral guide for believing Christians.

The *vita Hilarionis* seems intended by Jerome to give the widest possible picture of the whole extent of the Roman Empire. When the people of Gaza petition the emperor for the death of Hilarion, the imperial rescript is published for the whole world: *toto orbe scriptum erat* (*vH* 33).[80] The *vita* includes examples of representative geographical settings from all over the Empire. Hilarion, born in the village of Tabatha near Gaza, is educated in the imperial centre of Alexandria (*vH* 2).[81] People come to him for help from the city of Rome itself, as well as from the western barbarian outpost of Germania *nunc Francia* (*vH* 37). As a Palestinian monk, the natural arena for his activity is Palestine itself, and it is here that he visits the urban centres: the *urbs* of Gaza and the *oppida* of Elusa and Maiumas (*vH* 14; 25; 19, 20, 21). At Gaza he is involved in an incident at the circus, where his blessing ensures a Christian victory over the local god Marnas in a chariot race which is the central event and emotional peak of the *vita Hilarionis* (*vH* 20). The circus was often conceived as a microcosm of the pagan world, and Jerome's Christian hero is thus defeating his opponents at the symbolic centre of pagan urban life, site of the imperial cult. Jerome himself is most unlikely to have visited the circus in Palestine, although he does write elsewhere

---

[80] Presumably what is actually meant here is the whole *Roman* world.

[81] On Tabatha and its identification, see Y. Dan 'On the ownership of the village of Thavatha in the Byzantine period' *SCI* 5 (1979/80) 258–62 and bibliography *ad loc.*

of the circus as being a temptation for monks.[82] He depicts a different sort of cultural mixing in 'semi-barbarian' Elusa, with its large Saracen population and festival of Venus/Lucifer (*vH* 14).[83] The *vita Hilarionis* does not, however, show the hero in Jerusalem; Jerome tells us in *ep.* 13 that Hilarion was only there for one day in his whole life.[84] Hilarion also visits other towns around the Mediterranean, particularly in Egypt (*vH* 30–34). Other activities of his take place in the settled countryside around Gaza, with its monasteries, villages, large estates and vineyards (*vH* 24–28). Hilarion prefers the wilds: the robber-infested desert (*vH* 3–13), the coastal sands near Gaza (*vH* 19) or parts of Egypt (*vH* 30; 32–4). In Egypt, too, he visits the paradisial oasis where Antony lived (*vH* 31). Following this, he takes ship and lands on the island of Sicily (*vH* 35–38). He seeks the islands, Jerome says, *ut quem terra vulgaverat, saltem maria celarent.*[85] His final home is on another island, Cyprus, where he lives in the mountains (*vH* 41–43) in another paradisial setting. Hilarion also visits Jerome's native Dalmatia (*vH* 39–40), where he is involved with a dragon which is devastating the coast—the landscape here is the landscape of myth, as Christian hero defeats pagan cult. Jerome closes the circle by ending the *vita* where he began it, in Palestine.

1b. *The holy man and the social order*

Holy man and bishop   The spiritual authority wielded by Hilarion is sited outside the traditional centres of power in the city. It is the authority of the holy man outside the social order, not the bishop inside the city.[86] Christianity in the persons of the bishop and clergy eventually took over positions of power from the traditional ruling

---

[82] *Com. in Ps.* 90[91] (*CCSL* 72, 129–130) and see n. 162 below.

[83] See below 2.1b. The holy man and the social order: Elusa *semibarbarum oppidum*: Jerome's geography of language.

[84] Jerome's attitude to Jerusalem seems to vary according to his relationships with the Christian community there. For Jerome and Jerusalem see chapter 4.1.1 Jerome's mental map; 4.4.2b: Rhetorical construct: ruined cities.

[85] *vH* 34: so that him whom land had made known the sea might conceal (tr. Ewald).

[86] Cf. D. Brakke *Athanasius and the politics of asceticism* (Oxford, 1995) 81, who writes that the movement of hermits to the desert was 'fortuitous in its removal of competing male authority figures from the immediate proximity of insecure bishops.'

classes in the late antique city.[87] Jerome in the *vH* shows a mid-way position between these two extremes. Christianity is slowly infiltrating the army and the civil administration through individuals. Bishops, however, have not yet achieved the considerable degree of power and influence they would have later: they appear in the *vita* not as important figures in the city administration, but in exile or in marginal areas.[88] Jerome personally came into conflict often with authority figures in the Christian community. He refers disparagingly to the 'senate of Pharisees' who put him on trial.[89] They seem to have acquitted him, but he had to leave Rome. Later in his life he was to come into bitter conflict with Bishops John of Jerusalem and Theophilus of Alexandria,[90] although Epiphanius, at a safe distance in Cyprus, remained a respected friend. One of the bishops Hilarion does come into contact with, Dracontius, is on record as being most unwilling to be appointed bishop.[91] Jerome will have been aware that the authority wielded by bishops in Hilarion's time was far less than in his own time. He may well have felt considerable sympathy for a period in which the secular aspects of the church were less developed than in his own time. He will also have been aware of the growing power of the exocentric holy man—an image which he certainly cultivated for himself.

The cast of the vita Hilarionis   De Vogüé classifies the minor protagonists of this *vita* into groups of three men, three women, three people from Gaza and two appendices, which does not contribute much of an insight into the text.[92] Jerome was, in fact, both more

---

[87] Discussion of bishops: R. Lane Fox *Pagans and Christians* (Harmondsworth, repr. 1988) 493f.

[88] Bishops Dracontius and Baisane are in exile in the Egyptian desert: *vH* 30. Bishop Epiphanius of Salamis in Cyprus is mentioned in the introduction to the *vita Hilarionis*, but he belongs to Jerome's own time and has outlived the time of the action of the *vita*.

[89] For church courts, see *CAH* 13, chapter 8: The Church as a public institution, esp. vii Bishops and the Law (E.D. Hunt).

[90] E.A. Clark *The Origenist Controversy* (Princeton, 1992).

[91] There is a letter of Athanasius to Dracontius about this (*PG* 25, 524–533) cf. D. Brakke *op. cit.* n. 84 above, 99–110.

[92] A. de Vogüé *Histoire littéraire du mouvement monastique dans l'Antiquité: Première partie: Le monachisme latin ** de l'Itinéraire d'Égérie à l'éloge funèbre de Népotien (384–396)* (Paris, 1993) 197.

subtle and more wide-ranging than this. The action of the *vita Hilarionis* takes place against the backdrop of the whole Roman world; the *vita* thus includes a cast with large numbers of people, from all social classes and from many different walks of life. In describing Hilarion's social context Jerome sketches in microcosm the whole Roman world, with particular stress laid on the process of Christianisation. The Appendix to this chapter contains an annotated list of the *dramatis personae* of the *vita Hilarionis*.

Greek-speakers and Syriac speakers   In the discussion of the *vita Hilarionis* and the *Golden Ass* in part 1 of this chapter it was already noted that Jerome takes a particular interest in language, including the languages of different ethnic groups. Hilarion's contacts with various social and ethnic groups in Palestine reflect differential aspects of the process of Christianisation of the empire. His message is more successful with people outside the traditional Roman local power structure, and with Syriac speakers, rather than Greek speakers. Brock has pointed out that Jerome's contemporary, John Chrysostom, indicates that the demarcation between Greek speakers and Syriac speakers is 'essentially provided by the distinction between *polis* and *chora*.'[93] Many of those turning to Hilarion for help reflect the plight of the local rural poor and disabled, who were speakers of Aramaic, or as Jerome calls it, Syriac: *vo[x] Syra* (*vH* 25). Poverty and disability had changed little from biblical times:[94] Jerome reflects this in episodes reminiscent of the miracles related of Elijah and Elisha, or of Jesus himself. Jerome certainly recognised Syriac as being the local language of the province, as is seen in his comments about Laban from the book of Genesis:

---

[93] S.P. Brock 'Greek and Syriac in Late Antique Syria' in A.K. Bowman & G. Woolf (eds.) *Literacy and power in the ancient world* (Cambridge, 1994) 150. Brock also discusses the Christian literature written in Syriac, which Jerome does not mention in the *vita Hilarionis*. However in his *de viris illustribus* cxv, Jerome speaks highly of Ephrem of Edessa and his works in Syriac, one of which he had read in Greek translation. See also F. Millar 'Paul of Samosata, Zenobia and Aurelian: The Church, local culture and political allegiance in third-century Syria' *JRS* 61 (1971) 5–8.

[94] For analysis of the development of the church's attitudes to the poor in Late Antiquity: Peter Brown *Poverty and Leadership in Late Antiquity (Lectures in memory of Menachem Stern)* Jerusalem, May 16–22, 2000.

gentis suae sermone vocavit. Erat enim Syrus et antiquam linguam parentum provin-
ciae, in qua habitabat, sermone mutaverat.[95]

Laban spoke Syriac, says Jerome, having abandoned the Hebrew of
his parents for the language of the province in which he lived. Jerome
may even distinguish a particular dialect of Palestinian Syriac: as we
saw earlier,[96] when Hilarion converses with a demon inside the
Frankish *candidatus Constantii*, the speech he hears is idiomatic Palestinian
Syriac:

videres de ore barbaro . . . Syra ad purum resonare: ut non stridor, non aspiratio,
non idioma aliquod Palaestini deesset eloquii.

On the other hand, Hilarion is pursued by the city fathers of Gaza
with an imperial edict under Julian's rule. Gaza was a Greek city,[97]
though Jerome refers to the officials of Gaza by their Roman titles—
duumvir (*vH* 20), *decuriones* (*vH* 22), for Gaza was now a Roman *colo-*
nia.[98] He also notes the Roman nature of the ceremonies held at the
circus in honour of the god Consus and in memory of the Rape of
the Sabine women, for Jerome is aware of the complex cultural and
linguistic situation in the city and in the province of Syria/Palaestina.
Nearby, Hilarion does have a positive interaction with Italicus, the
municeps of Maiumas, but this Christian *oppidum* had lost its city status under Julian, and was in continuing conflict with its rich and
powerful neighbour, the *urbs* of Gaza, a conflict which is reflected
in the chariot race described so vividly in the *vita*.[99] Thus Italicus is
not part of the upper echelons of the mainstream establishment.
Similarly Orion, a rich man from the *urbs* of Aila who comes to
Hilarion for help, is described only vaguely as *ditissimus* and *primarius*,
not by the exact technical terms *clarissimus* or *illustris* which were

---

[95] *Hebrew Questions on Genesis* 31.46–7 (*CCSL* 72,40; *PL* 23,987): Tr. Hayward
op. cit. 69: '. . . in the language of his own people. For he was a Syrian, and he
had exchanged the ancient language of his ancestors for the tongue of the province
in which he was dwelling.' See also the discussion of this passage in chapter 3.2.2
below.

[96] Above, 2.1.1c. Interest in languages.

[97] On Gaza as a Greek city, see E. Schürer *The History of the Jewish People in the*
age of Jesus Christ II (rev. and ed. G. Vermes, F. Millar, M. Black, Edinburgh, 1979)
99.

[98] See on this F. Millar *The Roman Near East 31 BC–AD 337* (Cambridge,
Mass./London, 1993) 385 and refs.

[99] See below 2.2.2b Confrontation with paganism: Christians and the games; the
theme of the chariot.

used for those within the social power structure of the traditional city administration.[100] This is an interesting example of what was to become a future trend in the decay of the traditional structure of the city councils and the take-over by bishops, *primates* and *possessores*.[101] The noble lady Aristaenete, discussed below, appears at first sight to be an exception, as the wife of the future praetorian prefect, supreme commander of the Orient. However, even here Jerome is at pains to point out that her Christian husband's appointment to this powerful position is still in the future. And the position is held by her husband, not herself: Aristaenete, as a woman, is once again outside the traditional power structure. There are other examples of Hilarion's contact with people outside the establishment. The high-ranking *candidatus Constantii* who comes to Hilarion from outside Palestine is noted as a barbarian Frank. The pagan priest of Venus at Elusa is a Saracen, who, when he repudiates his cult, is recognised by Hilarion as a Christian priest. Jerome has already specified Elusa as an *oppidum semibarbarum*, inhabited by Saracens who greet Hilarion *voce Syra*,[102] and are eventually persuaded by his Christian argument. We may note that there are recorded episodes of Saracen Arabs becoming Christians in the fourth century[103] and Eusebius mentions a bishop of the Arabs called Beryllus at Bostra in the third century.[104] Jerome is here reflecting this potential in his story of Hilarion.

It is clear from the letters of Jerome's contemporary Libanius that there was also a considerable Greek-speaking element in Elusa, with

---

[100] On the '*urbs*' of Aila see Millar *op. cit.* n. 98 above, 399, with a useful discussion of languages.

[101] Just. *Nov* 128.16. See on this process the discussion of J.W.G. Liebeschuetz *Decline and fall of the Roman city* (Oxford, 2001) 110–136.

[102] *vH* 25. See section 2.2.1b on Elusa below for a discussion of this.

[103] The most famous of these is the Saracen queen Mavia: for the mixture of legend and history in the accounts of Mavia, see, among others: G.W. Bowersock 'Mavia, Queen of the Saracens' *Studien zur antiken Sozialgeschichte: Festschrift für F. Vittinghoff* (ed. W. Eck, H. Galsterer, H. Wolff, Köln, 1980) 477–95; I. Shahîd *Byzantium and the Arabs in the Fourth Century* (Washington, 1984) 138–202; J. Matthews *The Roman Empire of Ammianus Marcellinus* (London, 1989) 350–2; P. Mayerson 'Mauia, Queen of the Saracens—A cautionary note' *IEJ* 30 (1980) pp. 123–131 = *id. Monks, martyrs, soldiers and Saracens: Papers on the near East in Late Antiquity (1962–1993)* (Jerusalem, 1994) 164f.; *CAH* 13,447–9 (B. Isaac) For other accounts of conversions of Saracens, see another paper by Mayerson: 'Saracens and Romans: Micro-Macro Relationships' *BASOR* 274 (1989) 71–79 = *op. cit.* 313f. and Isaac *loc. cit.* 444–452.

[104] Eusebius *H.E.* 20.

a school of rhetoric.[105] However, Jerome nowhere implies that the conversion of Elusa included its Greek-speaking inhabitants. The pagan Greek-speakers in the cities, *gentili* or *ethnici* as he calls them using the terminology of the New Testament, remain mostly deaf to his message.[106] The antagonism to the saint from the Greek-speaking inhabitants of Gaza, '*urb[s] gentilium*' has already been noted.[107]

The demons comprise a further, very interesting group of Syriac-speakers in the *vita Hilarionis*. Both the Frankish *candidatus Constantii* and a Bactrian camel are noted as being possessed by demons which communicate in Syriac, a language which neither the *candidatus* nor the camel could be expected to speak. I have already noted above in part I how Jerome uses this as an occasion for a joke at the expense of the *candidatus*' translators, who only knew Greek and Latin.[108] The demons, of course, represent the forces of evil here, which are overcome by the Christian saint.[109] An interesting complement to the Syriac-speaking demons in the *vita Hilarionis* can be found in Greek-speaking divine voices in the early fifth century *vita Porphyrii*,[110] also set in Gaza. Here a normally Syriac-speaking peasant child becomes the vehicle for divine prophecy and speaks unexpectedly in Greek.[111] Part of Hilarion's process of overcoming the

---

[105] Libanius *epp* 54, 4; 132; 164; 318. See on this O. Seeck *Die Briefe des Libanius* (Leipzig, 1906; repr. Hildesheim, 1966) 131; 151. Cf. P. Mayerson 'The city of Elusa in the literary sources of the fourth-sixth centuries' *IEJ* 33 (1983) 248 = *id. op. cit.* n. 101 above, 198.

[106] *Gentiles*, together with *graeci*, is used by the Vulgate to translate N.T. Ἕλληνες. On the use of the terms *gentili* and *ethnici* see: I. Opelt 'Griechische und lateinische Bezeichnungen der Nichtchristen: ein terminologischer Versuch' *VChr* 19 (1965) 1–22; B. Isaac 'Ethnic groups in Judaea under Roman Rule' in *id. The Near East under Roman Rule Selected Papers* (Leiden etc., 1998) 257–267.

[107] *Urbe gentilium*: Josephus calls Gaza πόλις Ἑλληνίς: *Ant.* xvii,320; *BJ* ii,97. For Jerome's use of Josephus, see chapter 4.4.2: Jerome's Jewish geography: the boundaries of the Land of Israel.

[108] 2.1.1. Functional parallels: 1c Interest in languages, above.

[109] Cf. A. Momigliano 'Pagan and Christian historiography in the fourth century AD' in *id. Essays in Ancient and Modern Historiography* (Oxford, 1947, repr. 1977) 107f. = *id.* (ed.) *The conflict between Paganism and Christianity in the fourth century* (Oxford, 1963) 79–99: 'a mass invasion of devils into historiography preceded and accompanied the mass invasion of barbarians into the Roman empire.'

[110] For the *vita Porphyrii* see 2.2.2b: Confrontation with paganism: Confrontations with three cults: The cult of Marnas in late antique Gaza, below.

[111] *vPorph* 68. Theodoret of Cyr (born in Antioch in 393) who wrote his *Historia Religiosa* in Greek also records a demon or devil who spoke to him in Syriac. See on this Brock *op. cit.* 154; T. Urbainczyk '"The devil spoke Syriac to me": Theodoret

Syriac-speaking demon in the *candidatus* is forcing him to speak Greek. Greek was, of course, the written language of the New Testament and as such suited to Christian communication. On the other hand, the New Testament itself contains accounts of gentiles and Greeks who opposed the Christian message, particularly in the cities. It is thus not surprising that this ambivalence to Greek is present in the *vita Hilarionis*. On the one hand Hilarion forces the demon to speak Greek, the language of divine communication: on the other hand it is the Greek-speaking city fathers, the *gentili* and *ethnici*, who are antagonistic to Hilarion and pursue him.

Elusa—semibarbarum oppidum: *Jerome's geography of language*   I have already alluded to the visit of Hilarion to Elusa above, described by Jerome as a *semibarbarum oppidum*, where the saint is greeted by the Saracen population in what Jerome calls *voce Syra*, i.e. in Syriac, '*barech.*'[112] It has been suggested by Shahîd that the language used was in fact Arabic, since it was spoken by Saracen Arabs.[113] However, Hilarion is portrayed by Jerome as speaking both Greek and Syriac when necessary, and Jerome here appears to be showing the Saracens communicating with Hilarion in a language they could both understand. I find it hard to believe that Jerome, with his considerable interest in, and sensitivity to languages would have not realised that the Arabs were speaking Arabic had this been the case; he would surely have wanted to report this to show the Church reaching out to people of all languages. In his letter 106, for example, he writes to the Gothic monks, Sunnia and Fretela, saying how moved he is that speakers of Gothic should be interested in philological problems connected to the language of the Bible. Furthermore, in his preface to his translation of the book of Job in the Vulgate, he specifically distinguishes between Hebrew, Arabic and Syriac.[114]

The most extensive analysis of late antique Elusa known to me is that of Mayerson, in his article 'The City of Elusa in the Literary

---

in Syriac' in *Ethnicity and culture in Late Antiquity* (eds S. Mitchell & G. Greatrex, London/Swansea, 2000) 253–265; *ead. Theodoret of Cyrrhus* (Ann Arbor, 2002) Language pp. 72–79.

[112] *v. Hilarionis* 25.

[113] I. Shahîd *Byzantium and the Arabs in the Fourth Century* (Washington, 1984) 290–293.

[114] *Prol. in Iob* (Weber, 731): *hebraico, arabicoque sermone et interdum syro.*

Sources of the Fourth-Sixth Centuries,' and throughout his collection of papers *Monks, Martyrs, Soldiers and Saracens*.[115] Mayerson notes the evidence of the fourth-century Libanius, who was an orator in Antioch, and others, that there was a school of rhetoric at Elusa, while a recorded visit to the city by the *Comes Orientis*, he argues, 'shows that the city was in the mainstream of imperial life.' He notes the archaeological find of a theatre, which was in use in the Late Roman and Byzantine periods.[116] Based on this evidence, Mayerson rejects Jerome's adjective *semibarbarum*, which he translates as 'half-civilized.' Elusa, in Mayerson's view, was fully civilized.[117]

A similar interpretation of Jerome's use of the term *semibarbarus* in other works is made by Chauvot.[118] Chauvot in fact analyses all the uses of *semibarbarus* he could find in Latin literature: he found eleven examples in the *TLL*, of which eight are from the fourth century. Four of these come from Jerome. However, Chauvot does not mention the description of Elusa as *semibarbar[um]*, nor Jerome's use of *barbarus semisermo* in *ep.* 7. Chauvot considers that, in each of the cases he deals with, Jerome is using the term as a description of culture and ethnicity. Thus, on the passage in *ep.* 50:

> nec mirum si me et absentem et iam diu absque usu Latinae linguae semibarbarumque, homo Latinissimus et facundissimus superet,

Chauvot comments

> le terme s'applique, par autodérision, à l'auteur, qui se dit être en voie de barbarisation. Celle-ci s'accomplit par l'absence de la pratique du latin, fondement de l'appartenance à la romanité; il peut donc y avoir barbarisation en dehors de tout processus de nature ethnique.

---

[115] P. Mayerson *Monks, Martyrs, Soldiers and Saracens: Papers on the Near East in Late Antiquity (1962–1993)* (Jerusalem, 1994). This collection of papers includes the article 'The City of Elusa in the Literary sources of the Fourth–Sixth Centuries' (cited above, n. 105) 197–203, reprinted from *IEJ* 33 (1983) 247–253. See also Y. Dan 'Palaestina Salutaris (Tertia) and its capital' *IEJ* 32 (1982) 134–137, which argues that Elusa was the capital of Palaestina Tertia. For the archaeology of Elusa, see A. Negev *NEAEHL s.v.* Elusa, and bibliography *ad loc.*
[116] A. Negev 'Survey and trial excavations at Haluza (Elusa), 1973' *IEJ* 26 (1976) 92–93.
[117] *Contra*: Shahîd *op. cit.* above, 289: 'The clear implication of the account is that both Elusa and its vicinity were Arab.'
[118] A. Chauvot 'Remarques sur l'emploie de *semibarbarus*' in A. Rousselle (ed.) *Frontières terrestres, frontières célestes dans l'Antiquité* (Perpignan/Paris 1995) 255–271.

For Chauvot, the cultural and ethnic aspects are paramount, and language is merely a secondary phenomenon. He has problems therefore, with Jerome's descriptions of imperial Trèves [Trier] as the *Rheni semibarbaras ripas* (*ep.* 3, 5), and Leptis Magna: *in Lepti urbe semibarbara et posita in solitudine* (*adv Iouinianum* 1,48), and concludes that in both these cases 'Jérôme déforme la réalité,' just as Mayerson has concluded for Elusa.

Jerome is often guilty of exaggerations and rhetoric.[119] But it would seem to be unlikely that he should be so consistently inaccurate in his description of these places as 'half-civilized.' It is true that he does use the word *barbarus* to mean uncivilized or barbaric, especially in relation to various attacks by barbarian tribes on the Roman empire.[120] But Jerome just as often uses *barbarus* in its original meaning of non-Greek (or non-Latin) speaking. When it comes to the term *semibarbarus*, I would like to suggest that he uses this term to refer to language above all. Jerome, the translator of the Vulgate, the self-publicised *vir trilinguis*, was at all times exceptionally concerned with language, and in particular with the variety of spoken languages. He goes out of his way often to note language variety, for example when describing Paula's funeral, when psalms were sung in three languages (*ep.* 108). I already noted above how he writes to the Gothic monks Sunnia and Fretela that he is very touched by the fact that speakers of their tongue should be concerned with the meaning of the language of the Bible (*ep.* 106). The joke he makes in the *vita Hilarionis* at the expense of Frankish translators has also been noted already.[121] He is even interested in local dialects, noting that some of the expressions of Paul of Tarsus can be paralleled by contemporary local Cilician usages (*ep.* 121, 10), and his note of the Palestinian idioms in the Syriac of the demon Hilarion converses with has already been pointed out. Let us briefly review all his other uses of the term *semibarbarus* throughout his works.

---

[119] Cf. D. Wiesen *Jerome as a Satirist* (Ithaca/NY, 1964).

[120] See for example: *Com. in Hiez.*, *praef.*: *indigentium rabiem ... barbarorum; Praef. in Eusebii Caesarensis Chronicon: Dibacchantibus adhuc in terra nostra barbaris; ep.* 118, 2 *vastationem totius barbaro hoste provinciae.*

[121] *vH* 22.

1. He uses the word *semibarbarus* to refer to his own Latin slipping away in Bethlehem, where he was surrounded by speakers of other languages (*ep.* 50, 2):

> *Nec mirum si me et absentum, et iam diu absque usu Latinae linguae semibar-barumque, homo Latinissimus et facundissimus superet.*

Chauvot may be right here to understand that Jerome is deploring his own general cultural barbarisation as well, but what he actually says is that his language is deteriorating.

2. Jerome uses the term of his time at imperial Trier in 'semibarbaric' Rhineland (*ep.* 3, 5)

> *Cum post Romana studia ad Rheni semibarbaras ripas eodem cibo, pari fueremur hospitio*

It is hard to believe, as Chauvot rightly points out, that the seat of the imperial court was culturally 'semibarbarian.' It is much easier to understand Jerome's use of *semibarbar[us]* as meaning that there was a mixture of Latin and local languages in use in this city sited in the border province of Germany.[122]

3. Jerome also uses the term *semibarbar[us]* to describe the city of Leptis in the North African desert (*Adv. Iouinianum* 1):

> *in Lepti urbe semibarbara et posita in solitudine*

Jerome was never at Leptis: he most probably found his description of the city in Sallust, who writes of how the *language* of the place was influenced by the meeting of the culture of the Sidonian founders of the city with the local desert Numidians and the proximity of the desert:

---

[122] For a mixture of languages in Trier somewhat later cf. J.D. Harries 'The shifting frontiers of *romanitas*' in *Shifting frontiers in Late Antiquity* ed. R.W. Mathisen & H.S. Sivan (Aldershot/Brookfield, 1995) 31–44, who cites the bi-lingual Synagrius writing of the pure Latin of the barbarian *Comes* Arbogast of Trier in the late fifth century.

Chauvot notes that Jerome's expression here is possibly an echo of Symmachus *Laudatio in Valentinianum Augustum prior*, 14 (ed. Seeck, Berlin, 1883, *MGH* 6,1): *ipse supra inpacti Rheni semibarbaras ripas raptim vexilla constituens.* Tr Chauvot: (Valentinian) établissant aussitôt des détachements sur les rives semibarbares du Rhin non pacifié.

eius ciuitatis lingua modo conuorsa conubio Numidarum; legum cultusque pleraque Sidonica, quae eo facilius retinebant quod procul ab imperio regis aetatem agebant. Inter illos et frequentem Numidiam multi vastisque loci errant.[123]

That Jerome must have known this passage in Sallust can be deduced from the fact that he quotes the preceding sentence '*Syrtes ab tractu nominate*' in his *Lib. Nom. Heb.* (*PL* 23, 850) s.v. *Syrtim*:

melius autem Sallustius a tractu ait nomen impositum.[124]

Chauvot, indeed, notes how out of date his picture is. It should also be noted that the *Historia Augusta* implies that people from Leptis could hardly speak good Latin, or perhaps had a heavy local accent; the sister of the Emperor Septimius Severus is said to have been sent home because her poor Latin embarrassed her brother:

cum soror sua Leptitana ad eum venisset vix Latine loquens, ac de illa multum imperator erubesceret (*SHA Severus* xv,6).

The *Historia Augusta*, which is probably making a joke at the expense of the imperial family here, may however be pointing to a commonly held fourth-century prejudice about the Latin speakers of Leptis.[125] Both the *Historia Augusta* and Jerome note the distinctive sound of North African speech.[126]

4. To these uses of *semibarbarus* we should probably add the *barbarus semisermo* of the Syrian monks which Jerome complains of in *ep.* 7.[127]

---

[123] Sallust *Bell. Jug.* lxxix.

[124] For Jerome's knowledge of Sallust, (whom he calls '*auctor certissimus*' in his translation of Eusebius' *Onomasticon* 83, 7), see Hagendahl, 292: 'Besides Cicero, Sallustius is the only prose writer from the period of the Republic who occupies a considerable place in Jerome's works. Sallustius is, to Jerome, the Roman historian par préférence *nobilis historicus* (*Adv. Iov.* 2,10) or simply *historicus* (e.g. *Com. in Dan.* 3,46), to be compared with Thucydides.' Jerome quotes Sallust by name [Crispus] in the preface to the *vita Hilarionis*; see on this T.D. Barnes 'Jerome and the *Historia Augusta*' in *Historiae Augustae Colloquium Parisinum* (eds. G. Bonamente & N. Duval, Macerata, 1991) 23–28. See also below, chapter 3.3.2a Stereotypes of barbarian, on the use made of Sallust in the *v. Malchi*.

[125] See on this B. Isaac 'Orientals and Jews in the Historia Augusta: Fourth-Century Prejudice and Stereotypes' in I. Gafni, A. Oppenheimer, D.R. Schwartz (eds.) *Studies in Memory of Menahem Stern* (Jerusalem, 1996) 101*–118* = B. Isaac *The Near East under Roman Rule: Selected papers* (Leiden etc., 1998) 279–81.

[126] *SHA Severus*, xix, 10: *canorus voce, sed Afrum quiddam usque senectutem sonans*; Jerome *ep.* 130,5: *stridor linguae Punicae*.

[127] Jerome's uses of *barbarus* (106) and *semibarbarus* were checked on the *CETEDOC* CD-ROM database. There were 5 occurrences of *semibarbarus*, or 6 including

This clearly refers to language: as Chauvot notes, Jerome remarks on his stay in the 'desert of Chalcis' as being *iuncto barbariae fine.*

5. Finally, Jerome's description of Stilicho as a 'semibarbarian' traitor:

sed scelere semibarbari accidit proditoris (ep. 123,16)

is the one case where the association with language is less compelling. It is possible that Jerome is here referring to a low standard of Latin speaking, or an accent. However, this may be a piece of ethnic abuse or a genuine description of the level of culture of Honorius' half-Vandal commander-in-chief. I know of no way of deciding between the possibilities in this case.

It should be noted too, that one other of the fourth century sources cited by Chauvot as mentioning the word *semibarbarus,* the *Historia Augusta*'s account of the Emperor Maximinus, describes the emperor as *adulescens et semibarbarus et uix adhuc Latinae linguae.*[128] This clearly includes incompetence in the Latin language in the same breath as 'semibarbarian.'

To return to Elusa, it would seem that Jerome simply means that this town, like Leptis and Trier, is partly inhabited by non-Greek speakers, rather than that it is 'half-civilised.' He underlines this mixture of languages when he shows us the Saracens hailing Hilarion *'barech.'* Thus Jerome's geography of fourth century Palestine must be set in his own context, which is influenced by his concern for language. If he can be said to relate to culture, it is a culture typified by its use of language.[129] Civilization for Jerome is the use of a language of civilization, either Latin in Trier or Greek in Elusa, but not German or Syriac.

---

barbarus semisermo (the reading preferred by Kelly, p. 49 and S. Rebenich 'Asceticism, Orthodoxy and Patronage: Jerome in Constantinople' *Studia Patristica* 33 (1997) 363, over the *barbarus seni sermo* which Hilberg (*CSEL* 54, p. 27,6) prefers over the readings of four manuscripts).

[128] *SHA Maximini duo* ii, 5; ib i, 6–7. If 'semibarbarian' is taken to refer to ethnicity, this must be one of the jokes the *Historia Augusta* abounds in, for *both* Maximinus' parents have just been described as barbarians!

[129] Saracens will appear again in Jerome's *vita Malchi.* Here, unlike the *vita Hilarionis,* Jerome does relate to their culture, but this is because he wants to make symbolic use of them in his account of the Christian ascetic takeover of the human body.

Contacts with the nobility: Elpidius and Aristaenete Jerome records
Hilarion's contacts with the noble lady Aristaenete, wife of the future
praetorian prefect, Elpidius. The couple first appear in the *vita* on
their way back from a pilgrimage to Antony in Egypt (*vH* 14).
[H]Elpidius is documented in other sources, including Ammianus
and Libanius.[130] He was praetorian prefect from 360 to 361.[131] Jerome
writes of Aristaenete: *nihil de praefecti ambitu habens* (*vH* 29). Ewald
translates this as 'without any of [the prefect's] pretensions.' However,
Elpidius was a prefect known for his simplicity. Ammianus notes his
lower class origins and speech, and writes that he was too ingenu-
ous, and so mild that he resigned when asked by Constantius to torture an innocent man.[132] This may be Ammianus disapproving of
Elpidius' Christian principles, but it should be noted that he had to
be saved from lynching by his troops by the intervention of the
emperor Julian.[133] Perhaps Jerome is simply praising Aristaenete even
more by the comparision—she had not even the small degree of
ostentatiousness of a prefect known for his simplicity. However, maybe
it should be 'none of his display,' and Jerome could be referring literally to the display that went with the prefect's office: John Lydus
has left vivid details of the brilliant purple, gold and flame-coloured
clothes worn by a praetorian prefect.[134] Aristaenete may be presumed

---

[130] Ammianus xxi 6, 9; he appears in many letters of Libanius: qv *PRE sv* Claudius
Helpidius (2). *CIL* viii, 20542 notes him as *praeses* of Mauretania Sitifensis in 337
and various parts of the *CTh* record him receiving instructions from emperors. In
ep. 225 Libanius writes to Elpidius' assessors τοῖς Ἐλπιδίου παρέδροις to ask a
favour for a certain Acontius, who was to appear before the court. M. Schwabe
'Libanius' letters to the Patriarch in the Land of Israel' *Tarbiz* I/II (1930, Hebrew)
85–110 has suggested that this shows bad relationships between the pagan Libanius
and the Christian prefect, for Libanius should have written to Elpidius directly.
However, it could be that it reflects cool relations between Libanius and Acontius,
in that Libanius was not prepared to exert himself to the full on Acontius' behalf,
only writing to some lower officials.
[131] For the wrong dating of Ammianus xxi 6, 9, see A.H.M. Jones, J.R. Martindale,
J. Morris *The Prosopography of the Later Roman Empire* I: *AD 260–395* (Cambridge,
1971) 414 *s.v.* Helpidius 4, and stemma 18, p. 1141.
[132] *Loc. sit.: Aspectu vilis et lingua, sed simplicioris ingenii, incruentus et mitis, adeo cum ei
coram innocentem quendam torquere Constantius praecipisset, aequo animo abrogari sibi potestam
oraret.*
[133] Libanius *Or.* xxxvii, 11. For the debate on Ammianus' attitude to Christianity,
see now: T.D. Barnes *Ammianus Marcellinus and the Representation of Historical Reality*
(Ithaca/London, 1998).
[134] John Lydus: *de Mag.* xi, 13: a flame-coloured cloak striped with gold, purple
tunic and embellished crimson belt.

to prefer the sombre clothes Jerome thought were more suitable to Christan women: elsewhere he commends Paula for preferring goat's hair to linens and silks.[135]

The relationship of Hilarion to Aristaenete is built on the biblical type of the holy man Elisha and the high-born Shunamite woman (II Kings 4:8f.). The Shunamite woman came to Elisha on an ass to ask him to restore her only son to life. Aristaenete comes to Hilarion on an ass to ask him to restore all her three children to life—Jerome's Christian hero surpasses his Old Testament predecessor: he brings back three children to life, not just one. And as Jerome writes himself into all his saints' *Lives*, there are parallels too to the relationship between Jerome himself and the noble lady Paula, who is also commended by Jerome for renouncing much of the status due to her, both in her clothing and particularly in choosing to ride on a lowly ass.[136]

The advent of Elpidius and his wife Aristaenete after their pilgrimage to Antony is the event which brings Hilarion back into contact with society and also serves Jerome's purpose in showing the contacts of the saint with the Roman world, in this case with the upper classes.

Authority figures in late antique Palestine: Roman dux, *Jewish patriarch, Christian holy man*   Even if we only had the titles of Jerome's works, it would be clear that he was a polemicist—so many of them include the word *contra* or *adversus*.[137] He was heavily engaged in the controversies of his day, and his reputation was such that Augustine himself called on him for help against the Pelagians.[138] It has become a commonplace that the human being tends to define his or her own identity against that of 'the other.'[139] Thus Greek is set against

---

[135] *ep.* 108, 15. Cf. *epp.* 38, 4; 117, 6; 128, 2 etc.

[136] *ep.* 108, 7 (*CSEL* 55, p. 313).

[137] E.g. *Aduersus Heluidium de Mariae uirginitate perpetua; Aduersus Iouinianum; Contra Vigilantium; Contra Iohannem Hierosolymitanum; Apologia aduersus libros Rufini; Dialogi contra Pelagianos libri iii.*

[138] On Pelagius and his followers, see B.R. Rees *Pelagius: Life and Letters* (Woodbridge/Rochester, 1998).

[139] See e.g. F. Hartog *Le miroir d'Hérodote: essai sur la représentation de l'autre* (Mayenne, 1980); E. Hall *Inventing the Barbarian: Greek self-definition through tragedy* (Oxford, 1989); E.P. Sanders *et al.* (eds.) *Jewish and Christian self-definition* I–III (Philadelphia, 1980–1982); J. Neusner & E.S. Frerichs *To See Ourselves as Others See Us: Christians, Jews, 'Others'*

barbarian, Jew against pagan, and the Christians of late antiquity came to self-definition through their definitions of various heresies. This process is very clear in the works of Jerome filled with invective against his various adversaries, in his letters and even in his commentaries on the Bible. Jerome is Christian, as opposed to pagan or Jew, Latin-speaking and Western, as opposed to Greek-speaking and Eastern, Roman as opposed to barbarian, an ascetic without possessions as opposed to a rich noble man, a monk as opposed to a bishop, a man as opposed to a woman. These positions are usually spelled out and repeated in his more didactic and polemic works, with all the help that rhetoric can give.

When it comes to his saints' *Lives*, the position is less explicit. Here he is producing a literary work, written for consumption by the less learned and possibly less convinced. He himself notes what problems he had in adapting his style,[140] and indeed the story form lends itself less to polemic and learned discussion.[141] But it is nonetheless there. Even if Jerome could hardly expect his audience to pick up the references, he needed a sub-text of polemic dialogue with Roman authorities, Jews and bishops to arrive at his own self-definition, for all Jerome's saintly heroes contain a great deal of Jerome himself. Although the Christian hero is mostly engaged with the pagan Roman world in the *vita Hilarionis*, the authority of Judaism is still a factor to be reckoned with in the Holy Land itself.

Jerome drew his holy man, Hilarion, following Athanasius' very successful *Life of Antony*. Hilarion was later than Antony chronologically, but Jerome presents him at first as a Syro-Palestinian equal in spiritual authority to the Egyptian monk. Later, he even surpasses

---

in Late Antiquity (Chico, 1985), and now cf. A. Kobak 'From Belsen to Butlins' *TLS* 5054 (Feb. 11th 2000) 31, citing an anonymous American reviewer: "Lately it has become impossible to say whether such topics as 'Eat me: Captain Cook and the Ingestion of the Other' or 'The Semiotics of Sinatra' are parodies . . . or serious presentations by credentialed scholars." (The anonymous reviewer is in fact A. Delbanco 'The decline and fall of literature' *The New York Review* (November 4, 1999, 32.)

[140] *ep.* 10, 3. where he sends his 'Life of Paul' to the aged Paul of Concordia: *Misimus interim tibi, id est Paulo seni, Paulum seniorem, in quo propter simpliciores quosque multum in deiciendo sermone laboravimus* . . . See the discussion of this in chapter 1: Jerome's programmatic introduction to the vita Pauli: The letter to Paul of Concordia.

[141] See above chapter 1.4.4: The *vita Pauli* and the *aggadah* compared, with n. 109 *ad loc.*, on polemic in ancient biography.

him in symbolic spiritual authority. But Jerome is concerned not
only with symbolic spiritual authority but with the spiritual authority of the holy man in his everyday social context. Thus he implicitly contrasts his hero with the authority figures of late antique
Palestine, the Roman *dux* and the Jewish patriarch.

The Gaza area where Hilarion was active was well-known in late
antiquity for its wines.[142] There is a hint that the wine-industry may
have been a particularly Christian trade in the early fifth-century
vita Porphyrii, which notes the Christian population of Gaza's port of
Maiumas as being increased by Egyptian wine merchants.[143] During
his time as chief monk of Palestine (Antony's definition: *vH* 14;24),
Hilarion used to visit his monks 'on fixed days before the vintage'—
statibus diebus ante vindemiam—accompanied by many followers. On
such occasions he used his authority to bless or curse the produce,
depending on the spiritual deserts of the monks who produced the
wine. Hilarion's visits, said to have been accompanied by as many
as 2,000 and even 3,000[144] monks, are reminiscent of the tours of
inspection of the Roman emperors and governors. The large body
of thousands of soldiers, officials and administrative staff that was
attached to the Emperor and formed his government was called the
comitatus. It travelled with him all over the Empire, and similar bodies, though not so large, were attached to the provincial governors.[145]
Jones stresses the 'formidable spectacle' the *comitatus* must have presented on the roads,[146] and the problems that must have arisen of
billeting and accommodating such large numbers. The stingy monk
whose produce is later cursed by Hilarion was horrified at the thought

---

[142] P. Mayerson 'The Wine and Vineyards of Gaza in the Byzantine Period'
BASOR 257 (1986) 75–80 = *op. cit.* (n. 103 above) 250f., and see now S.A. Kingsley
*A Sixth-century AD Shipwreck off the Carmel coast, Israel: Dor D and the Holy Land Wine
Trade* (Oxford, 2002).

[143] *vita Porphyrii* 58.

[144] The thousands who need to be fed are an allusion to the miracles of Jesus
with the loaves and the fishes which fed thousands (Matthew 14:21; 15;38; Mark
6:36–44; 8:9; John 6:5–10).

[145] See, for the earlier period F. Millar *The Emperor in the Roman World* (London,
1977) 28–40; A.J. Marshall 'Governors in the Roman World' *Phoenix* 20 (1966)
231–246; G.P. Burton 'Proconsuls, Assizes and the Administration of Justice' *JRS*
65 (1975) 92–106, and for the fourth century, A.M.H. Jones *The Later Roman Empire*
(Oxford, 1990) 366–8.

[146] On the visual impact of the display of power in the massive accompaniment
of the emperor, see S.R.F. Price *Rituals and Power: the Roman Imperial Cult in Asia
Minor* (Cambridge, 1984).

of providing for Hilarion and his retinue (*vH* 26). Jerome's description of Hilarion's tours of the monasteries of Palestine leaves little
doubt that he had such a comparison in mind: the monks who
accompany Hilarion are described as *comitat[u/i] tali duce* (*vH* 25).
Hilarion's authority is being paralleled to that of the fourth century
dux, the highest ranking army commander in the region.

But it was not only the Roman officials who used to make tours
of inspection in order to legislate and solve disputes: from the first
century the Jewish Patriarch in Palestine used to make tours on this
model, and make halakhic decisions in the various communities he
visited. Aharon Oppenheimer writes of Rabban Gamaliel's tours in
the first century that 'there can be no doubt that the main purpose
of these tours and visits was to impose the authority of the [*sc.* Jewish]
leadership institutions on the [*sc.* Jewish] settlements in Palestine.'[147]
Some of the evidence for this comes from Lydda,[148] where Jerome
records contacts of his with Jews. Jerome writes in several places of
the Jewish Patriarch, his influence with the Roman authorities, his
wealth and his sending of *apostoli* to collect money abroad.[149] Some
of what he says is paralleled by Libanius, who wrote a number of
letters from Antioch to the Jewish Patriarch in Palestine asking for
his help and influence with the Roman authorities.[150] Some of Libanius'
letters are exactly contemporary with the writing of the *vita Hilarionis*.
The Patriarch could even assert himself against the Roman gover-

---

[147] A. Oppenheimer 'Rabban Gamaliel of Yavneh and his tours in Palestine'
Perlman Festschrift (Tel Aviv, 1988, Hebrew) 8 now translated as *id.* 'Rabban Gamaliel
of Yavneh and his circuits of Eretz Israel' in *id. Between Rome and Babylon: Jewish
leadership and society* (Tübingen, forthcoming, 2005).

[148] M. Fischer, B. Isaac, I. Roll *Roman Roads in Judaea* II: *The Jaffa—Jerusalem roads*
(Oxford, 1996) 204.

[149] E.g. *ep.* 57, 3 and see Newman 9f; 33f. Cf. *CTh* 16,8, 8–17. A good discussion of the status of the Patriarch in general and relevant parts of the *CTh* in particular is to be found in J.B. Rives *Religion and Authority in Roman Carthage from Augustus
to Constantine* (Oxford, 1995); M. Jacobs *Die Institution des jüdischen Patriarchen: eine
quellen- und traditionskritische Studie zur Geschichte der Juden in der Spätantike* (Tübingen,
1995) esp. 342ff.; L.I. Levine 'The status of the patriarch in the third and fourth
centuries: sources and methodology' *JJS* 47 (1996) 1–32. Cf. R. Syme 'Ipse ille
patriarcha' in *Emperors and biography: Studies in the Historia Augusta* (Oxford, 1971)
17–29.

[150] M. Schwabe 'Libanius' letters to the Patriarch in the Land of Israel' *Tarbiz*
I/II (1930, Hebrew) 85–110; E. Habas-Rubin *The Patriarch in the Roman-Byzantine
era—the making of a dynasty* (Doctoral thesis, Tel Aviv, 1991, Hebrew with English
summary).

nor, according to both Libanius and Jerome, writing of two separate incidents.[151]

Evidence for tours of inspection by the Patriarch has not been fully assembled for the fourth century, but the practice of tours by senior rabbis seems to have continued, as noted in various Talmudic sources. For example, Rabbi Abbahu, head of the *Bet Midrash* at Caesarea and contemporary with Hilarion, enjoyed a status somewhat similar to that of the Patriarch and is recorded as having close contacts with the Roman authorities.[152] He is also known to have had contacts with the Christian community,[153] and Jerome knew of some of his statements.[154] While allowing his daughters to learn Greek, Rabbi Abbahu was careful to define the boundaries between Jews, Christians and Samaritans.[155] He made many official trips, both in Palestine and abroad and sent senior rabbis on tours of inspection. There is an episode noted in the Jerusalem Talmud where R. Abbahu sends R. Ami, R. Assi and R. Hiyya, a group of senior rabbis, to inspect the vineyards of the Samaritans.[156] When they return he rules that their wine is halakhically impure. 'Why then was it permitted in our fathers' day?' they [the Samaritans] ask. 'You have deteriorated since,' he replies. If we place this episode side by side with Hilarion's tours of inspection of the monks' vineyards, we see that a different authority is being expressed by Jerome.[157] The concerns

---

[151] Libanius *ep.* 1105; Jerome *ep.* 57, 3 (*CSEL* 54, 506). See on this G. Stemberger *Jews and Christians in the Holy, Land: Palestine in the fourth century* (tr. R. Tuschling, Edinburgh, 2000) 'The Jewish Patriarch: power and political influence' 238f. with bibliography *ad loc.* Stemberger calls the Patriarch 'simply the highest-ranking man in Palestine.' For a detailed discussion see now S. Schwartz *Imperialism and Jewish Society 200 BCE to 640 CE* (Princeton, 2001) esp. 104f. 'Rabbis and patriarchs on the margins.'

[152] See for example the traditions about the matrons of the imperial house who sang for him (BT Ketubot 17a); or the request of the sages of Tiberias that Rabbi Abbahu should intercede on their behalf with the '*anthupatos* [governor] of Caesarea' (JT Megillah iii 74a).

[153] N. de Lange *Origen and the Jews* (Cambridge, 1976).

[154] R. Abbahu is cited in the Babylonian Talmud as identifying Ekron with Caesarea, an identification which Jerome quotes as 'some say' and adds to his translation of Eusebius' *Onomasticon*. Below, chapter 4.5.

[155] For example, he made it clear that he would not accept Christian claims, saying: 'If a man tells you "I am God", he is lying; "I am the son of man", he will eventually regret it; "I shall go up to heaven", he promises but will not fulfill.' (JT Ta'anit ii 65b).

[156] JT Avodah Zarah v,4: 44d.

[157] Mayerson (*op. cit.* n. 142 above) 251 suggests that Hilarion is visiting the vineyards presumably in order to give a blessing to the vintage. This is true, in so far

here are not the rules of the *halakhah*, but the moral behaviour of the monk. Hilarion as a Christian holy man is concerned not with the letter, but the spirit of the law. The stingy monk is condemned with laying up things on earth, rather than in heaven. He has deteriorated morally, in contrast to the ascetic Hilarion, who has voluntarily given up all, and from this derives his authority. Jerome's holy man has authority equivalent to that of a Roman *dux*, or a Jewish patriarch, but it is neither the *potestas* backed up by force of arms, nor the legal authority of the *halakhah*.[158] It is a spiritual authority which still enables him to actualize his leadership over activities of everyday life such as the viticulture around Gaza, an area famed in late antiquity for its wines.

2.2.2. *From Classical to Christian world*

2a. *The Apostolic Constitutions*
When Hilarion is first introduced he is described as one who, believing in Lord Jesus, was not pleased by *circi furoribus . . . arenae sanguine . . . theatri luxuria* (*vH* 2). These words are reminiscent of Tertullian, of Augustine and of Jerome's own letter of advice and encouragement to Marcella.[159] But they are not just a literary allusion or moral reference: these were spheres of life specifically forbidden to a Christian according to regulations listed in a group of documents that are called the *Apostolic Constitutions*. These documents exist in various ver-

---

as it goes, but it does not take into account the political implications of giving and receiving blessings, where the act of receiving a blessing is tantamount to recognition of the authority of the giver. In the 1996 Israeli parliamentary elections, the blessings handed out by the modern holy man, Rabbi Kadourie, in Netivot, a town not far from Gaza, were an important factor in expressing the political identification of the recipients. I have no reason to suspect that things were any different in the fourth century.

[158] For the difference between *auctoritas* and *potestas*, see Augustus *Res gestae* 34 and the discussion of this by K. Galinsky *Augustan Culture: An interpretive introduction* Princeton, 1996) esp. 11–12. On p. 12 Galinsky discusses *auctoritas* as 'moral leadership.'

[159] Tertullian Adv. Marcionem 1: 27, 5: *circus furens, cavea saeviens, scaena lasciviens*; Augustine Sermones 199, 3: *turpitudines variae theatrorum, insania circi, crudelitas amphitheatri*: Jerome *ep.* 43, 3 *harena saevit, circus insanit, theatra luxuriant*; cf. Jerome Com. in Hiez. xx, 7 (CCSL 75, 258; PL 25, 197): *a spectaculis. . . . removeamus oculos, arenae, circi theatrorum*. See now on this: S. Rebenich 'Insania circi. Eine Tertullianreminiszenz bei Hieronymus und Augustinus' *Latomus* 53 (1994) 155–158.

sions and languages: Greek, Latin, Arabic, Syriac, Sahidic, Bohairic and Ethiopian. While the earliest are attributed to Hippolytus of Rome in the early third century, there is a Greek version from the fourth century from Antioch.[160] This version of the *Apostolic Constitutions* appears to incorporate the document known as the *Apostolic Tradition* in its eighth book. Its editor, Metzger, dates its compilation to a short time before the council of Constantinople in 381. Jerome was in Antioch in the late 370's, and went from there to Constantinople at an unknown date shortly before the council of 381. There is a considerable degree of correspondence between the list of forbidden occupations in the eighth book of the fourth-century Antiochene version of the *Apostolic Constitutions* (viii, 32) and the occupations of Hilarion's antagonists.[161] The *Apostolic Constitutions* forbid the baptizing of anyone possessed by a demon, as well as a maker of idols, a procurer, a prostitute, anyone connected to the theatre (whether male or female), a charioteer, a gladiator, a racer in the stadium, a curator of the games, an Olympic official, various sorts of musicians and a huckster.[162] A soldier was to swear he would 'do violence to no

---

[160] These are grouped under the heading *Iuris Pseudo-Apostolici: Opera Singula* in M. Geerard *Clavis Patrum Graecorum I: Patres Antenicaeni* (Turnhout, 1983) nos. 1730–1743. For discussion, and translated and reconstituted text of the *Apostolic Tradition* see G. Dix (rev. H. Chadwick) *The treatise on the Apostolic Tradition of St Hippolytus of Rome* (London, 1968). For the *Apostolic Constitutions* see: F.X. Funk *Didascalia et Constitutiones Apostolorum* (Paderborn, 1905); M. Metzger *Les Constitutions Apostoliques* i-iii (*Sources Chrétiennes* 320, 329, 336, Paris, 1985–7). After many attempts to place these and related documents in a chronological derivative order (q.v. the series of articles by C.H. Turner *JThS (OS)* 13 (1911) 492f.; 15 (1913) 53f.; 16 (1914) 54f.; 21 (1919) 160f.; 31 (1929) 128f.), the modern tendency is to see in them a genre of parallel texts with no original 'real author.' However, it seems to be generally agreed that the source for the fourth-century Antiochene eighth book of the *Apostolic Constitutions* was the *Apostolic Tradition*, originating in third-century Rome and attributed to Hippolytus. For a brief statement of the present consensus, see C. Jones, G. Wainwright, E. Yarnold, P. Bradshaw *The Study of Liturgy* (London/NY/Oxford, 1992²) 88 (the editors); 90 (Yarnold) and now cf. A. Brent *Hippolytus and the Roman Church in the Third Century: Communities in tension before the emergence of a Monarch-Bishop* (Leiden, 1995) 184f.
[161] There is a further list of forbidden professions in the *Apostolic Constitutions* iv, 6, but this seems to be more a condemnation of what was seen as immoral behaviour than a list of occupations which were intrinsically forbidden: thus the list includes oppressors of widows and orphans, lawyers who support injustice, makers of false weights, drunkards etc.
[162] Some of these would have been despised by any traditional Roman of good family: *saltator* is the worst Cicero could call an enemy (*Mur.* 6,13: *saltatorem appellat L. murenam. Maledictum est . . .; Off.* 1, 42, 150: *minimeque artes eae probandae . . . saltatores totumque ludum talarium*), while gladiators were considered the dregs of society:

man, neither accuse any falsely; and be content with [his] wages.'[163]
Also forbidden were people who indulged in various sorts of forbidden sexual practices, different kinds of magicians and makers of
amulets, and those who refused to give up a pagan or Jewish way
of life.[164]

This list finds many parallels in the cast of the *vita Hilarionis*.[165]
There are several people possessed by demons (*vH* 16; 17; 18; 21;
22; 23; 42), a maker of pagan amulets who uses them to procure a
girl (*ib.* 21), naked female temptresses (7), a charioteer (16), gladiators (7), a chariot race (20), officials responsible for games (20), two
soldiers: a high-up *candidatus Constantii* (22) and a *scutarius* (37). There
are references to forbidden use of magic arts, incantations and magic
figures (20; 21). There is also a pagan priest of Venus *sacerdos ut erat
coronatus* (25) and a Jewish huckster (38).

Dix, the editor of the *Apostolic Tradition*, has pointed out that the
earlier versions of these regulations forbid the baptism of generals
or other officials of the Roman empire, but that these classes are
omitted from the list of exclusions by the fourth century, when this
became irrelevant due to the Christianisation of the empire. Thus
the *vita Hilarionis* shows high Roman officials, including a *candidatus
Constantii*, coming to the saint for help. Particularly interesting is the
case of the *scutarius* who comes from Rome for help from Hilarion
(37). The imperial guard at Rome included the *schola scutariorum prima*,
which had as its shield-emblem the chi-rho.[166] It was because of this

---

cf. T. Wiedemann *Emperors and Gladiators* (London/NY, 1992, repr. 1995) 102–127;
C. Edwards 'Unspeakable professions: public performance and prostitution in ancient
Rome' in J.P. Hallet, M.B. Skinner (eds.) *Roman sexualities* (Princeton, 1997) 66–95.

[163] Cf. Luke 3:14. This is particularly interesting as it shows what was the norm
for an ordinary soldier.

[164] The Jerusalem Talmud (Ta'anit i, 4, 64b) relates an incident associated with
Rabbi Abbahu (Caesarea, third century) which records Jewish rabbinical disapproval
of people associated with the theatre: 'This man commits five sins every day: he
adorns the theatre, engages the *hetaerae*, brings their clothes to the bathhouse, claps
hands and dances before them, and clashes the cymbals before them.' See on this
Z. Weiss 'Adopting a novelty: the Jews and the Roman games in Palestine' in *The
Roman and Byzantine Near East 2: Some recent archaeological research* (ed. J. Humphrey,
Portsmouth, Rhode Island, 1999) 33 with bibliography *ad. loc.*

[165] See Appendix to this chapter: The *dramatis personae* of the *vita Hilarionis*.

[166] D. Woods 'The Emperor Julian and the Passion of Sergius and Bacchus' *JECS*
5 (1997) 345–367 with bibliography *ad loc.* See also R. Tomlin 'Christianity and
the Late Roman Army' in S.C.N. Lieu, D. Montserrat (eds.) *Constantine: History, historiography and legend* (London/NY, 1998) 21–51 esp. p. 26 on the transitional period.

sign that Constantine had claimed he won the battle of the Milvian Bridge, which led to the Christianisation of the empire.[167] Thus the *scutarius* bears the symbol of the Christianisation of the Roman army. Jerome reflects the same process of change as the *Apostolic Constitutions*, the beginning of the Christianisation of the army and the administration. The *Apostolic Constitutions* also forbid the baptism of a curator of the games and an Olympic official. Games in general, and the Olympics in particular, were essentially pagan cult events and as such irreconcilable with a Christian way of life. There would also have been considerable conflicts for Christian office-holders having to officiate at civic ceremonies, which were inevitably still pagan in some of their content. Jerome presents a vivid picture of a change of Christian attitude in the episode of Italicus, who is a councillor (*municeps*) in the mostly Christian *oppidum* of Maiumas, the port of Gaza. He supports a team of horses, and comes to the saint for help in the contest between him and his pagan rival from the city of Gaza. When Hilarion protests that he is wasting money which could have helped the poor, Italicus tells him that sponsorship of horse racing is part of his civic duty, a claim which the saint accepts.[168] However, other occupations closer to the games themselves and voluntarily chosen remained completely unacceptable for Christians: Hilarion tells the *auriga*, the charioteer who comes to him for cure, that he must give up his job if he wants his help—as the *Apostolic Constitutions* put it 'either he repudiates it, or he is rejected.' (viii, 32,9) Thus, too, the pagan priest of Venus at Elusa, having repudiated his cult, is recognised as a Christian priest (*vH* 25).

2b. *Confrontation with paganism*

Christians and the games   I have already noted that the emotional high point of the *Life of Hilarion* is the chariot race in the circus of Gaza. From early times the Roman public was devoted to spectacles—the *ludi* or games often had a religious character, and included both chariot races and theatrical shows in the circus, while the *munera*

---

[167] For a clarification of the differing accounts of this in Lactantius and Eusebius, see Averil Cameron and S.G. Hall (eds. and trs.) *Eusebius: Life of Constantine* (Oxford, 1999) 207–210. In his *ep.* 107, 1–2 Jerome writes of the symbol on the *labarum: vexilla militum crucis insignia sunt.*

[168] *vH* 20.

included gladiatorial contests and *venationes*—wild beast shows in the amphitheatre.[169] We know from Jerome's slightly older contemporary Libanius and others that chariot racing played an important part in the municipal life of the east in late antiquity, especially in Constantinople and Antioch. The mid fourth century *Expositio totius mundi* also notes the fame of Antioch's circus, together with those of Laodicia, Tyre, Berytus and Caesarea; Gaza and Ascalon were famed for their boxers, and athletes and pankratists.[170] As is clear from the mosaics of North Africa, late Roman charioteers came in for an immense amount of adulation.[171]

By late antiquity these clear distinctions had become eroded, and Christian writers condemn all together.[172] In one of his sermons, Jerome tells his audience of monks to avoid the temptation of going to the circus.[173] Under the 'persecuting emperors' Christians had

---

[169] For a useful summary: H. Dodge 'Amusing the masses: Building for entertainment and leisure in the Roman world' in *Life, Death and Entertainment in the Roman World* (eds. D.S. Potter, D.J. Mattingly, Ann Arbor, 1999) 205f., esp. 206 (*ludi*); 224 (*munera*). A. Futrell *Blood in the Arena* (Austin, 1997) 169f.: 'Human sacrifice in the arena,' writes of the *munera* as ritualised human sacrifice, the gladiators engaging in 'ritual combat at the heart of the Roman state' (205). See now D. Kyle *Spectacles of Death in Ancient Rome* (London/NY, 1998).

[170] Constantinople: *LRE* 539; 706; 1017–9; Alan Cameron *Circus Factions* (Oxford, 1976). Antioch: P. Petit *Libanius et la vie municipale à Antioche au IVᵉ siècle après J.-C.* (Paris, 1955) ch. 3: 'Les jeux et les spectacles' 123–144; G. Downey *A History of Antioch in Syria from Seleucus to the Arab Conquest* (Princeton, 1961); J.H.G.W. Liebeschuetz *Antioch: City and Imperial Administration in the Later Roman Empire* (Oxford, 1972). *Expositio*: J. Rougé (ed. and tr.) *Expositio totius mundi et gentium: Introduction, texte critique, traduction, notes et commentaire* (*SC* 124, Paris, 1966) xxxii. Boxing and athletic contests were traditionally part of the *ludi* which took place in the circus together with chariot racing: Cicero *de legibus* 2, 38. Pankratists: D.S. Potter 'Entertainers in the Roman Empire' in Potter and Mattingly (*op. cit.* above, n. 167) 256 and bibliography *ad loc.*

[171] Cf. K.M.D. Dunbabin *The mosaics of Roman North Africa* (Oxford, 1978).

[172] The classic work on gladiators in the east is L. Robert *Les Gladiateurs dans l'Orient grec* (Paris, 1940). For a general discussion see: Wiedemann (*op. cit.* n.160 above) ch. 1, p. 1f.; for a slightly earlier period: M. Sartre *L'Orient romain: provinces et sociétées provinciales en Méditerranée orientale d'Auguste aux Sévères (31 avant J.-C.—235 après J.-C.)* (Paris, 1991) 186; for the later period Alan Cameron *op. cit.* n. 168 above; for Christian condemnation Wiedemann *op. cit.* 147f., and see now D.G. Kyle 'Rethinking the Roman arena: Gladiators, sorrows and games' *Ancient History Bulletin* 11 (1997) 94–7; A. Futrell *op. cit* n. 169 above. On Christians and the games see S. Rebenich '*Insania circi*. Eine Tertulliansreminiszenz bei Hieronymus und Augustin' *Latomus* 53 (1994) 153–158 amd bibliography *ad loc.*

[173] *Com. in Ps.* 90[91] *CCSL* 72 pp. 129–130: *si ieris in civitatem, monachus solus, et coeperis deambulare, et audieris clamorem in circo, et aliquis tibi dixerit: 'veni et specta, circus est'; et coeperis ei tu dicere: 'Non licet, non possum ire.'* That monks had to be told not

often been condemned to *damnatio ad bestias* and it may be partly as a result of this that gladiatorial shows decline in popularity[174] and chariot racing becomes a popular craze, with growing political involvement in the circus parties or factions by the fifth and sixth centuries.[175] One of Eusebius' martyrs of Palestine, Timotheos, came from Gaza, and was put to death in the context of a pagan festival with horse-racing and wild beasts.[176] In the *vita Hilarionis* a chariot race between the supporters of Christ from Christian Maiumas and the supporters of Marnas from pagan Gaza becomes a pivotal event. It is preceded by terrible animal and human noises, recalling the *venationes*, the wild animal contests held in the amphitheatre, where the noise made by the animals must have contributed to the atmosphere.[177] Following this, Hilarion is tempted by scenes reminiscent

---

to go to the circus is interesting in itself, and evidently reflects an early stage in the development of monastic discipline, when they were free to go to town and open to its temptations.

[174] For Constantine's disapproval: *CTh* 15.12.1. See on this T. Barnes: *Constantine and Eusebius* (Cambridge/London, 1981 repr. 1993) 53 and nn. 98–100 with bibliography.

[175] For *damnatio ad bestias* see K. Coleman 'Fatal Charades: Roman executions staged as mythological enactments' *JRS* 80 (1990) 44–73; G. Bowersock *Martyrdom and Rome* (Cambridge, 1995) and now D.S. Potter *loc. cit.* n. 170 above, p. 26. That the move from gladiatorial games to chariot racing was not so clear a progression as has hitherto been understood, at least in late antique Palestine, may be seen from recent discoveries in Beit She'an/Scythopolis, where Y. Tsafrir has uncovered evidence that the circus was converted into an amphitheatre in the fifth century. Similar processes occurred at Neapolis and Gerasa. For a convenient summary and recent bibliography, see B. Isaac 'Between the old Schürer and the new: archaeology and geography' in: A. Oppenheimer (ed.) *Jüdische Geschichte in hellenistisch-römischer Zeit: Wege der Forschung: Vom alten zum neuen Schürer* (Munich, 1999) 181–91, and see now Z. Weiss *op. cit.* n. 164 above.

[176] *Mart. Pal.* 3, 1 (*PG* 20, 1469) This occurred in 304/5. See F. Millar *The Roman Near East 31 B.C.–A.D. 337* (Cambridge, Mass./London, 1993) 199 for a discussion.

[177] In the sermon quoted in n. 173 above, where Jerome is warning his audience against the temptations of the circus, the first sign of it is the noise: *audieris clamorem in circo*.
It may be noted here that Jerome's contemporary, the poet Rutilius Namatianus, waiting in Pato [present-day Fiumicino] for a favourable wind for sailing, said he could hear—or imagine—the beloved sounds of the amphitheatre at Rome (*de reditu suo*, ll. 201–4):

> *saepius attonitae resonant circensibus aures,*
> *nuntiat accensus plena theatra favor;*
> *pulsato notae redduntur ab aethere voces,*
> *vel quia perveniunt vel quia fingit amor.*

That Rutilius could not have heard this at such a distance is immaterial—it is clear that the noise of the amphitheatre must have been considerable, and enjoyed by many.

of the *arenae sanguine* and *theatri luxuria* at least as they appear in
Apuleius—naked women and huge banquets.[178] Later, dying gladiators plead with him for burial.

Jerome's *vita Hilarionis*, written at the end of the fourth century,
while seeking to reflect the reality earlier in the century, may be
seen to provide a mid-way picture—gladiators receive bare mention
as an evil and temptation of the Devil, but great stress is placed on
chariot-racing. Not only does a vivid description of the chariot race
between supporters of Jesus and supporters of the local god Marnas
form a high point of the *vita Hilarionis*, but Jerome also includes discussion of its importance and function in municipal life.

Chariots in the vita Hilarionis   In the *vita Hilarionis* Jerome makes
use of the wide popularity of chariot racing on different levels. Not
only is the high point of the *vita* his description of a real and very
exciting chariot race between the supporters of Christianity and
paganism, but there are also other chariots and charioteers, real,
visionary and metaphorical, which Jerome interweaves in his text
and which act as a connecting thread between the different parts of
the story.

In late antiquity the only rival to the charioteer superstar was the
holy man.[179] Jerome goes even further. For him, the *auriga*, the charioteer *par excellence*, was God Himself, as he makes clear on numer-
ous occasions. When Jerome uses *auriga* for a late antique human
charioteer it is usually to condemn, and as such, charioteers appear
together with other undesirables such as *mimi, sacerdotes idolorum, scortae*
etc.[180] For Jerome, a human charioteer was committing the ultimate
blasphemy, like Pharoah in the book of Exodus, in trying to rival
God.[181]

---

[178] *vita Hilarionis* 7: *Quoties illi nudae mulieres cubanti, quoties esurienti largissimae apparuere
dapes?* . . . *psallentique gladiatorum pugna spectaculum praebuit* etc. The parallel with Apuleius
has already been noted. Apuleius' feasts and naked women are actually sited in an
amphitheatre.

[179] 'The citizen of the East Roman Empire had in fact two heroes—the winner
in the chariot race and the ascetic saint.' N. Baynes *The Byzantine Empire* (London,
1925) 33, cited by Alan Cameron *Porphyrius the Charioteer* (Oxford, 1973) 3.

[180] E.g. *Com. in Naum; ep.* 52; *ep.* 69.

[181] A search of the CETEDOC CD-ROM of Jerome's works produced 30 uses
of the word *auriga*, other than the two in the *vita Hilarionis*. Of these, 16 referred
to God, Christ or the Holy Spirit as *auriga* (*Com. in Es.* [3]; *Com. in Hiez.* [2]; *Com.
in Os.; epp.* 52; 64; 69, etc.) and four more appeared to interpret Elisha's words

In the *vita Hilarionis* 4–6 Jerome describes Hilarion's struggle with the Devil. The Devil's account of his proud attempt to rival God is cited:

> *In coelum ascendo . . . et ero similis Altissimo.*[182]

But the Devil fears he is being vanquished by the saintly hero, and sets out to assail him. He makes a series of attacks on Hilarion, attempting to distract him from his prayers with fearful demonic visions. Hilarion arms himself with the sign of the cross. First kneeling, then actually prostrated in prayer, he resists the fearful distraction of the chariot in the moonlight which threatens to run him down with galloping horses—

> *cernit rhedam ferventibus equis super se irruere.*[183]

Hilarion calls on Jesus for help and the chariot is swallowed up in a cleft of the earth.[184] Hilarion praises God in response, quoting the song of Moses from the book of Exodus, after the Children of Israel had passed safely through the Red Sea but Pharoah and his chariots who pursued them were swallowed up:

> *Equum et ascensorem projecit in mare.*[185]

Moses had continued his description of the defeat of God's enemies: *inruat super eos formido*[186] which is reminiscent of the chariot Hilarion saw *super se irruere*. Hilarion continues his response to his deliverance from the Devil's chariot with a statement of his trust in God, not in horses and chariots:

---

when Elijah was taken up to Heaven in a fiery chariot (Kings II[IV]2:12) as addressed to God, not Elijah: *pater mi pater mi currus Israhel et auriga eius* (*Com. in Es.; Com. in Hiez.* [2]; *Com. in Zach.*). Jerome's *ep.* 53, addressed to Paulinus of Nola, contains a vividly sustained development of this image, where the *quadriga Domini* is drawn by four horses who are the four Evangelists. This letter had a wide influence on later Christian thought and art. For a full discussion with bibliography, see M. Jacoff *The Horses of San Marco and the Quadriga of the Lord* (Princeton, 1993) 12–17; 126–131. Jesus as Helios in his chariot also appears on a mosaic underneath St. Peter's in Rome: J. Stevenson *The Catacombs: Rediscovered monuments of early Christianity* (London, 1978) 75.

[182] Isaiah 14:14.

[183] *vH*6: *provolutus genibis, Christi crucem signavit in fronte: talique armatus, jacens fortius praeliabatur; . . . splendente luna cernit rhedam ferventibus equis super se irruere.*

[184] *Cumque inclamasset Jesum, ante oculos ejus repentino terrae hiatu, pompa omnis absorpta est.*

[185] Exodus 15:1.

[186] *Loc. cit.* verse 16.

hi in curribus, hi in equis nos autem in nomine Dei nostri . . .[187]

This time the horses and chariots come from Psalms 19:8–9, which is also cited in the *vita Antonii.*

It is not always possible to be sure how far a writer could expect his audience to pick up his references, even when taken from the Bible, for we cannot always know how familiar people were with all parts of the Bible. Here, however, Jerome is stressing the story of the crossing of the Red Sea, which is also noted by the pilgrim Egeria and which played an important part in the Easter liturgy.[188] The crossing of the Red Sea also appears in the iconography of this period. It may therefore be fairly assumed to have been familiar to even the less learned of his audience.[189]

Later, a paralysed human charioteer is brought to the saint for help, which Hilarion provides, on condition the charioteer changes his occupation.[190] As already noted, the *Apostolic Constitutions* required this—either the charioteer repudiates his calling or he is rejected as a candidate for the church. The church wanted no internal rivals for popular acclaim within its ranks. But although it was possible to repudiate the individual, the church still had problems with the institution—it was not possible yet to dismantle the whole civic structure of the late antique city, with its compulsory *munera* and games related to the cult of pagan gods, as Jerome points out. Indeed, the hippodrome had become an image for the whole pagan cosmos in microcosm.[191] This is reflected in yet another episode relating to

---

[187] I showed above (chapter 2.1.6: the Christian Ass) how Jerome connects this image with Jesus' Entry into Jerusalem riding on an ass in his *Com. in Zach.*, where he talks of the victory of peace and the transfer of the chariots of war (including Pharoah's chariots) to the service of the Lord.

[188] Liturgy: Armenian lectionary in J. Wikinson *Egeria's Travels* (Warminster, 1999³) 193. It has also been an important part of the Jewish liturgy from Second Temple times to the present day: I. Elbogen *Der Judische Gottesdienst in seiner geschichtlichen Entwicklung* (rev. and tr. Y. Amir, J. Heinemann *et al.* Tel Aviv, 1988, Heb) 67; 89.

[189] Egeria vii, 1–4 (*CCSL* 175, 46–48) visits the Red Sea; iconography: sarcophagi from Rome and Dalmatia (as well as Gaul): q.v. on this M. Lawrence 'Columnar sarcophagi in the Latin West' *Art Bulletin* 14 (1932) 175f.; wall paintings in the Roman catacombs: for bibliography see J. Kollwitz *et al.* (eds.) *Lexikon der Christlichen Ikonographie* II, (Rome etc., 1970) *s.v.* Durchzug durch das Rote Meer.

[190] *vH* 16.

[191] G. Wuilleumier 'Cirque et astrologie' *MEFRA* (1927) 184–209, based on the evidence of Tertullian and Isidore of Seville, esp. p. 193: 'l'hippodrome était conçu comme un monde en miniature.' Cf. A. Futrell *op. cit.* n. 169 above: 'The arena was the embodiment of the empire.'

chariots in the *vita* Hilarionis, the story of Italicus. Italicus, the Christian *municeps* of Maiumas, and his sponsorship of chariot racing has already been mentioned, together with the problems of holding public office for a Christian.[192] Jerome relates a conversation between Italicus and Hilarion where this is spelled out:

'Why don't you rather spend the price of horses on the poor for the salvation of your soul?' [Italicus] answered that the contest was his public duty and it was not that he wanted to do it, but that he was forced to.[193]

The people of Gaza, the owners of the opposing chariot team are, he says, enemies of God: *adversarios Dei*.

The saint provides holy water to sprinkle on the chariot and Jerome provides his readers with the exciting spectacle of a real chariot race, no mere demonic temptation, where, of course, the Christians' team wins and the crowd roars 'Christ has beaten Marnas.' As with his pornographic text converted to Christian ends, Jerome is now showing the victory over the very epitome of paganism on its own terms. Christians had early taken over the language, first of athletic contests, and later of gladiatorial combat, to convey their message.[194] Here Jerome is appropriating the language and imagery of the circus. Eusebius had recorded the martyrdom of the Christian Timotheos at Gaza, at a pagan festival which included horse-racing and wild beasts.[195] Jerome is here showing a Christian triumph in Gaza, where his ascetic hero now comes to the very place of Timotheos' martyrdom and aids Italicus' team to achieve a Christian victory. This victory is by no means final, but marks a milestone in the long process of Christianisation. The first victory over paganism had begun when Jesus died on the cross—and this process is now inevitably fulfilling itself in history.[196]

The story of Hilarion continues, with the saint once more victorious

---

[192] Above, 2.2.2a: The Apostolic Constitutions.

[193] *vH* 20: *Cur non magis equorum pretium pro salute animae tuae pauperibus erogas? Ille respondit, functionem esse publicam; et hoc se non tam velle, quam cogi.*

[194] See on this R. Merkelbach 'Der griechische Wortschatz und die Christen' *ZPE* 18 (1975) 101–48, especially the section 'Griechische Athletik, Gladiatorenkämpfe und Kaiserkult' and the following discussion by Youtie.

[195] Timotheos of Gaza: Eusebius, *Mart. Pal.* 3, 1 (*PG* 20, 1469).

[196] On this see Peter Brown *Authority and the Sacred: Aspects of the Christianisation of the Roman World* (Cambridge, 1995).

over chariots of evil, this time metaphorical ones. Hilarion finds himself on board a ship threatened by pirates (*vH* 41). Once again the saint's speech compares the threat to that of Pharoah's army, overcome in the Red Sea:

> *Numquid plures sunt hi quam Pharaonis exercitus? Tamen omnes Deo volente submersi sunt.*

The ship with the saint on board escapes from the pirates, just as Moses and the Children of Israel had escaped from Pharoah and his army of chariots. Thus chariots appear again and again in the text of the *vita Hilarionis*, linking the various parts of this otherwise rather rambling narrative. Pharoah and his chariots drowning in the Red Sea had already been used by Eusebius, both in his Church History and in his *Life of Constantine*, as a metaphor for the defeat of Maxentius and the victory of Constantine in the name of Christianity at the Milvian Bridge.[197] Jerome has chosen a Biblical story which already had strong associations with the Christianisation of the Roman Empire.[198]

At the Red Sea, the leader of the Children of Israel had been Moses, the Lawgiver. But the Law of Moses for the Christian Jerome was the Old Law, now superseded by Jesus as the fulfillment of all of the Law and the Prophets, just as the Church was the New Israel.[199] For Jerome, one of the types of Jesus in the Old Testament was Moses' successor Joshua.[200] So as a prelude to Hilarion's eventual victory over the chariots of evil, where Pharoah and his hosts drown in the Red Sea, Jerome refers to the crossing of the Jordan led by Joshua, where the new takes over from the old. This is not a direct reference as in the other passages, but the vocabulary of *vH* 40 where the saint holds up a tidal wave is clearly taken from the account of Joshua holding up the waters of the Jordan (Joshua 3):

---

[197] Eusebius *HE* ix, 9. See on this A. Alföldi *The conversion of Constantine and pagan Rome* (Oxford, 1948, repr. 1969); *vita Constantini* i, 38; on this Cameron and Hall (*op. cit.* n. 165 above) 215.

[198] Judas Maccabeus also calls on his men to remember God's defeat of Pharoah at the Red Sea in I Macc 4:8–11, before the battle of Emmaus, but it is hardly surprising that there is no trace of the Jewish hero in his nationalist guise in Jerome.

[199] For a contemporary iconographic image of Jesus as Lawgiver, in Santa Constanza at Rome (c. 350) the so-called *Traditio legis*, see A. Grabar *Christian Iconography: A study of its origins* (Princeton, 1968, repr. 1980) 42 and plate 101.

[200] For Jerome on Christian typology see his *ep.* 53, 4 where he also points out that Joshua (Iesus Naue) and Jesus have the same name: *Iesum Naue, typum domini non solum in gestis, uerum et in nomine.*

Joshua 3	*vita Hilarionis* 40
13: *posuerint vestigia pedum . . . in aquis Iordanis*	*posuerunt [Hilarion] in littore*
14: *egressus est populus de tabernaculis suis*	*Epidauritani . . . ingressi sunt ad senum*
16: *steterunt aquae descendentes in uno loco et instar montis* Joshua 3 (cont.)	*montes gurgitum littoribus . . .* *vita Hilarionis* 40 (cont.)
intumescentes	*intumescens mare ante eum steterit*

The passage in the book of Joshua ends with Joshua setting up stones[201] as a memorial of the crossing (Jos. 4:6–7):

> *. . . quando interrogaverint vos filii vestri cras dicentes quid sibi volunt isti lapides, respondebitis eis defecerunt aquae Iordanis ante arcam foederis Domini cum transiret eum idcirco positi sunt lapides isti in monumentum filiorum Israhel usque in aeternum.*

The episode in the *vita Hilarionis* ends with Jerome recording mothers telling their children of the miracle as a memorial for the future. The triple cross drawn by the saint stops the destructive and apparently overwhelming tidal wave of paganism and New Israel, the Church, can be led into the Promised Land, by Joshua/Jesus. Jerome has developed his chariots through demonic temptation, via an exciting use of every-day life, to a spiritual triumph.

The *vita Hilarionis* deals with the Christian saint in a pagan world, a world which assails and competes with Christianity, but where Christianity is beginning to win notable victories. Although these victories are still for Jerome's Roman world only partial, the eventual spiritual triumph, Jerome assures his audience, is certain.

Confrontations with three cults   I shall turn now to consider Jerome's portrayal of Hilarion's confrontations with three important pagan

---

[201] These stones are mentioned as still visible by the Bordeaux pilgrim *It. Burd.* 597 (*CCSL* 175, 19) and in the *Onomasticon* 64,24f. = 65,25f.: *Galgala. Haec est quam supra posuimus Golgol, ad orientalem plagam antiquae Ierichus cis Iordanem, ubi Iesus secundo populum circumcidit . . . in ipso loco lapides quoque, quos de alueo Iordanis tulerunt, statuerunt . . . et ostenditur usque hodie locus desertus in secundo Ierichus miliario, ab illius regionis mortalibus miro cultu habitus.*

cults, Marnas at Gaza; Venus at Elusa and Paphos; and Cadmus in
Illyria, Jerome's birthplace.

The cult of Marnas in late antique Gaza   The pivotal event of the
vita Hilarionis, as already mentioned a number of times above, is
the chariot race between the team of the Christian Italicus and the
pagan *duumvir* of Gaza, worshipper of the god Marnas (*vH* 21). The
cult of Marnas at Gaza appears to have been widely known: *O
Marna! O Iuppiter!* exclaims the Syrian-born emperor Severus Alexander
in the *Historia Augusta*.[202] This would seem to imply mockery of the
emperor's provincial origin by association with this local provincial
cult. A huge, twice life-size statue identified as Zeus/Marnas and
found in Gaza is still extant in the Archaeological Museum at
Istanbul,[203] and the cult of the god is mentioned in the *vita Porphyrii*
by Mark the Deacon.[204] Marnas also appears identified by name on
city coins of Gaza.[205]

Hilarion scores a notable victory at the chariot race: the crowd
roars: 'Christ has beaten Marnas'. But circus crowds were fickle in
their allegiances to parties and although a battle has been won, the
war continued, and Jerome knew very well that the victory over
paganism was far from complete.[206] At the time he wrote his *vita
Hilarionis* Jerome was under no illusions as to the progress of Christianity

---

[202] *SHA* Severus Alexander 17,3–4. For discussion of Marnas, see H. Grégoire,
M.-A. Kugener *Marc le Diacre: Vie de Porphyre, évêque de Gaza* (Paris, 1930) p. xlviif.;
for bibliography on Marnas, see G. Mussies 'Marnas god of Gaza' *ANRW* 18.4,
2312f., and F.R. Trombley *Hellenic Religion and Christianization, c. 370–529*, I (Leiden
etc., 1993).

[203] Personal observation, February 1999.

[204] *vPorph* 19. The *vita Porphyrii* records seven other temples in Gaza (*vPorph.* 64),
including a cult of the naked Venus (*vPorph.* 59).

[205] Coins: Y. Meshorer *The City Coins of Eretz-Israel and the Decapolis in the Roman
Period* (Jerusalem, 1984, in Hebrew) 29–30, nos. 56, 62, 64, 65. Coins 62 and 64
also show the Temple of Marnas, the Marneion. Meshorer notes (*op. cit.*, 29) that
the symbol of the mint at Gaza was Phoenician *mem*, the first letter of the name
Marnas. See too *Lexicon Iconographicum Mythologiae Classicae* vol. viii, I, supplementum
s.v. Marnas II (M. Dennert).

[206] The slow rate of the Christianisation of the Holy Land has been stressed by
Z. Rubin: 'Jerome's *Vita Hilarionis* and the Conflict of Religions in Palestine in Late
Antiquity' (Paper given at the 25th Annual Conference of the Israel Society for the
Promotion of Classical Studies, Ramat Gan, 1996). See too G.W. Bowersock *Hellenism
in Late Antiquity* (Cambridge etc., 1990) for the survival of pagan Hellenism in
Palestine.

at Gaza as opposed to the more Christian port of Maiumas. Thus Jerome's hero must acknowledge the god's presence and be seen to contend with him, but cannot be seen to supplant him totally. It has already been noted above that the *vita Hilarionis* was written no later than 393. Thus it was written before Theodosius' series of anti-pagan laws of 395–6.[207] Jerome later rejoiced to see the end of the public cult of Marnas in his letter 107, written sometime between 400–402:

> *Marnas Gazae luget inclusus et euersionem templi iugiter pertremescit.*[208]

But even then the cult of Marnas continued secretly. It is clear from the early fifth century *vita Porphyrii* that there were still many conflicts between pagans and Christians in Gaza at this period.[209] Thus Jerome's Hilarion had to refuse the request of Aristaenete who wanted him to overthrow the idol of Marnas at Gaza. It is not until his Commentary on Isaiah nearly a decade later that Jerome can write of the final victory over Marnas:

> *hoc et nostris temporibus uidemus esse completum: Sarapium Alexandriae et Marnae templum Gazae in ecclesias Domini surrexerunt.*[210]

Marnas was originally a rain god,[211] and it is interesting to note that both the *vita Hilarionis* (*vH* 32) and the *vita Porphyrii* (20) show their Christian heroes praying (successfully) for rain. But even here Hilarion does not compete with Marnas on his own territory—his rain miracle occurs just after he has left Gaza for Egypt.

I have already noted above that Hilarion is described as a 'rose

---

[207] *C.Th.* 16,10 *de paganis sacrificiis et templis*. This series of laws actually begins with a law passed by Constantine in 321, but most of the legislation cited comes from Theodosius.

[208] *ep.* 107.2 Tr. Marnas mourns, imprisoned in Gaza, and greatly fears the overthrow of his temple. Kelly, 273 dates the letter to 401 or early 402; Cavallera II, 162 puts it between 400–402.

[209] See discussion in Trombley *op. cit* (n. 200 above) chapter 3: Gaza. For the disputed dating of the *vita Porphyrii* see Z. Rubin 'Porphyrius of Gaza and the conflict between Christianity and paganism in southern Palestine' in *Sharing the Sacred: Religious Contacts and Conflicts in the Holy Land First-Fifteenth centuries CE* (ed. A. Kofsky, G. Stroumsa, Jerusalem, 1998) 31–66.

[210] *Com. in Es.* 17,1 (text after R. Gryson *Commentaires de Jérôme sur le prophète Isaïe* (Freiburg, 1994) 778; dated by both Kelly and Cavallera between 408 and 410.

[211] *vPorph* 19: ἔλεγον γὰρ τὸν Μαρνᾶν κύριον εἶναι τῶν ὄμβρων τὸν δὲ Μαρνᾶν λέγουσί εἶναι τὸν Δία.

among thorns', and discussed the significance of roses in the context of Jerome's use of Apuleius' *Golden Ass*.[212] It is interesting to note that there is evidence of an actual pagan Festival of Roses in late antique Gaza from the sixth century author Choricius.[213] It is unclear whether this festival was celebrated earlier in the fourth century as well, although it would seem unlikely that a new pagan festival would have been introduced between the fourth and sixth centuries. However, both the Jerusalem Talmud and the Babylonian Talmud quote a discussion of the festive fair at Gaza by the third century Palestinian rabbi, Resh Laqish. In the Babylonian Talmud version (Avodah Zarah 12b), Resh Laqish notes that pagan participators in the festival can be identified by the fact that their shops are decorated with garlands of roses and myrtle (the Jerusalem Talmud Avodah Zarah i, 4, 39d has myrtle and decorative leaves). In this case, he rules, Jews are forbidden to buy in these shops. It may be that this is referring to the same rose festival as Choricius.

Thus Hilarion competes with Marnas on his own territory, winning a notable battle, although final Christian victory over the pagan god is yet to come.

Venus at Elusa and Paphos   Mention has already been made of the important part played by the goddess Venus in the *vita Hilarionis*. Venus, as goddess of sex and love, was the complete antithesis of Jerome's Christian asceticism. Venus was also an important representative of the Roman world as the mother of Aeneas, the founder of Rome:[214] one of the largest temples in Rome was the temple to Venus and Rome between the Forum and the Colosseum.[215] In the Holy Land, Eusebius had written that the Church of the Holy Sepulchre was built over a temple of Venus/Aphrodite,[216] and Jerome says in *ep.* 58 that there had been a marble statue of Venus on the rock of the Cross.[217] In the same letter, Jerome also writes of the site of the Church of the Nativity in Bethlehem:

---

[212] 2.1.3: Shared images: 3a. Roses and thorns.

[213] Festival of Roses at Gaza: Choricius: *Dialectis* 32, 365; 16, 196 (ed. Foerster & Richsteig, Leipzig, 1929).

[214] For Jerome's use of this aspect of Venus in the *vita Malchi* see chapter 3 below.

[215] Temple of Venus and Rome: J.B. Ward-Perkins *Roman Imperial Architecture* (Harmondsworth, 1981² repr. 1983) 122f.

[216] Eusebius *vita Constantini* 3, 26–8.

[217] *ep.* 58, 3–4 (*CSEL* 54, 531f.) and see Wilkinson 82f.

in specu, ubi quondam Christus paruulus uagit, Ueneris amasius plangebatur.[218]

The historicity of this account has been doubted, but Jerome's polemic intent in writing it is clear.[219] The pagan Roman emperor Hadrian had defiled a Christian holy site with a cult of Venus' lover Adonis. Now Christian churches had taken the place of the worship of Venus.

Jerome's picture of the Christian takeover of the Roman world shows Hilarion struggling with this important goddess. It was already noted above that there was a cult of Venus as well as Marnas in late antique Gaza,[220] while *vita Hilarionis* 25 shows Venus worshipped by the Saracens of Elusa as Lucifer.[221] On her festal day Hilarion arrives in town to find all the population in her temple:

> *quo anniversaria solemnitas omnem oppidi populum in templum Veneris congregaverunt.*

Hilarion is known to the Saracens, for he has exorcised many demons from them, and on this occasion he persuades them of their error in worshipping mere stones, so that they agree to convert to Christianity. Hilarion makes the sign of the cross over their priest and marks the outline of a church for them: *limitem mitteret.* This act signifies a new foundation—there is a similar description in the *vita Porphyrii*, when the Empress Eudoxia commands a church which is built only subsequently.[222] Roman colonies were founded by the act of marking city-boundaries; the same seems to be done here for a Christian building. ΚΤΙΣΙΣ, the personification of the act of foundation, is portrayed on an early fifth century Christian mosaic from a bath-house at Curium in Cyprus holding a measuring instrument in her hand, from the time of the re-foundation of the Christian city.[223]

---

[218] Tr. In the cave where the Christ child once cried, the lover of Venus was bewailed.

[219] R.W. Hamilton *The Church of the Nativity in Bethlehem* (Great Britain, 1947² repr. Jerusalem, 1968) 109f. and cf. P. Welten 'Bethlehem und die Klage um Adonis' *ZDPV* 99 (1983) 189–203.

[220] *vPorph* 59.

[221] Epiphanius *Pan.* 51, 22, 9–11 (*GCS* Epiphanius II, ed. J. Dummer, Berlin, 1980) 286–7 writes of a virgin goddess worshipped at Elusa and Petra: καλοῦντες αὐτὴν Ἀραβιστὶ Χααμου τουτέστιν Κόρην εἶτ' οὖ παρθένον. While Venus was hardly virgin, this may be a garbled reference to this cult.

[222] *vPorph* 78.

[223] Curium mosaic: D. Christou *Kourion: Its monuments and local museum* (Nicosia, 1996) 26–32. Another inscription in the same building makes it clear that the town is now in the care of the Christian patron Eustolios, not the god ΦΟΙΒΟΣ [Apollo]. For Hilarion at Curium, see below.

The building at Curium is described in an inscription as being 'gir-dled' ΖΩΣΑΝΤΟ with the signs of Christ—ΣΗΜΑΤΑ ΧΡΙΣΤΟΥ. Thus in the *vita Hilarionis*, pagan Elusa, which had worshipped Venus, is being given a new Christian foundation.

This is not Hilarion's only confrontation with Venus and her cult, although the goddess is not again mentioned by name. Hilarion's final home is in Cyprus, at the ruins of Paphos (*vita Hilarionis* 42–3). Jerome reminds his readers of the city's famous past as the home of Venus:

> [*Hilarion*] *ingressus ergo Paphum, urbem Cypri nobilem carminibus poetarum, . . .*
> *nunc ruinarum tantum vestigiis quid olim fuerit.*[224]

Jerome was aware of the power of names, and does not deign to name the famous patroness of the city. The ancient temple of Venus may be in ruins, but its power has not been forgotten: Hilarion turns with joy to the remaining innumerable demons he must struggle with and attempt to overcome.[225]

The serpent of Epidaurum: the cult of Cadmus in Illyria   After leaving Palestine, Hilarion wanders all over the Mediterranean before he eventually settles in Cyprus. He stays briefly in Sicily, but because of the pursuing crowds, he leaves for Jerome's native Dalmatia.[226] Here he finds that a great dragon is devastating the lands around Epidaurum. The dragon, Jerome tells us, is called *boa* in the language of the Greek-speaking gentiles—*gentili sermone*—because it ate cattle (*boves*). Hilarion commands the dragon to mount the pyre he

---

[224] Venus on Paphos is mentioned e.g. by Virgil *Aeneid* x, 51, cf. discussion in 2.1.3b above.

[225] *vH* 43. *antiquissimi juxta templi ruinam ex quo . . . tam innumerabilium per noctes et dies daemonum voces resonabant . . . Quo ille valde delectatus, quo scilicet antagonistas haberet in proximo.* For the temple of Venus/Aphrodite at Paphos, identified by a Greek inscription, see F.G. Maier 'Der Tempel der paphischen Aphrodite in der Kaiserzeit' in G. Wirth *et al.* (eds.) *Romanitas Christianitas: Untersuchungen zur Geschicht und Literatur der römischen Kaiserzeit: Johannes Straub zum 70. Geburtstag* (Berlin/NY, 1982) 768f. For an excellent collection of sources on Paphos and the temple of Venus see M.R. James 'On the History and Antiquities of Paphos' *JHS* 9 (1888) 175–89 and more recently I. Opelt 'Des Hieronymus Heiligenbiographien als Quellen der historischen Topographie des östlichen Mittelmeerraumes' *Römische Quartalschrift für christliche Altertumskunde und Kirchengeschichte* 74 (1979) 176, n. 78 on *Venus Paphia*. T. Bruce Mitford 'The Cults of Roman Cyprus' *ANRW* 18.3, 2178f., *s.v.* Paphos, is disappointing.

[226] *vH* 39.

has prepared for it, which he sets alight, burning the great serpent to ashes.

This serpent obviously owes something to the snake the Apostle Paul encountered in Melita (Acts 28:3) as well as the serpents in the book of Numbers (21:6–9). Jerome variously calls the beast *draco* and *serpens*. These words would remind his readers of the Devil himself, and in particular of his defeat in the book of Revelation, where both words are used together.[227] But the picture of the dragon laying waste the countryside until destroyed by the hero clearly has pagan connotations too.[228] Not far south of Epidaurum, on the Roman road that ran along the coast of Dalmatia, lay the town of Butua/Βουθόη. The name of this town is derived from βοῦς, an ox or cow (the same root as Jerome's *boves*), according to Stephen of Byzantium.[229] In this town there was a local cult of Cadmus, as the father of the eponymous founder of Illyria. (The Illyrians were the people in whose territory the Roman province of Dalmatia was situated.) The myth of Cadmus has the hero following a cow to the site of his city of Thebes, and killing a dragon.[230] In his old age, Cadmus went to Illyria with his wife Harmonia in a cart drawn by oxen (ζεῦγος βοῶν). It was from these oxen that the town of Butua/Βουθόη received its name.[231] Cadmus and Harmonia were finally turned into serpents.[232] There were two rocks bearing the names of Cadmus and Harmonia near Butua/Βουθόη and Epidaurum.[233] The serpent, indeed, has been

---

[227] Rev. 12.9: *et proiectus est draco ille magnus serpens antiquus qui vocatur Diabolus et Satanas qui seducit universum orbem.*

[228] Cf. e.g. the myth of Perseus and Andromeda, which was known to Jerome: see: P.B. Harvey, Jr., 'The Death of Mythology: The case of Joppa' *JECS* 2 (1994) 1–14.

[229] Stephen of Byzantium: *Ethnika* (ed. Meineke, Berlin, 1849, repr. Graz, 1958) 180f:

Βουθόη, πόλις Ἰλλυρίδος, ὡς Φίλων, διὰ τὸ Κάδμον ἐπὶ ζεύγους βοῶν ὀχούμενον ταχέως ἀνύσαι τὴν ἐς Ἰλλυριοὺς ὁδόν. οἱ δὲ τὸν Κάδμον ἀπὸ τῆς Αἰγυπτίας Βουτοῦς ὀνομάσαι αὐτήν, καὶ παραφθαρεῖσαν καλεῖσθαι Βουθόην. ἔχει δ'ἐπὶ τοῦ μυχοῦ Ῥίζονα πόλιν καὶ ποταμὸν ὁμώνυμον. τὸ ἐθνικόν Βουθοαῖος. There is also an island off the Dalmatian coast near Epidaurum called Boas, as noted by Rosweyde in his commentary on the *vita Hilarionis, PL* 73 *ad loc.*

[230] Roscher II, 849, *s.v.* Kadmos and see R.B. Edwards *Kadmos the Phoenician: A study in Greek legends and the Mycenaean age* (Amsterdam, 1979).

[231] Stephen *loc. cit.*

[232] See Apollodorus: *The Library* III, v 4 (tr. and ed. J.G. Frazer, Cambridge/London 1976) with note by Frazer and bibliography *ad loc.* Further bibliography in Roscher II, 849.

[233] Cf. C. Müller *Geographii Graeci Minores* I (Paris, 1861, repr. Hildesheim 1990)

claimed to have been a particularly important symbol in this area of Dalmatia. Many pieces of jewellery discovered in this area are ornamented with serpents.[234] Illyrian Epidaurum bore the same name as Epidauros in Greece with its famous cult of the healing god Aesculapius, the subject of earlier triumphs of Hilarion,[235] where snakes were particularly prominent.

As a former inhabitant of Dalmatia, it is reasonable to assume that Jerome would have known of the local pagan cult, especially in view of its connections with the eponymous hero. He often goes out of his way to discuss origins and meanings of names, particularly geographical names—at times he can even be said to write philological geography. It is therefore very likely that he knew the explanation given by Stephen of the derivation of the name of Butua/Βουθόη from βοῦς, a cow or ox, and as noted above, Jerome explains the name of the *boa* which was devastating Epidaurum as being due to the serpent's diet of cattle—*boves*. This explanation appears to be unique to Jerome in the ancient literature: Lewis and Short cite him as the only source for it.[236] By causing the serpent of Epidaurum to self-destruct, then, Hilarion is symbolically making local paganism destroy itself at the command of Christianity. Just as Hilarion has chalked up victories over paganism in Jerome's new home of Palestine, so now the saint is victorious over the pagan cult of Cadmus in Jerome's old home country. Hilarion here is successful in his encounter with the serpent, foreshadowing the second coming of Jesus and the final days foretold in the book of Revelation with its defeat of the dragon. And just as with Venus on Paphos, Jerome is aware of the power of names and has deleted the very name of the pagan hero from his account. Here, then, Hilarion's victory is complete.

Having looked at these three pagan sites and their cults, I shall turn now to Jerome's treatment of Christian holy places in the *vita Hilarionis*.

31: the periplus of pseudo-Scylax (mid 4th cent. BCE) discussed by J. Wilkes *The Illyrians* (Oxford/Cambridge, 1992) pp. 94–99.

[234] This is noted by Wilkes *op. cit.* 245. Serpents are a not uncommon decorative feature on jewellery, and it is not clear from what he writes whether in fact there are more in Illyria than anywhere else. Wilkes relates to Jerome's account, saying that 'the slaying of the serpent by St. Hilarion must have had a symbolic impact on the people of that region.'

[235] *vH* 21.

[236] L&S *s.v. boa*.

2.2.3. *The rise and development of Christian holy places*

3a. *Competing identifications: Hilarion and the Apostle Paul on Melita*

The saint's victory over the serpent of Epidaurum which has just been described appears to owe something to the New Testament account of the Apostle Paul on Melita. Hilarion, indeed, has many attributes in common with the apostle: just as Paul of Thebes in Jerome's *vita Pauli* has prototypes in both the prophet Elijah and John the Baptist, so Hilarion's forerunners include Elijah's successor Elisha and the apostle Paul. Paul it was, of course, who was particularly charged with the mission to the Gentiles, and Hilarion has had successes in this area at Elusa and Gaza. Hilarion, like Paul, journeys far, all over the Mediterranean. Indeed, both the Acts of the Apostles and the *vita Hilarionis* have proved goldmines of information for historians of ancient shipping.[237] Jerome uses the Greek word *nauclerus* as used in Acts for the owner of Hilarion's ship, rather than the Latin *navicularis*.[238] Jerome, as always, has a tendency to try to go one better—both Acts and the *vH* have an account of a ship in peril with fearful sailors, but where Paul's ship is wrecked, Hilarion's is saved by the action of the saint.

There may be a further resemblance. After his shipwreck, Paul arrives at the island of Melita.[239] Here the local barbarians light a fire to warm the shipwreck survivors, and a snake fastens itself onto Paul's hand. When he manages to shake this off and is clearly unharmed, the natives are sure he is a god. It is clear that this New Testament story was well-known in the late fourth century, for it became the subject of contemporary art—it is the central scene on one of the leaves of the so-called Carrand diptych, where other scenes have also been identified as belonging to the story of Paul on Melita, while Adam in Eden faces them on the other leaf.[240]

---

[237] L. Casson *Ships and seamanship in the ancient world* (Princeton, 1971).

[238] For the terminology of the merchant ship's crew, see Casson *op. cit.* above, 314f.

[239] Acts 28.

[240] The scenes in the fourth-century Carrand Diptych have been discussed in detail: E. Konowitz 'The program of the Carrand Diptych' *Art Bulletin* 66 (1984) 484–488; K. Shelton 'Roman aristocrats, Christian commissions: The Carrand Diptych *JACh* 29 (1986) 166–180; H. Maguire 'Adam and the animals: Allegory and literal sense in Early Christian Art' *DOP* 41 (1987) 363–373. Shelton (170–1) notes that the scenes on this diptych were originally identified with the life of Jerome

Paul's Melita is now generally identified with the island of Malta, but other identifications have been proposed.[241] One of these suggestions is the island of Mjlet, also called Melita in antiquity, situated off the coast of Dalmatia, where it is the southernmost of a group of islands north of Epidaurum.[242] The third century Antonine Itinerary gives its position as being in the Dalmatian group of islands, 200 stadia (i.e. 25 miles) from Epidaurum.[243] There is a ninth-century tradition that Mjlet, not present-day Malta, was Paul's Melita, but no earlier evidence of this tradition. Most modern scholars do not accept this identification of Melita with Mjlet, in spite of evidence about snakes, mongooses etc. adduced by its supporters.[244] None of the scholars involved in the debate, however, have noted the presence of a cult of Cadmus and his snake-connections on the Dalmatian coast, and none have mentioned the *vita Hilarionis*. The presence of a local cult of Cadmus as a divine serpent could explain why the barbarian inhabitants of the island thought Paul was a god when he defeated a snake.[245] The opponents of the identification of Mjlet with Paul's Melita have pointed out that there is no extant evidence earlier than the ninth century that this Melita was identified with Paul's island. Without entering into the debate as to the cor-

---

by the early cXIX scholar C.-M. Grivaud de la Vincelle (*non vidi*). Perhaps this is tribute to Grivaud's understanding of how far Jerome identifies with his heroes. Shelton reads the depiction of the scenes from the episode of Paul on Malta (sic), which include a high Roman official and Paul healing the sick, as showing the encounter of Christianity with the late antique Roman world (178f.), and especially its high officials. This is an important theme of the *vita Hilarionis*. The presence of Adam in Eden on the other leaf of the diptych should also be noted—Konowitz (488) shows that Paul and Adam were linked by Ambrose and Basil. Hilarion, as discussed above, is associated both with Adam in his paradisial abode (*vH* 31; 43: see chapter 2.1.4 above) and with Paul here, and on his sea journeys.

[241] For an up-to-date survey of the evidence, with full bibliography see B. Rapske 'Acts, travel and shipwreck,' p. 1f. in D.W.J. Gill & C. Gempf (eds.) *The Book of Acts in its First Century setting* II: *The Book of Acts in its Graeco-Roman setting* (Grand Rapids/Carlisle, 1991) esp. 36f.

[242] Müller *loc. cit.* n. 233 above.

[243] O. Cuntz (ed.) *Itineraria Romana* I: *Itineraria Antonini Augusti et Burdigalense* (Stuttgardt, 1990²) p. 83: 520, 2 *s.v.: insulae inter Dalmatiam et Histriam: a Melta Epidauros stadia CC.*

[244] See e.g. A. Acworth 'Where was St. Paul shipwrecked? A re-examination of the evidence' *JThS* n.s. 24 (1973) 190–3; O.F.A. Meinardus 'St. Paul shipwrecked in Dalmatia' *BA* 39 (1976) 145–7; *id.* 'Melita Illyrica or Africana? An examination of the site of St. Paul's shipwreck' *Ostkirchliche Studien* 23 (1974) 21–36.

[245] Cf. Acts 14:8–12, where Paul and Barnabas are identified with Jupiter and Mercurius by the inhabitants of Lycaonia.

rectness of the identification, it does seem possible that there could already have been a local identification of Mjlet with Paul's Melita in the fourth century, which Jerome was aware of. After the conversion of Constantine early in the fourth century, there was a massive interest in identifying sites connected with the Hebrew Bible and New Testament all over the Roman Empire, especially in the Holy Land, and there were often competing identifications, which Jerome was aware of, and even on occasion corrected.[246] I shall discuss below in chapter 4 the translation and corrections he made for Eusebius' *Onomasticon*, which identified Biblical sites in the Holy Land. To return to the *vita Hilarionis*: it is quite possible that Jerome was aware of a contemporary identification of Mjlet with Paul's Melita, under the influence of the Cadmus legend, which is why he brought his saint Hilarion to contend with a snake on the coast of Dalmatia. It is also possible that Jerome rejected this identification, as do the majority of modern scholars, which is another reason why his account remains anonymous, with no explicit mention of either Paul or Cadmus.

3b. *The new Christian geography: a Christian eponymous heroine*
In the *vita Hilarionis*, which deals with the spread of Christianity through the Greek and Roman world, Jerome is also involved in creating a new Christian mythological geography. Nineteenth century scholarship analysed Greek myths of colonisation and settlement on their face value, as if they reflected the actual travels of ancient peoples. But by the middle of the twentieth century, the displaced scholar Elias Bickerman had produced a far more sophisticated analysis of the myths of *origines gentium*.[247] The Greeks, he claimed, were

---

[246] There is a huge literature on fourth-century identifications of Holy Land sites, starting with Eusebius' *Onomasticon*, which Jerome translated and corrected: see below: chapter 4.5. A recent selection: E.D. Hunt *Holy Land Pilgrimage in the Later Roman Empire AD 312–460* (Oxford, 1982); P. Maraval *Lieux saints et pèlerinages d'Orient. Histoire et géographie. Des origines à la conquête arabe* (Paris, 1985); P.W.L. Walker *Holy City, Holy Places?* (Oxford, 1990); R.L. Wilken *The Land Called Holy* (New Haven/London, 1992); J.E. Taylor, *Christians and the Holy Places: The myth of Jewish-Christian origins* (Oxford, 1993).
For Jerome on competing identifications of sites, see e.g.: *Com. in Ion. prol.*: Geth (*CCSL* 76, 378; *PL* 25, 1172).
[247] E. Bickerman 'Origines gentium' *Classical Philology* 47 (1952) 65–81; cf. E. Hall *Inventing the Barbarian: Greek self-definition through tragedy* (Oxford, 1989) 36; 48.

highly ethnocentric and thus selected myths about the barbarians which reflected their own Greek world view, or even rewrote them to prefigure or legitimise their own colonisation of foreign parts. I have shown above how Jerome replaces the mythical Cadmus in conflict with the dragon by his Christian hero's victory over the dragon of Epidaurum. In the episode of Constantia he goes further, creating an entirely new phenomenon—the eponymous Christian heroine.

In the final episode of the *vita Hilarionis* Jerome presents the story of the pious woman Constantia, whose family Hilarion had healed, and whom he charges to bury him in Cyprus. She does so, but his disciples in Palestine steal Hilarion's body and take it back to Maiumas in Palestine. Constantia drops dead when she hears this. Jerome ends his *vita* recording the conflict between Palestine and Cyprus over Hilarion, the one having his body, and the other his spirit. Finally it is in Cyprus 'perhaps because the place was dearer to him' where the greater number of miracles associated with him occur.[248] Hilarion had spent the end of his life in Cyprus in a deserted spot outside Paphos fighting the demons in an 'ancient temple', presumably that of his old adversary Venus (*vH* 42).[249] Paphos is in the west of the island, but Jerome is careful to point out that Hilarion was also present in 'Salamis, Curium, Lapetha and other cities' (*vH* 42)—i.e. in the east, south and north of Cyprus as well—the whole island is covered by his activities. The *vH* began by telling of the earlier account of the saint's life written by the bishop Epiphanius. Epiphanius was metropolitan archbishop of Salamis between 368–403 CE, and was finally buried in the great basilical church he had built there on the model of the Church of the Holy Sepulchre.[250] Salamis, as metropolis, must stand for the whole island.

Constantia, the holy woman connected with the saint, is on one level clearly like Aristaenete, another allusion to Paula and her relationship with Jerome.[251] However, apart from this function on the

---

[248] *vH* 47: *tamen in utrisque locis magna quotidie signa fiunt, sed magis in hortulo Cypri, forsitan quia plus illum locum dilexerit.*

[249] See above 2b: Confrontation with paganism: Venus at Elusa and Paphos.

[250] *vita Epiph.* (*PG* 41, 112f.) and see A.H.J. Megaw 'Byzantine architecture and decoration in Cyprus: metropolitan or provincial?' *Dumbarton Oaks Papers* 28 (1974) 59f.

[251] Being an idealised figure, however, Constantia does not predecease Hilarion and is thus able to bury him.

personal level, she also has a further function in Jerome's account of the Christian geography of the Roman world. The holy Constantia herself is not recorded elsewhere, to my knowledge, and I have not found any discussion of her by anyone.[252] However, both Salamis in Cyprus and Maiumas of Gaza were re-named 'Constantia' in the fourth century.[253] The sources differ as to why: it is unclear whether the name is from a son or sister of Constantine.[254] In the *vita Hilarionis*, Jerome seems to be providing his own explanation. His Christian holy woman, he implies, is the mythical eponymous heroine linking these two towns. I do not know of any other case of an eponymous heroine, rather than a hero, although in late antiquity it was still common to find female personifications representing a city or country—the city *tyche*.[255] Even the Christian city of Constantinople appears as a female personification on the *Tabula Peutingeriana*.[256] Toynbee has noted this phenomenon and suggests that the *tyche* of the city seems to have been viewed by Christians more as an abstract personification, unlike the actual pagan gods.[257] She points out that Zosimus reports that Constantine himself actually set up a statue of Roma in a temple in Constantinople, his new Rome.[258] Thus also, as already noted above, the act of Christian re-foundation was depicted in an early fifth century bath-house at Curium as a mosaic portrayal of a female bust inscribed ΚΤΙΣΙΣ.[259] Jerome had portrayed Rome as the Babylonian

---

[252] I. Opelt 'Des Hieronymus Heiligenbiographien als Quellen der historischen Topographie des östlichen Mittelmeerraumes' *Römische Quartalschrift für christliche Altertumskunde und Kirchengeschichte* 74 (1979) mentions both Salamis Constantia (p. 173 n. 74) and the woman Constantia who buries Hilarion (p. 176) but does not make any connection between them, and has no further discussion of the holy woman other than what is provided by Jerome. Constantia does not appear in the *PLRE*.

[253] Constantia: *PRE*: Maiumas-Constantia; Sozomen *HE* 5.

[254] Eusebius wrote a letter to Constantia, sister of Constantine: *PG* 20, 1545, and see C. Mango *Art of the Byzantine Empire* (Toronto, 1986) 17.

[255] P. Gardner 'Cities and countries in ancient art' *Journal of Hellenic Studies* 9 (1888) 47–81.

[256] See below chapter 4.1.3: *breuis tabella*.

[257] Apparent neutralisation of minor pagan gods in late antiquity has been discussed a great deal with regard to Jewish art, where, for example, Helios appears on several synagogue floors; the classic work is still E.E. Urbach 'The rabbinical laws of idolatry in the second and third centuries in the light of archaeological and historical facts' *IEJ* 9 (1959) 149–165; 229–245.

[258] J.M.C. Toynbee 'Roma and Constantinopolis in Late Antique Art from 312–365.' *Journal of Roman Studies* 37 (1947) 135f.

[259] Curium mosaic: Christou (*op. cit.* n. 223 above) 26–32.

whore:[260] Now he represents Christian cities by a Christian holy woman.

Hilarion has contended with Marnas in the circus of Gaza and with Venus in her temple at Paphos, and now the Roman world is changing: Jesus has beaten Marnas and Paphos lies in ruins after earthquakes.[261] Now Salamis in Cyprus and Maiumas near Gaza bear the name of a Christian holy woman, based on the name of Constantine himself, the first Christian emperor, and both contend for the body and spirit of Saint Hilarion.

3c. *Competing for the remains of the saint*

It has already been reiterated that the Christian holy man in his tomb functioned for the believer as a conduit of holiness between heaven and earth.[262] The site of a tomb of a holy man, especially a martyr, gave status and power to its keepers and to the local inhabitants, and acted as a magnet to draw worshippers and pilgrims. Newly Christian towns did not have such resources, so that one solution was to import them.[263] Thus the transfer, *translatio*, of the relics of saints became common practice, and the Holy Land exported to new cities like Constantinople.[264] Jerome writes of the *translatio* of the relics of Andrew, Luke and Timothy to Constantinople in the time of Constantius. Later he notes Arcadius moving the relics of Samuel from Judaea to Thrace, and the cheering crowds that lined the streets all the way from the Holy Land to Chalcedon.[265] This was an officially approved act, although some churchmen like Vigilantius bitterly opposed it.[266] High church officials could get approval and presum-

---

[260] *de Spiritu Sancti in Didymo: Praef.: cum in Babylone* [*sc.* Rome] *versarer, et purpuratae meretricis essem colonis . . . (PL* 23, 101–2).

[261] *vH* 42: . . . *Paphum . . . quae frequenter terrae motu lapsa, nunc ruinarum tantum vestigiis . . . ostendit.* It has been generally accepted that there were earthquakes in Cyprus in 332 and 342, which caused widespread destruction: see Megaw *art. cit. supra.*

[262] Peter Brown *The Cult of the Saints* (Chicago, 1981).

[263] See on this *CAH* 13, 254f. (E.D. Hunt).

[264] The *translatio* of what were claimed to be Jerome's own remains was recorded at the end of the 13th century in the *Translatio corporis beati Hieronymi* (*PL* 22, 237–40). See on this E.F. Rice *Saint Jerome in the Renaissance* (Baltimore/London, 1985) 55f.

[265] *contra Vigilantium* 5 (*PL* 23, 343); Chronicon: Constantius 19–20: *Reliquiae apostoli Timothei Constantinopolim inuectae . . . Constantio Romam ingresso ossa Andreae apostoli et Lucae euangelistae a Constantinopolitanis miro fauore suscepta.*

[266] See now D.G. Hunter 'Vigilantius of Calagurris and Victricius of Rouen: Ascetics, Relics and Clerics in Late Antique Gaul' *JECS* 7 (1999) 401–430. Hunter notes that the practice of *translatio* was still officially illegal under *CTh* 9.17.7, issued

ably money for relics; less politically well-placed Christians had to resort to other methods. In mediaeval Europe a whole trade in dubiously acquired relics developed, with unscrupulous dealers like Chaucer's Pardoner passing off pillow cases and pigs' bones as genuine relics.[267] The only ways a newly Christian site had of acquiring relics, as analysed by Geary, were by purchase, gift, *inventio* or theft.[268] The power struggle among different monasteries was often expressed by the sacred theft, for the owners of the relics could thereby increase their status. The problems of the dating of events in the *vita Hilarionis* have already been noted above. In some episodes it is clear that Jerome is writing about early fourth-century events from his own late fourth-century stance. Both Salamis-Constantia and Maiumas-Constantia were new Christian foundations, Salamis being re-built as a Christian city after mid-fourth century earthquakes. It became the seat of the Bishop Epiphanius, a most belligerent and political man, friend and patron of Jerome, and the author of the version of the *vita Hilarionis* that Jerome used for his source. It was obviously very much in Epiphanius' interests in his search for status to have a tomb of Hilarion in Cyprus. But Jerome was obviously aware of the rival claims of Maiumas, which had been given independent status as a Christian city and made a bishopric by Constantine, only to have its status revoked by Julian the Apostate. The inhabitants then applied to the next Christian emperor to regain their status. In this context, a tomb of Hilarion would have been a useful card to hold for the local inhabitants here also. A tomb of Hilarion near

---

in 386 in Constantinople, and that imperial permission had to be obtained for relic transfer.

[267] P. Geary *Furta Sacra*, (Princeton, 1990²) and cf. Augustine *de opere monachorum* 28, (*PL* 40, 575): *alii membra martyrum, si tamen martyrum, venditant.*

Cf. *The Works of Geoffrey Chaucer* (ed. F.N. Robinson, Oxford, 1957²): *General Prologue to the Canterbury Tales* pp. 23–4, ll. 694–700:

For in his male he hadde a pilwe-beer
Which that he seyde was Oure Lady veyl;
He seyde he had a gobet of the seyl
That seint Peter hadde, whan that he wente
Upon the see, til Jhesu Christ hym hente.
He hadde a croys of latoun ful of stones,
And in a glas he hadde pigges bones.

[268] The head of Jerome himself at Nepi (other heads were sited in the Escorial and at Cluny) was claimed to have been stolen from S. Maria Maggiore in 1527 during the sack of Rome: qv. Rice (*op. cit.* n. 264 above) pp. 57–8 and n. 24.

Gaza is noted by the pilgrim from Piacenza in the sixth century and has been identified from a fragmentary inscription on the Madeba map.[269] There is no evidence other than Jerome for the story of the sacred theft of Hilarion's mortal remains, but such deeds were certainly not uncommon: this appears to have been one of the first Christian thefts recorded.[270] There would have been good political reason for it. Jerome's discomfort with the situation, given his friendship with Epiphanius, is evident. A 'singular rivalry' *miram . . . contentionem* grew up between the people of Palestine and the people of Cyprus, the former claiming to possess Hilarion's body, the latter his spirit, he writes.[271] Jerome eventually comes down on the side of the empty tomb in Cyprus, where, he says, and we may be sure the locals claimed, more miracles took place than in Palestine 'perhaps because that place was dearer to [Hilarion].'

There are, of course, echoes here of Jesus in the empty tomb in the garden. And although the people of Palestine have the physical remains, it is the people of Cyprus who have the spirit—for Jerome, the land of Palestine, albeit physical site of holiness, no longer has the monopoly on miracles now the Church has spread to other places in the Roman world.

---

[269] Ant. Placentius 33 (*CCSL* 175, 145) *Ad secundum miliarium Gazae requiescit sanctus pater Hilario.* Madeba Map: sect. IX (black), no 126: E. Alliata *et al.* 'The Legends of the Madeba Map' in M. Piccirillo, E. Alliata (eds.) *The Madeba Map Centenary 1897–1997: Travelling through the Byzantine Ummayad Period* (Jerusalem, 1999) 93.

[270] There are, however, pagan precedents: Herodotus (i, 67) records the trick by which the Spartans obtained the bones of Orestes from Tegea, and Plutarch (*Theseus* 36) tells how Kimon found the bones of Theseus and brought them back to Athens: both are noted by Pausanias (3.3.9). I am grateful to Andrew Jacobs for this reference. In view of Jerome's knowledge of the *aggadot* about Rabbi Shim'on bar Yohai discussed in chapter 1, it is interesting to note that the Pesiqta deRav Kahana records a dispute over the body of R El'azar, the son of R Shim'on, when the inhabitants of Meron stole the body from Giscala on the Day of Atonement, after R Shim'on appeared to them in a dream. (There is a parallel in the BT Bava Metzia 84b.) The Pesiqta is dated to the fifth century by G. Stemberger *Introduction to the Talmud and Midrash* (Edinburgh, 1996²), but B.-Z. Rosenfeld 'R. Simeon b. Yohai: wonder worker and magician: scholar, *saddiq* and *hasid*' *REJ* 158 (1999) 361 and bibliography *ad loc.* suggests there are indications for dating the redaction of this particular episode 'even to the fourth century.'

[271] *vH* 47. The discomfort of the translator Sister Marie Liguori Ewald with this episode is evident: she translates *miram . . . contentionem* as a 'wonderful and *holy* rivalry.'

Summary

To sum up, in his *vita Hilarionis* Jerome presents a picture of the process of the christianisation of the Roman world. For him, the world of literature was a vital part of this world which the Christian must come to terms with. This entailed the appropriation of one of the most popular and threatening forms of literature, the ancient novel. Jerome takes the central event of Apuleius' novel, *Golden Ass*, the conversion of the hero to an ass, and uses it as a metaphor for his Christian hero. Not only does the hero, Hilarion overtly compare himself to an ass but the *vita Hilarionis* as a whole contains many parallels to Apuleius. There are parallels in background and contents, on both micro and macro levels, as well as shared images; there are even biographical parallels between the lives of both Jerome and Apuleius, both of whom are to some extent identified with their heroes. I have tried to show how part of this Christian *vita* is written in deliberate counterpoint to Apuleius' pagan pornographic novel. Thus Jerome succeeded in converting this literary form and creating his new Christian genre of hagiography written in Latin.

Jerome was also concerned with Roman society. Hilarion, like Jerome, fails to distance himself from the Roman world around him and so the *vita Hilarionis* is also a portrayal of the holy man and his relationship to society. Jerome seems deliberately to have included representatives from almost all classes and occupations as the *dramatis personae* of his *vita*. He shows the holy man relating more successfully to people outside the traditional Roman establishment, to Syriac speakers rather than to Greek speakers, and in this context it is significant that for Jerome the term *semi-barbarus* refers to language rather than to culture. The *vita* is set at a time when the civic and secular powers of the church were less developed than in Jerome's own day: bishops appear only in marginal areas. Hilarion, the holy man, in contrast, is explicitly compared with a Roman *dux*, and implicitly with the Jewish patriarch. The *vita* shows the Roman world in transition to becoming a Christian world, and the Christian world developing to accommodate it. Christians had begun by refusing to allow baptism to civic officials: Jerome shows Hilarion giving help to a Christian civic official to carry out the duties forced upon him. A similar change is recorded in the contemporary version of the Apostolic Constitutions produced in Antioch, which has other parallels to the *vita Hilarionis*. Christians and pagans inevitably came into conflict during this transition, and Jerome expresses this excitingly in a chariot race between the supporters of Christ and the supporters of Marnas, the local god of Gaza. Here the Christians win, but it is clear this is not a complete victory. Hilarion also confronts other pagan cults—Venus/Lucifer at Elusa and at Paphos is mentioned by name but the cult of Cadmus in Illyria is only implicit. Chariots—real, demonic and metaphorical—appear several times in the *vita Hilarionis*, and are used to signify the forces of evil overcome by the Christian saint, just as the chariots of Pharoah were defeated at the Red Sea in the book of Exodus.

The fourth century was a time when Christian holy places were being established in the Holy Land and other parts of the empire. Jerome shows some of the complexities of this process in this *vita*: there are allusions to the competing identifications of the site of Melita, and he begins the creation of a new Christian geography with an eponymous heroine at Constantia. He also records one of the first Christian examples of the *furta sacra*—the theft of the remains of the saint, and the competing claims of those who had his body in Palestine and those who had his spirit in Cyprus, coming down on the side of the spirit and thus making it clear that the physical Holy Land alone could no longer contain the spread of Christianity.

The conflict between body and spirit leads us now to the next chapter and the *vita Malchi*. The subject of this *vita* is once more intimately connected to Jerome's own life: the ascetic saint's struggle with his own body, a struggle Jerome had already described graphically relating to himself.[272] Malchus, like Jerome, begins with a failed attempt at monasticism, and again like Jerome, ends living chastely side by side with a woman.

---

[272] *Ep.* 22,7. Kelly p. 100 dates this letter to 384.

APPENDIX: *DRAMATIS PERSONAE* OF THE *VITA HILARIONIS*
(Classified, and in order of appearance)

MEN

CHURCHMEN AND OTHER HOLY MEN

episcopus (*vH* 1)

episcopum et confessorem (*vH* 30)

The bishop was the official local leader of the church, parallel to the secular administration, whereas the status of the holy man was unofficial.

The bishops Dracontius and Philo whom Hilarion met in Egypt are mentioned by Athanasius *Historia Arianorum ad monachos* 72 (*PG* 25, 780). There is also a letter of Athanasius to Dracontius, who was most unwilling to be appointed bishop. (*PG* 25, 524–533) Cf. D. Brakke *Athanasius and the politics of asceticism* (Oxford, 1995) 99–110.

congregatione Ecclesiae (*vH* 2)

fratribus (*vH* 3) brothers = monks

monachus (*vH* 3)

beatus Antonius (*vH* 4; 14) Saint Antony of Egypt, subject of the first saint's life in Greek, the *vita Antonii*, attributed to Athanasius. Antony appears in Jerome's *vita Pauli*, where he acknowledges Paul as his predecessor, as well as in the *vita Hilarionis*, where he is the senior monk of Egypt, as Hilarion is the junior in Syria/Palaestina.

servo Dei/Christi (*vH* 14)

presbyter clericorum et monachorum greges (*vH* 30)

diacono Baisano (*vH* 30)
The term clericus was used of priests and deacons, but sometimes included other ranks. See the discussion in the context of Egeria's

contemporary journey in J. Wilkinson *Egeria's travels in the Holy Land*
(Jerusalem/Warminster, 1981²) 32. The deacon Baisanus, like some
of the other *clerici* encountered by Egeria, appears to have had a
further function as a pilgrim guide, for he kept camels for pilgrims
to Saint Antony: *qui locatis dromadibus camelis, ob aquae in eremo penuriam
consuerat euntes ad Antonium ducere.*

prophetam Christianorum (vH 38)

PAGAN HOLY MEN

vatibus Aesculapii (vH 21) See under Aesculapius below.

sacerdos ut erat coronatus (vH 25) Pagan officiants at sacrificial rites were
often crowned. Cf. Pliny xvi,4; Tertullian *de corona* 10 (*PL* 2,89–91)

magus (vH 33)

CIRCUS AND AMPHITHEATRE

gladiatores (vH 7) See 2.2.2b Confrontation with paganism: Christians
and the games for bibliography on gladiators.

agitator (vH 8) circus driver: Cicero *Academica* iv; *CTh* 15,7,7 and cf.
Virgil *Georgics* 1, 273: *agitator aselli* (lit. ass driver) = peasant

auriga (vH 16)

palaestritam (vH 18) wrestler in the *palaestra* = gymnasium This word
is also used by Apuleius in *Met.* i 15.

ARMY

tirunculus (vH 5)

exercitus (vH 6; 41)

legione (vH 18)

candidatus Constantii imperatoris (vH 22) The *candidati* of the emperor
Constantius were a sub-division of the *scholae palatinae*, the imperial

guard, 40 white-uniformed soldiers who formed the emperor's personal bodyguard. They often as here included Germans: *LRE,* 613; 621.

agmen (vH 25)

scutarius (vH 37) lit. shield bearer. Name of a regiment of the imperial guard, *scholae palatinae (LRE* 613). The *scholae palatinae* included the *scholae scutariorum* of which the most senior, the *schola scutariorum prima* had as its shield-emblem the chi-rho, because of which sign Constantine claimed he had won the battle of the Milvian Bridge, which led to the Christianisation of the empire. Cf. D. Woods 'The Emperor Julian and the Passion of Sergius and Bacchus' *JECS* 5 (1997) 345–367 with bibliography *ad loc.*

for *dux* and *comitatus* see below: sv UPPER CLASSES

CITY FUNCTIONARIES

oppidi municeps (vH 20) burgher of a town (as opposed to a city).

duumvirum Gazensem (vH 20) one of the two chief magistrates of the city council (*curia* or *boule*) of Gaza; *LRE* 725. As noted by C.A.M. Glucker *The City of Gaza in the Roman and Byzantine Period* (Oxford, 1987), the presence of a *duumvir* indicates that the city had the status of a Roman *colonia*.

decurionibus Gazae (vH 22) the ten magistrates of the Gaza city council *LRE* 737f. esp. 748 who 'collected and underwrote the imperial levies and taxes, repaired the roads, administered the public post, conscripted recruits for the army, managed the mines—in cities maintained amenities of urban life, in particular the baths and the games.'

apparatoribus (vH 22) servants, esp. public servants or military aides.

cum lictoribus praefecti (vH 33) The prefects with their lictors. Bastiaensen *ad loc.* suggests that the term *praefecti* here is most likely to be the nominative plural referring to the *duumviri* of Gaza accompanied by their lictors in a police function. This seems more likely than seeing it as genitive singular like Rosweyde (com.on *vita Hilarionis, PL*

73) and C.A.M.Glucker *op. cit.*, who thinks it refers to the Prefect of Egypt.

LOWER CLASSES AND SLAVES

latrones (*vH* 3; 4; 12)

eunuchis (*vH* 14) Jerome often notes with great disapproval the use of eunuchs as slaves by the rich; eg in *ep.* 22,16 he refers to the *greges eunuchorum* accompanying rich women, and later refers satirically to the *ordo semivir* cf. also *ep.* 107, 11 on mixed bathing with eunuchs. Eunuchs sometimes attained positions of power and even held high office at court at this time: for an interesting discussion of eunuchs in Late Antique society see J. Matthews *The Roman Empire of Ammianus Marcellinus* (London 1989) 274f.; on Constantine's ban see F. Millar *The Roman Near East 31 BC–AD 337* (Cambridge Mass/London 1993) 213.

pauperes (*vH* 18)

servis (*vH* 22)

vulgus ignobile (*vH* 30)

mendicus (*vH* 36)

servulis (*vH* 37) The diminutive by the fourth century has lost much of its original meaning, and is used sometimes as a stylistic alternative, although it can have a contemptuous tone cf. e.g. *Com. in Soph.* i 15–16 (*CCSL* 76A, 673; *PL* 25, 1419) of Jewish women: *decrepitas mulierculas.*

plebe (*vH* 39)

UPPER CLASSES

consularis (*vH* 13) consular [governor of the province]

Praefecti praetorio (*vH* 14) *LRE* 370. Prefect of the Emperor, 2nd in command to him, ruled group of provinces in the East—Thrace,

Asiana, Pontica and Oriens—even appointed provincial governors *ib.* 372.

Imperatore (vH 22)

duce (vH 25) The *dux* was the chief general: *LRE* 609. There were two *duces* in Africa and seven along the eastern frontier at the end of the reign of Theodosius I (Palestine, Arabia, Phoenice, Syria, Osrhoene, Mesopotamia and Armenia).

comitatu[s] (vH 25) The *comitatus LRE* 366–7 was a migratory body attached to emperor's person, which included some thousands of people, The 'task of billeting the *comitatus* on its journeys must have taxed the energies of the imperial mensores who went ahead to requisition lodgings'. However, this was originally a military term applied to soldiers under the immediate command of the emperor, so it is not by accident that Jerome, who is anyway using this term metaphorically, uses it together with the word *dux* (see above).

Constantius rex (vH 30) In the reign of Constantius II, one of Constantine's three sons, who ruled the Orient from 337 and the whole empire from 350–67.

potentes viri, judices (vH 30)

vir primarius et ditissimus urbis (vH 30) Cf. the official ranks called (*viri*) *clarissimi*—men of senatorial rank, and *perfectissimi*—men of equestrian rank *LRE* 730–1

PAGANS AND BARBARIANS

urbe gentilium (vH 14) Gentiles, together with *graeci*, is used by the Vulgate to translate N.T. Ἕλληνες.

ethnici (vH 20) pagans N.T. ἐθνικοί.

Saxones et Alemanos gens (vH 22) Fustel de Coulanges observed that at this time for many Germans, the Roman army was not an enemy, but a career: *CAH* 13,223.

Saracenorum natio (*vH* 25)

barbaras nationes (*vH* 38) There is a discussion of Jerome's use of the term *barbari*, and in particular *semibarbari*, in the context of the city of Elusa in 2.2.1b of this chapter.

SEAFARERS

piratae (*vH* 21)

naucleri (*vH* 35; 36) The use of the Greek term ναύκληρος, rather than the Latin *navicularis*, links the voyage of Hilarion with that of Paul (Acts 27, 11).

nautae (*vH* 35)

MISCELLANEOUS OCCUPATIONS

medicos (*vH* 15)

interpres (*vH* 22; 30) This was an official function in the multi-lingual society of the east, in government, church and synagogue. The *interpres* in the church translated from Greek to Aramaic or Syriac and sometimes to Latin (Egeria 47, 3–5) and Jerome notes that at Paula's funeral psalms were sung in three languages *ep*. 108, 29: *Graeco, Latino Syroque*. The *meturgeman* in the synagogue translated the Bible from Hebrew to Aramaic: S.D. Fraade 'Rabbinic views on the practice of Targum and multi-lingualism in Jewish Galilee in the third–sixth centuries' in L.I. Levine *The Galilee in Late Antiquity* (NY/ Jerusalem, 1992) 253–288.

negotiatores (*vH* 35; 37)

Judaeo vilia populis scruta vendente (*vH* 38) Cf. Horace *lib*. i, *ep*. 7: *vilia vendentem tunicato scruta popello*. A *scrutarius* was a dealer in second-hand clothes, a trade in which Jews were to be very much involved. Jerome may well be writing metaphorically here, implying that what Jews have to sell, i.e. Judaism, is worthless.

agricolas (*vH* 39)

pastores (*vH* 39)

SCHOOL AND LETTERS

Homerus (*vH* 1) There is no evidence that Jerome had any first hand acquaintance with his works in Greek.

Crispus (*vH* 1) G. Sallustius Crispus, the first century historian, much quoted by Jerome.

grammaticus (*vH* 2) See now Robert A. Kaster *Guardians of Language: The Grammarian and Society in Late Antiquity* (Berkeley/LA/London, 1988). Kaster sees the grammarian as a 'pivotal figure' and the 'role of the grammarian as a guarantor of social as well as cultural continuity' (p. ix). He also discusses his place among the middle classes, his *mediocritas*. He was never a *vir primarius*, but he would educate the children of this group, and be well acquainted with them (132–3).

discipulis (*vH* 25)

magistri (*vH* 34)

poetarum (*vH* 42)

HEROES

Alexander Magnus Macedo (*vH* 1) Alexander the Great. Jerome is here quoting Sallust. The similarity of this passage to the *SHA Life of Probus* has given rise to a scholarly debate as to whether Jerome used the *Historia Augusta* or vice versa: T.D. Barnes 'Jerome and the "Historia Augusta"' in *Historiae Augustae Colloquium Parisinum* (edd. G. Bonamente, N. Duval, Macerata, 1991) 22f.

Achillis (*vH* 1) Achilles, hero of the *Iliad*.

BIBLICAL CHARACTERS

Daniel (*vH* 1) the prophet Daniel

Joannis (*vH* 1) John the Baptist

Geizi (*vH* 19) Gehazi, servant of Elisha (II Kings 5:20–27)

PAGAN GODS

Consus (*vH* 11; 4; 20) The Roman god associated with the circus. Cf. Cicero *Rep.* ii, 7, 12; Ovid *Fasti* iii 199f.; Varro *de ling. lat.* v; Tertullian *de spect* 5.

Marnas (*vH* 14;20) Zeus/Marnas was the local god of Gaza: see discussion above, 2.2.2b: Confrontations with three cults.

Aesculapii (*vH* 21) Aesculapius was the god of medicine, and is set by Jerome as against Jesus as the true healer.

Venus/Lucifer (*vH* 25). Venus the pagan goddess of love and sex was the antithesis of Christian asceticism. For Venus worshipped as Lucifer by the Saracens cf. *Com. in Amos* (*CCSL* 76, II, v, 25–27, 296; *PL* 25, 1106). There was a cult of the naked Venus in late antique Gaza: cf. *vita Porphyrii* 59; For Hilarion's symbolic conquest of the unchaste Venus of Paphos, see discussion above, 2.2.2b: Confrontations with three cults.

WOMEN

UPPER CLASSES

matronalis pompae (*vH* 14)

Aristaenete uxor praefecti praetorio (*vH* 29) Aristaenete, wife of the praetorian prefect, Elpidius. She is discussed in 2.2.1b: Elpidius and Aristaenete.

Constantia (*vH* 44) Constantia is discussed above in 2.2.3b: An eponymous Christian heroine.

LOWER OR UNDIFFERENTIATED CLASSES

mulier sterilis (*vH* 13) There are many episodes of women being cured of barrenness, in both the Hebrew Bible (e.g. Sarah, Rachel, Hannah, the Shunamite woman etc.) and the New Testament (many miracles of Jesus).

ancillulis (vH 14)

caeca mulier (vH 15)

HOLY WOMEN

virginem Dei (vH 21) In the fourth century women 'dedicated themselves to God' through a public profession of their intention to preserve their virginity. Some sources imply a quasi-legal obligation. qv
S. Elm *Virgins of God: The making of asceticism in antiquity* (Oxford, 1996).

sancta femina (vH 44)

sanctissime mulieris (vH 47)

WOMEN AS SEXUAL BEINGS

nudae mulieres cubanti (vH 7)

raptum Sabinarum (vH 20) An account of the famous legend of the
rape of the Sabine women is to be found together with the rites of
the god Consus in Varro, *de lingua latina* v.

matronarum Christianarum (grandis tentatio) (vH 30) For Jerome's condemnation of Christian women at Rome for their unchaste relationships with church men, see e.g. *ep.* 22, 28.

CHAPTER THREE

THE *VITA MALCHI*: JEROME'S CHRISTIAN
APPROPRIATION OF THE HUMAN BODY

INTRODUCTION

The previous chapter examined Jerome's portrayal of the saint and
his relationship with society, indeed with the whole Roman world.
The *vita Hilarionis* ended with contention over the body and spirit
of Hilarion. Jerome uses this as a metaphor for the conflict between
matter and spirit, to show us that the spirit of Christianity has now
outgrown its origins in the Holy Land and must spread over the
whole world. But the body, as Jerome himself found, is not so easily subdued. The *vita Malchi* is about a monk's ascetic struggle to
subdue his own body and achieve complete sexual abstinence. It has
been described (by a Jesuit) as a 'paean in praise of life-long chastity.'[1]

Jerome tells us that he actually met the monk Malchus, the hero
of the *vita Malchi*, in person, and heard his story from his own mouth.
There seems little reason to doubt this, but the story has been written up in the form of a new literary creation, more tightly controlled
than the lengthy and rather rambling *vita Hilarionis*. Jerome sets his
hero against an apparently realistic background of fourth century
Mesopotamia, but this apparent realism is interwoven with metaphorical and stereotypical material. This background too is charged with
sexuality, in order to set off Malchus' victory in subjugating his body.
This chapter will attempt to unravel Jerome's closely knit fabric using
contemporary local material from Ammianus and the Babylonian
Talmud. We will also see how he makes use of both biblical and
classical models to make up his picture of the ascetic subjugation of
sexuality, which once again contains many autobiographical elements.

---

[1] Kelly, 171. *Contra*: S. Rubenson 'Philosophy and Simplicity: the problem of
classical education in early Christian biography' in *Greek Biography and Panegyric in
Late Antiquity* (eds. T. Hägg, P. Rousseau, Berkeley etc., 2000) 122: 'the entire story
is told not to edify but to amuse.'

I shall attempt to disentangle reality from metaphor, stereotype and prejudice to see how Jerome achieves his end:

> *ut sciant, inter gladios et inter deserta et bestias pudicitiam nunquam esse capti-vam.*[2]

Summary of vita Malchi

The *vita Malchi monachi captivi* tells of Malchus, a *colonus*[3] of Nisibis at the very edge of the Roman empire in the East, some time in the mid fourth century. Jerome says he actually met Malchus in his old age and heard his story from his own mouth.[4] Malchus, an only son, flees from home when pressed by his family to marry and produce an heir, since he preferred to remain chaste and become a monk. Thus he joins a community in the desert of Chalcis,[5] to the south of Antioch, hundreds of kilometres from Nisibis and in a different province. However, after years in the monastery he decides to return home to claim his patrimony. His abbot, of course, is most

---

[2] *vita Malchi* 10: that they [sc. posterity] may know that purity is never taken captive amid sword, and amid deserts and wild beasts (tr. Mierow, 1946).

[3] In the classical period *colonus* was used to mean a husbandman but also a citizen of a *colonia* (Nisibis had received colonial status under the Severans q.v. B. Isaac *Limits of Empire: The Roman Army in the East* (Oxford, 1990[1]) 360 with bibliography *ad loc.*). By the fourth century *colonus* often meant a peasant farmer tied to his land but Malchus was not tied, for he was able to leave for the monastery. Later in the *vita Malchi* Jerome writes of Malchus claiming his inheritance, so his parents evidently owned some property. In his other works Jerome sometimes uses *colonus* to refer to the inhabitants of Paradise, engaged in cultivating its soil eg *epp.* 10, 1; 52, 5, and at other times he seems to use it to mean a settler from outside as opposed to indigenous inhabitants e.g. *Com. in Amos* iii. 8 (*CCSL* 76, 330; *PL* 25, 1134): *non colonus et aduena, sed habitator*. On *coloni* in the fourth century see: *CAH* 13, 287f. (C.R. Whittaker, P. Garnsey); 357 (A. Marcone).

[4] Jerome, writing sometime between 386 and 390, relates that he met Malchus at Antioch and heard his story. There is no reason to disbelieve this, and some of the vivid geographical and historical details may well point to a local source: see below and Kelly 170–2. The events described in the *vita Malchi* as belonging to Malchus' younger days must have taken place at least twenty years earlier if not more. Jerome was in Antioch some time between 373 and 380—the dates are not certain. S. Rebenich *Hieronymus und sein Kreis*, (1992), 76 n. 331; 117–8 n. 571 has a full discussion and bibliography, and see now A.A.R. Bastiaensen 'Jérôme hagiographe' *CC Hagiographies: International History of the Latin and Vernacular Hagiographical Literature in the West from its origins to 1550*, vol. I (Turnhout, 1994) 106.

[5] The classic work on this area in antiquity is still A. Poidebard, P. Mouterde *Le limes de Chalcis: Organisation de la steppe en Haute-Syrie romaine* (Paris, 1945), and see now G.W. Bowersock 'Chalcis ad Belum and Anasartha in Byzantine Syria' in *Travaux et Mémoires: Mélanges Gilbert Dagron* 14 (2002) 47–55.

disapproving and tells him that he has been ensnared by the Devil. But Malchus refuses to listen to his pleas, and his abbot escorts him from the monastery, as he says, as if at his funeral. On his way home Malchus takes the main Roman road which ran from Beroea to Edessa, travelling in a convoy of about seventy souls. But the convoy is attacked by camel-riding Saracens, and Malchus and his companions are taken into captivity by these nomads. Once in captivity Malchus learns to re-appreciate the spiritual life, tending his master's flocks. He is tempted by an enforced marriage to a fellow slave. They are allotted a cave to live in, but she turns out to be Christian too, and married; her own husband was also enslaved, but serving another master. So by mutual agreement Malchus and the woman decide to live together in chaste *contubernium*,[6] without sexual intercourse. Eventually they decide to escape, and after floating down the Euphrates on inflated bladders are pursued by their Saracen master into another cave. Here a lioness saves them miraculously by eating their pursuers. They arrive at a *castra Romana* and finally end their lives in chaste companionship on the estate of Bishop Evagrius near Antioch.

3.1. THE BODY

Introduction

In the *vita Hilarionis* Jerome had used classical pagan sources for his literary reworking of what he claimed was a biography of a real person, basing it on an extant letter by Epiphanius, combined with elements from Apuleius' *Golden Ass*. The *vita Malchi*, in contrast, Jerome says, was based on a story told him by Malchus in person. Few have seen reason to doubt this statement. This *vita* was written, Jerome says, for the chaste about the chaste—and, as goes without saying, by the chaste Jerome: *castis historiam castitatis exposui* (*vMal* 10). Having worked through the process of the Christian takeover of pagan Roman literature, Jerome here presents the Christian takeover of the human body.

Human perception of the body is socially determined,[7] and Jerome

---

[6] *Contubernium:* see below, n. 29.
[7] See on this: B.S. Turner *The Body and Society* (London etc. 1996²) p. 66, not to

is here re-constructing the body through the eyes of a Christian. The *vita Malchi* is about ownership and use of the body by the idealised Christian holy man. With his Roman legal training, Jerome was aware of the legal aspects of ownership of the body.[8] Thus, as will be shown below, he quite deliberately uses Roman legal terminology about body-ownership, and converts it to Christian metaphor.

Looking at the social and cultural background he creates with its perceptions and prejudices about the body and society can enlighten the modern reader about the perceptions of Jerome's contemporary world. Jerome had for many years been an avowed ascetic, abnegating the enjoyment of property, the bodily pleasures of sex and all but the most basic food.[9] Now in the *vita Malchi* he is constructing a blueprint for monastic asceticism not in theory, but in the real context of his late antique world. And even here, where Jerome is using local eyewitness evidence mixed with biblical metaphor, his classical heritage is still present. Virgil, one of his favourite poets,[10] is never far from Jerome's mind: the central episode of Malchus in his cave is constructed in implied contrast to the fourth book of the Aeneid, as will be shown below. Thus this chapter will also be looking at aspects of what Jerome can show us of sex and society, comparing it with contemporary pagan and Jewish conceptions.

---

be confused with: Peter Brown *The Body and Society* (New York, 1988) which traces the development of Jerome's attitudes to sexuality, including the *vita Hilarionis*, but not the *vita Malchi*. The importance of the body in modern discussions of Christianity can be seen from the fact that in the recent *Critical Terms for Religious Studies* (ed. M.C.Taylor, Chicago, 1998) the chapter on 'The Body' (W.R. LaFleur, p. 36f.) comes second after 'Beliefs' and before 'God,' 'Rationality,' 'Relics' etc.

[8] Jerome's legal training: see below, n. 17.

[9] A selection of recent writing on asceticism in general and Jerome's asceticism in particular: D. Brakke *Athanasius and the politics of asceticism* (Oxford, 1995); Peter Brown 'Asceticism: Pagan and Christian' *CAH* 13, 601; E.A. Clark *The Origenist Controversy: The cultural construction of an early Christian debate* (Princeton, 1992); P. Cox Miller 'The Blazing Body: Desire and Language in Jerome's Letter to Eustochium' *JECS* 1 (1993) 21–45; S. Elm *Virgins of God: The making of asceticism in Late Antiquity* (Oxford, 1994); V. Grimm *From Feasting to Fasting, The evolution of a sin: Attitudes to food in late antiquity* (London, 1996), esp. 157f.: 'Jerome and ascetic propaganda;' G.G. Harpham *The Ascetic Imperative in Culture and Criticism* (Chicago, 1987); P. Rousseau *Ascetics, Authority and the Church in the age of Jerome and Cassian* (Oxford, 1978); A. Vööbus *A History of Asceticism in the Syrian Orient* (Louvain, 1960); V.L. Wimbush (ed.) *Ascetic Behavior in Greco-Roman Antiquity* (Minneapolis, 1990); V.L. Wimbush, R. Valantasis *et al. Asceticism* (NY/Oxford, 1995).

[10] H. Hagendahl *Latin Fathers and the Classics* (Göteborg, 1958).

3.1.1. *The body in law*—postliminium[11]

We shall start by looking at legal aspects of ownership of the body in the *vita Malchi*. As already noted above, the *vita* tells of Malchus, a *colonus* of Nisibis in the mid fourth century, renouncing his inheritance and going to become a monk in another province. Later he changes his mind, leaves his monastery and goes back to reclaim his property, but is captured instead. At this point he describes himself as

longo postliminio hereditarius possessor

the legal heir by long right of *postliminium*, who is now by contrast reduced to servitude.[12]

The Roman legal concept of *postliminium* is defined for us by Cicero[13] as well as in the Theodosian Code of laws.[14] These both make it clear that any Roman captured by the enemy was considered as legally dead—however, if he managed to escape he could come back and exercise the right of *postliminium* and reclaim his title to his property.[15]

It would seem at first glance that here there is a different use of the legal term, for Malchus simply moved province when he entered the monastery and was not captured by the enemy. A different *local* use of the term *postliminium* would seem unlikely, in view of the fact

---

[11] A more detailed treatment of this episode and the concept of *postliminium* is to be found in my paper: S. Weingarten '*Postliminium* in Jerome: A Roman legal term as Christian metaphor' *SCI* 14 (1995) 143–150.

[12] *vita Malchi* 4.

[13] Cicero: *Topica* 8, 36 *Scaevola autem P.F. iunctum putat esse verbum, ut sit in eo et post et limen; ut, quae a nobis alienata, cum ad hostem pervenerint, ex suo tamquam limine exierint, hinc ea cum redierint post ad idem limen, postliminio redisse videantur.*

[14] *Cod. Theod.* 5, 7 Mommsen and Meyer: *de postliminio* (dated 366): *Si quos forte necessitas captivitatis abduxit, sciant, si non transierunt, sed hostilis inruptionis necessitate transducti sunt, ad proprias terras festinare debere recepturos iure postliminii ea, quae in agris vel mancipiis ante tenuerunt, sive a fisco nostro possideantur, sive in aliquem principali liberalitate transfusa sunt. Nec timeat quisquam alicuius contradictionis moram, cum hoc solum requirendum sit, utrum aliquis cum barbaris voluntate fuerit an coactus.*

[15] For a discussion of the Roman legal concept of *postliminium* and bibliography on the subject, see P. Varon, '*Ius postliminii* and the soldier' in *Roman Frontier Studies 1989: Proceedings of the XVth International Congress of Roman Frontier Studies*, (edd. V.A. Maxfield & M.J. Dobson, Exeter, 1991) 407–409. To the bibliography cited there may be added the discussion of the development of the concept at an earlier period to be found in A. Watson, *The Law of Persons in the Later Roman Republic* (Oxford, 1967) 162–163; 237f. I am grateful to Perlina Varon for introducing me to this subject.

that Ammianus at almost the same time and in almost the same place (the environs of Nisibis) uses the term as it appears in the Theodosian Code.[16] Mere carelessness is also to be ruled out in view of Jerome's own evidence of his legal training.[17]

Another work by Jerome, the preface to his translation of Didymus' treatise *de Spiritu Sanctu*,[18] gives a clue. Here Jerome writes *metaphorically* of his own flight from Rome to Jerusalem as his return from captivity in Babylon (quoting Ps. 137) *velut postliminio*—he is reclaiming his spiritual inheritance in the celestial Jerusalem, for at this time he had not yet visited the earthly city and thus could only return metaphorically. The use of *postliminium* here within a metaphor in a work written at almost the same time,[19] alerts us to the possibility that in the *vita Malchi* too, Jerome is using the term spiritually.

Thus turning back again to the *vita Malchi*, it is now clear that Jerome is saying that in leaving his monastery and attempting to reclaim his earthly property Malchus has fallen into the power of the arch-enemy—Satan—and is thus regarded as dead by his abbot. Malchus' spiritual return is brought about by his subsequent capture by Saracen nomads, which leads him to return to the true values of his monastery. Paradoxically, the physical enslavement of his body leads to his spiritual liberation and rehabilitation. This is the heir returning from the dead to reclaim his heavenly portion by *postliminium*. Jerome has taken a Roman legal term and used it to enrich the various levels of Christian metaphor in his story. The body of the Christian saint, he shows us here, has a legal right to its spiritual inheritance.

---

[16] Ammianus: 19, 9, 6–8.
[17] For Jerome's legal training see e.g. *Apol. contra Ruf.* 1, 30, (*CCSL* 79, 30) and Introduction: Jerome's Life. For Jerome's legal concepts see: G. Violardo *Il pensiero giuridico di San Girolamo* (Roma, 1937). However, Violardo does no more than mention Jerome's use of *postliminium*.
[18] *In Didymum de Spiritu Sancto*: Praef. (*PL* 23, 101–103). It is interesting to note that Jerome here describes *himself* as a *colonus* of Babylon (*i.e.* of Rome, the scarlet whore) cf. n. 3 above.
[19] Cavallera II, 27, *contra* Kelly 142; 170. Jerome uses the same image of wiping rust off his tongue in both the *vita Malchi* and the translation of Didymus; both seem to have been written after the long silence due to his travels.

3.1.2. *Christian and pagan bodies*

The *vita Malchi*, Jerome tells us, is based on the Syrian Malchus' own account: perhaps it is because of this that there are no direct citations from Latin literature which might look incongruous. However, Jerome does use Virgil's pagan material to provide an opposing contrast and a countertext against which to construct Malchus, his Christian hero. This material would, of course, have been very familiar to Jerome's Roman audience, whom he could have expected to pick up his allusions.

De Vogüé has noted that the episode of Malchus and his woman companion in the cave is reminiscent of and opposed to the episode of Dido and Aeneas in the cave in book iv of Virgil's Aeneid.[20] His is just a brief note, however, and de Vogüé does not analyse either the structural or the verbal parallels. The structural parallels are considerable, for Jerome creates a series of antitheses opposed one by one to the elements of the Aeneid narrative. There are verbal parallels too, not with the actual very brief episode of Dido and Aeneas in the cave in Aeneid book iv, 165–172, but with Dido's deliberations with herself at the beginning of this same book (iv, 9f.).[21] Virgil begins with a speech by Dido, who has sworn to be true to the memory of her dead husband, but is now wavering because of the love Aeneas has awakened in her. Dido addresses her own *pudor*, her feelings of shame and propriety (iv, 27). At first she intends to keep firm, but love for Aeneas inflames her soul: *animum inflammant amore* (*ib*. 54) and causes her to abandon her modesty: *solvit pudorem* (*ib*. 55).[22]

In Jerome's story, Malchus is provided with a wife by his Saracen master who forces them into a cave to consummate their union. In his cave Malchus addresses his *anima*:[23] *Quid agimus anima?* What do we do, my soul? And in contrast to Dido he replies that it is better for his body *corp[us]* to die, preserving his chastity, his *pudicitia*.[24]

---

[20] De Vogüé *Histoire littéraire du mouvement monastique dans l'Antiquité: Première partie: Le monachisme latin ** de l'itinéraire d'Égérie à l'éloge funèbre de Népotien (384–396)* (Paris, 1993), 91. De Vogüé merely notes the parallel between the *spelunca* of Malchus and that of Aeneas.

[21] It is presumably because the verbal parallels are with Dido's earlier speech that de Vogüé missed them, even though he picked up Jerome's structural parallels.

[22] Jerome quotes from Anna's speech to Dido (*loc. cit.* 32–34) in *ep.* 123, 13.

[23] *vMal.* 6.

[24] On *pudor/pudicitia*, see: R.A. Kaster 'The Shame of the Romans' *TAPA* 127

His companion, at first an *infelix mulier*, just as Dido is *infelix Dido* (*Aen* iv, 68), becomes the wife of his chastity *conjugem pudicitiae*, while the unchaste union of Dido and Aeneas is only *called* a marriage by Dido: *conjugium vocat* (*ib.* 172). Following their union in the cave, Aeneas prepares to leave Dido, and Virgil describes his men scurrying to depart as being like a colony of ants (*ib.* 402–407). The episode in the cave in the *vita Malchi* is also followed by a description of a colony of ants which Malchus observes, and from which he draws a Christian lesson (*vMal* 7).[25] Hagendahl has pointed out the close verbal similarities between these two passages about ants.[26]

Thus Malchus is prepared to kill himself in order not to marry: instead he kills his desire for his companion's body and takes control over his own, even in her presence. Sex is transferred to the mind:

> *magis animae copulam amato quam corporis.*

This is the central event in this *vita* written to display *castitas*. By denying himself sexual use of his own body, the Christian hero has taken over his own body for asceticism. It is no accident that his woman companion is unnamed: she is Christian womankind in general, who must submit to her fate of marriage if necessary. Having married she must then renounce all other sexual contact—but this is her duty, and therefore not so commendable as the unmarried male saint's voluntary renunciation.

In the Aeneid, Dido finally kills herself because of her desire. Recently it has been argued that the human body 'lies at the centre of the narrative of the Aeneid.' Analysing and summarising Angus Bowie's discussion of 'Dido, Aeneas and the body as a sign,' D. Montserrat writes that 'bodies in the Aeneid are a metaphor for decoding the text itself; the reader's desire to explore Virgil's bodies parallels their desire to master the text's symbolic system.'[27] While

---

(1997) 1f. esp. 9–10: 'women certainly possessed a capacity for *pudor* but it was largely limited to a single frame of reference, the sexual: the *pudor* of women is, in effect, congruent with their *pudicitia*, or sexual respectability . . . *Pudicitia* . . . reduces *pudor* to the appropriate gender roles of both sexes.'

[25] On Augustine's Christian use of this passage, see S. MacCormack *The shadows of poetry: Virgil in the mind of Augustus* (Berkelely/LA/London, 1998) 94.

[26] H. Hagendahl *Latin Fathers and the Classics* (Göteborg, 1958) 118.

[27] D. Monserrat (ed.) *Changing Bodies: Changing Meanings: Studies on the Human Body in Antiquity* (London/NY, 1998) introduction p. 7, referring to A. Bowie *'Exuvias effigiemque*: Dido, Aeneas and the body as a sign' *op. cit.* 57f.

I would not go quite as far as Bowie in seeing Virgil's epic as cen-
tering on the human body, it is clear that the episode of Dido and
Aeneas was a very important and moving part of the Aeneid for
readers in late antiquity—Augustine records that he wept over Dido.[28]
And the bodies of Dido and Aeneas are indeed central to their story
within the poem, just as the bodies of Malchus and his companion
are central to the *vita Malchi*. If we set the two accounts side by side
we can see the contrasts and oppositions:

MALCHUS AND HIS 'WIFE'	AENEAS AND DIDO
Venus worshipped by Saracens—negative	Venus seen positively as mother of Aeneas—helps him and Dido

cave scene

rejection of sexual union	consummation of sexual union
marriage of soul, not body	sin [of body] rather than marriage
obedience to duty	dereliction of duty

subsequent life

contubernium[29]	parting

It is a magnificent paradox[30] that whereas consummation of sexual
union is followed by parting (and Dido's suicide)[31] for Dido and

---

[28] Augustine *Conf.* I, xiii, 20. See on this S. MacCormack, *op. cit.* n. 25 above, chapter 3, 'the tears run down in vain': emotions, soul and body' 89f., esp. 90. On Virgil and the body see also: P. Heuzé *L'image du corps dans l'oeuvre de Virgile* (Rome, 1985), on real and imaginary bodies: 1–2; on Dido's body and its betrayal of her 'moral degradation,' 515f.

[29] *Contubernium* was originally used of soldiers living together in the same tent. It then became used of other forms of living together, including concubinage and other non-legalized marriages, especially of slaves, as opposed to *conubium*, legal marriage (L&S).

[30] On paradox as a feature of Christian rhetoric see Averil Cameron *Christianity and the Rhetoric of Empire: The development of Christian discourse* (Berkeley, 1991) 155–88, which includes a useful discussion of Jerome's saints' *Lives*.

[31] On Dido's death, surrounded by curses and magical rites, as a sort of human sacrifice see A.M. Tupet 'Didon magicienne' *REL* 48 (1970) 229f. In contrast, Malchus and his companion are repeatedly saved from death and live long and blessed lives. Jerome also uses the fate of Dido as part of his argument against

Aeneas, rejection of sexual union is followed by living together for the rest of their lives for Malchus and his companion. Malchus, of course, will go to Heaven: Aeneas later meets Dido in Hades.[32] Jerome has underlined his narrative of the Christian takeover of the body for asceticism by setting it against the contrasting background of one of the most famous pagan narratives, and he makes clear the Christian victory. Ascetic renunciation has its compensations.

3.2. Distinguishing Biblical Metaphor from Local Setting

Jerome's account of the Christian appropriation of the body in the *vita Malchi* is set against the background of fourth century Syria and Mesopotamia. As with the other *vitae*, it is not always easy to separate Jerome's accounts of fourth century *realia* from his biblical metaphors or contemporary stereotypes. 3.2 will attempt to separate out biblical aspects while 3.3 will look at *realia* vis à vis contemporary stereotypes.

3.2.1. *Biblical typology in Jerome's saints' Lives*

We have already seen how Jerome makes use of the Christian habit of typological comparisons to express various aspects of his saintly heroes.[33] The *vita Pauli* mentions types of Paul the hermit explicitly in the narrative: the prophet Elijah, John the Baptist and Jesus, all of whom are strongly associated with asceticism and the desert. In the *vita Hilarionis*, the narrative of the saint, his travels all over the Mediterranean world and his contacts with pagan society are modelled on the type of the Apostle Paul, who also travelled around the Mediterranean on his missions to the gentiles. Hilarion's prototypes also include Adam in paradise and Elisha. Elisha indeed is used to express various aspects of the saint: his taking over the succession

---

remarriage in his letter to Geruchia (*ep.* 123): quoting *Aen.* iv 548–552, he writes: *proponis mihi gaudia nuptiarum; ego tibi opponam pyram, gladium, incendium.*

[32] Bowie also notes the use made of Aeneas' sword in the Aeneid: a sword three times fails to harm Malchus in the *vita Malchi*: his master's sword in *vMal* 6 and again in *vMal* 9, and his own sword in *vMal* 6. The sexual overtones of the sword are made clear by the description of his master's sword on both occasions: *evaginato gladio.*

[33] Cf. Rom. 5:14. Jerome discusses the typology of a number of Biblical figures (but none of those under discussion here, unfortunately) in his *ep.* 53.

from Antony/Elijah, his relationship with the rich widow who is the
type of Aristaenete, the wife of the *praefectus praetorii Orientis*.[34] Hilarion's
relationship with his disciple Hadrian is also built on that of Elisha
and Gehazi, his greedy disciple who accepted gifts.[35] Some of these
types are explicitly named in the text, others are just implied, to be
inferred by the biblically well-read reader.[36] In *ep.* 108 the relationship between Jerome and his widowed friend Paula is also partly
modeled on the relationship between Elisha and the widow. In the
vita Malchi, once again, there are named types: Jacob and Moses as
faithful shepherds (*vita Malchi* 5), with Jesus the Good Shepherd to
be inferred. But there is another very interesting Biblical type implicit
in Jerome's text, the patriarch Jacob's son Joseph. Malchus is taken
captive by camel-riding Saracens, also called Ishmaelites, and as de
Vogüé has noted:

"Ismaelite" fait penser à la captivité du chaste Josèphe.[37]

The significance of this for the plot of the *vita Malchi* will be discussed below. The biblical Joseph became the Christian type of
chastity as he refused the sexual advances of Potiphar's wife;[38] he
was also a type of Jesus, being sold for pieces of silver.

3.2.2. *Biblical metaphor or local setting?*

The discussion of the *vita Pauli* in chapter 1 demonstrated how
Jerome's picture of the Egyptian setting in which Paul lived has some
elements which are paralleled in Jerome's own Syrian setting, and
could have been based on his local knowledge, rather than his vivid
imagination, as some scholars have suggested.[39] The *vita Malchi* is set

---

[34] For this see Appendix to chapter 2 on the *vita Hilarionis*.

[35] II[IV] Kings 5.20–27; *vHil* 34, and cf. *vHil* 18 where Gehazi [Giezi] is actually mentioned by name.

[36] It is not always possible to be sure which Bible stories were known to Jerome's
audience. However, some stories are found depicted in fourth century art in the
catacombs and on sarcophagi—the ascent of Elijah to heaven in a fiery chariot,
for example. We can assume that others were widely known from references to
them in the accounts of other fourth century pilgrims, such as the Traveller from
Bordeaux (see below, chapter 4) who includes a variety of references to stories about
Elijah and Elisha. See on this S. Weingarten 'Was the pilgrim from Bordeaux a
woman? A reply to Laurie Douglass' *JECS* 7 (1999) 291–297.

[37] de Vogüé (*op. cit.* n. 20 above) 88–9, referring to Gen. 37: 25–28.

[38] Gen. 39: 7–21.

[39] See above on *vPauli*: chapter 1.2.1.

partly in the Syrian desert which Jerome had himself experienced, and partly further away in Mesopotamia towards the border with Persia,[40] as Malchus says:

> *ad Orientem ire non poteram propter vicinam Persidem* (*vita Malchi* 3).

What is more, Jerome says that much of the description is based on the eyewitness evidence of Malchus himself, whom Jerome met as an old man and from whom he heard his story.[41] Thus it is not surprising that there should be some elements which can be paralleled in other sources dealing with this area. However, although on the one hand, apparently lurid details in Jerome's saints' *Lives* are not always spurious exaggerations, on the other hand, apparent details of fourth-century daily life should not always be taken at their face-value. Jerome interweaves biblical material in his text so that his writing often has the quality of cinema, whereby the action of his story flashes back and forth between biblical narrative and the circumstances of the fourth century. Thus Malchus took the main Roman road which ran from Beroea to Edessa, travelling in a convoy of 'about seventy souls' (*vita Malchi* 4). The convoy was attacked by camel-riding Saracens armed with bows and spears, and Malchus and his companions were taken into captivity by these nomads (*ib.*). The Roman road from Beroea to Edessa certainly exists—archaeologists have measured and photographed it.[42] So scholars have usually taken this episode as fairly realistic: Matthews notes 'its vivid and on the whole persuasive detail,' and compares Jerome's Saracens to those of Ammianus (14.4), where he has warned against abandoning all as mere stereotypes. Millar, while cautious about the 'stereotypical and over-dramatised elements' takes it as a 'genuine reflection of social contrasts and conflicts at the edge of the steppe.'[43]

---

[40] By this he meant the Sassanian part of Iraq, not modern Persia. See on this B. Isaac 'Rome and Persia' in 'The Eastern Frontier' *CAH* 13, 437f.

[41] On ancient historians' use of 'eyewitness evidence' see J. Marincola *Authority and tradition in ancient historiography* (Cambridge, 1997) 63f. and G. Frank *The Memory of the Eyes: Pilgrims to Living Saints in Christian Late Antiquity* (Univ. of California, 2000).

[42] See R. Dussaud, *Topographie historique de la Syrie antique et médiévale* (Paris, 1927), map xiv, with V. Chapot, *La Frontière de l'Euphrate de Pompée à la conquête arabe* (Paris, 1907), ch. v esp. 342, and for photographs and sections of the continuation of this road west of Immae: A. Poidebard, 'Coupes de la chassée romaine Antioche-Chalcis' *Syria* 10 (1929) 22–29. The road appears on the Peutinger Map, and was used by Jerome's contemporary, the pilgrim Egeria: *It. Egeriae* 18, 2 (*CCSL* 175,59).

[43] F. Millar *The Roman Near East 31 BC–AD 337* (Cambridge, Mass/London 1993) 484–5.

Piccirillo notes the similarity of Jerome's 'Arabs, Ishmaelites and Saracens' to a late antique mosaic in the church of Kaianus at 'Uyun Musa in present-day Jordan showing an Arab camel driver.[44] Only Opelt is dubious, seeing the camels in particular as part of the marvels of the east added for western audiences.[45] But the convoy of 'about seventy souls' should remind the reader of the seventy souls who went down to Egypt with the patriarch Jacob, in the story of Joseph in the book of Genesis.[46] Now the biblical text in Genesis has seventy souls, while Acts gives the number who accompanied Jacob as seventy-five. There was considerable rabbinic discussion on how this number was made up. So Jerome's 'about seventy'—*circiter septuaginta*—while looking like a vague estimate, is in fact a very exact biblical reference, showing he knew of the controversy surrounding this number.[47] The biblical allusion is underlined by Jerome's turning the Saracens into 'Ishmaelites' at the very point when they take Malchus captive, reminding his audience of the camel-riding Ishmaelites who took Joseph captive in the book of Genesis.[48] Joseph, as already noted, is a Christian type of *castitas*, and thus serves to underline Jerome's interest in the Christian ascetic body.

Jerome, then, at his apparently most realistic, has interwoven biblical types into his world picture. He later makes this even more clear, explicitly comparing Malchus to Jacob and Moses (*vita Malchi* 5).[49]

---

[44] M. Piccirillo *The Mosaics of Jordan* (Amman, 1993) 40. Piccirillo identifies the camel driver as Christian Arab Ghassanid on the basis of parallels with Ammianus and Jerome, as well as Safaitic and Thamudic graffiti of the desert.

[45] I. Opelt 'Des Hieronymus Heiligenbiographien als Quellen der Historischen Topographie des östlichen Mittelmeerraums' *Römische Quartalschrift für christliche Altertumskunde und Kirchengeschichte* 74 (1979) 151.

[46] Gen. 46:27; Acts 7:14. The area around Carrhae, south east of the Beroea-Edessa road is noted by Egeria in 384 for its associations with the patriarchs: Egeria was shown the well where Jacob met Rachel tending her sheep *qui puteus sexto milliario est a Charris*: It. *Egeriae* 21, 1 (*CCSL* 175,65). See P. Maraval *Égérie: Journal de voyage (Itinéraire)*, 1972 for discussion and bibliography.

[47] Jerome discusses this problem in *QHG ad loc.* (*CCSL* 72, 49; *PL* 23, 1001f.) including the fact that the LXX is also inconsistent—once saying 75 and once 70.

[48] Gen. 37: 25–28 cf. de Vogüé *op. cit.* 88–9 cited in n. 20 *supra*. On the identification of the Saracens with Ishmaelites, see F. Millar 'Hagar, Ishmael, Josephus and the origins of Islam' *JJS* 44 (1993) 23–45.

[49] At the beginning of the *vita* Jerome says Malchus was *Syrus natione et lingua* (*vMal* 2). It is difficult to understand the specific force of *natio* here in the context of the fourth century (q.v. Millar *op. cit.* n. 43 for extensive discussions of Syrian culture at this period, and his paper 'Ethnic identity in the Roman Near East, 325–450: Language, religion and culture' *Mediterranean Archaeology* 11 (1998) 159–176). It is just possible that the description is referring to the biblical context, rather than

The Bible is an inextricable part of his perception of his late antique world.

3.3. Distinguishing *Realia* from Stereotypes

Having looked at how it is possible to distinguish Biblical metaphors from Jerome's account of the real world of Mesopotamia, we turn now to try to disentangle his *realia* from his contemporary stereotypes.

3.3.1. *Realia*

1a. *Local knowledge or literary borrowing? Jerome and Ammianus*
The discussion of Jerome's Saracens has demonstrated that some parts of his description are made up of biblical metaphors. It will be made clear below that he does also use contemporary material, in this case contemporary stereotypes. There are also descriptions of the local material culture which can be paralleled in contemporary written sources, and archaeologically. Thus Malchus and his 'wife' float down the Euphrates using inflated goatskins. There is a parallel to this in Ammianus (*Hist.* 25, 8, 1–2), who has an account of the soldiers of Jovian who escaped pursuit by crossing the Euphrates on inflated bladders in 364 CE. Ammianus was actually present himself in the area: Jerome says Malchus was too. There is also other independent evidence of the use of bladders as a means of transport on the Euphrates.[50] Thus both Jerome and Ammianus are clearly aware of local customs. The relationship between Ammianus and Jerome is unclear,[51] but here they are both writing about the same

---

the fourth century: cf.: Jacob's uncle Laban, whom Jerome describes in his *Hebrew Questions on Genesis* 31.46–7 (*CCSL* 72, 40; *PL* 23, 987): *gentis suae sermone vocavit. Erat enim Syrus et antiquam linguam parentum provinciae, in qua habitabat, sermone mutaverat.* Cf. the discussion of this passage in chapter 1.2.1b above.

[50] The earliest evidence of the use of inflated bladders for transport on the Euphrates comes from an Assyrian relief dated to about 700 BCE. Assyrian soldiers appear to have carried inflatable skins as standard equipment: L. Casson *Ships and Seamanship in the Ancient World* (Princeton, 1971) p. 3. For exhaustive discussion with extensive bibliography, of bladders and *keleks* (rafts made of bladders) in ancient and modern Mesopotamia see M. Tardieu *Les paysages reliques: routes et haltes syriennes d'Isidore à Simplicius* (Louvain/Paris, 1990), ch. 2 coutumes nautîques Mésopotamiennes 71–102; ch. 4 137–147 and plates. For a vivid account in early 20th century Albania cf. Edith Durham *High Albania* (London, 1909 repr. 1985) 179–80.

[51] See J. Matthews *The Roman Empire of Ammianus* (London, 1986) 529–30, citing R. Syme *Ammianus and the Historia Augusta* (Oxford, 1968) 19 and Alan Cameron's

part of the world, at the same time, with the same details. Furthermore, there are a number of other parallels between Jerome's *vita Malchi* and the later books of Ammianus. As already noted, both deal with the area of Nisibis and the border with the Persians;[52] both recount an episode about the use of the legal term *postliminium*;[53] both recount (in the first person) an exiting escape and pursuit by night;[54] both tell of lions in the vicinity of the Euphrates;[55] Ammianus also notes a Saracen chief (*phylarchus*) called Malechus:[56] Jerome notes Malchus' name means king—*rex*—in Syriac. Both note a highly placed official called Sabinianus/Sabianus.[57] Syme, Alan Cameron and Matthews have touched on possible relationships between Jerome and Ammianus, but there would appear to be a larger number of parallels than hitherto noted between the *vita Malchi* and Ammianus.[58]

---

review of Syme in *JRS* 61 (1971) 259 and now T.D. Barnes 'Jerome and the "Historia Augusta"' in *Historiae Augustae Colloquium Parisinum* (edd. G. Bonamente, N. Duval, Macerata, 1991) 22.

[52] Nisibis: *vita Malchi* 3; Amm. xviii 6.8. Persian border: *vita Malchi* 3, cited above; Amm. xvii, 5.3: *ad extremas Romani limitis partes*.

[53] *postliminium*: *vMal* 4; Amm xix, 9, 6, and above 3.1.2.

[54] *vita Malchi* 8; Amm. xviii 6. Cf. J. Marincola *Authority and tradition in ancient historiography* (Cambridge, 1997) 201f., on Ammianus' account of his own escape from Amida: 'the most exciting escape narrative in an ancient historian, told in the first person with a series of first-person verbs conveying the rapid movement.' Much the same could be said of Jerome's narrative.

[55] Lions: *vita Malchi* 9; Amm. xviii, 7.5. J. Matthews *The Roman Empire of Ammianus* (London, 1986) 487, notes the presence of lions on Assyrian and Sassanian reliefs. The BT Niddah 67b allows women to undergo ritual immersion by daylight for fear of lions in the area of Nares east of the Euphrates: see on this A. Oppenheimer (with B. Isaac and M. Lecker) *Babylonia Judaica in the Talmudic Period* (Wiesbaden, 1983) 265f.; 347.

[56] Amm. xxiv, 2,4. Matthews *op. cit.* p. 352 notes this "name (if Ammianus has not confused it with a title) is the Semitic 'malik' or 'king'." See also P. Mayerson 'The use of the term *phylarchos* in the Roman-Byzantine east' *Zeitschrift für Papyrologie und Epigraphik* 88 (1991) 295 = *ib. Monks, Martyrs, Soldiers and Saracens: Papers on the Near East in Antiquity (1962–1993)* (NY/Jerusalem, 1994) 346.

[57] Sabianus in the *vita Malchi* is the *dux Mesopotamiae;* Sabinianus in Ammianus is the *magister eq. per Orientem* in 359/60. Vallarsi (*PL* 23, 62, n. 9) suggested that they are the same man, and this proposal has been generally accepted q.v. *PLRE*, I, 388; Rebenich p. 130.

[58] See bibliography in n. 51 above. S. Rubenson 'Philosophy and Simplicity: the problem of classical education in early Christian biography' in *Greek Biography and Panegyric in Late Antiquity* (eds. T. Hägg, P. Rousseau, Berkeley etc., 2000) 123 points out how the piling up of many of these elements—escape by night, pursuers, a lion and a happy ending—give a novelistic quality to the *vita*.

1b. *Local customs or literary stereotype?* Carnes semi-crudae

It has already been noted how one apparently realistic contemporary description in the *vita Malchi* proved on further analysis to come from the world of the Bible. The converse is also true. Apparently unreal and stereotypical elements sometimes reflect more of Jerome's fourth-century world than is first evident. Jerome describes the invading Huns—*Hunorum nova feritas*—in 393 as living on half-raw meat.[59] Ammianus does the same: his Huns (31.2) also live on half-raw meat:

> *semicruda pecoris carne vescantur.*

Syme and Alan Cameron have used this to try to work out the literary relations between Ammianus and Jerome. Matthews writes 'that Huns . . . ate [their meat] 'half-cooked', is a characteristic exaggeration to the point of incongruity of a barbarian habit widely assumed in Classical sources of consuming meat in its raw state . . . In fact as the discovery of many copper cauldrons shows the Huns were quite capable of cooking meat.' He then notes that Syme and Cameron ignore the fact that Jerome also says of the Saracens who captured Malchus that

> *carnes semicrudae cibus et lac camelorum potus erat.*

He sums up by saying that 'the consumption of uncooked or 'half-raw' meat is another rhetorical motif of the life of nomadic steppe people, being assigned in similar terms by Ammianus to the Huns as by Jerome to the Saracens.' Scholarly opinion, then, makes the half-raw flesh a stereotypical symbol of the barbarian worthy of Lévi-Strauss.[60] There is, however, evidence from the Babylonian Talmud of a local vocabulary for half-raw meat in late antique Babylonia. In a discussion about the eating and cooking of בשר נא—half-raw, half-roasted meat (BT Pesahim 41a) based on the biblical verse in Exodus 12:9, the Talmud clarifies what is meant by the term by explaining it 'this is in Persian—*abarnim*.'[61] The Talmud is not dealing in stereotypes here, but in exact definitions in order to establish

---

[59] *Adv. Iovinianum* 2.7 (*PL* 23, 308).

[60] C. Lévi-Strauss *The Raw and the Cooked: Introduction to a science of mythology* (Eng. trans. London, 1969).

[61] Prof. Aharon Oppenheimer informs me that *abarnim* אברנים—evidently represents the Persian word *biyārnim* half-cooked.

halakhic status. If there was a separate word for it, half-raw meat as such must have been part of everyday life in Persia in late antiquity.

Malchus and his Saracen captors are at the edge of Roman Mesopotamia—as noted above, he had originally been unable to go further east because of the Persians and the Roman frontier.[62] It seems, then, that Jerome in the *vita Malchi* is referring to real local food, not just a literary stereotype.

3.3.2. *Stereotypes*

2a. *Stereotypes of barbarian*

Turning now to discuss Jerome's use of stereotypes, we shall begin by looking at stereotypes of the barbarian in general. It has already been noted in chapter 2 that one of the ways in which a society defines itself is by defining those who do not belong, the cultural 'others.'[63] Indeed, authors writing in the classical tradition developed a picture of outsiders, barbarians, which was often defined more by where they differed from classical culture than by what they were actually like. Thus descriptions of different groups of barbarians in different classical authors owe as much to the Roman idea of what a barbarian should be—and what a Roman is not—as they do to the actual culture of the particular barbarians discussed. It is possible to point to several characteristics of barbarians in the classical sources.[64] Thus descriptions of barbarians show them living in a marginal area (to symbolize their marginality to Roman society),[65]

---

[62] *vMalchi* 3, cited above. This is very similar to the pilgrim Egeria in 384 CE, who was told she could not go beyond Nisibis into Persian territory: *Locus ille, filia, quem requiris, decima mansione est hinc intus in Persida. Nam hinc usque ad Nisibin mansiones sunt quinque, et inde usque Hur . . . aliae mansiones sunt quinque; sed modo ibi accessus Romanorum non est, totum enim illud Persae tenent. (Itinerarium Egeriae* 22,12 (*CCSL* 175, 64). And cf. Ammianus' account of Craugasius of Nisibis who deserts to the Persians (xix 9,6–8).

[63] See on this: F. Hartog *Le miroir d'Hérodote* (Paris, 1980) and the references above, Chapter 2.2.1b; the excellent analysis of B.D. Shaw 'Rebels and outsiders' *CAH* 11 (2000) 361–403; and now B. Isaac *The Invention of Racism in Classical Antiquity* (Princeton, 2004).

[64] cf. T.E.J. Wiedemann 'Between man and beasts. Barbarians in Ammianus Marcellinus' in I.S. Moxon, J.D. Smart, A. Woodman (eds.) *Past Perspectives: Studies in Greek and Roman historical writing* (Cambridge, 1986) 189–211. Wiedemann also suggests that it is possible to set up a type of the 'ideal barbarian,' but this does not allow enough for the very considerable differences in ancient pictures of the barbarian.

[65] Early classical barbarians often lived on islands, such as the Cyclops which Odysseus meets, or at the edges of the known world, like Herodotus' Scythians in the North and Ethiopians in the South, with farther away still the fabled Androphages.

wearing few or no clothes,[66] living somewhere other than in a house, such as a cave or a tent.[67] They tend to be nomads rather than sedentary farmers, and have limited social structures.[68] They may be cannibals or so 'just' that they abstain from all meat:[69] in other words they eat curious food, and drink something other than the regular Graeco-Roman wine and water.[70] Finally, they would have either strange sexual customs or, at the very least, rôle-reversal between the sexes.[71] In other words, classical descriptions of barbarians developed into literary *topoi*. Thus in the *vita Malchi*, Jerome's Saracens have some characteristics borrowed from Sallust's African tribes.[72] Sallust's African tribes, in their turn, are derived from literary sources, even though Sallust himself was governor of an African province and might have been thought to have access to first-hand knowledge rather than literary precedent.[73]

Cf. J. Romm *The Edges of the Earth in Ancient Thought: Geography, Exploration and Fiction* (Princeton, 1992).

[66] Naked barbarians: eg Strabo xvii 2,1,8 (small naked nomads); Dio 76.12.2.5 on the Britons calls them naked and unshod. Cf. the letters from Vindolanda probably describing *nudi Brittones*, later referred to scornfully as '*Brittunculi*': A.K. Bowman, J.D. Thomas 'New texts from Vindolanda' *Britannia* 18 (1987) 136–7. It is unclear here how far the scornful diminutive reflects reality or is merely a *topos* used to denigrate. On the gymnosophists, naked Indian philosophers, see G. Stroumsa 'Philosophy of the Barbarians: On Early Christian Ethnological Representations' in *Geschichte—Tradition—Reflexion: Festschrift für Martin Hengel zum 70. Geburtstag* (eds. H. von Hubert *et al.*, Tübingen, 1996) 339–368 and bibliography *ad loc.*

[67] Cf. Tacitus' cynical account of the Romanisation of the British barbarians, which included the active promotion of villa building: *Agricola* 21, and similarly Strabo vii.3.7 (301).

[68] Lack of sociability: e.g. Strabo vi.4.2 (288); absence of laws: Sallust; Ammianus n. 77 below.

[69] Strabo vii.3.9 (302).

[70] see B. Shaw: 'Eaters of Flesh, Drinkers of Milk' *Ancient Society* 13/14 (1982/3) 5–31 and cf. Jerome's long description of strange foods in *adv. Iov.* ii 7, including worms, crocodiles and ancestors.

[71] Dio *loc. cit.* n. 66 above.

[72] Compare *v Malchi* 4: *Saraceni incertis sedibus huc atque illuc semper vagantur* with Sallust *Jug.* xviii on the African tribes, the Gaetuli and the Libyes: *vagi, palantes, quas nox coegerat sedes habebant* and *Cat.* vi, 1: on the Trojans and the Aborigines: *sedibus incertis vagabantur*.

[73] Sallust actually says that it was not possible to get first-hand information, because of the heat and the difficult and desert terrain: *ob calorem aut asperitatem item solitudines* (*Jug.* xvii, 2; *ib*, 7). He therefore discusses only the literary traditions and puts all responsibility for the truth on his *auctores*.

2b. *The specific barbarian: sex and the Saracens*

Yet, in spite of the common use of stereotypes when talking about barbarians, it is sometimes possible to disentangle some characteristics from these descriptions which look as if they might point to something specific to a certain group of barbarians, rather than to barbarians in general. John Matthews has thus analysed in some detail several groups of barbarians who appear in the work of Ammianus—Huns, Goths, Saracens etc.[74] In order to see Jerome's Saracens and their sexual behaviour against the background of the concepts of his contemporaries, I should like to look again at one characteristic of the Saracens noted by Ammianus which Matthews just mentions in passing, their sexual behaviour, for it may be that Ammianus is reflecting here, if not an actual characteristic of the Saracens, then at least a widely held fourth century view about these particular barbarians, as opposed to a mere *topos* about barbarians in general. I shall use the collateral evidence of the Babylonian Talmud, and the fourth century Latin *Historia Augusta* (*HA*).

First I shall sum up briefly the general characteristics of

'the Scenite Arabs whom we now call Saracens': *Scenitas Arabas quos Saracenos nunc appellamus*[75]

in the history written by Jerome's contemporary Ammianus. Wiedemann has pointed out quite rightly that they appear here in an *excursus* (xiv, 4)—Ammianus is writing here in a distinctively literary form. It is clear at once they have many of the traditional characteristics of the barbarian: they are nomads, moving from place to place, not subsisting on the produce of settled farming—unless at second-hand, by plunder. They live in tents, at the edges of the empire: they are literally marginal people. They eat strange food—half-raw meat— and drink camels' milk, and Ammianus further notes that he has seen some who were wholly unacquainted with corn and wine. In the terms of Lévi-Strauss' oppositions of the raw and the cooked[76] when analyzing primitive and civilized peoples, they are most definitely far out on the primitive side. They rove around half-naked—*seminudi*—and, in a passage remarkably reminiscent of Sallust, Ammianus notes that they have no fixed laws:

---

[74] J. Matthews *The Roman Empire of Ammianus Marcellinus* (London, 1989) ch. 14: Barbarians and Bandits 304f.
[75] 22.15.2.
[76] C. Lévi-Strauss *op. cit.* n. 60 above.

errant semper per spatia longe lateque distenta, sine lare sine sedibus fixis aut legibus.[77]

They swoop down on their prey *milvorum rapacium similes,* and are desirable neither as friend or foe. Finally, Ammianus notes their strange sexual behaviour: the woman has the right to leave her husband if she wants, and, amazingly to a Roman used to arranged marriages, it is 'unbelievable with what passion both partners have sex'—

incredibile est quo ardore apud eos in venerem uterque sovitur sexus.

At first sight it might seem that this last comment is simply a variation on the strange-sexual-mores-of-barbarians *topos.* However, there is parallel material in other sources dealing with the Saracen Arabs in the same place at the same time.

Turning to the *Historia Augusta,* this is now generally accepted to be the work of a single author who often indulges in jokes and parody in his or her lurid scenes from Roman history.[78] Saracens appear briefly in a few places and especially in connection with Zenobia, the famous Arab barbarian queen. The *topos* of the barbarian warrior queen and her attractiveness to civilized classical heroes begins with the Amazons of Greek mythology, where Penthesilea and Achilles were the subjects of Greek vase painting.[79] The historian Cassius Dio develops Boadicea as the noble savage queen, putting into her mouth a rhetorical expression of the barbarian versus the civilized Roman.[80] And it is no accident that the *Historia Augusta* has Zenobia claim Cleopatra as her ancestor, for by the fourth century Cleopatra was a by-word for her sexuality. The portrait of Zenobia is built up with all the 'imagination and fabrication' the *Historia Augusta* could muster.[81] Zenobia was in fact a most successful commander and a respectable enemy for the Romans. However, in the *Historia Augusta* a fictitious letter from Aurelian describes her as

---

[77] cf. Sallust *Cat.* vi 1, cited in n. 72 above. This passage, on the wandering Trojans who joined the primitive Aborigini to found Rome, is also cited by Augustine *de civ. Dei* iii 3.

[78] See *CAH* (13) 685 (Averil Cameron).

[79] On the famous vase painting of these two by Exekias: J. Boardman *Athenian Black Figure Vases* (London, 1974, repr. Singapore, 1980) 230, pl. 98.

[80] Boadicea [Boudicca]: Dio lxii,6,2–5.

[81] Syme *op. cit.* 76.

quam prudens in consiliis, quam constans in dispositionibus, quam erga milites gravis.[82]

This exaggerated description of virtues that would suit a very tradi-tional Roman general—*prudentia, constantia, gravitas* etc.—is obviously satirical when applied to a barbarian Arab queen who would have achieved her victories by unconventional methods of fighting. The satire continues, mingling un-Roman attributes such as facility in languages including Egyptian, with the latest Roman literary fash-ion: *dicatur epitomasse*—the writing of epitomes had become very pop-ular in the fourth century,[83] but it is ludicrous to attribute this learned activity to Zenobia. The *Historia Augusta* also notes that the queen was dark-skinned and unbelievably beautiful; this too is presumably satirical. Great stress is placed on her extravagant jewels: so large that she had to have a slave to take the weight off her neck, while on her head she wore a jewel commonly borne by horses! As a bar-barian who wanted badly to be accepted into Roman society she is mocked for her efforts—she insisted so hard that her sons spoke Latin that they lost their competence in Greek, while she herself is described as setting up house in Rome and living

cum liberis matronae iam more Romanae.

The joke is even more pointed when we remember Jerome's Malchus among the Saracens having to bend his neck

adorare dominam liberosque ex more gentis.

The *Historia Augusta* produces yet another satirical effect in its descrip-tion of Zenobia's marital life, attributing extreme continence to her:

cuius ea castitas fuisse dicitur ut ne virum suum quidem scieret nisi temptandis conceptionibus.

Since Ammianus attributes incredible ardour to the Saracens within their marriages, and, as we shall see, Jerome's Saracens are set up as the complete opposite of the chaste Malchus, so it must have seemed quite incongruous to the audience of the *Historia Augusta* to

---

[82] *SHA* XXX Tyr. 30.
[83] For a good discussion of the epitome as a fourth century fashion see J.J. O'Donnell's review of R. Herzog *Restauration et Renouveau: La littérature latine de 284 à 374 après J-C* (Turnhout, 1993) in *Bryn Mawr Classical Review* 5,5 (1994) 415–426.

think of an Arab queen as continent—particularly a descendent of
the notorious Cleopatra.[84]

Returning now to Jerome, his works contain several references to
Saracens, and even a definition. Jerome lived for some years in the
desert of Chalcis:

> in ea . . . heremi parte . . . quae inter Syros ac Sarracenos uastum limitem ducit[85]

although, as noted above, recent scholarship tends to see the account
of his lone cell as somewhat exaggerated.[86] However, there can be
no doubt that the picture he gives of the area and the Saracens
includes elements that can be geographically and archaeologically
identified, although as shown above, and as is usual with Jerome,
they are also placed in a literary and Biblical context. Interestingly,
like Ammianus, he too implies that the name 'Saracens' has recently
come into fashion as a name for the people otherwise called
Ismahelitae, Agareni or Arabi.[87] The Saracen Arabs he describes in
his *ep.* 129 are ranged around all the borders of the empire from
Mauretania to Persia and even as far as India. They are inhabitants
of the *vasta solitudine* which is seen as being threateningly full of barbarians—*plena ferocium barbarorum.*[88] Jerome, like Ammianus, uses literary material in his descriptions of the Saracens, including a quotation

---

[84] For a suggestion that the *Historia Augusta*'s portrayal of Zenobia's chastity owes
something to the Christian ascetic movement, see J.F. Gilliam 'Three passages in
the *Historia Augusta*: Gord. 21, 5 and 34, 2–6; Tyr. Trig. 30, 12' *Bonner Historia-
Augusta-Colloquium 1968/9* (Bonn, 1970) 107–111.

[85] *ep.* 7, 1, written in 374 (*CSEL* 54, 26).

[86] Rebenich 85–98.

[87] In *ep.* 129, 4, 2 he writes *Arabas et Agarenos quos nunc Saracenos vocant.* It should
be noted, also, that in his translation of Eusebius' Chronicle we find *Ismahel a quo
Ismahelitorum genus qui postea Agareni et postremum Saraceni dicti* (Helm, 24), even though
the version of Eusebius preserved in the later *Chronicon Paschale* 94.18 (ed. Schoene
Eusebi Chronicorum Canonum, Zurich, 1866 repr. Dublin, 1967) 13 has: Οἱ δ'αὐτοί
εἰσιν Ἀγαρηνοὶ οἱ καὶ Σαρακηνοὶ καλούμενοι with no mention of 'most recently.'
Jerome says that the first part of his translation of Eusebius '*pura Graeca translatio
est*' (Helm, 6) but it has been shown that Jerome does in fact add to text which
he says he only translated as noted by T.D. Barnes *Eusebius and Constantine*
(Cambridge/London, 1981) 113. Eusebius does use the term Σαρακηνοί in other
contexts. G.W. Bowersock 'Arabs and Saracens in the Historia Augusta' *Historia
Augusta Colloquium, Bonn 1984/5* (Bonn, 1987) has argued that the term first came
into generalizing use in the third century, but then dropped out of use in the fourth
century, which is why Ammianus notes it as recent. He does not discuss Jerome's
parallel comments.

[88] *ep.* 129 *loc. cit.*

from Virgil about the wandering Barcae—which comes from a context which stresses the desert. (Unlike Ammianus he then carries on with a philological discussion of the various names.)

Saracens appear also in the *vita Hilarionis* and the *vita Malchi*. As noted in chapter 2 above, in the *vita Hilarionis* Jerome stresses the missionary activities of Hilarion, and his success in converting pagans to Christianity. He relates the visit of Saint Hilarion to Elusa,

> *oppidum magne parte semibarbarum . . . propter loci situm,*

where the Saracens worshipped Venus as Lucifer. There is epigraphic evidence that the Nabatean Arabs identified their goddess al-'Uzza with Venus/Aphrodite, and there was a cult of al-'Uzza at the Nabatean city of Petra.[89] Hilarion is extremely successful in converting the population of Elusa, and the priest of Venus, the goddess of love and sex, becomes the first bishop. However, Mayerson has pointed out that Elusa at the time was not really a half-civilized town, but could even be described as being 'in the mainstream of imperial life.'[90] He suggests that here Jerome seems to be using a *topos* of the Saracens 'a word most often used pejoratively to mean pagan Arabs, settled or unsettled (i.e. Bedouin) who inhabit desert regions,' in order to build up his picture of Hilarion.[91] As shown in chapter 2, it is probable that Jerome's description of Elusa as semibarbarian was referring to the language of the Saracens, which he calls *vo[x] Syra*.

The *vita Malchi*, however, written to advertise the virtue of chastity, has more details of Saracens in the unquestionably uncivilized wild, outside cities. The monk Malchus, travelling with a caravan along the road from Beroea to Edessa is attacked and captured by nomad Saracens. The barbarian threat has become a reality.[92] The Roman

---

[89] Bi-lingual Greek and Nabatean inscription (9 CE) from Cos: J. Patrich *The Formation of Nabatean Art* (Jerusalem, 1990) 86 and bibliography *ad loc.*; for the temple at Petra see: I. Browning *Petra* (London, 1989³) 147f. At Petra too there seems to be evidence of much earlier buildings being in use until the fourth century.

[90] P. Mayerson 'The City of Elusa in the Literary sources of the Fourth -Sixth Centuries' *IEJ* 33 (1983) 247–253 esp. 249 = *ib. Monks, Martyrs, Soldiers and Saracens: Papers on the Near East in Antiquity (1962–1993)* (NY/Jerusalem, 1994) 197–203.

[91] Mayerson *op. cit.* 248.

[92] For the reality of Saracen attacks on travellers cf. an inscription recording *insidiatos a Saracenos perisse*. J.H. Iliffe 'A building inscription from the Syrian limes AD 334' *QDAP* 10 (1944) 62.

highway from Beroea to Edessa where the Saracens attack is a real road, as shown above. But many of the other details, as with Ammianus,[93] are those of the literary *topos*, reminding the reader of Sallust and Virgil.[94]

Other details, as already noted, are also similar to Ammianus, especially with regard to food: the *carnes semi-crudae et lac camelorum*. Both authors specify the use of camels by the nomads, and their semi-naked state. Jerome's Saracens are armed—with bows and arrows and spears. Later Malchus' master makes use of a sword.

In captivity Malchus is required to bend his neck to the *dominam liberosque ex more gentis*. The customs here are far distant from Jerome as a Roman or a Christian. Ammianus has hinted at the relative independence of the Saracen women—who, shockingly to him, make up their own minds about their choice of sexual partner: Jerome also seems to imply a higher status for Saracen women than he is used to. Shahîd notes that the author of the contemporary *Expositio totius mundi et gentium* writes of the Saracens: *et mulieres aiunt in eos regnare* and suggests that this is evidence of a matriarchal system.[95] Rougé has suggested that this may be a reference to Mavia, the Saracen queen who fought Rome in the fourth century.[96] However, Mayerson doubts that these hints can be used as hard evidence of the fourth century.[97]

Malchus is put to work tending his captor's flocks and herds, and living in a cave. These Saracens are half-way between true nomads and settled people. His Saracen master then forces Malchus at swordpoint to take another captive as his wife, even though Malchus pleads to be allowed to preserve his chastity. They retire to his cave, and in a scene which has already been presented as a negative counterpart of the union of Dido and Aeneas presided over by the goddess Venus, Malchus' fellow captive reveals herself as a married

---

[93] Ammianus is fanciful in his geographical excursus; he often writes as if he was a second century author: in his excursus on Arabia he implies that the Nabataeans were still around. See chapter 4 below.

[94] Cf. n. 72 above.

[95] *Expositio* xx. I. Shahîd *Byzantium and the Arabs in the Fourth Century* (Washington, 1984) 286.

[96] J. Rougé (ed.) *Expositio totius mundi et gentium* (Paris, 1966) 24–6.

[97] P. Mayerson 'Mauia, Queen of the Saracens—A Cautionary note' *IEJ* 30 (1980) 123–131 = ib. *Monks, Martyrs, Soldiers and Saracens: Papers on the Near East in Antiquity (1962–1993)* (NY/Jerusalem, 1994) 164–172.

Christian and proposes they should live together in chastity. This 'marriage' Malchus says, made them more pleasing—*amabiliores*—to their masters, the Saracens. Jerome here is using the Saracens, worshippers of Venus, the goddess of sex, and insistent on marriage on pain of death, as an extreme contrast to his chaste hero Malchus. As well as the polarities of civilised Roman versus barbarian, and Christian versus pagan, he includes an implicit contrast of sexuality versus chastity.

Thus both classical sources and Jerome provide us with a picture of the Saracen Arabs made up of a mixture of *topos*, reality and commonly held stereotype.

In the latter category, it can often be difficult to distinguish between common human attitudes at any time or place, and attitudes that were specific to a certain time or place. The imperial instability of the third century seems to have gone hand in hand with attacks by marauding nomads in border areas of Palaestina and Mesopotamia, and by the fourth century there appears to have been a tendency towards consolidation of these Saracen Arabs into stronger tribal groupings. It is noteworthy that all the three sources looked at so far have presented the Saracens as violent and threatening, which would seem to be a reasonable human reaction to the fourth century situation. When people are threatened by attack from outside, they naturally fear the worst—murder, pillage and rape. Could the picture of the unbridled sexuality of the Saracens come simply from a common fear of rape?

One answer to this question is to be found in a different type of source, the Babylonian Talmud, which was written as a legal and moral guide, rather than a literary production. Editing finished around the seventh century in Babylonia, but it contains much earlier material, and fourth-century material can be distinguished through careful scholarship.[98] The attitude of the rabbis of Babylonia towards the Saracen Arabs has been studied recently by Aharon Oppenheimer.[99]

---

[98] Dating of Babylonian Talmud: G. Stemberger *Introduction to the Talmud and Midrash* (tr. M. Bockmuel Edinburgh, 1996²) 190f.

[99] A. Oppenheimer 'The attitude of the sages towards the Arabs' in *Jewish Studies in a New Europe* (ed. U. Haxen *et al.*, Copenhagen, 1998) 572–9. The Talmudic sources have various names for Arabs: *Arava'ae* (i.e. Arabs), *Sarqayin* (Saracens), *Navataya'ae* (Nabataeans), *Yishma'elim* (Ishmaelites cf. Jerome), *Hagariya'ae* (i.e. children of Hagar, the mother of Ishmael), *Taya'ae* (the name of a local Babylonian tribe of Arabs).

The Arabs are presented at first neutrally and there is evidence of an uneasy co-existence—Arabs are employed as shepherds for flocks belonging to Jews, although they have to be closely supervised because of their unreliability.[100] This is obviously the other side of the picture from the *vita Malchi*, where Malchus is employed as a shepherd for the Saracens and under suspicion at first. But by the third and fourth centuries the Arabs take on the *persona* of attackers, as the threat to the border settlements along the Euphrates increases.[101] As with the classical sources already noted, the Talmudic sources also stress the sexuality, and what they saw as immorality, of the Arabs: 'Ten *qabs* of promiscuity came down to this world: nine were taken by the Arabs, one by the rest of the world.'[102] It might be thought, as suggested above, that such a picture is due to a natural fear of attack and rape. However one very interesting tannaitic source makes it clear that this was not the case, and that the Arabs had a reputation for not actually raping their captives, but merely harassing them sexually:

> 'What after all is it' said Rabbi Dosa 'that that Arab has done to her? Has he made her unfit to be a priest's wife [sc. by rape] merely because he squeezed her between her breasts?' (Babylonian Talmud Qetubot 36b).

Talmudic sources made careful distinctions between the different sorts of sexual behaviour to be expected of captors because this would affect the subsequent status of their prisoners.[103] Thus these sources show the Saracen Arabs as well-known for their pronounced sexuality, but as they present them as engaging in sexual harassment, not rape, they do not appear to be simply showing a stereotypical picture of fantasies of rape by the barbarian 'other,' but to be presenting a picture of what was commonly believed to be the nature of the Saracen.

---

[100] BT Bava Batra 36a and Sukkah 47a.

[101] See Oppenheimer *op. cit.* n. 99 above for a careful analysis of the complex group of Talmudic sources which deal with this.

[102] BT Qetubot 36b and cf. BT Avodah Zara 22b.

[103] Cf. Tosefta Qetubot iv, 5 and BT Qetubot 51b and the discussion by B. Isaac 'Bandits in Judaea and Arabia' *HSCP* 88 (1974) 171f. = *id. The Near East under Roman Rule* (Leiden, 1998) 132–3.

Thus this consistent picture of the emphatic sexuality of the Arabs would seem to have been a widely held popular stereotype in the fourth century, distinguishable from other classical literary *topoi* about non-Roman barbarians, in that it is found in pagan Roman serious and satirical literature alike, and also in both Christian and Talmudic sources. Jerome is therefore pointing up the extreme chastity of his hero Malchus by setting him against a background of stereotypical Saracens whose sexual reputation would have been familiar to audiences within and without the empire. Malchus' body is enslaved by the Saracens, but he is free from their enslavement to sexuality.

Summary: Biography and autobiography in Jerome's saints' Lives[104]

In our discussion of the *vita Pauli* we saw how Jerome writes himself into his work, as it were, making plain his own desire to be seen as Paul's true successor.[105] In the *vita Hilarionis* we saw how the hero Hilarion is set up to take over the pagan literature of Apuleius and his *Golden Ass*—and there are a number of parallels between the life of Jerome and that of Apuleius.[106] The *vita Malchi* too has parallels to Jerome's own life. Jerome describes Malchus as a *colonus* of Nisibis in the *vita*, just as he calls himself a *colonus* of Babylon/Rome in his preface to his translation of Didymus, written around the same time. Both Jerome and Malchus had to flee from their enemies. Both of them were monks in the desert of Chalcis, and both lived afterwards with a woman in chastity, Malchus with his 'wife', Jerome and Paula in Bethlehem. There are clear parallels between the life of Jerome and the life of his hero, so that the transformation of the legal term *postliminium* into a Christian metaphor in the *vita Malchi* relates to an episode in the life of Jerome himself. Malchus' takeover of his body for Christian asceticism is like Jerome's own personal victory over his own body. Jerome, like Malchus, lived for a time in the desert of Chalcis and struggled with his own body, beset by sexual temptations and fantasies, as he describes graphically in *ep.* 22,7.[107] Should there be any lingering doubts that Jerome's heroes undergo the same

---

[104] On biography in late antiquity, see Introduction pp. 4–5 and bibliography *ad loc.*

[105] cf. E. Coleiro 'St Jerome's Lives of the Hermits' *VChr* 11 (1957) 171.

[106] Chapter 2.1.5.

[107] *O quotiens in heremo constitutus et in illa vasta solitudine . . . putavi me Romanis interesse deliciis . . . mens desideriis aestuabat . . . etc.*

conflicts as their author, these must be dispelled by the words Malchus uses at the height of his conflict with his body in the cave, when he asks himself rhetorically what to do about his woman companion: *quid agimus anima?* 'What do we do, my soul?' Jerome addresses exactly the same words to himself when writing his account of his companion Paula's life in his letter 108, 27,1: *quid agimus anima?*[108] Kelly has written very convincingly of the repressed sexuality of the relationship between Jerome and Paula, gossip about which was one of the factors in Jerome's disgrace and expulsion from Rome.[109]

The success of Jerome's mixture of biography with autobiography can be seen from the fact that later generations inextricably confused Jerome himself with his own heroes. In the discussion of the *vita Pauli* we noted how, from the Middle Ages onwards, St. Jerome in his cave in the desert, accompanied by a lion, was a very popular subject of paintings, and that this was probably partly due to a confusion of St. Jerome with St. Gerasimus.[110] The saint with a lioness and a cave play an important part in the *vita Malchi* too. Jerome took care to use his own literary creations to construct a literary *persona* for himself.[111] In writing the *vitae* of the saints Paul, Hilarion and Malchus he was also creating the *vita* of Saint Jerome.

The *Life* of Malchus is the last of Jerome's 'official' saint's *Lives*. It has many autobiographical elements, both in its subject matter and in many of its details, describing as it does Malchus' life, lived with his 'wife' in their cave, on their journey and finally settled, together yet apart. In the last chapter we now turn to Jerome's letter 108, addressed to Eustochium, the daughter of his saintly friend and companion Paula. Written after Paula's death, it describes her life, her journey through the Holy Land together with Jerome, and their life next to the Cave of the Nativity in Bethlehem, where they finally settled, living together yet apart.

---

[108] *ep.* 108 27, 1 (*CSEL* 55,1996²) 345.
[109] Kelly, 109.
[110] See Kelly, 333 with bibliography *ad loc.*
[111] For Jerome's creation of a literary *persona* for himself, M. Vessey 'Jerome's Origen: The Making of a Christian Literary *Persona*' Studia Patristica 28 (1993) 135f. and cf. C. Favez 'Saint Jérôme peint par lui-même' *Latomus* 16 (1957) 655f.; *ib.* 17 (1958) 81–96; 303–316. Both these articles relate to his letters and prefaces only and do not mention his saints' *Lives*. For Jerome in the *vita Pauli* see above, chapter 1 esp. 1.5: Jerome's literary methods.

CHAPTER FOUR

JEROME'S *EP.* 108 AND THE CHRISTIAN APPROPRIATION OF THE HOLY LAND

INTRODUCTION

We have looked at Jerome's three saints' *Lives*, written, as it were, in ascending order of reality, from Paul the hermit, who may never have existed, through Hilarion, whom Jerome knew of through Epiphanius, up to Malchus, whom he says he actually once met. In this chapter we shall be looking finally at Jerome's last saint's *Life*, *ep.* 108, which was written as a *Life* of Paula, who was undoubtedly his real friend and companion for many years.[1] It has long been used as a source of information about the Holy Land in the fourth century, with a notable tendency to detach the account of Paula's journey from its context and treat it as a document standing alone.[2] However, we will see that *ep.* 108, although it deals with a real woman, is in fact a carefully contrived rhetorical product, and by no means always reliable as evidence of the *realia* of fourth century Palestine. Analysis of its rhetorical form will prove rewarding here in disentangling Jerome's rhetoric from his *realia*. So we shall be looking at the rhetorical elements in the context of the various classical genre forms he uses in the letter: *consolatio, iter, propempticon, encomium, epitaphium.* Of these, the genre of *iter*, with its satirical antecedents, is of particular interest. Classical historians, including his contemporary Ammianus, commonly included geographical *excursus* in their works, and Jerome includes an *iter*, an account of the

---

[1] Cf. E. Hendrikx 'S. Jérôme en tant qu'hagiographe' *Ciudad Dios* 181 (1968) 661–7.

[2] General use of *ep.* 108 as historical information, for example, M. Avi-Yonah *Gazetteer of Roman Palestine* (Jerusalem, 1976); *TIR*. Paula's journey taken on its own out of context: A. Stewart, C.W. Wilson (ed. and tr.) *The Pilgrimage of the Holy Paula by St. Jerome* (PPTS, London, 1887); F. Stummer *Monumenta historiam et geographiam Terrae Sanctae illustrantia* (Bonn, 1935); J. Wilkinson *Jerusalem Pilgrims before the Crusades* (Jerusalem,1977); O. Limor *Holy Land Travels: Christian Pilgrims in Late Antiquity* (Jerusalem, 1998, in Hebrew).

pilgrimage he made together with Paula round the Holy Places. For
this *Life* deals with yet another Christian appropriation, that of the
Holy Land. Jerome had already appropriated the book of the Holy
Land as it was in ancient times, the Bible, for western Christians,
by translating it into Latin. Around 390 he had also set himself to
translate the book of the new Christian Holy Land, Eusebius'
Onomasticon. This was not merely a translation however, for he added
to the text details of the progressive Christianisation of the Holy
Land, with all the new churches built since Eusebius wrote. In chapter 2 we saw how Jerome began to create a new Christian geography of the Roman Empire. Here I shall expand the discussion by
looking at his geographical concepts in general and where they might
have originated, and in particular his Jewish and Christian geogra-
phies of the Holy Land. Finally, comparison of his translation of the
Onomasticon with the *iter* of the *Life* of Paula, together with a close
look at some of the vocabulary of the text, will be used as another
aid in disentangling his rhetoric from his *realia*.

Creation of a Christian literature: Jerome's translation of the Onomasticon and his ep. 108

Ancient Roman education focussed on literature, alongside rhetoric,
as the highest attainments of the upper classes. A Roman whose
career might entail army command and provincial administration
would be prepared for it by an education in literature. Historians
preferred descriptions taken from books to descriptions from real life,
no matter if they were centuries out of date. Jerome was employed
by Damasus, he tells us, to rewrite the translation of the Bible into
a form that would be more acceptable to an audience accustomed
to the best Latin literature—previous translations had sounded barbaric to Roman ears. Christians trained in classical Latin rhetoric
had all the glories of pagan literature before them, and no Christian
literature of their own, or very little by Jerome's day. It was clearly
necessary to create a Christian literature. In his saints' *Lives* Jerome
is attempting to do this, and if we judge from the number of surviving manuscripts alone, he was very successful.

   In the *vita Pauli* Jerome had created a Latin Christian literary
world by taking over elements from Greek Christian literature and
from Virgil, and I have proposed that he has also appropriated
Jewish *aggadah* for his Christian purpose. His *vita Hilarionis* had entailed

a Christian appropriation of the most popular of classical pagan literature—the ancient novel, as well as dealing with the creation of
a Christian geography. The *vita Malchi* is about the Christian appropriation of the human body with Jerome using Virgil to provide a
contrast to his chaste hero.

In *ep.* 108, his last saint's *Life*, Jerome proceeds to yet another sort
of Christian literary appropriation, that of the Holy Land. In the
commentaries he wrote, Jerome reads the Bible both historically and
spiritually. Where the Hebrew Bible's Land is that which it promised
to the Jews, Jerome uses Jewish commentaries to elucidate the geographical details, both Josephus and the *targumim*. There is, indeed,
little early Christian material on geographical questions, because for
the early Christians it was the spiritual aspect which was paramount:
not Jerusalem on earth but the heavenly Jerusalem. By the fourth
century, with the Christianisation of the empire, all this was changing.[3] Christian pilgrimage had led to a new trend in Christian interest in the Holy Land, and in particular an attempt to identify places
in the Bible with extant fourth century places. Eusebius had written
his *Onomasticon* identifying places in the Bible with places in his contemporary Palestine around the turn of the third and fourth centuries.[4]

Jerome even claims, in the context of a letter about the *spiritual*
significance of the Land of Israel, that the *physical* Holy Land was
now the Promised Land, *terra repromissionis*, for Christians, as a result
of the passion and resurrection of Jesus:

> *hanc terram* [sc. the Land of Israel] *quae nunc nobis Christi passione et
> resurrectione terra repromissione effecta est.*[5]

---

[3] This is only one aspect of the increasing Christian preoccupation with the physical, which it attempted to turn into a gateway to the spiritual, so that tombs and
relics were seen as a conduit to heaven. See on this Peter Brown *The Cult of the
Saints* (Chicago, 1981).

[4] T.D. Barnes 'The composition of Eusebius' *Onomasticon*' *JThS* 26 (1975) 412–5;
id. Constantine and Eusebius (Cambridge, Mass., 1981) 108–111; Hunt 97; and now
G.S.P. Freeman-Grenville, (tr.), J.E. Taylor, R.L. Chapman III, (eds) *The Onomasticon
by Eusebius of Caesarea: Palestine in the Fourth Century AD* (Jerusalem, 2003), but see
my review of this translation in *Scripta Classica Israelica* 23 (2004) pp. 312–314.

[5] *ep.* 129, 4. See on this R.L. Wilken *The Land Called Holy: Palestine in Christian
History and Thought* (New Haven/London, 1992) 128f. and n. 6, but Wilken is more
interested in Jerome's spiritual concepts of the Holy Land than his geographical
concepts.

This is paralleled later in his Com.in Ez. when he is discussing the centrality of Jerusalem:

> *Hierusalem in medio mundi sitam, hic idem propheta testatur, umbilicum terrae eam esse demonstrans. . . .*[6]

Around 390[7] Jerome set himself to translate the book that deals with the Holy Land of his own day and its relation to the Bible, the *Onomasticon* of Eusebius. And just as in his *vita Pauli* one of Paul's three questions was 'What new roofs appear in the ancient cities?', so here Jerome adds to Eusebius details of new churches at ancient sites. As already noted in chapter 1, he also discusses this subject in his *ep.* 120, 8, which talks of the new churches in Jerusalem with their crowds of Christian believers. In his revision of the *Onomasticon* he updates in the minutest detail the picture of the fourth-century Holy Land, in the light of the pilgrimage he made with Paula.[8] This pilgrimage is described in *ep.* 108, which includes descriptions of Paula's life and death at Bethlehem. Just as the Bible is the book of the Holy Land of ancient times, so Jerome has translated, updated and created his own books of the Holy Land for his own Christian

---

[6] *Com. in Hiez.* ii, 5: 5–6. (*CCSL* 75, 55–6; *PL* 25, 54).

[7] P. Nautin *TRE s.v.* Hieronymus, p. 306; cf. Cavallera *op. cit.* vol. II, p. 157: 389–392.

[8] It is interesting how little Jerome dwells on the 'True Cross' (*ep.* 108, 9). Walker *op. cit.* suggests that Eusebius' total silence on this subject can be presumed to derive from the political struggles for status between the sees of Jerusalem and Caesarea. (But see now Averil Cameron & S.G. Hall (eds and trs) *Eusebius: Life of Constantine* (Oxford, 1999) 279–81, who do not accept Walker's thesis.) It may be that for Jerome too, tensions between the Christian communities in Jerusalem and Bethlehem meant that Jerome was reluctant to stress this important relic which he had visited with Paula in the years before the quarrel broke out. J.W. Drijvers *Helena Augusta: The Mother of Constantine the Great and the Legend of the Finding of the Cross* (Leiden, etc., 1992) has written of how the story of its discovery by Helena had been included by Rufinus in his *HE* x, 7–8 (Drijvers, 79–80) and was thus particularly associated with Jerome's enemies. G. Stemberger *Jews and Christians in the Holy Land: Palestine in the fourth century* (tr. R. Tuschling, Edinburgh, 2000) 102 suggests this is why Jerome has so little to say on Jerusalem in general. Thus Jerome writes that he only wanted to hurry Paula away from the Cross: *nisi ad reliqua festinaret, a primis non posset abduci.* He further hints at implied doubts on its authenticity when he says that Paula adored it 'as if' she saw the Lord hanging on it: *prostrataque ante crucem, quasi pendentem dominum cerneret, adorabat.* In contrast, he seems to accept the authenticity of the 'sepulchre of the Resurrection': *ingressa sepulchrum resurrectionis, osculabatur lapidem, quem ab ostio sepulchri amouerat angelus, et ipsum corporis locum in quo dominus iacuerat . . . ore lambebat.* For his doubts over the nails from the Cross, see *Com. in Zach.* iii, 14, 20 (*CCSL* 76A, 898).

times. The Holy Land of his literary works is both the historically real Holy Land of the fourth century, with its official Roman administration and network of roads, as well as the spiritual centre where Paula can still see the infant Jesus in his manger at Bethlehem.

In this chapter I shall therefore be considering Jerome's geography in general, how far it is a literary construction and how far it is related to the historical reality of the world around him. Let us begin by looking at his mental map of the world.

4.1. JEROME'S WORLD CONCEPT—MENTAL MAPS AND REAL MAPS

4.1.1. *Jerome's mental map*

Before discussing Jerome's use of Jewish sources for his geography of the Holy Land, and his part in the creation of a Christian geography of Palestine, we need to begin with a brief look at his world concept, and in particular the question of his own mental map. Jerome's geographical descriptions in general do not make it clear whether he had a graphic or a verbal map at his disposal. His general world concept seems to be that familiar from Roman authors: Britain (or the Scythians) in the north, the Atlantic Ocean in the west, Ethiopia in the south and India in the east mark for him the farthest extents of the world.[9] Romans saw the world as centred on Rome, with countries decreasing in importance from Italy out to the extremes of the empire.[10] For Vitruvius, indeed, Rome at the centre of the world was aligned with heaven itself.[11]

Jerome reframes this imperial concept in creating a new Christian geography centred on the Holy Land.[12] Jerusalem or even Bethlehem

---

[9] *ep.* 146, 1: the world extends from Gaul in the west, via Britain in the north, Africa in the south and out to Persia and India in the east. For the Scythians as representing the north, see *Com. in Hiez.* ii, 5:5–6 (*CCSL* 75, 56; *PL* 25,54), discussed below. See on this concept in the Roman authors: C. Nicolet *Space, geography and politics in the early Roman empire* (tr. H. Leclerc, Ann Arbor, Mich., 1991).

[10] Appian *praef.* (P. Viereck & A.G. Roos (eds), E. Gabba (rev.) *Appiani Historia Romana* (Leipzig, 1961) p. 1f.

[11] Vitruvius vi, 1, 10–11. Cf. D. Edwards *Religion and Power: Pagans, Jews and Christians in the Greek East* (NY/Oxford, 1996) 72.

[12] For earlier Christian concepts of the Land, see W.D. Davies *The Gospel and the Land: Early Christianity and Jewish Territorial Doctrine* (Berkeley etc., 1974).

become for him the centre of the world.[13] He writes of Jerusalem
as the centre of the world in his Com. in Ez.:

> *Hierusalem in medio mundi sitam, hic idem propheta testatur, umbilicum terrae*
> *eam esse demonstrans.*[14]

The concept of Jerusalem as navel ὀμφαλός of Judaea is found earlier in Josephus, and as navel of the world טיבורו של עולם in the
Babylonian Talmud.[15] But it seems to have been Jerome who was
first to Christianise it. This concept of the geographical centrality of
Jerusalem was to be very influential, and was perhaps the origin of
mediaeval maps showing Jerusalem as the centre of the world.[16]
Jerome backs up the biblical statement that Jerusalem is *in medio gentium* with a geographical explanation:

> *A partibus enim orientis cingitur plaga quae apellatur Asia; a partibus occidentis*
> *eius quae vocatur Europa; a meridie et austro Libya et Africa; a septemtrione*
> *Scythis, Armenia atque Perside et cunctis Ponti nationibus.*[17]

> Tr. For from the eastern parts it is surrounded by the *plaga* which is
> called Asia; from the western parts, by that which is called Europa,
> from the south and south Libya and Africa; from the north, the
> Scythians, Armenia and Persia and together with the peoples of Pontus.

The mental world map here is not a note of the farthest extents of
the Roman empire, as in *ep.* 60, but a continental map of the world.
Apart from Jerusalem at the centre, this is also the conventional
Roman picture, more like the concept of Strabo, who talks about
the naming of Asia and Europe and the conceptual division of the
inhabited world into three continents:

---

[13] Jerome's fluctuating attitude to Jerusalem is dependent on the ups and downs
of his relationship with the Christian community there. On this see H.I. Newman
'Between Jerusalem and Bethlehem: Jerome and the Holy Places of Palestine' in
A. Houtman, M.J.H.M. Poorthuis, J. Schwartz (eds) *Sanctity of Time and Space in
Tradition and Modernity* (Leiden/Boston/Köln, 1998) 215–227, with bibliography *ad loc.*

[14] *Com. in Hiez.* ii, 5: 5–6. (*CCSL* 75, 56; *PL* 25, 54).

[15] Josephus *BJ* iii, 52; BT Sanhedrin 37a. In the BT this is found in commentary on the Song of Songs cited in the name of R. Aha bar Hanina, a Palestinian
sage of the second century. I have not seen M. Tilly *Jerusalem-Nabel der Welt: Über-
lieferung und Funktionen von Heiligtumstraditionen im antiken Judentum* (Stuttgart, 2002).

[16] See on this: I.M. Higgins 'Defining the Earth's center in a Medieval "Multi-
Text": Jerusalem in *The Book of John Mandeville*: # Jerusalem as the Center of the
Earth: From St. Jerome to Felix Fabri' in S. Tomasch & S. Gilles (eds) *Text and
Territory: geographical imagination in the European Middle Ages* (Philadelphia, 1998) 34,
without discussion of Jerome's possible sources.

[17] *Com. in Hiez. loc. cit.*

ἀλλ' οὔτε τὴν Ἀσίαν οὔτε τὴν Εὐρώπην ὠνόμαζόν πω οἱ τότε, οὐδὲ
διῄρητο οὕτως εἰς τρεῖς ἠπείρους ἡ οἰκουμένη.[18]

tr. *LCL* But the people of that time were not yet using either the name
'Asia' or 'Europe,' nor yet had the inhabited world been divided into
three continents.

The Jewish origin of Jerome's concept of Jerusalem at the centre
has already been noted: Jewish thought had seen the world as a
series of concentric circles of decreasing holiness from the sanctuary,
the home of the Divine presence, through the Temple, through
Jerusalem and through Judaea out to the rest of the world.[19] It will
be shown below, in the discussion of Jerome's Jewish geography,
how his concept of the Land of Israel is superimposed, as it were,
on the wider boundaries of the Land as Promised. But for Jerome,
after the incarnation and the passion of Jesus, the Holy Land is now
Christian, and with it the very centre of the world.[20] That this is a
conscious shift in the representation of the centre of the world is
apparent from, for example, Jerome's commentary on the book of
Daniel, where he compares the countries which lie around Judaea
with the countries surrounding the empire of Alexander the Great.[21]

4.1.2. *Did Jerome have actual maps?*

Having looked briefly at Jerome's overall concept of the world, centred on Jerusalem or Bethlehem, we now turn to look at the geographical information he provides to see if there is evidence that he
was acquainted with any form of real map.

Apart from Jerome's geography of the Holy Land, there appears
to be a difference in the quality of his descriptions of different parts

---

[18] Strabo xii, 3,27. Strabo says this conceptual division post-dated Homeric
geography.

[19] Cf. Mishnah Kelim i, 6–9 and see M. Goodman 'Sacred Space in Diaspora
Judaism' in B. Isaac, A. Oppenheimer (eds.) *Studies on the Jewish Diaspora in the
Hellenistic and Roman periods* (Tel Aviv, 1996) p. 1f.; S. Fine *This Holy Place* (Notre
Dame, 1997) 12–13.

[20] *ep.* 60, 4: *ante resurrectionem Christi notus erat in Iudaea deus . . . ubi tunc totius orbis
homines ab India usque ad Britanniam, a [f]rigida septentrionis plaga usque ad feruores Atlantici
oceani.*

[21] *Com. in Dan.* III, xi 4–5 (*CCSL* 75A, 899; *PL* 25, 584) compares what was
north, south, east and west of Alexander's empire with what lay in these directions
with respect to Iudaea.

of the empire. It may well be that this was due to differences in the sort of information available to him. His descriptions of the east in *ep.* 60, for example, seem to owe much to the Greek geographical tradition, with the lists of rivers from west to east, for example—Halys, Cydnus, Orontes, Euphrates—which is reminiscent of Greek geographers from Herodotos onwards. His descriptions of the west, in the context of the barbarian invasions, for example, the entities detailed *inter Constantinopolim et Alpes Iulias*, however, are more like the Roman traditions, with lists which relate not only to cities and tribes, but also to provinces:

> *Scythiam, Thraciam, Macedoniam, Thessaliam, Dardaniam, Daciam, Epiros, Dalmatiam cunctasque Pannonias.*[22]

Here the list generally follows the movement of the invaders, from east to west.

The general scholarly consensus today is that the Romans may have had schematic world maps, but no regional maps as we know them.[23] As will be noted in the section on *periploi* and *itinera* below, there were extant verbal descriptions of linear routes—*itineraria*—along coast lines or roads, as well as lists of places within a region—cities, provinces etc. In the fourth century, Vegetius refers to military *itineraria picta*, which has been taken to refer to strip-maps with cities, hills etc. drawn along the route,[24] on the model of the *Tabula Peutingeriana*.[25] This map includes the whole Roman empire on a strip

---

[22] On the provincial divisions here see J.H.D. Scourfield *Consoling Heliodorus, A commentary on Jerome, Letter 60* (Oxford, 1993) 209–10.

[23] R.J.A. Talbert 'Rome's empire and beyond: the spatial aspect' in *Gouvernants et gouvernés dans l'imperium Romanum (IIIe av. J.-C.–Ier ap. J.-C.) Cahiers des études anciennes* 26 (1989) 215f. with bibliography *ad loc.*; C. Nicolet *op. cit.* n. 8 above; A.D. Lee *Information and Frontiers: Roman foreign relations in Antiquity* (Cambridge, 1993) ch. 3 'Background assumptions and knowledge: Geographical knowledge,' 81–90 and bibliography *ad loc.*; K. Brodersen *Terra Cognita: Studien zur römischen Raumerfassung* (Hildesheim/Zurich/NY) 1995; A.C. Bertrand 'Stumbling through Gaul: Maps, Intelligence and Caesar's *Bellum Gallicum*' *Ancient History Bulletin* 11 (1998) 107–122; K. Brodersen 'The presentation of geographical knowledge for travel and transport in the Roman world: *itineraria non tantum adnotata sed etiam picta*' in C. Adams & R. Laurence (eds.) *Travel and geography in the Roman empire* (London/NY, 2001) 7–21

[24] Vegetius 3,6: *usque eo ut sollertiores duces itineraria provinciarum in quibus necessitas gerebatur [geritur] non tantum ad notata sed picta habuisse firmentur ut non solum consilio mentis verum aspectu oculorum viam profecturus eligeret.*

On *itineraria picta* see A.&M. Levi *Itineraria picta. Contributio allo studio della Tabula Peutingeriana* (Roma, 1967) and now Brodersen (2001) in n. 23 above.

[25] L. Bosio *La Tabula Peutingeriana: una descrizione pittorica del mondo antico* (Rimini,

24 feet long by 1 foot wide. The possibilities for distortion are thus obvious, and countries are ordered on a west-east axis, so that the Holy Land appears rotated, with west uppermost.[26] The information on the map is presented in strip format, as in modern strip-maps.[27] The map is illustrated with schematic, often tiny drawings of towns, single buildings, hills etc.

Information has recently become available of an original and even earlier, possibly mid-first century BCE, map drawn on papyrus along the same sort of lines, published by Galazzi and Kramer. This too is an elongated strip-map, in this case of Spain only, with the emphasis on roads and rivers, with the lines drawn east-west. It appears together with the text of Artemidorus' *Geographoumena* with a table of distances and a description of physical geography.[28]

4.1.3. breuis tabella

Thus there do seem to have been some sort of schematic maps available in the Roman world. Could Jerome have had access to these? It is very difficult to know, but on seven occasions[29] Jerome does refer to a *breu[is] tabella* on which there is a depiction of the whole world.[30] A look at each of these parallel passages shows that the sum total of the information is quite revealing.

1983); O.A.W. Dilke *Greek and Roman Maps* (London, 1985) 112–120. The so-called Dura-Europos shield, once thought to be a similar map, has now been shown convincingly to be part of a *periplus* of the Black Sea: P. Arnaud 'Observations sur l'original du fragment du pseudo-bouclier de Doura-Europos' *Revue des Études Anciennes* 90 (1988) 151–6.

[26] Dilke *op. cit.* above, 117.

[27] Strip-maps: A.M. MacEachren 'A linear view of the world: Strip maps as a unique form of cartographic representation' *The American Cartographer* 13 (1986) 7–25; A.M. MacEachren, G.B. Johnson 'The evolution, application and implications of strip format travel maps' *The Cartographic Journal* 24 (1987) 147–158 esp. 148 and fig. 1.

[28] C. Galazzi, B. Kramer 'Artemidor im Zeichensaal. Eine papyrusrolle mit Text, Landkarte und Skizzenbüchern aus späthellenistischer Zeit' *Archiv für Papyrusforschung* 44 (1998) 189f. I am grateful to Professor Kramer for sending me details of her paper prior to publication.

[29] *breu[is] tabell[a]* was searched for using the CETEDOC CD-ROM of the church fathers.

[30] Other *breves tabellae:* Florus *Epitome* pr. 3: *faciam qui solent qui terrarum situs pingunt: in brevi quasi tabella totam eius imaginem amplector;* Ausonius *Gratiarum actio* 2, 9: *signanter et breviter omnia . . . indicare . . . ut qui terrarum orbem unius tabulae ambitu circumscribant,* and cf. Martial *Epigrammata,* 14,6: *Quam brevis immensum cepit membrana Maronem! Ipsius vultus prima tabella gerit.* Martial is referring to a codex of Virgil's works with

1) *quod solent ii facere, qui in breui tabella terrarum et urbium situs pingunt, et latissimas regiones in modico spatio conantur ostendere*
(*Com. in Ps. Praef*)

As people usually do who paint the sites of cities and countries on a *small tablet*, and try to show the widest regions in a small confine

2) *quasi in quadam breui tabella, sicut pinxisse terrarum, totius que orbis uastitatem et ambitum oceani, angusto monstrasse compendio*
(*Com. in Eccl.* 12, 1)

As in some *small tablet* thus to paint the immensity of the whole world and the lands and to show in a narrow compass the circle of Ocean

3) *quomodo nos totius legis quasi uniuersi orbis descriptionem in breui tabella conamur ostendere*
(*Com. in Is.* 18; 66, 22)

How we try to show the delineation of the whole law like all the world on a *small tablet*

4) *sicut hi, qui in breui tabella terrarum situs pingunt*
(*ep.* 60, 7)

Like those who paint the sites of the lands on a *small tablet*[31]

5) *quasi latissimos terrarum situs in breui tabella uolui*
demonstrare non extendens spatia sensuum atque tractatuum, sed quibusdam punctis atque conpendiis infinita significans . . .
(*ep.* 73, 5)

I wanted, as it were, to demonstrate the widest regions of the lands on a *small tablet*, not treating extensively ideas or areas of thought, but signifying endless space by certain points and roads

6) *quasi in breui tabella latissimos terrarum situs ostendere uolui*
(*ep.* 123, 13)

I wanted to show the widest sites of lands as on a *small tablet*

7) *ut totam tibi scaenam operum tuorum quasi in breui*
depingerem tabella
(*ep.* 147, 12)

As if I were to paint the scene of your deeds for you as on a *small tablet*

---

the poet's picture at the beginning. Virgil's epic was seen 'immeasurable'—a world in itself.
   [31] Tr. *LCL*: 'As men draw the map of the world on one small tablet' . . .

If the information from these parallel texts is combined, it is clear that they are all talking about what is depicted (*pingunt, pinxisse, depingerem*) or shown (*ostendere, demonstrare*), on a small tablet (*in breui tabella*). This is reminiscent of Vegetius' *picta* above, which have been interpreted as illustrations on itineraries, as well as Florus' *brev[is] tabella*.[32] On Jerome's *tabellae* are the *situs latissimos terrarum* or the *situs terrarum et urbium*, or the *latissimos regiones* or the *terrarum totiusque orbis uastitatem et ambitum oceani*—ie wide regions of the earth, the sites of cities and lands, the immensity of the whole world and the circle of Ocean. These vast areas are shown in a small space, *in modico spatio*, and most interestingly, *angusto compendio*, in a narrow confine. While the term *angustus* was used as a general word for small, its original meaning referred to a narrow strip,[33] and there may be a hint here of a strip-map. This possibility is further strengthened by passage 5) above, from *ep.* 73:

> I wanted, as it were, to demonstrate the widest regions of the lands on a *small tablet*, not treating extensively ideas or areas of thought, but signifying endless space by certain points and roads ...

Here Jerome seems to be saying that wide areas are signified on tablets as points, *punctis* and roads, *conpendiis*. This might imply that he was familiar with the same sort of strip-map showing towns and roads in linear format as on the Artemidorus map and the *Tabula Peutingeriana*.[34]

In five of the works in which his *breu[is] tabella* appears there are also geographical passages.[35] Could Jerome then have had some sort

---

[32] Vegetius see above: n. 24; Florus: n. 30.

[33] L&S *s.v. angustus*. I owe this point to Dr Yuval Shahar.

[34] *Punctis* might seem to imply towns shown as dots, as on modern maps. On the *Tabula Peutingeriana* towns are shown by tiny drawings of buildings or as a kink in the road. The Artemidorus map is unclear. There is also the possibility that Jerome may have had some vague awareness of Ptolemaic geographical concepts: O.A.W. Dilke *op. cit.* n. 25 above.

[35] *Com. in Eccl.* 12,1: (*CCSL* 72, 349; *PL* 23, 1105–6); *Com. in Es.* 18; 66, 22: (*CCSL* 73A, 796; *PL* 24, 675); *ep.* 60, 4 extremes of the world from Britain to the Atlantic and India quoted above n. 8; *ib.* 16 area between Constantinople and the Julian Alps; *ib.* Antioch and rivers in east; *ib.* Arabia Phoenix, Palaestina, Aegyptus; *ep.* 73, 8: discussion of route of Abraham in Holy Land; *ep.* 123, 15: *quidquid inter Alpes et Pyrenaeum est ... quod oceano Rhenoque concluditur* with extensive details of Gaul (see below).

of schematic linear map on which he checked his geographical distances (or which he remembered when thinking geographically)?
There is not enough evidence to do more than suggest such a connection. The geographical information in *ep.* 123, 15 is particularly
suggestive in this context. Here Jerome, having mentioned his *breui[s]*
tabella, is describing the barbarian invasions of Gaul, and he lists the
places affected. He begins at the provincial boundary and then moves
westwards. The first list is the most detailed, and the places or tribes
are mentioned in geographical order as they occur on the known
Roman roads of Gaul:

> *Mogontiacus* [Mainz], *nobilis quondam ciuitas, capta atque subuersa est* . . .
> *Uangiones* [Worms] *longa obsidione finiti, Remorum* [Rheims] *urbs praepotens,*
> *Ambiani* [Amiens], *Atrabatae* [Arras] *extremi que homines Morini, Tornacus*
> [Tournai].³⁶

The only sizeable town omitted is Trier. Jerome then starts again
from the provincial border and moves westwards, but this time with
no towns beyond the border (except for Tolosa, where there was a
bishop), only provinces:

> *Nemetae* [Speyer], *Argentoratus* [Strasbourg] *translatae in Germaniam, Aquitaniae*
> *Nouemque populorum, Lugdunensis et Narbonensis prouinciae* . . . *Tolosae* . . .
> *Hispaniae.*

Jerome himself spent some time at Trier,³⁷ which could explain why
he might have had access to a map or *itinerarium* of the area.³⁸ It is
not clear to me why he omitted the name from his list: perhaps he
had not heard of barbarian attacks on the city, or perhaps the city
appeared graphically in a different form from the other towns on
his map or itinerary.³⁹

---

³⁶ See E.M. Wightman *Gallia Belgica* (London, 1985) ch. 14 and map pp. xi–xii
with roads and towns. All these towns are on roads appearing in the Antonine
Itinerary or the *Tabula Peutingeriana* or both. Wightman notes (301) 'Accounts [sc.
of the invasions] are more dramatic than clear' and continues with a citation of
this passage.

³⁷ Jerome at Trier: see Introduction.

³⁸ There is also an extant *itinerarium* on stone found at Atuatuca [Tongeren] mentioning some of these towns: Brodersen *op. cit.* n. 23 above, 181f. with bibliography *ad loc.* Recently Salway has suggested that this and other documents should be
seen as *tabellaria*, lists of towns along a route, displayed as stone tablets at various
places along the route: B. Salway 'Travel, *itineraria* and *tabellaria*' in C. Adams &
R. Laurence (eds.) *Travel and geography in the Roman empire* (London/NY, 2001) 22–66.
contra: Brodersen, *op. cit.*

³⁹ Different graphic formats: In the Antonine Itinerary 374, 1 there is a head-

If we compare Jerome's account with Ammianus' *excursus* on Gaul the difference is noticeable.[40] Ammianus notes many of the same places as Jerome (Mogontiacus, Vangiones, Nemetae, Ambiani etc.) but they are mostly not in geographical order along the roads of Roman Gaul. Plotted on a map of the roads they produce a criss-cross of movement in all directions. Ammianus tells us in his intro-duction to his *excursus* on Gaul that he took much of his information from Timagenes who was *et diligentia Graecus et lingua* and indeed his information is organised in a way more similar to, say, the Greek geographer Pausanias,[41] than to other Latin writers or to *itineraria* organised along roads. Ammianus goes from one provincial division to the next: *secunda Germania, prima Germania, Belgica prima, secunda Belgica* and so on. Within each division he cites the principal towns, only in a single case in geographical order—the towns along the River Rhine—but not along roads. Even in his up-dating of Timagenes, Ammianus would seem to have used a different kind of document from Jerome's first list here. Barnes suggests he might have found his information on 'a list of provinces and cities of Gaul similar to the later Notitiae Galliarum.'[42] It would seem likely that Ammianus, unlike Jerome, used lists or literary sources here rather than maps or itineraries.

Jerome's discussion in *ep.* 73 is also suggestive of the use of some kind of map or itinerary. Here Jerome is discussing the site of the palace of Melchizedek, king of Salem (Gen. 14.18). He notes that Abraham was coming from *Dan, quae hodie Paneas appellatur* to *Sichim* [Shechem] in the Biblical account, and thus would not have gone

---

ing *Item a Treveris[Trier] Argentorato.* Trier does not appear again separately, unlike Argentoratum. This itinerary also mentions Mogontiaco, Bormitomago [Uangiones], Noviomago [Nemetae].

Personifications: Rome, Antioch and Constantinople appear as personifications on the *Tabula Peutingeriana*: Bosio *op. cit.* n. 25 above: Rome p. 84, pl. 21; Constantinople p. 87, pl. 22; Antioch p. 88, pl. 23. The personification of Trier, Treveri, appears in the Filocalus Calendar of 354: see *Lexicon Iconographicum Mythologiae Classicae* (Zurich/Munich 1981–) *s.v.* Treveri (Rainer Volkammer).

[40] Ammianus 15,11: an excursus describing the *situ[s] locorum*. Unlike Jerome, he does mention Trier, *domicilium principum clarum*.

[41] On Pausanias' organisation of his material see A. Snodgrass *An Archaeology of Greece* (Berkeley, 1987) 75f.

[42] T.D. Barnes *Ammianus Marcellinus and the Representation of Historical Reality* (Ithaca/London, 1998) 99. Barnes continues 'or more probably a map or maps of Gaul from the mid-fourth century.'

via Jerusalem, although he could have gone via Salem, which was in the territory of Shechem according to some.[43] Jerome does not say that he himself visited Salem or nearby Aenon on his journey round the holy places with Paula. He may have done so, like the pilgrim Egeria,[44] especially since he does not tell us how he returned south from Galilee. But the presence of these details in *ep.* 73, together with his use of the image of a map in 73, 5 as we saw above may suggest that he used some sort of map here to check the details of Abraham's journey.

Eusebius' *Onomasticon* in its original version included a καταγραφή of Judaea, noted in the preface. Jerome translates this as *chorografia*. There was also an εἰκὼν διαχαράξας of Jerusalem and the Temple, which Jerome translates as *cum brevissima expositione picturam*. Καταγραφή can be used of a graphic work, but *chorografia* is usually used of a verbal description.[45] Both are evidently not the same as the εἰκών/*pictura* of Jerusalem.[46] It is even more difficult to know what might have been meant by the latter—a schematic presentation with a partial street-plan, like Jerusalem on the Madeba mosaic map, as is generally assumed?[47] A picture of Jerusalem with its buildings, as on the Umm al-Rasas mosaic? Or a personification of Jerusalem like Rome, Constantinople or Antioch on the *Tabula Peutingeriana*? Antioch, it may be noted, appears on the *Tabula Peutingeriana* as a seated figure together with her temple.[48]

---

[43] Jerome presents several different versions of the meaning and position of Salem: *On.* 41, 1; *ib.* 107, 1; *ib.* 151, 1; *QHG* on Gen. 14:18 and see C.T.R. Hayward *Saint Jerome's Hebrew Questions on Genesis* (Oxford, 1995) *ad loc.* as well as this discussion in *ep.* 73. Salem [Shalem] as belonging to Shechem is based on Gen. 33.18. See also Newman, 264–8 and Stemberger (*op. cit.* n. 8 above) 97–100 esp. 99–100.

[44] *Itinerarium Egeriae* xiii, 2–xv, 6 (*CCSL* 175, 54–56). Egeria saw a church and was shown the foundations of Melchisedech's palace at Sedima (Salem). She was also shown the road along the Jordan by which Abraham came back from the battle with Quodollagomor to Sodom: *ista via ... qua ... regressus est sanctus Abraam de cede Quodollagomor, regis gentium, reuertens in Sodomis, qua ei occurrit sanctus Melchisedech, rex Salem.*

[45] Cf. Pomponius Mela's book of world geography: *de chorographia*. This was also the title of a book by Cicero and a poem by Terence. The term is used of a verbal description in Ptolemy i, 1. But cf. Vitruvius 8, 2, 6: *capita fluminum, quae orbe terrarum chorographiis picta itemque scripta plurima maximaque inveniuntur.*

[46] Discussion of the meaning of καταγραφή with bibliography: M. Avi-Yonah *The Madaba Mosaic Map* (Jerusalem, 1954) 30.

[47] See the recent discusssion of L. Di Segni 'The "Onomasticon" of Eusebius and the Madeba Map' in M. Piccirillo, E. Alliata (eds.) *The Madeba Map Centenary 1897–1997: Travelling through the Byzantine Ummayad Period* (Jerusalem, 1999) 115–6.

[48] Jerusalem on the Madeba map (6th century): H. Donner, H. Cüppers *Die*

4.1.4. *The 'Jerome map'*

The so-called 'Jerome map' of the Holy Land is a mediaeval map
in Latin found together with a map of Asia in a copy of the *Onomasticon*
dated to the late twelfth century.[49] It has been suggested that it is
a copy of Eusebius' or Jerome's original map of the Holy Land mentioned in the preface of the *Onomasticon*.[50] This cannot be the case.[51]
Some strange things never mentioned by Jerome but marked on the
map, such as the Oracle of the Sun and Moon, could have been
added by a mediaeval copyist, but there are other integral data which
Jerome would never have approved, iconographically, philologically
or topographically. I shall take one example of each; there are more
which could be cited. They are all places which were visited by him.
Mount Tabor, remarked on by Jerome more than once as 'rounded
and sublime' as well as 'equal from all sides,'[52] appears on the map
iconographically as asymmetrically jagged peaks. Lida and Diospolis

---

Mosaikkarte von Madaba (Wiesbaden, 1977); P. Donceel-Voûte 'La carte de Madaba:
Cosmographie, anachronisme et propagande' *RB* 135 (1988) 519f.; For excellent
colour reproductions: M. Piccirillo *The Mosaics of Jordan* (Amman, 1993) pl. 63,
p. 83: Η ΑΓΙΑ ΠΟΛΙΣ ΙΕΡΟΥΣΑ[ΛΗΜ]; Umm al-Rasas [Kastron Mefaa] mosaic (8th
century): *ib.* pl. 344, p. 218: Η ΑΓΙΑ ΠΩΛΙΣ; Peutinger map (for date see n. 24
above): Bosio *op. cit.* n. 25 above: Rome p. 84, pl. 21; Constantinople p. 87, pl.
22; Antioch p. 88, pl. 23. Discussion of personifications: J.M.C. Toynbee 'Roma
and Constantinopolis in Late Antique Art from 312–365' *Journal of Roman Studies*
37 (1947) 135f.; Dilke *op. cit.* n. 25, p. 117; *LIMC s.v.* Antiocheia (J. Balty);
Constantinopolis (M. Vickers); Roma (E. di Filippo Balestrazzi); E. Weber 'The
Tabula Peutingeriana and the Madeba Map' in E. Alliata *et al.* 'The Legends of
the Madeba Map' in M. Piccirillo, E. Alliata (eds) *The Madeba Map Centenary
1897–1997: Travelling through the Byzantine Ummayad Period* (Jerusalem, 1999) 41–46.
[49] K. Miller *Mappaemundi: Die ältesten Weltkarten. III Die kleineren Weltkarten* (Stuttgart,
1865) 1–21, with map on p. 14; P.D.A. Harvey 'The twelfth-century Jerome maps
of Asia and Palestine,' (Paper given at the 17th international conference on the history of cartography, Lisbon, Thursday 10th July, 1997). I am grateful to Professor
Harvey for letting me have a copy of his paper prior to publication.
[50] Miller *loc. cit.*; C. Delano Smith 'Geography or Christianity? Maps of the Holy
Land before AD 1000' *Journal of Theological Studies* 42 (1991) 147–148 and fig. 2.
[51] Cf. Harvey, *op. cit.* n. 23 above; *id.* 'The Cartographic context of the Madeba
Map' in E. Alliata *et al.* 'The Legends of the Madeba Map' in M. Piccirillo,
E. Alliata (eds.) *The Madeba Map Centenary 1897–1997: Travelling through the Byzantine
Ummayad Period* (Jerusalem, 1999) 106.
[52] *Com. in Osee* i, v 1–2 (*CCSL* 76, 51; *PL* 25, 898): *Thabor mons in Galilea, situs in
campestribus, rotundus atque sublimis, et ex omni parte finitur aequaliter; Onomasticon* 99, 22:
mons in medio Galilaeae campo mira rotunditate, sublimis. It could, of course, be argued
that the jagged peaks are mere map-makers' convention, but Jerome would hardly
have approved.

appear as two separate towns (on the coast!), when Jerome writes in
ep. 108, 8 'Lydda, now known as Diospolis.' Jerome, as we have
seen, was very careful in his works over the identification and naming of towns in Palestine which appeared in the Hebrew Bible and
the New Testament. Finally, 'Emmas quae nunc Nicopolis' is sited
on the map south of Eleutheropolis and next to Gaza, when Jerome
in *ep.* 108, 8 writes of visiting this town on the road between Jaffa
and Jerusalem, and also notes the topography correctly in his commentary on Daniel: this is 'where the mountains of the province of
Judaea begin to rise.'[53]

It thus seems unlikely in the extreme that Jerome would have
countenanced all these discrepancies and more between the map and
his written works. It seems far more likely that the map was made
by someone less familiar than he was with the details of fourth century Palestinian geography.

Thus to sum up Jerome's general geographical concepts: Jerome may
have had access to real schematic maps or itineraries of parts of the
empire—Gaul and the Holy Land, although he would not have countenanced the so-called 'Jerome map'. He clearly christianises the
Roman mental map: his world has three continents, but the centre
has shifted from Rome to the Holy Land. Indeed, Jerome claims
that Christians now have title to the physical Holy Land following
the passion and crucifixion of Jesus. We shall turn now to look at
the part Jewish sources play in Jerome's geography of the Holy Land.

4.2. JEROME'S JEWISH GEOGRAPHY:
THE BOUNDARIES OF THE LAND OF ISRAEL

Before looking at Jerome's concept of the Holy Land in *ep.* 108, it
will be useful to examine the geographical use of Jewish sources in
his biblical commentary. Jerome's geography of the Hebrew Bible is
primarily a Jewish geography. Christian commentators on the Bible,
such as Origen, had related to geography almost exclusively alleg-
orically, so Jerome had little choice as regards sources. The first

---

[53] *ep.* 108, 8: [from Joppa] *repetito itinere, Nicopolim, quae prius Emmaus vocabatur . . .*
ingressa est Hierusolymam; Com. in Dan. iv, xi 44–45 (*CCSL* 75A, 933; *PL* 25, 600) *ubi*
incipiunt Judaeae prouinciae montana consurgere.

century Jewish historian Josephus is often used by Christian writers, and his *Bellum Judaicum* becomes their main source for descriptions of the destruction of the Temple in Jerusalem, which they saw as God's punishment to the Jews for their crucifixion of Jesus.[54] Thus Jerome uses Josephus often,[55] but where the Jewish historian does not provide the material he needs, he uses other Jewish material, including the *targumim*. Hayward has shown how many parallels there are to targumic material in Jerome's commentaries and especially in the *Hebrew Questions on Genesis* [*QHG*],[56] and McNamara has noted that Jerome makes use of targumic material not only in his commentaries, but even within the text of the Vulgate.[57] Jerome's Hebrew was learned from Jews in order to enable him to translate the Bible; it is therefore not surprising that he uses material from the Aramaic *targumim*, whose purpose was to translate the Hebrew biblical text into the local language for the Jews of Palestine, and which in the process provided commentary and exposition of the text.[58] In his commentary on the book of Ezekiel he wants to explain the sites mentioned as the boundaries of the Promised Land in Ezekiel 47:13–48:8. He notes that there are two other places in the Bible which deal with the boundaries of the land, Joshua 13:1–21; 15–21:43, and Numbers 34: 2–12. His exposition of the boundaries of the land

---

[54] H. Schreckenberg, K. Schubert *Jewish Historiography and Iconography in Early and Medieval Christianity* (Assen/Minneapolis 1992) 30: 'Jewish history as represented by Josephus became in the Christian assessment a sort of *praeparatio evangelica*'. See also eg Jerome *Com. in Es.* xvii: 64, 8/12 (*CCSL* 73A,739; *PL* 24, 626). For Josephus as a possible source for the Christian pilgrim from Bordeaux see: S. Weingarten 'Was the pilgrim from Bordeaux a woman? A reply to Laurie Douglass' *JECS* 7 (1999) 294.

[55] As noted above in chapter 2.1.8, there is no evidence that Jerome read secular literature in Greek, but Josephus can hardly be considered 'secular'—besides his re-writing of the Hebrew Bible in *AJ*, his historical account of the destruction of the Jewish Temple is used by Jerome often as Jewish evidence for Divine punishment of the Jews.

[56] Commentaries: R. Hayward 'Saint Jerome and the Aramaic targums' *Journal of Semitic Studies* 32 (1987) 105–123. *Id. op. cit.* n. 43 above esp. 21–2.

[57] M. McNamara *Targum and Testament* (Shannon, 1972) 89: 'Jerome. . . . makes several explicit references to the Jewish understanding of Scripture in his own day. At other times Jewish influence is present in his writings even when not specifically mentioned. The Jewish (and targumic) understanding of Scripture has even influenced his Vulgate rendering.' Newman 70f. also demonstrates Jerome's use of targumic materials.

[58] For a convenient summary: P.S. Alexander *Anchor Bible Dictionary* (NY, 1992) *s.v.* Targum, Targumim 320–331.

is clearly taken from Jewish sources: he introduces it with *dicunt...
Hebraei*, and follows this shortly with *Hebraei autumnant* then *Hebraei...
nominant*.[59] His identifications of places along these borders are very
close to those found in *Targum* Neofiti on Numbers. The text of
Targum Neofiti, apparently a Palestinian *targum*, was only discovered
in the 1950's, so it was not available to the 19th- and early 20th-
century scholars who dealt with concepts of the boundaries of the
land, such as Hildesheimer and Abel.[60] It is interesting that Jerome
begins with the verb *dicunt*, for the *targumim* began as verbal translation and commentary on the Hebrew Bible and it is not known
when they were committed to writing.

I have put Jerome's identifications side by side with those of the
targum for ease of comparison. Jerome discusses each border in turn,
taking first the text from Ezekiel and then the parallel text in Numbers.
As usual with him, he gives first the 'historical' i.e. geographical
identification, and then the allegorical meaning.

Jerome: *Com. in Hiez.*	*Targum* Neofiti[61]
North	
a Mari Magno	from the Great Sea
Palaestinae, Phoenicis Syriae	
quae appellatur Coele Ciliciae	
per Aegyptum	

---

[59] *Dicuntque Hebraei: Com. in Hiez.* xiv, xlvii, 15–17 (*CCSL* 75, 720; *PL* 25, 497f.)
Hebraei autumnant: ib. loc. cit. 721; *Hebraei... nominant: ib.* 18, 723. A. Kamesar 'The
evaluation of narrative aggadah in Greek and Latin patristic literature' *JThS* 45
(1994) 37–71 shows (p. 60) how Jerome distinguishes between what he sees as a
legitimate Jewish historical tradition, in which case he uses words such as *tradunt*
and *narrant*, and Jewish conjectures, where he uses *putant, autumnant* etc. Here he is
using *autumnant* for a case where Jewish tradition has two alternatives: *uel Ama-
num... uel Taurum*. Further discussion of this terminology: pp. 65–6.
For Jews as the authority in Christian eyes on individual sites in Palestine, see
O. Limor, 'Christian Sacred Space and the Jew' in *From Witness to Witchcraft: Jews
and Judaism in Medieval Christian Thought* (ed. J. Cohen, Wiesbaden, 1996) 55–77.
[60] N.H. Hildesheimer *Beiträge zur geographie Palästinas* (no place, 1885) = *ib.* 'Geography
of the Land of Israel' in H. Bar-Daroma (tr.) *The boundaries of the Land of Israel:
research papers* (Jerusalem, 1965, in Hebrew); F.-M. Abel *Géographie de la Palestine* I
(Paris, 1938) chap. 2 'Limites et noms de la Palestine' 298f. Abel remarks in a foot-
note that *Targum Ps-Jonathan* extends the borders of Palestine as far as Cilicia, and
that Jerome's concept of the boundaries of Palestine as shown in *ep.* 129 is 'prob-
ablement sous l'influence de ces vues juives.' Ps.-Jonathan and Neofiti share some
identifications (q.v. Diez Macho *ad loc.*), but Jerome is much closer to Neofiti than
to Ps.-Jonathan.
[61] *Targum* Neofiti: *Neophyti 1: Targum palestinense ms. de la biblioteca Vaticana*, vol. 4,
(ed. A. Diez Macho, Eng. tr. M. McNamara, Madrid, 1974) Numbers 34.

montem Altissimum =	
uel Amanum. . . . uel	Amanus
Taurum	Taurus
Emath quae	entrance of Antioch
nunc Epiphania nominatur	
ab Antiocho . . . nam	
cognomentum habuit	
Ἐπιφανής	

Sedada

Zephrona = Zephyrium	Zephirin
oppidum Ciliciae	gates of Cilicia
uilla Enan = Aser Enan,	Tirat [= castle, village of] ʻEnewata
Enan, atrio Enan	

Here Jerome ends his identifications *secundum historiam*, which have all followed Neofiti on Numbers. (For the problem of Emath, see the appendix to this chapter.) Jerome then turns to the remaining names in Ezekiel, which he is forced to explain *sequens* ἀναγογήν in the absence of any geographical-historical source. Because of his use of the two texts, the geographical order of places is not always completely clear. However, in his *ep.* 129 to Dardanus, Jerome has a further discussion of the borders of the Promised Land—*terra repromissionis.* I have used this much briefer outline to clarify his geographical picture of the borders of the Land of Israel. Here he is not bound to follow the order of the biblical text, and his descriptions are in strictly geographical order:

> *ab aquilone Taurum montem et Zephyrium usque Emath, quae appellatur Epiphania Syriae.*[62]

Returning to *Com. in Hiez.* and *Targum* Neofiti:

East

uilla Enan = Aser Enan,	Tirat [= castle, village of] ʻEnewata
Enan, atrio Enan	
de Apamia = Sephama	Apamea
. . . in Rebla = Antiochia	Antioch

---

[62] *ep.* 129, 5: In the north via the Taurus mountain and Zephyrium as far as Emath, which is called Syrian Epiphania.

fontem = Daphnem	Daphne, to the east of 'Ayna ['Ayna = fountain]
mare Chenereth = ad stagnum Tyberiadis	Sea of Gennesar
mari = Mortuo [orientale]	extremities of sea of salt

For the eastern border Jerome again follows the identifications of *targum* Neofiti, uilla Enan to Apamia, paralleled by Antioch to the Sea of Galilee. He then discusses whether the sea in the description of the eastern border

> *termini usque Iordanem, et ad ultimum claudentur mari* (Num. 34,12)

means the Dead Sea *mare Mortuum* or *ut alii putant,* the Red Sea

> *lingua maris Rubri, in cuius littore Ahila posita est ubi nunc moratur legio et praesidium Romanum.*

This second identification is not in the *targum* but the information about Ahila [Aila, modern Eilat] resembles that found in the *Onomasticon* (*On.* 7,25f.).[63] The information based on Numbers here is vague, he tells us, but the information in Ezekiel clarifies things: the border runs from Hauran, i.e. Damascus in the desert and Gilead, via the Jordan to the *mare orientale*. This can only mean the Dead Sea, not the Red Sea. Once again *ep.* 129 clarifies his geographical concept:

> *ad orientem uero per Antiochiam et lacum Cenereth, quae nunc Tiberias appellatur, et Iordanem, qui mari influit salinarum, quod nunc mortuum dicitur; trans Iordanem autem duarum et semis tribuum posessio est . . .*[64]

South

torrentum Aegypti iuxta urbem Rinocorurum mari influit	Nile of the Egyptians and its exits west
Thamar = Palmyra	
contradictionis Cades (see below)	

---

[63] *On.* 7,25f. *Ailath in extremis finibus Palaetinae iuncta . . . mari rubro. . . . sedet autem ibi legio Romana.*

[64] *Ib. loc. cit.* to the west indeed via Antioch and the Lake of Cenereth which is now called Tiberias, and the Jordan, which flows into the Salt Lake, which is now called Dead; while across the Jordan belongs to the two and a half tribes . . .

solitudine Sin iuxta	wilderness of Zin
Edom et Mari Rubro	boundaries Edom
Ascensum Scorpionis	Ascent of Akrabbim (of the Scorpions)
	Mount of Iron
Senna	
Cadesbarne in deserto	Rekem de-Gi'a
ad urbem Petram	
atrium Adar	Tirat [= castle, village of] Adarayya
	Shuq Masai
Asemona	Qesem

Here Jerome follows Numbers from the desert of Sin next to Edom noting the sites according to the text. He explains the 'torrent of Egypt' as flowing into the sea next to Rinocorura; Neofiti similarly explains it as a western branch of the Egyptian Nile. He then returns to the text of Ezekiel, and identifies Tamar in the east with Tadmor, Palmyra. Here he appears to have reverted to his philological geography.[65] Tadmor is indeed east of the Holy Land, but much farther east than the boundary according to Neofiti, although it is possible that Jerome was influenced here by the boundaries of the Land in Gen. 15, 18–21 which extend to the Euphrates. Unfortunately Jerome does not comment on this at all in *QHG*. Later he adds an explanation of Cadesbarne. This is identified by the targum with Rekem de-Gi'a, and Jerome notes it as being in the desert *ad Petram*. Petra was called Rekem *a Syris* as Jerome notes in the *Onomasticon.*[66] *Ep.* 129 has:

> *a meridie maris salinarum per Sina et Cades-Barne, usque ad torrentem Aegypti, qui iuxta Rinocoruram mari magno influit.*[67]

---

[65] See above, chapter 2 on the *vita Hilarionis*.

[66] *On.* 143, 7. See also: B. Maisler 'Reqem and Hagar' *Tarbiz* 20 (1949, in Hebrew) 316–319. Targum Ps.-Jonathan on Ezekiel also has Reqem for Qadesh (Ez. 47,19).

[67] *ep.* 129, 5: from the south of the Salt Sea via Senna [Sina] and Cades-Barne, as far as the River of Egypt, which flows into the Great Sea next to Rinocorura. Labourt here translates 'Sina' as 'mont Sina,' but Jerome, who calls it 'Senna' in the Vulgate and his commentary on Ezekiel, was aware that this was not the case. Jerome does not, however, seem to have realized that the Hebrew צִנָה is the locative of צִין which he correctly translates above as *solitud[ine] Sin*.

West

de mari usque ad	the Great Sea[West], the ocean
mare usque ad eum	
locum qui est contra	
Emath urbem Syriae	
de qua supra	
diximus	the Great Sea [= West] the ocean—these are
Occidens semper	the waters of the beginning—its islands,
in mari est, semper in	its ports, and the ships
salo et fluctibus	
ubi cotidie naufragia	
suscitantur et	
miserorum neces	
et diuitiarum	
et mercium amissio	

Jerome's west is, of course, the sea coast. Here it extends *ad eum locum qui est contra Emath*—i.e. לבו חמת [lit. to the entrance of Hamat] which the *targum*, as noted above on the northern boundary, has translated as the 'entrance of Antioch.' Jerome here is siting the entrance to his Emath/Epiphania/Antioch on the coast. Ancient Antioch was not on the coast, but it was on a navigable river, and Jerome actually relates that Paula sailed from Seleucia, which is on the coast, up the estuary of the Orontes, to Antioch. This, then, may be his understanding of the text. The *targum*'s expansion on the great sea with its islands, ports and the ships is paralleled by Jerome's sea as the site of many disasters—shipwrecks and lost merchandise. He notes too, quite correctly, that the sea and the west are always synonymous. The text of *ep.* 129 confirms this picture, and the order here is again strictly geographical, south to north:

> *ab occidente ipsum mare, quod Palaestinae, Phoenici, Syriae Coelae, Ciliciaeque praetenditur.*[68]

Jerome's Land of Israel, then, extends from Cilicia in the north-west to Egypt in the south, and as far as Palmyra in the east. This constitutes a problem, for it corresponds neither to his contemporary Judaea-Palestina nor to any historical time. The problem is dis-

---

[68] *Ib. loc. cit.*: from the west, the same sea which lies all along Palestine, Phoenicia, Coele Syria and Cilicia.

cussed in his *ep.* 129 where, as shown above, the boundaries of the Promised Land are presented with reasonable geographical accuracy. However, Jerome is well aware that the picture thus obtained does not correspond with any historical reality—the promise, he explains, was never actually fulfilled: *haec tibi repromissa, non tradita.* The actual land of Israel is pathetically tiny: one has only to read Joshua and Judges to understand this:

> *Lege librum Iosue et Iudicum et quantis possessionum angustiis sis coartatus, intelleges.*

On his wider concept of the promise he proceeds to superimpose the picture of the smaller reality. The dimensions he gives for the smaller land of Israel are reasonably accurate. The distance quoted from Jaffa to Bethlehem is 46 miles. The distance is in fact 48 miles via Jerusalem, and it may have been possible to cut this down by not going through the centre of the city.[69] The text of *ep.* 129 in Labourt, Hilberg and the Cetedoc CD-ROM gives a distance of *uix septuaginta quinque* 'scarcely 75' miles between Idumea and Jerusalem. Jerome saw Idumaea as a wide region corresponding to biblical Edom, which extended from Eleutheropolis as far as Petra and Aila, as he writes (*Com. in Abdiam* 5, 6–7):

> *omnia australis regio Idumaeorum de Eleutheropoli usque Petram et Ailam.*

75 miles from Jerusalem would bring us to some unspecified spot within this wide region. However, this letter was cited, not long after it was written, in a document attributed to Eucherius, bishop of Lyons in the mid-fifth century.[70] The distance here is given as 'scarcely 25', not 75, miles, which fits the distance from Jerusalem to Eleutheropolis.[71] The distance from Dan [Paneas] to Beersheba Jerome records as 'hardly 160 miles;' it is, in fact, nearer 180 miles.

---

[69] For distances along the roads between Jaffa and Jerusalem, see: M. Fischer, B. Isaac, I. Roll: *Roman roads in Judaea* II: *The Jaffa-Jerusalem roads* (Oxford, 1996) 296–7.

[70] (Pseudo) Eucherius *Eucherii quae fertur de situ Hierusolimae epistula ad Faustum presbyterum* ed. I. Fraipont in *Itineraria et alia geographica* (*CCSL* 175) 17, 240; H. Donner *Pilgerfahrt ins Heilige Land: Die ältesten Berichte christlicher Palästinapilger (4.–7. Jahrhundert)* (Stuttgart, 1979) 171f.

[71] Hilberg 170 n. 5 also gives *uiginti quinqe* as a variation in ms. Vaticanus lat. 355 + 356 (ix–x century).

216 CHAPTER FOUR

The question of where Jerome could have obtained his contemporary information is interesting. He certainly went from Jaffa to Bethlehem himself, as recorded in *ep.* 108. However, the distance of 48 miles is measured along the road to Jerusalem via Abu Gosh, whereas in *ep.* 108 Jerome records taking the longer but easier road via Beit Horon where the distance would have been 52 miles.[72] The roads from Jaffa-Jerusalem were official roads marked by milestones. Thus Jerome may have obtained his information from an official document, even from milestones, or from an itinerary or map.[73] Eleutheropolis, which marked the beginning of Idumaea, is also a *caput viarum* and connected to Jerusalem by an official road with milestones. Beersheba, site of a Roman camp, was not on an official highway marked with milestones, but the Onomasticon (*On.* 50,2 = 51,2) notes it as being 20 miles from Chebron, which in turn is 22 miles from Jerusalem (*On.* 6,11 = 7,17). There were official highways connecting Jerusalem with Paneas/Dan. No extant Christian itinerary before the late sixth century includes Beersheba. The *Itinerarium Burdigalense* (333 CE), indeed, has a marked dearth of information about facilities south of Jerusalem—there are no *mansiones* or *mutationes* noted as in other parts of the country.

Thus in the absence of Christian geographical sources Jerome appears to makes use of contemporary Jewish information to identify the boundaries of the Land of Israel, although he may have had some further documentation for the distances he gives. We shall turn now to see how he uses his translation of Eusebius' *Onomasticon* and his description of Paula's *iter* through the Holy Places to create a Christian geography of the Holy Land.

4.3. JEROME'S CHRISTIAN GEOGRAPHY

4.3.1. *Spiritual and material geography*

In his commentaries on the books of the New Testament Jerome is hardly concerned with geographical questions at all—the spiritual meaning of the text is paramount. However, although he does say in *ep.* 58, 3 that access to the courts of heaven is as easy from Britain

---

[72] Fischer, Isaac and Roll *loc. cit.* n. 69 above.
[73] See below: 4.4.

as it is from Jerusalem, he is well aware that his own behaviour in coming to the Holy Land appears to contradict this (*ib. loc. cit.*).[74] Like it or not, the physical realities took on a new importance now the Christians were in charge. It was impossible for the monk to remain in his cave oblivious of the outside world. Christians were staking their claim to the land, identifying sites and sanctifying them.[75] The Holy Land, Jerome says, 'has now become for us a promised land because of the passion and resurrection of Christ.'[76] Jerome had tried and abandoned the way of total secession from the world; but now he chooses to settle in Bethlehem. He sets himself to re-write the birth-place of Jesus as the historical source of the spiritual in the Holy Land and indeed the whole world. The site of the crucifixion, Jerusalem, was occupied by his rivals.

Deeply involved in translating the bible into Latin and making clear its historical and spiritual meaning in his commentaries, he now turns to Eusebius' *Onomasticon*, the book of the Holy Land of his own fourth-century Christian material reality. This he translates and updates,[77] adding yet more evidence of the Christian appropriation of the land. The *Onomasticon* becomes for him a new statement of historical and geographical reality. In his preface to the Book of Chronicles (Septuagint version), he writes that, just as seeing Greece and Rome helps in understanding the classical writers:

> *ita sanctam Scripturam lucidius intuebitur, qui Judaeam oculis contemplatus est [sit] et antiquarum urbium memorias, locorumque vel eadem vocabula, vel mutata cognoverit.*[78]

Tr. Hunt: The man who has seen Judaea with his own eyes and who knows the sites of ancient cities and their names, whether the same or changed, will gaze more clearly upon the Holy Scripture.

---

[74] *ep.* 58, 3: *de Hierosolymis et de Britannia aequaliter patet aula caelestis.*
His inconsistency: *neque uero hoc dicens memet ipsum inconstantiae redarguo damnoque, quod facio.*
[75] Hunt, esp. chapter 4 'Pilgrims and the Bible (1) The Holy Places; R.L. Wilken *The Land Called Holy: Palestine in Christian history and thought* (New Haven/London, 1992).
[76] *ep.* 129, 4: *nunc nobis Christi passione et resurrectione terra repromissionis effecta est.*
[77] As already noted above, Eusebius' *Onomasticon* was written around the turn of the third and fourth century: for Jerome's revision around 390: see n. 7 above.
[78] *Praef. in lib. Paralipomenon juxta LXX* (*PL* 29, 423): Trans. Hunt, 94. This was written about the same time as his version of the *Onomasticon* (Cavallera, II, 157; Kelly, 158).

The knowledge possessed by the Jews, he continues, has been used by him for his journey in what is now the Christian land:

> unde et nobis curae fuit cum eruditissimis Hebraeorum hunc laborem subire, ut circuiremus provinciam quam uniuersae Christi Ecclesiae sonant (ib. loc. cit.).

Hunt has pointed out how similar in wording the beginning of this passage is to the preface to the *Onomasticon*, where the task is:

> ut congregaret nobis de sancta scriptura omnium paene urbium, montium, fluminum, uiculorum et diuersorum locorum, quae uel eadem manent uel immutata sunt postea.[79]

> Tr. Hunt (adapted) to extract for us the names of almost all the cities, mountains, rivers and villages mentioned in the Bible, describing the location of these places and the names by which they are known today—whether these are the same as of old or have been changed.

But the *Onomasticon* leaves little room for the spiritual aspects. Jerome therefore completes his Christian re-writing of the land by adding the spiritual aspects seen through the eyes of the saintly Paula—and the saintly Jerome—in his *ep.* 108. So the Holy Land of these literary works is both the contemporary reality of fourth century Palestine, with its official Roman administration and its concrete Roman roads, as well as the spiritual centre where Paula can still see the infant Jesus in his manger at Bethlehem.[80]

4.3.2. *Geography as metaphor:*
The journey to the Holy Land in Jerome's ep. 76

Geography for Jerome had many uses. Besides recording the physical and spiritual realities of the Christian Holy Land, it could also be used purely metaphorically. An example of this can be seen in his *ep.* 76, written around 399. Here Jerome writes to the blind priest Abigaus in Spain, asking him to help the widow Theodora lest she be tempted into remarriage.[81] He writes of Theodora and her life

---

[79] *On. Praef*: Trans. Hunt (adapted) 96.

[80] For 'geographical terrain serv[ing] as a springboard to visionary experience' in Jerome, see B. Leyerle 'Landscape as cartography in early Christian pilgrimage narratives' *Journal of the American Academy of Religion* 64 (1996) 119–143, esp. 130. Leyerle does not distinguish between Jerome and Paula here: in fact the visionary experiences in *ep.* 108 and 46 are attributed to Paula and Eustiochium, in whose name Jerome wrote *ep.* 46.

[81] Kelly, 216.

as a sort of pilgrim's progress: he uses the geographical metaphor of the journey of the Children of Israel from Egypt to the Holy Land, hoping Theodora will not leave the path she has begun to tread:

> *ut in coepto itinere non lassetur, ut ad terram sanctam multo per heremum labore perueniat.*

Many of the geographical stations of the Israelites are used to signify stations on her way. Unlike in his *ep.* 78[82] where Jerome is also concerned to identify the stations of the Children of Israel in the wilderness with contemporary places, here they are only used to signify landmarks in Theodora's life:

> *... exisse de Aegypto ... per innumerabiles insidias ad montem Nebo et ad Iordanem fluuium perueniri, ut accipiat secundum in Galgalam circumcisionem, ut illi Hiericho corruat sacerdotalium tubarum subuersa clangoribus ... ut Gai et Asor pulcherrimae quondam corruant ciuitates ...*

The landscape of Egypt, Sinai, Transjordan and Canaan is here purely metaphorical—the journey through the desert is fraught with *insidias*—the devil lies in wait with temptations, and Theodora must use the sacred trumpets to bring about the downfall of the *pulcherrimae quondam civitates*, the pagan strongholds in the Holy Land. Like a much later Christian author,[83] Jerome has written here a metaphorical Pilgrim's Progress.

4.4. Jerome's *Ep.* 108: Literary Form and Material Context

In contrast to the purely metaphorical use of the Holy Land in *ep.* 76, *ep.* 108 begins with the same image of life as a journey and Paula as a pilgrim, but also includes a description of the actual journey she took, written in the form of an *iter* in Palestine. Paula, says Jerome, created a new spiritual reality in her material world. Her whole life was a pilgrimage in this world. The words *peregrina* or *peregrinatio* and variants appear four times in the first paragraph of *ep.* 108, and Jerome plays on the spectrum of meanings between

---

[82] *ep.* 78 *ad Fabiolam de mansionibus filiorum Israhel per heremum* (*CSEL* 55) 49f.

[83] J. Bunyan *The Pilgrim's Progress from this World to that which is to come* (London, 1678, repr. Oxford, 1966).

'exile' and 'pilgrimage.' Within this larger metaphorical pilgrimage,
he sets the smaller pilgrimage which actually took place through
fourth century Palestine. And he shows how Palestine, the Roman
province and site of the events of the Hebrew Bible, is appropriated
by Paula for Christianity. The *iter* of his pagan contemporary Rutilius
Namatianus includes an *encomium* of Rome:[84] Paula's *iter*, in contrast,
has an *encomium* of Bethlehem, new small centre of the world.

4.4.1. *Literary form: The influence of the literary genres*

Ep. 108, then, is a metaphorical *iter* of Paula's pilgrimage through
life, written as an *encomium*, an *epitaphium*, a *consolatio*. This section
considers the influence of these literary forms on the content.

This metaphorical *iter* contains within it a smaller *iter* describing
Jerome's actual journey with Paula and her companions around the
Holy Places. In his introduction to the account of this journey Jerome
writes that he will omit the *Syriae Coeles et Phoenicis iter* for he does
not intend to write *eius odoeporicum*—a ὁδοιπορικόν (= *iter*) *of them*. By
'them' he means the Roman provinces of Coele Syria and Phoenice,
which are of no interest to him. He will concentrate, he says, on
biblical sites.[85] Thus *ep.* 108 contains an *iter* or *odoeporicum* of their
actual journey in the Holy Land, together with a visit to the monks
of Egypt, beginning just outside the northern border of Palestine (*ep.*
108, 8) and ending when Jerome and Paula return from Egypt to
settle permanently in Bethlehem (108, 14):

> *huc usque iter eius descriptum sit.*

The first city Jerome mentions does not appear in the Scriptures at
all, *Beryt[us] Romana colonia*, but belongs to his classical literary heritage, being a city famed for its law school,[86] but Paula turns her
back on this—*derelicta*—to enter Sarepta [Zarephath], with its associations with the prophet Elijah.[87] Sarepta is outside the borders of

---

[84] Rutilius Claudius Namatianus *De Reditu suo sive Iter Gallicum*.

[85] *ep.* 108, 8: *Omitto Syriae Coeles et Phoenicis iter—neque enim odoeporicum eius dispo-
sui scribere—ea tantum loca nominabo, quae sacris uoluminibus continentur.*

[86] On Berytus see F. Millar *The Roman Near East: 31 BC–AD 337* (Harvard, 1993)
279–281; 527–8, and now L. Jones Hall *Roman Berytus: Beirut in Late Antiquity* (London,
2004).

[87] Elijah and the widow at Sarepta: I Kings 17,9.

the Roman province, but for Christian pilgrims it marked the beginning of the Holy Land. This is clear from the *Itinerarium Burdigalense*,
the account of a Christian pilgrim who travelled from Bordeaux in
Gaul to the Holy Land in 333 CE, and left an itinerary with very
basic details for Europe and Asia Minor, but filled in far more details
for the Holy Land.[88] The pilgrim from Bordeaux also begins his or
her itinerary in the Holy Land at Sarepta.[89] Jerome's presentation
of the Holy Land in *ep.* 108 shows the biblical associations taking
over from the classical. Jaffa is the site of both Andromeda and of
Jonah, but Andromeda belongs merely to the *fabulis poetarum* (108,
8), as opposed to the biblical truth.[90] It will become clear how his
rhetoric pairs off Christian and non-Christian sites, to show the
Christian supremacy, and how without corroboration from his translation of the *Onomasticon* we cannot take at face value his descriptions of sites, nor be sure of his routes. As often with problematic
texts, however, incidental information with no visible literary or religious purpose, can be taken as representative, especially if it fits the
picture taken from other sources. I shall begin here with an examination of the various genres of geographical and travel writing, in
both literary and practical forms, to see where Jerome bases himself on them, and where he departs from them.

1a. *Geographical literature*
Travellers' aids   periploi and *itineraria*   The first genres to be considered
here belong to the geographical literature. Descriptions of journeys
are found in this literature as early as the fourth century BCE. These
are the *periploi*, coastal journeys, lists of places along the coast in
geographical order written to help sailors following the coastline and
sometimes including details of places along the way and distances.[91]
Yuval Shahar has recently shown how, in the Roman period, this

---

[88] *Itinerarium Burdigalense* (*CCSL* 175, 1–26). On this see: *LRE* 832–3; L. Douglass
'A New Look at the *Itinerarium Burdigalense*' *JECS* 4 (1996) 313–333; S. Weingarten
(1999) *op. cit.* n. 54 above and now J. Elsner 'The *Itinerarium Burdigalense:* Politics
and salvation in the geography of Constantine's empire' *JRS* 90 (2000) 181–195.
[89] *It Burd.* 58, 3, 12: *inde Sarepta ibi Helias ad uiduam ascendit et petiit sibi cibum.*
[90] See on this P.B. Harvey, Jr., 'The Death of Mythology: The case of Joppa'
JECS 2 (1994) 1–14.
[91] O.A.W. Dilke *Greek and Roman Maps* (London, 1985), 130–144 and extensive
bibliography *ad loc.*

'linear concept' of a journey along the coast was transferred to journeys on dry land, using the line of the Roman road system.[92] Thus
we find non-literary '*itineraria*' written as travellers' aids, such as the
mid-third century Antonine itinerary, probably written as an aid to
tax collecting, with lists of roads, places along them and the distances between, as well as a similar document covering sea routes.[93]
There were also military *itineraria* prepared for soldiers to show them
the route to take, along which they would find lodgings and sup-
plies.[94] As well as verbal descriptions, there also appear to have been
cartographic *itineraria* in strip-map format and this may be what
Vegetius is referring to when he talks of *itineraria picta*.[95] Just as the
basic *periploi* sometimes contained details of harbours and products
to aid sailors and traders, so *itineraria* were not always bare lists of
places and distances but sometimes developed into works which contained details of places along the way as a guide to travellers of what
they might find. This was particularly the case with pilgrim *itineraria*,
both pagan, such as Pausanias,[96] and Christian, such as the *Itinerarium
Burdigalense*.[97]

Literary genres   iter, or *hodoeporicon*   Turning now to the literary genres, it is clear that side by side with these practical guides, journey
descriptions also developed as a literary form, often in verse. The
earliest example in the Latin literature of this kind of literary work,

---

[92] Y. Shahar *Josephus Geographicus* (Tübingen, 2004) 'Linear geography': 39–48 I
am grateful to my friend and colleague Dr Yuval Shahar for showing me pre-
publication drafts of his book and discussing this subject on many occasions. Cf.
N. Purcell 'Maps, Lists, Money and Power' *JRS* 80 (1990) 178–82.
[93] Antonine Itinerary, Palestine section: *Itineraria Romana* I: *Itineraria Antonini Augusti*
ed. O. Cuntz, rev. G. Wirth, (Stuttgardt, 1990) 21; 23. The introduction of Rivet
is still useful: A.L.F. Rivet 'The British section of the Antonine Itinerary' *Britannia*
1 (1950) 34–39, and see D. van Berchem 'L'itinéraire Antonin et le voyage en orient de Caracalla 214–5 *CRAI* (1973) 123–126; N. Reed 'Pattern and purpose in
the Antonine Itinerary' *AJPh* 99 (1978) 228–254.
[94] Ambrose *Expositio psalmo cxviii*, 33, 5, 2 (*PL* 15, 1250–1); Vegetius 3, 6.
[95] See above: Jerome's maps.
[96] Pausanias as a pilgrim: J. Elsner *Art and the Roman viewer: the transformation of art
from the pagan world to Christianity* (Cambridge, 1995) 125–55; I. Rutherford 'Tourism
and the sacred: Pausanias and the traditions of Greek pilgrimage' in S.E. Alcock,
J.F. Cherry, J. Elsner (eds.) *Pausanias: travel and memory in Roman Greece* (Oxford, 2001)
40–52.
[97] See above, n. 88.

known as an *iter,* or *hodoeporicon*[98]—ὁδοιπορικόν, is the *Iter Siculum* written by Lucilius.[99] Lucilius was seen as the father of satire, and does
not appear to have written anything else.[100] Jerome mentions him
twice in his Chronicon, once as *satyrarum scriptor.*[101] The *Iter Siculum*
is a poem which survives only in fragments, but we know that it
described in order the stages of a journey by land and sea from
Rome to Sicily in 119–116 BCE. In one case at least, there was a
numerical statement of the distance covered. The poem contained
descriptions of places and incidents along the way, including apparently realistic and often humorous personal details of the experience
of the journey—the mud (3, 5 [109]), the food (3,30 [133]), the
accommodation (run by a *caupona Syra*) (3,32 [128]) and the characters encountered. Fortunately our next example of an *iter,* Horace's
Iter Brundisinum, written about a journey in 37 BCE, is complete.
Jerome knew Horace's works well and cites him frequently.[102] Horace's
poem is also written as satire, on the model of Lucilius, and tells of
a journey by land and water from Rome to Brindisi. It details the
stages of the journey in order and describes the places along the
way, with a humorous focus on the discomforts of the journey and
the grotesque encounters. Some of the material can be paralleled in
Lucilius.[103] Lucilius had said (in another poem) that he could not fit
the name of a festival into his hexameters: Horace mentions an
oppidulum whose name does not fit his metre and where he had to
pay for water, although the bread was so good that travellers stocked
up by the cartful. Recently it has been questioned how far Horace
was really describing real events and how far he was merely adapting the literary model of Lucilius, whom he cites as his model in
his *Satires.*[104] What is clear, however, is the fact that Horace was

---

[98] *Hodoeporicon*: this is the form given by L&S, quoting Jerome *ep.* 108, 8; Hilberg
ad loc. prefers *odoeporicum.*

[99] Lucilius *Satires* I (ed. F. Charpin, Paris, 1978).

[100] On Lucilius as father of satire see M. Coffey *Roman Satire* (Bristol, 1989²).

[101] Chronicon: OL. 158.32; 169.13. On his dates for Lucilius, see G. Herbert-
Brown 'Jerome's dates for Gaius Lucilius: *satyrarum scriptor*' *CQ* 49 (1999) 535–543.

[102] A. Lübeck *Hieronymus quos noverit scriptores et ex quibus hauserit* (Leipzig, 1872);
H. Hagendahl *Latin Fathers and the Classics* (Göteborg, 1958).

[103] E. Gowers 'Horace, *Satires* 1.5: An inconsequential journey' *Proceedings of the
Cambridge Philological Society* 39 (1993) 48–66 esp. 49; A. Cucchiarelli '*Iter satyricum*:
Le voyage à Brindes et le satire d'Horace' *Latomus* 61 (2002) 842–851.

[104] Coffey (*op. cit.* n. 100) 76, and Gowers (*op. cit.* n. 103 *supra*) 61: 'a poem that
stops short of its full potential and turns out to have been a shaggy dog story all
along.'

familiar with the route travelled, and that even if this is not a real
report of a particular journey, it does contain reliable information about the road, which probably resulted from previous journeys
along it.[105]

Christian writers also used this literary genre. In his *de viris illustribus*
Jerome records that the Latin church father Lactantius wrote a verse
ὁδοιπορικόν of his journey from Africa to Nicomedia, and that the
Spanish Acilius Severus wrote a metaphorical—*quasi* ὁδοιπορικόν—
work about the events of his own life.[106] Neither of these works
survives.

As the practical *itineraria* became more detailed, the distance between
them and the literary form of the *iter* grew smaller and the genre
categories less clear. The *Itinerarium Burdigalense*, with its rather basic
Latin prose, like the account of the fourth-century pilgrim Egeria,[107]
is not a literary product of the upper classes schooled in rhetoric
like Lucilius or Horace, but it is not a mere list of stopping places
either.

Indeed, although the classical teachers of rhetoric defined distinct
literary genre forms, even in classical literary works these sometimes
shaded into one another, so that a *propempticon*, a poem bidding
farewell, became the beginning of an *iter*, a poem about a journey.
It is thus sometimes difficult to attribute a work to any one particular genre.[108] This problem is even more noticeable in Late Antiquity

---

[105] Horace had started by taking the *via Appia*, but after Beneventum takes an
old branch road, the *via Minucia*, clearly neglected: *inde Rubos fessi pervenimus, utpote
longum carpentes iter et factum corruptius imbri. Postera tempestas melior, via peior ad usque Bari
moenia piscosi.* The road was later reconstructed by Trajan. See on this G. Radke
'Topographische Betrachtungen zum Iter Brundisinum des Horaz' *Rheinisches Museum*
132 (1989), 54–72, and bibliography *ad loc.* This demonstrates knowledge of the
local topography which is consistent with first-hand acquaintance. I am grateful to
Prof. B. Isaac for clarification of this point.

[106] Lactantius (3rd cent.): *de vir.* lxxx; Acilius Severus: *de vir.* cxi.

[107] *Itinerarium Egeriae* ed. A. Franceschini, R. Weber (*CCSL* 175, 29–90); P. Maraval
Égérie. Journal de voyage (*SC* 296, Paris, 1982); J. Wilkinson (ed. and tr.) *Egeria's Travels
in the Holy Land* (Warminster, 1999³).

[108] For example, Statius *Silvae* 3,2 is often included in lists of *itinera*. The poem
begins with a *propempticon* bidding farewell to the poet's patron, and continues with
a list of places the latter *may* go and see at his destination in Egypt, rather than a
list of places he *has* seen (or says he has seen). Thus I do not think this should
really be called an *iter*—note that Statius' modern editors have not provided the
reader with a map of places to visit, unlike the modern editors of undubitable *itinera*
e.g.: Lucilius: *Satires* livres i–viii ed. F. Charpin (Paris, 1978) endpaper; Horace: *The
Satires of Horace and Persius* tr. N. Rudd (Harmondsworth, 1973) p. 50; Ovid: *Sorrows*

when, as Fontaine has noted, a kind of mixing of genres, frowned upon by the classical grammarians, apparently became positively desirable.[109] Thus Jerome's contemporary, the poet Rutilius Namatianus, in his account of his journey from Rome to Gaul, begins with an *encomium* of Rome, continues with an account of parting from his friends built on the classical *propempticon* and only then proceeds with the *iter*, the account of his journey, mentioning the places visited, with details of people and incidents along the way.[110]

Apart from the elements officially seen as belonging to any particular genre, the influence of the great classical writers was such that elements they had included in their works also became archetypes for the genre. Thus Rutilius includes satirical elements in his *iter*, following Horace and Lucilius—Lucilius' *caupona Syra* is succeeded by Rutilius' Jewish landlord.[111]

The geographical *excursus*   The *iter* is primarily a verse form. In prose, historical literature in Latin often contained passages of geographical information written in the form of an *excursus*. The Latin historians appear to have regarded such passages as more ornamental than practical: the information they contained was often long out of date, and owed more to literary precedent than to personal experience. Jerome's contemporary Ammianus, in his geographical *excursus* on Gaul, which has already been noted above, notes that he is basing himself on Timagenes, a Greek historian who wrote several hundred

---

of an exile: Tristia tr. A. Melville (Oxford, 1995) map I; Rutilius Namatianus: *De reditu suo sive Iter Gallicum* ed. E. Doblhofer (Heidelberg, 1972) frontispiece; Ausonius: *Mosella* ed. B.K. Weis (Darmstadt, 1989) front endpapers. Jerome's *ep.* 108, 6 contains a moving *propempticon* with a description of Paula's family bidding her farewell before her voyage to the Holy Land: on the grounds for taking this as rhetoric, rather than a realistic description, see A.E. Hickey *Women of the Roman aristocracy as Christian monastics* (Ann Arbor, 1987) 24–5.

[109] J. Fontaine 'Unité et diversité du mélange des genres et des tons chez quelques écrivains latins de la fin du IVᵉ siècle: Ausone, Ambroise, Ammien' in *Christianisme et formes littéraires de l'antiquité tardive en occident* (Fondation Hardt: Entretiens sur l'antiquité classique 33, Vandoeuvres, 1976) 432–434; M. Roberts *The Jeweled Style: Poetry and poetics in Late Antiquity* (Ithaca/London, 1986).

[110] F. Paschoud 'A quel genre littéraire le poème de Rutilius Namatianus appartient-il?' *Revue des Études Latines* (1979) 315–322 identifies the following genres included in the poem: 'récit de voyage, description des côtes, panégyrique, éloge, poème didactique.

[111] Lucilius: *Iter Siculum: Satires*, Bk. III frag. 97–148; Horace *iter Brundisinum: Sat.* i, 5. Cf. Rutilius Namatianus *de Reditu* i, 381f.

years earlier.[112] Ammianus introduces his *excursus* carefully: he will
show us the regions and situation of Gaul:

> *Galliarum tractus et situm ostendere puto.*[113]

He ends his long digression clearly, returning to his main subject:

> *Evectus sum longius; sed remeabo tandem ad coepta.*[114]

Between these framing sentences are descriptions of the origins of
the Gauls, the history of the Alpine passes, and a description of the
cities, rivers and mountains of Gaul. The latter is again marked off
from the final passage describing the customs of its people:

> *Sit satis de situ locorum. Nunc figuras et mores hominum designabo.*[115]

The information in such excursus was often out of date: Ammianus'
excursus on Arabia implies that the Nabataeans were still around in
the fourth century.[116]

In his *ep.* 108, Jerome introduces his account of his journey with
Paula around the Holy Places calling it an *iter*, and closes it as such
too, just like an *excursus*. Like Ammianus, he too uses the device of
framing statements: having begun his account of Paula's life:

> *Carpamus igitur narrandi ordinem,*[117]

he then marks off the portion dealing with the iter around the holy
places:

> *Omitto Syriae Coeles et Phoenicis iter—neque enim odoeporicum eius disposui
> scribere—ea tantum loca nominabo, quae sacris uoluminibus continentur.*[118]

He finishes the iter after Paula settles in Bethlehem, and builds a
hostel for other pilgrims:

> *huc usque iter eius descriptum sit.*

---

[112] Ammianus xv, 9, 2.
[113] *Ib.* xv, 9, 1.
[114] *Ib.* xv, 12, 6.
[115] *Ib.* xv, 11, 18.
[116] Ammianus on the Nabataeans: xiv, 8, 13. On the 'strong air of archaism' in
this description: J Matthews *The Roman Empire of Ammianus Marcellinus* (London, 1989)
342–3.
[117] *ep.* 108, 3.
[118] *Ib.*, 8.

His account here fulfils some of the same functions as Ammianus' excursus. It too contains geographical information in a form that is written with its full quota of rhetorical embellishment. Ammianus notes the tomb of the eponymous King Cottius in the Cottian Alps;[119] Jerome notes tombs of biblical heroes.[120] Ammianus notes the citadel founded by Hercules;[121] Jerome notes the towns and citadel built by King Solomon and David.[122] Ammianus notes the half-ruined city of Aventicum, once powerful;[123] Jerome also notes ruined and half-ruined, once powerful cities, which form part of his Christian polemic, as will be seen below.[124] It is interesting that he insists, when talking of Paula's virtues, that his work is a work of history, and that he has not invented or exaggerated her virtues.[125]

The *consolatio* and its geographical traditions   The classical genre of *consolatio* provided solace for the bereaved. Bereavement was, of course, more problematic for pagans than for Christian authors, with their expectations of heaven, but the Christian *consolatio* developed from the classical pagan genre.[126] The most famous classical example, Cicero's *de Consolatione*, was written by him when his daughter Tullia died. Jerome tells us that he read it,[127] but unfortunately it is no longer extant. What does survive, however, is the letter written to Cicero by his friend Servius Sulpicius Rufus on this occasion, included among Cicero's own letters. This included geographical elements, in particular, ruined cities:

> *ex Asia rediens cum ab Aegina Megaram versus navigarem, coepi regiones circumcirca prospicere. post me erat Aegina, ante me Megara, dextra Piraeus, sinistra Corinthus,*

---

[119] Ammianus xv, 10, 1–7.

[120] *ep.* 108, 10: *sepulchrum Rachel; ib.* 12 *sepulchrum Lazari; ib.* 13 *sepulchra Hiesu . . . filii Naue, et Eleazari filii Aaron sacerdotis* etc.

[121] Ammianus xv, 10, 9: *Monoeci arcem*

[122] *ep.* 108, 8–9: *urbes a Salomone conditas; Sion, quae in 'arcem' . . . uertitur . . . hanc urbem quondam expugnauit et aedificauit Dauid.*

[123] Ammianus xv, 11, 12: *Aventicum, desertam quidem civitatem sed non ignobilem quondam, ut aedificia semiruta nunc quoque demonstrant.*

[124] See below: 4.2.2b: Rhetorical construct: ruined cities

[125] *ep.* 108, 21: *testor Iesum . . . me in utraque parte nihil fingere, sed . . . quae sunt uera, proferre, id est historiam scribere, non panegyricum . . .*

[126] See C. Favez *La consolation latine chrétienne* (Paris, 1937), and the excellent discussion by J.H.D. Scourfield in his monograph on Jerome's *ep.* 60: 'Letter 60 and the consolatory tradition' in *op. cit.* (n. 22 above) 15f.

[127] *ep.* 60, 5, 3.

quae oppida quodam tempore florentissima fuerunt, nunc prostrata et diruta ante oculos iacent . . . uno loco tot oppidum cadavera proiecta iaceant.[128]

Later authors writing a *consolatio*, such as Jerome's contemporary Ambrose, writing between 387 and 394, took up these same geographical elements, which became typical of the genre:

sed doles quod dudum florentissima repente occiderit. Verum hoc nobis commune non solum cum hominibus sed etiam civitatibus terrisque ipsis. Nempe de Bononiensi veniens urbe a tergo Claternam . . . in dextera erat Brixillum, a fronte occurrebat Placentia. . . . tot igitur semirutarum urbium cadavera terrarumque . . .[129]

Rutilius also compares dead cities and dead men:

non indignemur mortalia corpora solvi:
cernimus exemplis oppida posse mori.

Ammianus, too, as noted above, decorates his *excursus* on Gaul with the half-ruined city of Aventicum.[130]

This image of dead cities compared with the corpses of men becomes a *topos* of moralising writing. As such it was particularly appropriate to the *consolatio*. The adjective *semirutus [dirutus]* thus became associated with these rhetorical descriptions of cities, which often seem to indicate an ethical picture of decline rather than an indication of their physical state.

The question of the relationship of the passage by Ambrose to the reality of fourth century Italy has been discussed by Cracco Ruggini. Bringing parallel statements by Rutilius and Jerome (*ep.* 1, 3), where he writes of the state of the Italian town of Vercellae as *semi-*

---

[128] Cic. *Ad Fam.* 4.5: Servius Sulpicius Rufus to M.T. Cicero, 45 BCE: On my return from Asia, as I was sailing from Aegina towards Megara, I began to survey the regions round about. Behind me was Aegina, before me Megara, on my right hand the Piraeus, on my left Corinth, at one time most flourishing towns, now lying prostrate and ruined before one's eyes . . . in this one land alone there lie flung down before us the corpses of so many towns. Tr. W. Glynn Williams, *LCL*, adapted.

[129] Ambrose *ep.* 39 to Faustinus (*ep.* 73 in *St Ambrose: Letters*, ed. M.M. Beyenka, Fathers of the Church 26, Washington, 1954): You are sad because she who was most flourishing for a long time died unexpectedly. This is an experience which we share not only with men but also with cities and countries. As you left Claterna behind . . . Brescello . . . was on your right hand and ahead Piacenza meets you . . . the corpses of so many half-ruined cities and so many lands . . . . Tr. Beyenka, adapted.

[130] Above n. 123.

ruta, she compares these descriptions with the conflicting archaeological evidence of the Italian towns, which seem to have been far
from rubble heaps. She notes that a few lines after writing of Vercellae
as *raro habitatore semiruta* (1, 3), Jerome himself refers to soldiers crowd-
ing the streets of the town (1, 7), a fact which can be confirmed by
epigraphical evidence. Thus she concludes that such passages fulfilled
a decorative and ethical function, rather than being literally descrip-
tive of reality—Ambrose, Rutilius and Jerome all appear to exag-
gerate the physical destruction of the cities of Northern Italy.[131] For
them, what seems to be at issue is the change in the classical city
in their period—the decline of previously flourishing civic institutions, rather than of physical amenities.

The influence of the genre of *consolatio* on Jerome's description of
Paula's *iter* in Palestine will be discussed below.[132] By the time he
wrote *ep.* 108, Jerome had written nine earlier *consolationes*. These
have been discussed by Favez and Scourfield,[133] so we shall just note
here that Jerome also included geographical details in one of these,
ep. 60, both real and metaphorical. The real details have been discussed above in 4.1.

1b. *Marvels at the edge of the world*

Marvels were an accepted and expected part of ancient travel writing from Herodotus onward, Christian pilgrim accounts not excepted.[134]
The further one travelled from civilised urban life, the more likely
one was to encounter the marvellous, especially at the edge of the
world.[135] Works such as Philostratus' biography of Apollonius of

---

[131] L. Cracco Ruggini, G. Cracco 'Changing fortunes of the Italian city from
Late Antiquity to Early Middle Ages' *Rivista di Filologia e di Istruzione Classica* 105
(1977) 448–475.

[132] Below: 4.2.2b: Rherorical construct: ruined cities.

[133] Scourfield *op. cit.* n. 22 above; Favez *op. cit.* n. 126 above . . .

[134] R. Wittkower 'Marvels of the East: A Study in the History of Monsters' *Journal
of the Warburg and Courtauld Institutes*, 5 (1942) 159f.; M.B. Campbell *The Witness and
the other World: Exotic European Travel Writing 400–1600* (Ithaca, 1988); on Christian
pilgrim literature see especially G. Frank 'The *Historia Monachorum in Aegypto* and
ancient travel writing' *Studia Patristica* 30 (1997) 191–195; *ead.* 'Miracles, monks and
monuments: the *Historia Monachorum in Aegypto* as pilgrims' tales' in D. Frankfurter
(ed.) *Pilgrimage and holy space in late antique Egypt* (Leiden etc. 1998) 487f. and now
A.H. Merrills 'Monks, monsters and barbarians: re-defining the African periphery
in late antiquity' *JECS* 12 (2004) 217–244.

[135] J. Romm *The Edges of the Earth in Ancient Thought: Geography, Exploration and
Fiction* (Princeton, 1992).

Tyana, show the pagan holy man on his travels encountering marvels in distant countries.[136] This work was translated into Latin,[137]
and Jerome recounts the list of countries Apollonius is said to have
visited in *ep.* 53,1. Jerome himself, when lashing his Christian oppo-
nent Vigilantius with abuse, calls him a monster who should be sent
to the farthest ends of the earth:

> *portentum in terras ultimas deportandum!*[138]

The Holy Land was not far from the legendary edges of the world
in the eyes of a western audience.[139] Jerome has indeed presented a
picture of the Holy Land as the centre of the world, and Bethlehem,
the site of the Incarnation, as its centre. But he is also writing for
a western Latin-speaking audience for whom the east was distant
and exotic. I noted above in chapter 1, how when sending a copy
of his *vita Pauli* to Paul of Concordia he refers to his work as valuable oriental merchandise.[140] Some fourth-century western Christian
pilgrims to the Holy Land, such as the pilgrim from Bordeaux and
Egeria, seem to have found being at the places where biblical miracles had occurred in the past was marvel enough. But meantime
Jerome's contemporary and friend-turned-enemy Rufinus had translated and edited the *Historia Monachorum in Aegypto*, a work full of
marvels.[141] Jerome himself had added mythical beings to his saints'
Lives: a centaur and a satyr in the *vita Pauli*, and a self-destructing
dragon in the *vita Hilarionis*. Hilarion has many encounters with
demons, being tempted by them, talking to them, exorcising them
and struggling with them. As noted above, Jerome's saints' *Lives* were
very successful. So when Jerome came to write the account of Paula's

---

[136] J. Elsner 'Hagiographic geography: Travel and allegory in the *Life of Apollonius
of Tyana*' *Journal of Hellenic Studies* 117 (1997) 22–37.

[137] Elsner *op. cit.* 24.

[138] *Contra Vig.* 8.

[139] On this cf. Romm *op. cit.* n. 133 above, 82f.: 'Wonders of the East,' on India;
149f.: on the Nile conceived as one of the ancient world's 'most remote and alien
frontiers.'

[140] *Ep.* 10, 3: *alia condita quae cum plurimis orientalibus mercibus ad te . . . nauigabunt.*
Cf. *QHG Praef.: peregrinae merces tantum volentibus navigent: balsamum, piper et poma palmarum rustici non emant.*

[141] Rufinus' translation of the *Historia Monachorum in Aegypto: PL* 21, 387–462. See
discussion by B. Ward in her introduction to the *Lives of the Desert Fathers* (tr. N. Russell,
Oxford/Kalamazoo, 1981).

and his own travels he again wrote of demonic marvels as well as the places where biblical miracles had occurred. Jerome's Paula, like Egeria, is filled with awe at simply being at the places where miracles happened in the Bible. Unlike Egeria, however, she sees demons hanging upside down in the air at the tomb of John the Baptist (108, 13).

1c. *Satire and humour in ep. 108*

Fourth century Latin literature abounds in humorous and satirical writing. The *Historia Augusta*, for example, has long been accepted by many scholars as a work of this kind, and Ammianus makes good use of satirical passages in his historical works. However, twentieth century readers are so far distant in time and culture that it is sometimes difficult for them to decide whether any particular piece of writing was intended as satirical or not. Humour is often achieved by the juxtaposition of the incongruous, and the perception of incongruity must be culturally determined. What is incongruous in one culture is not always so in another. The dependence of Christianity on holy paradox serves to complicate the matter even further. It was already noted in the discussion of the *vita Pauli* in chapter 1, that the episode of Paul and Antony struggling over a loaf of bread has embarrassed modern critics, who see it as ludicrous, while Jerome seems to have intended it as an expression of extreme abnegation.

Jerome himself, with his rhetorical training, clearly tends to the satirical: his invective is full of satire and humour, particularly the *reductio ad absurdum*. Many clear examples of this have been fully treated by Wiesen in his book *St. Jerome as a Satirist*.[142] However, while satire is generally characteristic of Jerome's writing, it is not always completely clear in any particular case whether he is writing with satirical intent or not. In the case of *ep.* 108, at first sight it might seem unlikely that an epitaph of a loved and saintly friend should contain satire—this would seem out of place to a modern audience. However, Wiesen notes that 'satiric comments ... frequently obtrude themselves incongruously into [Jerome's] exegesis.'[143]

---

[142] D. Wiesen *St. Jerome as a Satirist* (Ithaca/NY, 1964), and see also J. Lössl 'Satire, fiction and reference to reality in Jerome's *epistula* 117' *Vigilae Christianae* 52 (1998) 172–92.

[143] Wiesen *op. cit.* p. 160.

Furthermore, as already noted, in *ep.* 108 Jerome was using a mixture of genres, including the genre of the *iter*, the literary account
of a journey. It was noted above that the classic exponent of the *iter*
was one of Jerome's favourite authors, Horace, whose Satire i, 5
about his journey from Rome to Brundisium undoubtedly contains
humorous and satirical material about the discomforts of his trip.[144]

Thus it may be possible to distinguish satirical elements in *ep.* 108,
even satire of Paula herself. Kelly has already noted that Jerome
'extolling Paula's virtues, lashes out against the vanities and self-
indulgence of lesser women.'[145] Jerome is known to have been im-
patient and irascible in personality.[146] It could be that these personality
traits show through here, especially as he is using one of the genres which tended towards this sort of writing. For example, he
describes at some length Paula's enthusiasm for the places they visited together in the Holy Land. He notes her reluctance to leave
any one site except to see the next:

> *cuncta loca tanto ardore ac studio circumiuit, ut, nisi ad reliqua festinaret, a primis
> non posset abduci* (108, 9).

On the face of it, this is a compliment, but it could well have been
rather trying in reality for her companions on the journey. This
impression is strengthened by the description of Paula on the banks
of the Jordan, remembering the biblical events which had taken place
there:

> *feruentissimo aestu uenit ad Iordanem; stetit in ripa fluminis et orto sole solis iust-
> itiae recordata est, quomodo* ... (108, 12)

Feruentissimo aestu has been translated by Wilkinson as 'with burning
devotion.'[147] But it could just as well mean 'in the blazing heat'; it
is, indeed, used twice to mean just this later in the letter (108, 14),
where once the *feruentissimos aestus* are given as the reason for leaving Egypt and returning full speed to Bethlehem, and later Paula in

---

[144] Horace *Sat.* i, 5. Problems of journey: bad water l. 7; no sleep because of
frogs: l. 14–15; a girl who does not turn up l. 81–82; rain l. 95; bad road l. 96
etc., etc.

[145] Kelly, 279.

[146] Jerome's irascible personality: C. Favez *Saint Jérôme peint par lui-même.* (Bruxelles,
1958) 34f.

[147] J. Wilkinson *Jerusalem pilgrims before the Crusades* (Jerusalem, 1977) 51.

her last illness burns with fever in the blazing heat of July: *mense Iulio feruentissibus aestuis* (108,21). The Jordan valley at most times of the year indeed suffers from extreme, oppressive heat.[148] The ambiguity of the phrase allows Jerome a hint of satire at Paula's lengthy devotions in difficult conditions, which must have been trying for him, her captive audience. It would certainly be in the classical tradition of Lucilius and Horace remarking on the discomforts of their journey. And there is yet another possible appearance of satire on the same subject in the description of Egypt, where Paula enthusiastically visits hermit after hermit in the hot desert: *cuius non intrauit cellulam?* asks Jerome rhetorically: *quorum non pedibus aduoluta est?*[149] Once again we may be able to hear the groan in his voice. Jerome did not take kindly to competition.[150] It is with relief that very soon after he describes how they fled the heat to sail back 'like a bird' to the Holy Land.

Jerome also makes use of satire, albeit not humorously but in earnest, for his Christian purpose in his description of Bethlehem in *ep.* 108. I noted above how Jerome's contemporary, the pagan poet Rutilius Namatianus, spends many lines of his *iter* on praise of the city of Rome. This sort of *encomium* of their own city was popular in the fourth and fifth centuries among Christian writers too— Ausonius writes at length in praise of Bordeaux.[151] Praise of Rome, of course, is based on earlier literature, particularly that dealing with imperial themes. For example, Rutilius says that Rome is endlessly delightful: *sine fine placet.*[152] This may be an allusion to Virgil's Aeneid,

---

[148] A. Bitan, S. Rubin *Climatic Atlas of Israel for Physical and Environmental Planning and Design* (Tel Aviv, 1992). On 25th May 1999, Israel Radio reported a temperature of 49° C. near Jericho.

[149] *Ep.* 108,14: Whose cell did she not enter? Whose feet did she not prostrate herself at?

[150] Jerome's intolerance of competition as moral mentor is nowhere more apparent than in his description of his and Paula's visit to Mount Tabor (*ep.* 108, 13) where he alludes to the book of Judges, chapter 4. Here one might have expected that the *encomium* of a woman like Paula, head of three nunneries, would have mentioned the prophetess and judge Deborah, who plays the major rôle in the biblical account. But Jerome only mentions the secondary character in the Judges account, the male general Barak, and his victory over Sisera, and the name of Deborah does not appear at all. Even in his epitaph, Jerome takes care that Paula should be no challenge to his leadership rôle.

[151] Ausonius: *Ordo Urbium Nobilium: Burdigala* 126, 168.

[152] Rutilius Namatianus: *De reditu* i, 4.

where Jupiter promises the Romans an *imperium sine fine* and domin-
ion over her subjects.[153] Jerome too was conscious of the glory and
power of Rome, the city which had taken over the whole world.[154]
But Jerome had left Rome and rejected all she stood for, calling her
Babylon, the purple whore.[155] The 'city' whose praises he sings and
which he places at the centre of his work and his world is the tiny
village of Bethlehem. Bethlehem, site of the incarnation, is described
in implied contrast to Rome as her new rival. Jerome is here writing Christian satire.[156] With the eyes of faith Paula sees Jesus himself, the word made flesh, as an infant in his crib (108, 10). Jerome
quotes her praise of Bethlehem:

> *Salue, Bethlem, domus panis, in qua nata est ille panis, qui de caelo descendit*
> (108, 10).

And by judicious choice of biblical quotations and prophecies he
underlines his effect: from Bethlehem the smallest of villages will
come forth the ruler of Israel:

> *Bethleem . . . nonne minima es in milibus Iuda? Ex te mihi egredietur, qui sit prin-*
> *ceps in Israhel, et egressus eius ab initio, a diebus aeternis* (108, 10: Michah,
> 5: 2–3).

The *princeps* who has set forth from *diebus aeternis* is a satire on *Roma*
aeterna and her merely mundane *princeps*.[157] Later in the same paragraph (108, 10) Jerome quotes Luke:[158]

---

[153] *Aeneid* i, 279.

[154] *Ep.* 127, 12: *urbs quae totum cepit orbem*. This is taken from his mourning over
the capture of the city. For an analysis of the complexities and ambivalences of his
attitude to Rome, which I have simplified in my argument, see P. Antin, 'La ville
chez Saint Jérôme' *Latomus* 20 (1961) 298–311 (= *Recueil sur Saint Jérôme* Bruxelles,
1969, 375–389); P. Laurence 'Rome et Jérôme: des amours contrariées' *Révue*
Bénédictine 107 (1997) 227–249, including p. 240 on Rome and Bethlehem, although
in my opinion Laurence goes too far when he seeks to identify in 'l'âme hiéronymi-
enne' both 'Rome terrestre' and 'Rome céleste.' I have not seen K. Sugano *Das*
Rombild des Hieronymus (Frankfurt am Main, 1983). On Rome, Jerusalem and Bethlehem
in Jerome, see C. Krumeich *Hieronymus und die christlichen Feminae clarissimae* (Bonn,
1993) 355 on *ep.* 46.

[155] *In Didymum de Spiritu Sancto:* Praef. (*PL* 23 [1845] 101–103) and cf. *ep.* 45, 6.

[156] For a sensitive analysis of Jerome's Christian satire and its seriousness, see
J.R. Curran *Pagan city and Christian capital: Rome in the fourth century* (Oxford, 2000)
280–2.

[157] On *Roma aeterna* see also: B. Isaac 'Roma Aeterna' *Historia* 2 (1998, in Hebrew)
19–31 and bibliography *ad. loc.*

[158] Luke 2, 14, differing slightly from the Vulgate version.

gloria in excelsis deo et super terram pax,

implicitly contrasting with the *pax Romana*.[159] The choice of language in the translation of the Vulgate was made very deliberately by Jerome himself, and his selection of biblical verses here is also deliberate. For the pagan Rutilius writing in the shade of the late fourth-century barbarian incursions, Rome's vaunted empire without end had become merely Rome's endless capacity to please. For Jerome, the world and its ruler with Rome at the centre had been replaced by the infant who is the ruler of heaven and all the earth—the *princeps*, the *imperium* and *Roma aeterna* have been replaced by the *infantem uagientem in praesepe*, in Bethlehem *minima*, but the promise is of true *super terram pax*, from heaven, and not by force of Roman arms.

The presence or absence of satire naturally influences the interpretation of Jerome's depiction of the material context of his journey, as we will see below.

4.4.2. *Material context: Jerome's fourth century Palestine:* ep. *108 and the geography of the Holy Land*

In *ep.* 108, Jerome was developing a new Latin Christian genre of hagiography, and writing an allegorical account of the life of the saint as if it were a pilgrimage. Just as the Latin historians had included decorative geographical *excursus* in their histories, so Jerome included Paula's actual *iter* in the Holy Land within his allegory of the saint's life as pilgrimage. And just as the geographical *excursus* and the classical *iter* used details from the material world as part of a literary construction, so Jerome used details from the material world of fourth century Palestine. But he did not take even these details at their face value: Jerome's Palestine is the Holy Land, and the places he saw were seen with the eyes of a Christian. So although he describes Paula's journey through fourth-century Palestine, and actual information about the material conditions of the country can be found in this work, we must always be aware that he both saw places with Christian eyes and is using the account for an allegorical purpose.

---

[159] For various Christian attitudes to the *pax Romana* see: K. Wengst *Pax Romana and the peace of Jesus Christ* (tr. J. Bowden, London, 1987).

2a. ep. *108: Rhetorical construct or account of realia?*

There is general scholarly agreement that the journey Jerome and Paula appear to have made together around the holy places of Palestine and Egypt did actually take place, and is not entirely a literary creation of Jerome's.[160] Duval, indeed, did doubt that Jerome ever visited Joppa, suggesting that his description of Andromeda there was based on Pliny.[161] This has, however, been discussed fully by Harvey, who shows that in other places where Jerome mentions Joppa, he does seem to show real knowledge of the place that could not have been derived from Pliny.[162] It may be added that when Jerome uses the descriptions of classical authors in his works (as seen above in chapter 1 on the *vita Pauli*) there are usually traces of this in his language, and there are no traces of Pliny's words in Jerome's description of Joppa. I shall concentrate here on Jerome's actual journey, and the places he visited *en route*. The route Jerome describes can be traced on the familiar modern map of fourth-century Roman roads in Palestine and has many parallels in other contemporary itineraries.[163] It is marked on the map on page 271, which is based on the information in Israel Roll's map.[164] However, there are problems of verification of some parts of his route and especially his descriptions of some of the sites. I shall try to distinguish the separate layers from which Jerome made up his picture—the classical *consolatio*, the *iter* and its geographical and satirical components, and the biblical allegorising, through all of which Jerome's Palestine may be glimpsed.

---

[160] Kelly, 134. Jerome nowhere actually says he accompanied Paula 'but it is obvious' writes Kelly '. . . that at any rate from Antioch onwards he was accompanying the noble widow and her daughter.' See on this Kelly, pp. 116–7 with further bibliography on what is now the scholarly consensus.

[161] Y.-M. Duval (ed.) *Saint Jérôme: commentaire sur Jonas* (*SC* 323, Paris, 1985) 345. On Joppa [Jaffa, Iope, Ioppe] see now Fischer, Isaac, Roll (*op. cit.* n. 69) 180f.

[162] P.B. Harvey, Jr., 'The Death of Mythology: The case of Joppa' *JECS* 2 (1994) 1–14.

[163] I. Roll 'Roads and transportation in the Holy Land in the early Christian and Byzantine times' *Akten des xii. internationalen Kongress für christliche Archäologie* teil II (Jahrbuch für Antike und Christentum Ergänzungband, 20,2, Münster, 1995) 1166–70, tafel 164. This map is more up-to-date than the larger scale maps of Roman roads published previously by Roll: Y. Tsafrir, L. Di Segni, J. Green with I. Roll: *Tabula Imperii Romani: Iudaea/Palaestina* (Jerusalem, 1994) insert (I. Roll).

[164] I am grateful to Professor I. Roll for permission to use his map, which I have adapted.

2b. *Rhetorical construct: ruined cities*

It has already been noted that the primary literary form of Jerome's letter was that of a *consolatio*. The Christian *consolatio*, like its pagan predecessors, liked to extract moralising reflections from ruined towns. The letter written to Cicero to console him on the death of his daughter was used as a model by Ambrose, bishop of Milan. In *ep.* 108 Jerome in his turn talks of Dor as a ruined town—contrasting it with the thriving city and provincial capital, Caesarea, with its various Roman and Christian associations, next to which, *uersa uice*, lie the remains of Dor, once powerful, now in ruins, for Dor had been a well-known pagan Hellenistic city (108, 8).[165] The whole passage can be read as rhetorically pairing the ruins of pagan or Jewish sites against sites with a visible Christian presence—dead or dying Judaism and paganism against living Christianity. Jerome is stressing the Christian appropriation of the Holy Land. Thus he may also be exaggerating somewhat to gain his effect.

Herod's town of Antipatris had received city status under the Severans—there are coins from the city mint advertising this fact[166]—and there is archaeological evidence that there was quite a lot of building undertaken there in late antiquity.[167] Even though this appears to have been cut short by an earthquake in 363—the odeum appears not to have been finished—to call it a *semirutum oppidulum*, would appear to be yet another example of rhetorical exaggeration.

---

[165] *NEAEHL s.v.* Dor (E. Stern) with bibliography *ad loc.* Claudine Dauphin, who excavated at Dor, found a large church which she claims should have been there for Jerome to see. Her dating appears to have been based on a single bronze coin of Constantius II (337–356 CE) found between two floors: C. Dauphin 'Chronique archéologique: Dor 1979' *RB* 88, (1981) 591–592; *ead.* 'Chronique archéologique: Dor: Église byzantine' *RB* 91 (1984) 256–258. Dr Alla Stein points out to me that this coin can only represent a *terminus post quem*, and this sort of bronze coin continued to be used well into the fifth century, so that the situation in the later fourth century is far from clear, since E. Stern *Excavations at Dor: Final Report* (Qedem Reports 2, Jerusalem, 1995) vol. Ib, 471 (cf. *id. Dor, Ruler of the Seas* [Jerusalem, 1994] p. 320, ill. 227) has only published part of his coin finds so far. However, even this partial evidence hints at some sort of fourth century habitation of the site, contrary to Stern's conclusions, as the coins represent a continuous series.

[166] *BMC Palestine* xvf.; Y. Meshorer *The City Coins of Eretz-Israel and the Decapolis in the Roman Period* (Jerusalem, 1984, Heb.) p. 54 and cat. no. 150 ob.: ΑΥΤΚ-ΜΑΥΡΑΝΤΩΝΙΝΟΣ rev: ΜΑΥΡΑΝΤ/ΑΝΤΙΙΑ/ΤΡΙΣ and cf. nos. 149–152; A. Kindler, A. Stein *A Bibliography of the City Coinage of Palestine from the 2nd Century BC to the 3rd Century AD* (*BAR*, Oxford, 1987).

[167] *NEAEHL s.v.* Aphek-Antipatris (P. Beck, M. Kochavi).

It is also possible that in this rhetorical composition the diminutive *oppidulum* applied to Antipatris does not refer to its size. It may allude to Horace's satirised *oppidulum*, where he had to pay for water. Perhaps Jerome too had to pay for clean water at Antipatris. The river on which Antipatris was sited was called the Yarqon after the green colour of its murky water and Talmudic sources ban the use of the local water for ritual purposes.[168] Or perhaps the diminutive is being used, as is common with Jerome, as a term of scorn for this non-Christian site—in the New Testament it was the place where Paul was imprisoned on his way from Jerusalem to Caesarea.[169] Or perhaps, as often in fourth century literature, Jerome is using the diminutive as a totally meaningless variant.[170]

I have summarised in table form the paired sites with which Jerome begins his treatment of Paula's journey. It is clear that these fall into two categories, pagan or Jewish decline or ruins, and thriving Christian sites.

PAGAN/JEWISH SITE	CHRISTIAN SITE
Dor *ruinas urbis quondam potentissimae*	Caesarea/Stratonis Turris *Cornelii domum, Christi ecclesiam etc.*
Antipatri[s] *semirutum oppidulum (Herodes)*	[Lydda/Diospolis] *Dorcadis atque Aeneae resurrectio*

---

[168] BTBava Batra 74b: the waters of Pegae (= Antipatris) are forbidden because they are swamp waters.

[169] Acts 23,31. Jerome often uses the diminutive ending as a term of denigration e.g. *mulierculae*—little women.

[170] On the fourth century diminutive as a totally meaningless variant: cf. G.M. Bartelink *Hieronymus: Liber de optimo genere interpretandi (epistula 57): Ein Kommentar* (Lugduni Batavorum, 1980) 39 with bibliography *ad loc.*

It should be noted that in 333 the *Itinararium Burdigalense* notes Antipatris as a *mutatio* like Betthar and unlike Lidda and Nicopolis, each of which are listed as a *ciuitas*. The archive of Theophanes (ca. 325 CE), on the other hand, refers both to τῇ ἀλλαγῇ Βητάρου = *mutatio Betthar*, as well as to what its editors have restored as Ἀντ[ιπατρίδα καὶ εἰς τὴν]

Ἀλλαγ(ὴν) ἀ(πὸ) [Ἀντι]π(ατρίδος) [

ἀπὸ τῆς [Ἀλλαγῆ]ς εἰς Κε[σαρίαν. (Pap. Ryl. 4, 633, 399 and 628, 16f.)

If the restoration of τὴν ἀλλαγὴν ἀπὸ Ἀντιπατρίδος is correct, this could mean that there was also a *mutatio* near Antipatris rather than that the town had declined to the size of a *mutatio*.

Nob   [Arimathia]
urbem quondam sacerdotum nunc   *viculam Ioseph qui dominum sepeliuit*
tumulos occisorum

Ioppe   Emmaus/Nicopolis
fugientis portum Ionae   *cognitus dominus Cleopae*
—de fabulis—   *domum in ecclesiam deicauit*
Andromedae spectatricem

Jerome does not actually indicate fourth century Christian activity
at Lydda and Arimathia, but it is clear from his descriptions that
here the Christian associations are uppermost, which is not the case
with Ioppe [Joppa, Jaffa] where he only mentions the Jewish and
pagan associations, not the activities of Peter.[171] Jerome also sites the
miracle of Dorcas in Lydda, when it actually took place in Joppa,
according to the text in Acts.[172] However, it says in Acts that the
people sent for Peter from 'Lydda which is near Joppa.'[173] Lydda at
this time was a thriving town, and there is evidence of a Christian
community. Ioppe seems to have been in decline. Jerome thus seems
to prefer to identify the thriving town of Lydda with Christianity,
rather than the declining Ioppe.[174]

Jerome also uses the rhetorical *topos* of ruined cities when he talks
about the ruined cities of the Holy Land in his commentary on
Zephaniah, where he is commenting on *Dies irae dies illa*, the day of
judgement which befalls the Jews as a result of the crucifixion of
Jesus:

> *uix ruinarum parua uestigia in magnis quondam urbibus cernimus:* ... *Gabaa* ...
> *diruta est. Rama et Bethoron et reliquae urbes nobiles a Salomone constructae,*
> *parui uiculi demonstrantur.*[175]

He continues the image of the journey with an image of the roads
to heaven and hell. In other words, here in his biblical commentary

---

[171] Peter in Ioppe: Acts 9:36–10:23.
[172] Acts 9:36.
[173] Acts 9:38.
[174] On Joppa at this period, with the possibility that it was a mainly Jewish city
and not a thriving one: Fischer, Isaac & Roll *op. cit.* n. 69 184–5; Lydda as a thriving city is mentioned by the fourth century *Expositio Totius Mundi and Gentium* 13;
in 415 the church synod of Diospolis was held there: Kelly 318. On Christian
Lydda see Fischer, Isaac & Roll *ib.* 205f. with bibliography *ad loc.*
[175] *Com. in Sophoniam* i, 15/16 (*CCSL* 76A, 673; *PL* 25, 1418).

too, the description of these ruined cities on the road to Jerusalem is part of a polemical picture of triumphant Christianity as opposed to ruined Judaism.

To return to *ep.* 108, here Paula looks at these same ruined sites to the right and left of her road:

> *inde proficiscens ascendit Bethoron inferiorem et superiorem , urbes a Salomone conditas et ... postea ... deletas, ad dextram aspiciens Aialon et Gabaon ... in Gabaa urbe usque ad solum diruta paululum substitit ... ad laeuam mausoleo Helenae derelicto ...*

The sites serve to demonstrate the same moral, but the letter also includes real information: in the commentary on Zephaniah, Bethoron is simply a small ruined village used to point the message of ruined Judaism: in *ep.* 108 the description of the real journey is more exact: 'setting out from there' [sc. Emmaus], Paula 'ascended Lower and Upper Bethoron' i.e. she actually went up the famous pass between these two villages, and saw the other villages from there. But the ruins to the left and right of her path remind the reader of the classical model of the *consolatio*, of Servius Sulpicius and Ambrose as noted above.

The rhetorical use of ruins culminates in Paula's visit to Jerusalem. Newman has pointed out how concerned Jerome is to express the ruin of the city and its Temple in his anti-Jewish polemic. In his view, the destruction of the Jewish city is mentioned disproportionately often, on no less than eighteen separate occasions.[176] In *ep.* 108, 9, Jerome contrasts the ruined gates of the earthly city with the gates of the eternal city above:

> *diligit dominus portas Sion super omnia tabernacula Iacob* (Ps. 86 [87]:1f.): *non eas portas, quas hodie cernimus in fauillam et cinerem dissolutas, sed portas, quibus infernus non praeualet ...*

Jerome's geographical representations here in his literary work may be contrasted with his translation of the *Onomasticon*, where he is very concerned to give an accurate picture, as will be seen below. However, once we have taken into account rhetorical exaggeration, the list of places visited or seen can be used to check against the information of the *Onomasticon*, and help verify problems in the interpretation of

---

[176] Newman 226f.

this latter work. Similarly, philological analysis of the text can also help in ascertaining his motives and its reliability.

2c. *Account of* realia: *the route of the journey*

Having looked at the rhetorical elements in Jerome's description of their journey, it is now time to turn to the *realia*. I shall begin with Jerome's account of the routes they took, comparing them with contemporary accounts, and with archaeological evidence from fourth century Palestine. I shall then move on to look at the evidence of *ep.* 108 together with Jerome's translation of Eusebius' *Onomasticon*, and see how the two documents can be used together to provide a clearer picture of the *realia* of the Christian Holy Land.

The roads of Roman Palestine   Pilgrims coming to *provincia Palaestina*, the Christian Holy Land, found a Roman-built network of engineered roads—over one thousand miles of them, connecting the principal towns and cities.[177] The Roman authorities had paved the north-south arteries running from Syria to Egypt as well as building east-west roads connecting the coastal cities with the interior, and especially with Jerusalem. Roman roads were originally built primarily for military and administrative needs and included a system of road stations and staging posts which together made up the system of *vehiculatio*, which had taken over from the *cursus publicus*, the government post.[178] Much of the road system of Palestine is still extant in the field today, together with the milestone pillars which marked official Roman highways. However, even when a milestone still has an inscription which can be dated, this does not provide the complete answer as to when a particular road was actually in use. Roads normally continued in use for an unspecifiable time after the milestone was put up. So we are obliged to turn to the evidence of the written sources. Here careful use of Jerome's *ep.* 108 can

---

[177] I. Roll *op. cit.* n. 163 above. For earlier roads and milestones, see B. Isaac 'Milestones in Judaea, from Vespasian to Constantine' *PEQ* 110 (1978) 46–60; D. Graf, B. Isaac, I. Roll *s.v.* 'Roman roads' in *The Anchor Bible Dictionary* vol. 5 (ed. D.N. Freedman, 1992) 782–7. A larger scale map of the roads is to be found in the *Tabula Imperii Romani: Iudaea/Palaestina* cited in n. 163 above.

[178] *vehiculatio*: Dig. 50,4,1. For a convenient summary of the *cursus publicus* in general with bibliography: L. Casson *Travel in the Ancient World* (Baltimore/London, 1994²) 182–190.

CHAPTER FOUR

provide evidence that one road actually appears to have gone out
of use in the fourth century, as we will see. We shall turn now to
look at Jerome's routes in the holy land.

Detour via Antipatris   The *Tabula Peutingeriana* has already been noted
as a later copy of an ancient map with a schematic diagram of roads
and related sites and other features all over the Roman empire and
other parts of the ancient world. It shows a road running along the
coast of Palestine between Caesarea and Jaffa.[179] The information in
the map appears to come from different periods. Some is as late as
the fourth century, as evidenced by the presence of Constantinople,
which appears as a personification, and which must postdate the
foundation of the city by Constantine, but the information about
Palestine seems to pre-date the early third century Severan urban
changes in the province—the map shows Betogabra [Beit Guvrin]
rather than Eleutheropolis, Amavante [Emmaus] rather than Nicopolis,
and Lydda instead of Diospolis.[180] However, the third century Antonine
Itinerary does not mention the coast road south of Caesarea, nor
did Theophanes (324 or 325 CE) or the traveller from Bordeaux
(333 CE) use this road.[181] There is no record of this section of the
coast road in the *Onomasticon*.[182] A fourth century pagan document,
the *Expositio totius mundi et gentium*, which gives details of cities all over
the Roman empire, but concentrates on the East,[183] mentions a string

---

[179] A. & M. Levi *op. cit.* n. 24 above; L. Bosio *La Tabula Peuteringiana: una descrizione pittorica del mondo antico* (Rimini, 1983); O.A.W. Dilke *Greek and Roman Maps* (London, 1985) 112–120.

[180] See the discussion of the date of the Palestinian section of the *Tabula Peutingeriana* in Isaac and Roll *Roman roads in Judaea I; The Legio Scythopolis road* (Oxford, BAR 1982) 9–10, which they summarise: 'it is clear that the Palestinian section of the Tabula Peutingeriana reflects the situation from Hadrian till Septimius Severus' and in G.W. Bowersock *Roman Arabia* (Cambridge, Mass./London, 1983, repr. 1994) 164f. For a discussion of the roads to Jerusalem including Emmaus/Amavante see Fischer, Isaac & Roll *op. cit.* n. 69 above, 298.

[181] Antonine Itinerary: n. 93 above; Theophanes: C.H. Roberts, E.G. Turner, *Catalogue of the Greek and Latin Papyri in the John Rylands Library Manchester* vol. IV (Manchester, 1952); traveller from Bordeaux (*Itinerarium Burdigalense*): nn. 54, 88.

[182] This was already noted by P. Thomsen 'Palästina nach dem Onomasticon des Eusebius' *ZDPV* 26 (1903) 170.

[183] *Expositio totius mundi et gentium* (ed. J. Rougé, Paris, 1966) with notes and bibliography. See also M. Stern *Greek and Latin authors on Jews and Judaism* II (Jerusalem, 1980) 495f.; H.-J. Drexhage 'Die "Expositio totius mundi et gentium". Ein Handelsgeographie aus dem 4. Jahrhundert n. Chr. eingeleitet, übersetzt und mit ein-

of cities along the Syro-Palestinian coast, from Seleucia, the port of Antioch, southwards through Byblos, Sidon, Sarepta and Tyre to Ptolemais and Caesarea, but does not mention any town on the coast between Caesarea and Ascalon. The route taken by Jerome and Paula in *ep.* 108 provides the final convincing evidence that this road along the coast south of Caesarea was not in use at this period. Jerome and Paula travel from Caesarea to Lydda, via Antipatris, which Jerome describes merely as a miserable half-ruined town, not as a biblical site. They then travel to Joppa from Lydda, to see the sites associated with Jonah (and Andromeda), and return the same way as they came, doubling back on their tracks. It would have been more logical to have travelled south from Caesarea along the coastal road and then turned east inland to Lydda. However, neither Jerome nor any other travellers whose route can be traced did this in the fourth century. Presumably the reason for this was that the coast road was not in use at this time, and all travellers had to make a detour via Antipatris and Lydda.[184] Jerome mentions the necessity to return the way they came as an incidental fact of the journey. It can in no way be seen as a literary embellishment, or rhetorical device, nor as part of a Christian description, and it is therefore to be taken on its face value, as part of the actual experiences of his real journey giving valuable evidence of use (or rather disuse) of roads in his contemporary Palestine.[185]

North or south of Mount Carmel? There are various problems in determining the route taken by Jerome and Paula on their trip round

---

führender Literatur (Kap. xxii–lxvii) versehen.' *Münstersche Beiträge z. antiken Handelsgeschichte* 2,1 (1983) 3–41.

[184] Encroaching sand along the coast was a problem during the Byzantine period: Procopius: *Pan. in Emp. Anas.* xix (*PG* 87 iii, 2817) and cf. A. Raban, 'The Inner Harbor Basin of Caesarea: Archaeological Evidence for its Gradual Demise' A. Raban, K.G. Holum (eds.) *Caesarea Maritima: A Retrospective after Two Millenia* (Leiden, 1996) 628–666 esp. 657. The road was back in use by the sixth century as recorded by Theodosius (after 518): from Joppa it is 30 miles to Caesarea Palestinae: *de Ioppe ad Casarea Palaestinae milia XXX. De situ terrae sanctae* 4, (*CCSL* 175 ed. Geyer) 116. Cf. Wilkinson, 187; O. Limor *Holy Land Travels: Christian Pilgrims in Late Antiquity* (Jerusalem, 1998, in Hebrew) 179.

[185] See now for a more detailed discussion of the coastal road: S. Weingarten 'Road use in late antique Palestine' *Limes XVIII. Proceedings of the XVIIIth International Congress of Roman Frontier Studies held in Amman, Jordan* (September 2000) (Edited by P. Freeman, J. Bennett, Z.T. Fiema & B. Hoffman. British Archaeological Reports 1084. Oxford, 2002) 243–257.

the holy sites of Palestine. They arrive from Antioch and the North, like the traveller from Bordeaux but unlike Theophanes, who, how-ever, does go back that way. Jerome then writes that, having left Accho-Ptolemais, they then entered the plain of Megiddo:

> peruenit Accho, quae nunc Ptolomais dicitur, et per campos Mageddo Iosiae necis conscios intrauit terram Phylistiim. mirata ruinas Dor, urbis quondam potentis-simae, et uersa uice Stratonis turrem ab Herode, rege Iudaeae, in honorem Caesaris Augusti Caesaream nuncupatam, in qua Cornelii domum Christi uidit ecclesiam. . . . (108, 8).

If Jerome and Paula had gone along the coastal road from Ptolemais to Caesarea via Dor, like all the other recorded travellers of the fourth century, they would not have gone via the plain of Megiddo, which is east of the road and not visible from it. Thus Wilkinson, for example, suggests that Jerome 'mixed up' the plain of Megiddo with the plain of Accho/Ptolemais. This is possible, for Jerome was writing years later, and he did pass through Megiddo some time later on the same journey. There was a road to Megiddo which branched off from the coastal road to run via Gaba to Megiddo. Perhaps this was pointed out to Jerome or he saw a milestone with the distance from Megiddo, and this caused his confusion of the two plains. However, it is also possible that the plains of Ptolemais and Legio/Megiddo were seen by Jerome as one continuous entity: this can be inferred from the entry in the *Onomasticon s.v.* Camon:

> autem hodieque uicus Cimona in campo latissimo sex milibus a Legione ad septen-trionalem plagam pergentibus Ptolomaidem. (*On.* 117,18).[186]

There is a further problem with Jerome's description of Dor, as once powerful, now ruined, in view of the fact that a large church has been found at the site. However, as already noted above, the basis for the dating of this is uncertain.[187] Furthermore, the excavation showed signs of destruction of the church by fire,[188] so that even if the date given by Dauphin is correct, it could have been in ruins when Jerome passed. The other possibility, accepted by Aharoni, George Adam Smith and Isaac and Roll,[189] is that Jerome and Paula

---

[186] See discussion of *campus maximus Legionis* in Isaac and Roll *op. cit.* n. 180 above.
[187] Above, n. 165.
[188] Dauphin *op. cit.* n. 165 above.
[189] Y. Aharoni *The Land of the Bible: A Historical Geography* (Philadelphia, 1967) 46; George Adam Smith *The Historical Geography of the Holy Land* (London/Glasgow,

indeed took the road via Megiddo which skirts the Carmel range from the south before turning west again to Caesarea. This way they would not have passed Dor, and in fact Jerome does not actually say that Paula visited the ruins of the town, just that she marvelled at it—*mirata*—which she could have done looking from a distance once she got to Caesarea. This could explain why there is no mention of the church, for it would not have been visible from a distance. The text of Eusebius' *Onomasticon* in Klostermann's edition referring to Dor as desert—ἔρημος—has been reconstructed from Jerome's translation, so cannot help here.[190] Thus it is unclear from the text of *ep.* 108 alone which route Jerome actually took.

In Jerome's translation of Eusebius' *Onomasticon*, it appears that in his entry on Magdiel (130,21 = 131,20) five miles from Dor on the road to Ptolemais, Jerome translates Eusebius' κώμη μεγάλη as *parvus vicus*. He also makes a change for another site along this road, Sycaminum (108,20 = 109,25), which Eusebius calls a κώμη and he changes to *oppidum*. Eusebius calls Ioppe [Jaffa] a πόλις, Jerome calls it an *oppidum*, and it is indeed likely, as already noted, that the town was now in decline. Eusebius calls Sarepta a κώμη, but Jerome calls it an *oppidulum*: here we have complementary evidence from the *Expositio totius mundi et gentium* which calls Sarepta a *civitas* and includes it with Caesarea, Neapolis and Lydda as involved in purple dye.[191] The remaining sites are on the road from Ptolemais to Caesarea. There would seem to be no reason why Jerome should change κώμη μεγάλη to *parvus vicus*, and κώμη to *oppidum*, which we shall see below is contrary to his normal practice, unless he himself had indeed travelled this road, and was correcting Eusebius in the light of his more recent experience. It would thus seem likely that these changes result from his knowledge of these settlements from his journey along this road. Since Magdiel and Sycaminum are situated between Ptolemais and Dor, it now seems clear that Jerome did indeed go via Dor.

1931,[25] repr. 1966) chapters 19, 20; Isaac and Roll *op. cit.* n. 180 above. Professor Isaac now informs me that he is no longer so convinced that Jerome used this route. He had been convinced by Smith and Aharoni of the difficulties of the route north of the Carmel, but now thinks these may not have been so great, given the presence of stopping places like Sycaminum.

[190] *On.* 78,10. In the parallels in *On.* 136,16 = 137,19 only Jerome speaks of the site as desert *iam desertum*.

[191] *Expositio* xxx.

Jerome appears at first sight to mix his terms in translating Eusebius, but close analysis of his descriptions of the sites on the roads reveals him to be surprisingly consistent. Most of the differences between him and Eusebius appear to be cases of sites he himself had visited.

Fast road through Galilee It is clear from *ep.* 108, 12–13 that Paula and Jerome went down to Jericho and the Jordan sites and then west via *valis Achor* to join the Jerusalem-Neapolis road. From here she and her companions turn—*devertit*—east to Samaria-Sebaste. From here they presumably travelled north via Legio/Megiddo to Galilee. Corroborating evidence that they probably did take this road can be found in Jerome's additions to Eusebius' *Onomasticon* entry on Thaanac, which Eusebius describes as being now at the fourth milestone from Legio, to which Jerome adds the description *oppid[um]* and says that a village of that name is pointed out—*ostenditur*—there.[192] Jerome describes the next stage of the journey as follows:

> *cito itinere percucurrit Nazaram, nutriculam domini, Canam et Capharnaum, signorum eius familiares, lacum Tiberiadis. . . . . . . scandebat montem Thabor, in quo transfiguratus est dominus. aspiciebat procul montes Hermon et Hermonim, et campos latissimos Galilaeae . . .* (108, 13).

Unlike the emotional descriptions of her visit to Jerusalem (108, 9), where Paula only agreed to leave one sacred spot because she wanted to go on to another, and Bethlehem, where she claimed to see the infant Jesus lying in his crib (108, 10), there is no mention of anything seen by Paula in Nazareth, the *nutricul[a] domini*. Wilkinson suggests that this may have been because no holy sites had yet been identified there. I would suggest that it may also have been because Jerome and Paula did not actually go there. The main Roman road via Sepphoris to Tiberias, which they would have reached travelling north from Legio/Megiddo, does not pass through Nazareth, but skirts it to the north. Nazareth is relatively inaccessible on a hilltop—even today the road up is difficult, with hair-pin bends. Jerome writes:

> *cito itinere percucurrit Nazaram . . . Canam et Capharnaum*: 'she traversed Nazareth . . . Cana and Capharnaum by a quick route.'

---

[192] Thaanac cf *On.* 98,10 = 99,10; *TIR: Thaanach*, 246 = GR 170.214. See below for a discussion of the significance of Jerome's use of *ostenditur*.

Their speed is emphasised by the fact that the verb is in the perfect tense. The verb *percurrere* is used elsewhere by Jerome to denote traversing wide areas—of the invading Huns overrunning the province, of the conquests of Alexander the Great,[193] but not of simply travelling through small towns or villages. Thus we are led to conclude that the 'quick route' must have been the main Roman road through Galilee, from which the sites of Nazareth to the left and Cana[194] to the right were pointed out to Jerome and Paula as they passed through on their way to Capharnaum and the Lake of Tiberias. As Wilkinson says, there were probably no Christian sites there yet for them to see. This road from Sepphoris to Tiberias is one of the very few that Jerome mentions outside the *Onomasticon*. In his Commentary on Jonah he discusses the site of Geth, situated, he says:

> *in secundo Sapphorim miliario, quae hodie appellatur Diocaesarea euntibus Tyberiadem.*[195]

Deviation from the road system   Jerome and Paula are the first travellers we hear of who deviate from the known official Roman road system of the province, for Paula wished to climb Mount Tabor. No official Roman road has been recorded in this area, but there does seem to have been a secondary road running south from the cross roads at Hirbet Meskene excavated by Isaac, Roll and their team.[196]

---

[193] 52 uses of *percurrere* were found in a search of Jerome's works on the CETE-DOC CD-ROM of the Latin Fathers. Of these 47 were figurative uses, referring mostly to scanning literature. Of the five literal uses, one (*Tract.* lix *in Ps.* 76) referred to a chariot running over the ground; two (*ep.* 60,16 [*CSEL* 54]; *ep.* 126,2 [*CSEL* 56]) to the invasions of the barbarian hordes, one (*Com. in Dan.* 2, 7) to the conquests of Alexander the Great and the last to Paula and Jerome in Galilee above. Note that Jerome uses the verb a second time in the same paragraph under discussion, this time figuratively—*dies me prius quam sermo deficiet, si uoluero cuncta percurrere, quae Paula . . . peruagata est*—'the day would end before my words, if I were to run through at once all that Paula ranged through.'

[194] There is more than one site identified with Cana of Galilee, but the consensus of scholarly opinion now accepts the site north of the Roman road as Cana of Galilee. Like Nazareth, this site was inconveniently far from the main road, which was probably one of the factors which led to the site south of the road and east of Nazareth being identified later as Cana. This latter identification, however, does not seem to pre-date the seventeenth century. See R. Mackowski S.J.: 'Scholars' Qanah', *Biblische Zeitschrift* 23, 2 (1979) 278f. which includes a summary of the debate and bibliography.

[195] *Com in Jon. prol.* (*CCSL* 76, p. 378, *PL* 25, 1119).

[196] Road south of cross roads at Meskene: I. Roll 'Survey of Roman roads in Lower Galilee' *Excavations and surveys in Israel* 14 (1994) 38–40; Y. Stempinski 'Horvat

This is the road on which the large Khan Tujjar was built later, and
it is not impossible that there was a previous road and even lodging-
place here at this period. Constantine's foundation of Helenoupolis,
named after his mother Helena, if it existed, would also have been
somewhere in this area.[197] The settlement fortified by Josephus,
Itabyrium, was situated on top of Mount Tabor, so there must have
been some sort of access route up the hill earlier, even if this was
not a well-paved Roman road.[198] Jerome uses the imperfect tense—
ascendebat—as opposed to the perfect tense, to describe the slow climb
up this steep hill, which was undoubtedly difficult, even if a road
did exist by his time.

From Mount Tabor Jerome describes the view seen by Paula:

> *aspiciebat procul montes Hermon et Hermonim, et campos latissimos Galilaeae, in*
> *quibus Sisara et omnis eius exercitus Barach uincente prostratus est. torrens Cison*
> *mediam planitiem diuidebat, et oppidum iuxta Naim, in quo uiduae suscitatus est*
> *filius, monstrabatur.*

It is clear from the biblical account (Judges ch. 4–5) that the battle between Barak and Sisera took place in the Jezreel valley. Jerome
here includes Jezreel in his concept of 'Galilee,' calling it *'campos
latissimos Galilaeae.'*[199] Similarly, in his *ep.* 46,2 he writes of the Virgin
Mary leaving Galilee and going to Jerusalem:

> *derelictis campestribus ad montana perrexit*—'leaving the valleys she arrived
> at the mountains.'

Perrone has commented here: 'th[e] physical characterization is taken
as an allegory of spiritual ascent—even at the cost of forcing some-
how the geographical evidence.' While it is certainly true that Jerome
is using geography as allegory in this passage of *ep.* 46, given that
he includes Jezreel in his concept of Galilee in *ep.* 108, it is not

---

Maskana: Roman road' *Hadashot Arkheologiot* 108 (1998, in Hebrew) 175. Khan
Tujjar: C.W. Conder, H.H. Kitchener *Survey of Western Palestine* (London, 1881)
vol. i, *Galilee* pp. 394f. with plans.

[197] Helenoupolis: Sozomen *Hist. Ec.* ii, 2, 5; Hierocles *Synecdemus* 720,8 (*PG* 113,153).
Cf. J.W. Drijvers *Helena Augusta: The Mother of Constantine the Great and the Legend of
the Finding of the Cross* (Leiden, 1992) 9–10.

[198] Itabyrium: fortification: Josephus *vita* 188; Vespasian cannot access: *BJ* 54f.

[199] Josephus also appears to include the valley of Jezreel in his 'Galilee,' for he
writes in *BJ* iii, 37 that 'in the south [of Galilee] lie Samaria and the territory of
Scythopolis.' On this see George Adam Smith, *op. cit.* n. 189 above 246f.; 271.

really necessary to see him as 'forcing' the evidence: for him 'Galilee' evidently included the valley of Jezreel.[200]

To return to *ep.* 108, Jerome indicates by an imperfect tense—*aspiciebat*—that he and Paula spent some time looking at biblical sites from the top of Mount Tabor. This enabled Jerome later to correct Eusebius' descriptions in the *Onomasticon*.[201] Thus *ep.* 108 notes that *oppidum . . . Naim monstrabatur*. Eusebius' entry for Naim (*On.* 140,3) reads Ναείν κώμη but Jerome (*On.* 141,4) has 'oppidum' instead.

Roads south of Jerusalem On their journey south, Jerome and Paula set out on the old road which leads to Gaza (108, 11) and turn right to go to Bethsur. From there they go to Eschol and then to the sites connected with Abraham, presumably at Mambre [Terebinthos] although Jerome does not mention this name, only *Sarrae cellulas, incunabula Isaac, uestigia quercus Abraham*, before ascending to Chebron. After this Paula refuses to go to Cariath Sepher, but does see the *superiores et inferiores aquas* of Gothonihel, *filius* Iephone Cenez. The next day at sunrise she stands *in supercilio Caphar Baruchae* and looks out over the desert to see Sodom, Gomorrhae, Adama and Seboim, the balsam plantations in Engaddi, Zoar and Lot's cave. She returns to Jerusalem via *Thecuam atque Amos*, seeing the cross glinting from the top of the Mount of Olives (108, 12).

The beginning of Paula and Jerome's route here is not totally clear. We do not know for sure which was 'the old road to Gaza,' but it looks as if they went from Jerusalem, not Bethlehem, which is why they turned right to Bethsur. The road from Jerusalem via Bethsur to Hebron is an official Roman road with milestones. It was also used by the Bordeaux pilgrim in 333.[202] This pilgrim makes no mention of any *mansiones* or *mutationes* along this route, as opposed to routes north of Jerusalem. The return route of the Bordeaux pilgrim is unclear, but Paula and Jerome go via Caphar Barucha and Thecua [Tekoa] to Jerusalem. This was not an official road. A series

---

[200] L. Perrone 'The mystery of Judaea; [Jerome *ep.* 46] The holy city of Jerusalem between history and symbol in early Christian thought:' Paper given at conference on *Jerusalem: its sanctity and centrality in Judaism, Christianity and Islam* (June 23–28, 1996, Tantur, Jerusalem). I am grateful to Prof. Perrone for giving me a copy of his paper prior to publication.

[201] See below for discussion of Jerome's changes to the *Onomasticon*.

[202] *It. Burd.* 598, 4–599, 9.

of buildings has been found along it south of Thecua, together with
a stretch of paving. Such installations are difficult to date. Hirschfeld,
their first excavator, who does not relate to Jerome, put them around
the beginning of the fifth century, connecting their building with
attacks by Saracens near Thecua reported by John Cassian.[203] Some
of these have now been re-excavated, re-surveyed and re-dated by
Y. Barouch to the first century BCE—first century CE, but there is
evidence of later re-occupation in the Byzantine period.[204] No remains
of a road connecting Thecua with Jerusalem have been found,
although remains of the road south of Thecua are clear. However,
from *ep.* 108 it is clear that there was indeed some sort of road all
the way from Caphar Barucha to Jerusalem which was in use at the
end of the fourth century. Caphar Barucha was the site of a monastery
in the fifth century.[205] This monastery might have already existed at
the time of Jerome's journey, as Paula is reported to have looked
out from Caphar Barucha over the desert at sunrise—*orto iam sole.*
She is not likely to have travelled there by night, so must have stayed
in the vicinity. However, Barouch has suggested that some of the
buildings on the sites along this road, originally described as 'forts,'
may in fact have been road-stations.[206]

Thus looking carefully at Jerome's *ep.* 108 together with the archaeological evidence can give us important evidence about the fourth
century roads of Palestine. We turn now to look at Jerome's revision of Eusebius' *Onomasticon* together with *ep.* 108 to see how comparison of these two sources can further increase our knowledge of
the Holy Land in late antiquity.

---

[203] Y. Hirschfeld 'The series of Byzantine forts along the eastern local road in
the Hebron hill-country' *Qadmoniot* 46–47 (1980, in Hebrew) 78–84; John Cassian
Coll. 6, 1 (*PL* 49, 643–5).
[204] See the analysis by J. Magness 'Redating the forts at Ein Boqeq, Upper Zohar,
and other sites in SE Judaea, and the implications for the nature of the *Limes
Palaestinae*' in J.H. Humphrey (ed.) The Roman and Byzantine Near East 2: Some
recent archaeological research (Portsmouth, Rhode Island, 1999) pp. 189–206) with
bibliography *ad loc.* Magness (205) suggests a connection of the structures with
pilgrims.
[205] Caphar Barucha: *TIR s.v.* and bibliography *ad loc.*
[206] Y. Barouch 'Road stations in Judea during the Second Temple period' in
Y. Eshel (ed.) *Judea and Samaria research studies: Proceedings of the 6th annual meeting—
1996* (Kedumim-Ariel, 1997, Hebrew) 125–35.

4.5. JEROME'S REVISION OF EUSEBIUS' *ONOMASTICON*:
EP. 108 AS COLLATERAL

I shall now examine Jerome's translation and revision of Eusebius'
Onomasticon, showing how we can use details of his route in letter
108 as collateral evidence for the revisions relating to places that he
had actually seen. In his preface to the *Onomasticon*, Jerome claims
to have made many changes. This has generally been taken as an
exaggeration, but there are quite a number of small but significant
changes which have not all received comprehensive scholarly analysis up to now, although Thomsen and Wilkinson have made valuable contributions.[207] Klostermann, in his edition of the *Onomasticon*,
italicises some, but by no means all, of Jerome's additions.[208] Some
of Jerome's changes concern the terminology which he used to translate Eusebius' work, written to identify places mentioned in the Bible
for contemporary readers. Looking at these together with Jerome's
ep. 108, can show something of the changes that had taken place in
Palestine between Eusebius and Jerome, and clarify the routes Jerome
took on his pilgrimage with Paula. They also demonstrate how reliable Jerome is in a work of this kind, where there are no consid-
erations of rhetoric, although there does still remain the question of
style. It is also relevant that here Jerome is translating a work which
identifies sites in the Bible. He himself says in *ep.* 57 that translation of the Bible necessitates more word for word accuracy than
other, freer, translations,[209] so that his geography can be expected
to be much more exact in a work of this kind.

4.5.1. *Terminology: Eusebius and Jerome*

I have looked at the terminology used by Jerome and Eusebius for
359 sites, that is, all the sites where any sort of description of the

---

[207] P. Thomsen 'Palästina nach dem Onomasticon des Eusebius' *ZDPV* 26, (1903,
repr. 1970) 97f.; J. Wilkinson 'L'apport de Saint Jérôme à la topographie' *RB* 81
(1974) 245f.

[208] Regrettably the new English translation of the *Onomasticon* by Freeman-Grenville
in G.S.P. Freeman-Grenville, (tr.) J.E. Taylor, R.L. Chapman III, (eds), *The Onomasticon
by Eusebius of Caesarea: Palestine in the Fourth Century AD* (Jerusalem, 2003) is not consistent enough to give an accurate picture of Jerome's changes to Eusebius' text.

[209] *Ep.* 57, 5: *ego enim non solum fateor sed libera voce profiteor me in interpretatione Graecorum
absque scripturis sanctis, ubi et verborum ordo mysterium est, non verbum e verbo, sed sensum
exprimere de sensu.*

site is given, even one word, except for those mentioning the camping places of the children of Israel in the desert.[210] Thus sites such
as Dadan (*On.* 79,18) noted merely as *in tribu Iudae* following the biblical text, were not included. At first sight Jerome appears very inconsistent in his translations, but on a closer look a consistent pattern
emerges. It is clear that Jerome does not always use the same Latin
word to translate Eusebius' Greek term. This would seem to be a
stylistic consideration: Jerome was at all times exceptionally conscious
of style.[211] Here he appears to be using the stylistic principle of *variatio*, recommended by Quintilian to relieve boredom. It was a feature of Latin literature at all periods and students at school were
required to memorise lists of synonyms.[212] Even in his translation of
the Bible, where he insisted on literal translation, Jerome seems to
go out of his way not to use the same Latin word each time for a
particular Hebrew word, but to draw on a selection of synonyms.[213]

In the *Onomasticon* Jerome translates Eusebius' πόλις as *urbs* in 51
cases; in 141 cases he translates πόλις as *civitas*.[214] But on two occasions, both referring to Biblical times, he translates πόλις as *oppidum*.[215]
He translates κώμη as *uicus* (67 times) or *uilla* (74 times), less often
as *uillula* (5 times) or *uiculus* (7 times), or as *castellum* (4 times), especially if there is an army unit, as at Thamara or Adommim.[216]

---

[210] Here Jerome consistently translates (e.g. *On.* 126,8 = 127,8) σταθμός as *castra*.

[211] Style: cf. Jerome's biographies of Christian writers, *de viris illustribus*, where one
would have expected him to judge each writer by criteria such as Biblical knowledge, orthodoxy etc., but where 'le plus important critère selon lequel Jérôme juge
les écrivains est leur style': M. Starowieski 'Les commentaires bibliques patristiques dans le *Des viris illustribus* de S. Jérôme,' *Studia Patristica* 34 (2001) 459–469.
I am grateful to Professor Starowieski for sending me a copy of his paper prior to
publication.

[212] For a useful discussion of *variatio* in prose as well as poetry, and bibliography
ad loc., see M. Roberts *op. cit.* n. 109 above, 44f.

[213] For example, I Sam. 22–28 repeats the same Hebrew word נער five times;
Jerome uses three different Latin words, including a diminutive—*infans, infantulus*
and *puer*.

[214] E.g. *On.* 30,26 Αἰλών πόλις = 31,24 Ailon *urbs*; *On.* 32,1 Ἀράδ πόλις = 33,1
Arad *ciuitas*. Jerome does translate Eusebius' πόλις in *On.* 22,11 Ἄζωτος/Ἀσδώδ
as *municipium* (23,13). However, a page earlier Eusebius, under Ἀσδώδ/Ἄζωτος *On.*
20,19, wrote πολίχνη which Jerome translated (21,23) as *oppidum*.

[215] *On.* 12,6 = 13,5 Aroer; *On.* 174,21 = 175,22 Chelon. On two other occasions Jerome adds *oppidum* to Eusebius' description of the Biblical status of a site:
On. 54,8 = 55,8 Bethsan; *On.* 36,10 = 37,10 Asima.

[216] E.g. *On.* 34,21 Ἀβελμαελαί. κώμη = 35,18 Abelmela *uicus*; *On.* 44,17 κώμη
Βηθναμβρὶς = 45,22 *uilla* Bethnamaris; *On.* 76,13 Δάν. κώμη = 77,10 Dan *uiculus*;

Μεγίστη becomes *grandis* (14 times) or *pergrandis* (16 times), and on one occasion *non parvus*.[217] Μεγάλη, which is much rarer, is once each *grandis*, *pergrandis* and *magna*.[218] Πολίχνη becomes *oppidum* (5 times).[219]

If Eusebius has a number of terms in his description of a site, Jerome is careful to distinguish them in translation. Thus in the entry on Gabathon (*On.* 70,7 = 71,8) Eusebius successively mentions πόλις πολίχνη κώμη κώμη. Jerome translates *ciuitas*, *oppidum*, *uilla*, *uicul[us]*, showing his preference for stylistic variation rather than repeating the word *uilla* twice. It is clear from this that *uiculus*, as was common in the fourth century, no longer had the force of a diminutive, but was simply an alternative for *uicus* or *uilla*.

There are, however, occasions where Jerome differs from Eusebius. Sometimes he is simply filling in information not present in Eusebius' text, but which could be understood from the context, as when he adds that a place mentioned in the Bible is now identified as a village, e.g. (*On.* 26,13 = 27,14) *Anim . . . est uicus Anea iuxta alterum de quo supra diximus*, where Eusebius simply does not have the word for village. Sometimes his changes are a result of a rationalisation or correction of Eusebius, where Eusebius has two conflicting entries and Jerome chooses to be consistent. Thus Eusebius (*On.* 32,5 =

On. 24,18 κώμη Ἀσθὼ = 25,24 *uillula* Astho; *On.* 8,8 Θαμαρὰ κώμη . . . φρούριον = 9,6 *castellum* Thamara . . . *praesidium*; *On.* 24,10 Μαληδομνεῖ . . . φρούριον = 25,10 Maledomni *castellum militum*. In *On.* 22,19 Ἀφεκά. κώμη μεγάλη becomes *castellum grande* Afeca in 23,21. Here Jerome may have been thinking of the Afec (Vulgate *civitas*) where the defeated Syrian king took refuge from Ahab's pursuit in I Kings 20,26f. In *On.* 117,14 Jerome translates φρούριον as *castellum*. On *castellum* as not necessarily having a connection with the military, see P. Mayerson 'The Saracens and the *limes*' *Bulletin of the American Schools of Oriental Research* 262 (1986) p. 45, n. 4 = *ib. Monks, Martyrs, Soldiers and Saracens* (NY/Jerusalem, 1994) p. 281. n. 4.

[217] C. Dauphin 'Les "kômai" de Palestine' *Proche-orient chrétien* 36 (1987) 254, selects this exceptional '*non parvus*' as her single example of Jerome's translation of Eusebius' κώμη μεγίστη, ignoring the other 30 occasions. She also writes 'le site double de Beth Horon—qualifié de *kômai* par Eusèbe—est catalogué parmi les *parvi viculi* par St. Jérôme, with a reference to *On.* 46,21. However, Jerome's translation of Eusebius' κῶμαι β′ here in *On.* 47,19 is quite correctly and consistently *duo vici*, with no further qualification at all. It is only in the context of his Christian rhetoric in the *Com. in Sophoniam* i, 15/16 (*CCSL* 76a, p. 673, *PL* 25, 1418), as seen above, that he describes the villages as small, not in his more exact translation of the *Onomasticon*.

[218] E.g. *On.* 124,20 κώμη μεγίστη Μαβσαρὰ = 125,17 *uicus grandis* Mabsara; *On.* 108,8 Ἰεττάν. κώμη μεγίστη = 109,7 Ietan *uicus pergrandis*; *On.* 96,24 Ταμνά. κώμη μεγάλη = 97,21 Thamna *uicus pergrandis*; *On.* 90, 6 Ἐμάθ ἡ μεγάλη = 91, 11 Emath *magna*.

[219] E.g. *On.* 130,7 Μηνοεὶς . . . πολίχνη = 131,7 Menois *oppidum*.

33,5: Arisoth) describes Ἰάβις, once a πόλις (in Biblical times) now a μεγίστη πόλις. Jerome says once a *ciuitas*, now a *uilla pergrandis*. This is in keeping with *On.* 110,11–111,11 Iabis Galaad, where Eusebius has νῦν . . . κώμη and Jerome *nunc uicus*. Similarly, as already noted above, Eusebius calls Azotus/Asdod a πόλις (*On.* 22,11 = 23,13), which Jerome translates *municipium*, which is more in keeping with *On.* 20,18 = 21,21, where Eusebius has πολίχνη and Jerome *oppidum* for Asdod/Azotus.

It has been seen throughout how much importance Jerome attached to philology, and how he can even be said to write philological geography. This is clear from his translation of the *Onomasticon* too. He corrects Eusebius' mistaken notion that certain Hebrew words are names of sites, e.g. Enacim (*On.* 84,28 = 85,28) which he correctly notes as a name for the giants, inhabitants of Chebron, not a place name.

Sometimes Jerome adds a further identification of a site. In a few cases he notes that this identification or information was given to him by Jews,[220] or by unidentified informants: *pleri affirmant*. At least one of these unidentified sources can be paralleled in Talmudic literature—he notes that *quidem putant* that Accaron was Turris Stratonis (the old name for Caesarea Palaestinae). This identification is attributed in Talmudic sources to Rabbi Abbahu, who was a contemporary of Origen in third century Caesarea.[221]

Otherwise Jerome's changes to Eusebius' descriptions often seem to refer to places which it is clear he actually visited or saw. He adds churches he has seen, as at Bethel, Arboc, Sychar, Bethania and Gethsemani, and the tomb of John the Baptist at Someron.[222] He adds to Eusebius' description of the position of Mt. Tabor the evidence of an eyewitness, that the mount is *mira rotunditate*.[223] As a Christian eyewitness he adds the word *sublimis* as well. On three occasions he adds the information that a particular site is on the

---

[220] Achad: *On.* 5,22; Aenam: *On.* 9,11; Aialon: *On.* 19,13; Aermon: *On.* 21,6; Nageb, Theman, Darom: *On.* 137,14.

[221] BT Megilla 6a; Hildesheimer *op. cit.* p. 26, n. 37.

[222] Bethel: *On.* 5,26; Arboc: *On.* 7,11; Bethania: *On.* 59,16 cf. *ep.* 108, 12: *sepulchrum* Lazari; Gethsemani: *On.* 75,19; Sychar: *On.* 165,1 cf. *ep.* 108, 12; Someron: *On.* 155,19 cf. *ep.* 108, 12.

[223] *On.* 99,23. Compare his description in *Com. in Osee* i, v 1–2 (*CCSL* 76, p. 51; *PL* 25, 888): *Thabor mons in Galilea, situs in campestribus, rotundus atque sublimis, et ex omni parte finitur aequaliter.*

main road—*via publica.* In each of these cases these are roads he travelled on according to *ep.* 108, and thus may point to a memory of his journey.[224] Thomsen has pointed out that Jerome's comment that Rachel's tomb is on the road is undoubtedly a memory of Genesis 35,19, where Rachel is said to be buried next to the 'road which leads to Efrata'—*via quae ducit Efratham.*[225] However, Jerome has updated this biblical allusion, for he uses the technical term of the Roman province in referring to the road as a *viam publicam,* which it undoubtedly was. Naim, which he and Paula were shown from the top of Mt. Tabor, is changed from κώμη to *oppidum,* which is also the way he describes seeing it in *ep.* 108.[226] Capharnaum is also changed from κώμη to *oppidum* (Vulgate *ciuitas*).[227] Ioppe is changed from πόλις to *oppidum;*[228] Sarepta is changed from κώμη to *oppidulum.*[229] Jerome's downgrading of Ioppe and upgrading of Sarepta have some support from the fact that the fourth century *Expositio totius mundi et gentium* has Sarepta as a commercially significant town but does not mention Ioppe at all in its long list of the towns of the Syro-Palestinian coast.[230]

Jerome also changes Magdiel from κώμη μεγάλη to *paruus uicus,* and Sycaminum from κώμη to *oppidum.*[231] Both these sites are on the

---

[224] Sarepta (on the Tyre-Ptolomais road) *On.* 163,1; Socho (on the Aelia-Eleutheropolis road) *On.* 157,18; Efrata *On.* 45,2.

[225] Thomsen *op. cit.*

[226] Naim: *On.* 140,3 κώμη = 141,4 *oppidum; oppidum iuxta Naim . . . monstrabatur. ep.* 108, 14.

[227] *On.* 120,3 κώμη = 121,2 *oppidum.*

[228] *On.* 110,24 πόλις = 111,25 *oppidum.*

[229] *On.* 162,1 κώμη Σιδῶνος ἐπίσημος = 163,1 *oppidulum Sidoniorum.* It should be noted here that the epithet '*Sidoniorum*' does not necessarily refer to fourth century affiliation, but is a quotation from the NT Luke 4.26, as is clear from Eusebius' ἐπίσημος—famous (The discussion in Luke is bringing well-known examples to show that no prophet is accepted in his own country, only outside, like Elias in Σάρεπτα τῆς Σιδωνίας). At a later period Sarepta became known as an exceptionally long village—q.v. *Life of Peter the Iberian,* ed. Raabe pp. 111, 114; trans. pp. 105, 107: *Qrta arikta.* A fragment of the Madeba map (now lost) published by R.P. Germer-Durand 'Inscriptions romaines et byzantines de Palestine: Medaba' *RB* (1895) 588–589 has: ΣΑΡΕΦΘΑ ΜΑΚΡΑ ΚΩ[ΜΗ]: see discussion of this by F.-M. Abel 'Bulletin: Palestine' *RB* 29 (1920) 157–9.

[230] *Expositio* xxx, Sarepta is mentioned with Sidon, Ptolemais and Eleutheropolis as *ciuitates . . . optimae.*

[231] Magdiel: *On.* 130, 21 κώμη μεγάλη = 131,20 *paruus uicus;* Ἰάφεθ . . . Συκάμινος . . . κώμη: *On.* 108, 30 = 109, 134 Iafthie *oppidum Sycaminum.* For Sycaminum see now L. Ullman, E. Galili 'A Greek inscription mentioning ΣΥΚΑΜΙΝΩΝ' *SCI* 13, (1994) 116–122 with bibliography; *NEAEHL* s.v.

coastal road between Ptolemais, Dor and Caesarea. I have thus concluded above[232] that Jerome must have used this coastal road via
Dor, rather than the road via Legio/Megiddo south of the Carmel,
when travelling from Ptolemais to Caesarea. Eusebius never calls
anything 'small'—the only uses of *paruus* in the *Onomasticon* are connected to places where Jerome has been—Bethel he tells us 'was
shown'—*ostenditur*—as a *paruus vicus*; Ἀγγαὶ τόπος ἔρημος αὐτὸ μόνον
δείκνυται. Jerome adds .... *paruae ruinae*.... and as already noted,
he changes Magdiel from κώμη μεγάλη to *paruus uicus*, so that this is
even more likely to have been a deliberate change.

When it comes to Faran, which Eusebius calls a πόλις, referring
to Biblical times, Jerome writes *nunc oppidum*, just as he adds to
Eusebius' Ishmaelites *nunc Saraceni* in the same passage (*On.* 166,12f.;
167,13f.).[233]

To sum up: Using *ep.* 108 to corroborate the evidence of the *Onomasticon*, makes it clear that Jerome is very careful to translate Eusebius'
site descriptions accurately, when it is a question of size or type of
site. He is consistent within his own terms of reference, preferring
to vary his language, but keeping it accurate. He corrects Eusebius
when the latter appears to have made philological mistakes, and
when his information is out of date—he adds information about new
churches and corrects descriptions of the size of sites. He also expands
some of the Biblical details.

4.5.2. *Jerome's details of distances*

Jerome does not usually correct indications of distance or direction.
This would seem even more to indicate that his corrections are those
of an eye-witness. It is easy to see whether a village is large or small
when just passing by—it is more difficult to ascertain exact directions
or distances unless the traveller takes particular trouble to do so. On
the few occasions when he seems to do so, they are mostly places
where he has been, or just possibly problems with the manuscript.
For example, there are three entries on page 32 of Klostermann's

---

[232] Above, 2c: North or south of Mount Carmel?
[233] *On.* 22,11 = 23,13. There is no evidence, however, that Jerome ever was at
Faran.

edition very close to one another: Arisoth (*On.* 32,5 = 33,6), Aruir (*On.* 32,9 = 33,10); Abel (*On.* 32,14 = 33,15). In all these cases the distance of each site from Eusebius' reference point is given as ϛ′, i.e. six miles. Jerome, on the other hand, has *sex* for Arisoth, but *vicesm[o]* for Aruir and *septim[o]* for Abel, which is a small site across the Jordan where it is unlikely that he went. It would seem most likely that the text of Eusebius repeats ϛ by dittography, and that here Jerome has preserved the original version, rather than that he has corrected Eusebius' text. The cases where Jerome or Eusebius has only one of a two digit number and vice versa, may also be due to manuscript variants.[234]

However, Jerome was at Selo [biblical Shilo] *On.* 156, 28 ιβ′ = 157,28 *decim[o]* and as just noted, he saw Naim from the top of Mount Tabor: Naim *On.* 140,3 ιβ′ = 141,4 *secund[o]*, so he may have corrected these distances in the light of his actual experience. This is probably the case with Efratha next to Bethlehem *On.* 82,10 δ′ = 83,12 *quint[o]* and Luza *On.* 120,11 θ′ = 121,12 *terti[o]*. In one case Jerome adds a distance: he notes for Carnaim *On.* 113,1 that it is nine miles from Jerusalem. This would refer to the Jerusalem-Jericho road, which we know he took.

There is one case where Jerome is clearly mistaken over a distance to a village he undoubtedly knew—Elthece [Tekoa] *On.* 86,12 ιβ′ = 87,13 *non[o]* but as Wilkinson points out, he corrects this elsewhere on several occasions.[235] In another case he fails to correct a small discrepancy: Cariathiarim appears twice, once in *On.* 114,23 θ′ = 115,23 *non[o]*, and once in *On.* 48,22 ι′ = 49,19 *decimo*.[236]

Thus the impression given is that Jerome does not usually correct small discrepancies of distance in his translation of the *Onomasticon*.

4.5.3. *Eye-witness evidence: Jerome's use of* ostenditur

We can also use *ep.* 108 to tell us where Jerome is using his own eye-witness evidence about sites in the Holy Land in the *Onomasticon*.

---

[234] Anua *On.* 28,18 ιε′ = 29,17 *decimo;* Theman *On.* 96,18 ιε′ = 97,14 *quinqe.*

[235] *Com. in Amos prol.* (*CCSL* 76, 211,12); *Com. in Jer.* ii, 6,1 (*CCSL* 74, 63,8 18–20). Wilkinson *op. cit.* p. 246 n. 15.

[236] Cf. also Odollam *On.* 24,21 δέκα = 25,26 *decim[o];* *ib. On.* 84,22 ι′ = 85,22 *duodecim[o].*

3a. *Sites Jerome certainly saw: routes mentioned in* ep. *108*

When Jerome has visited or seen a site himself he often adds the
note *ostenditur*—it was shown[237]—and sometimes more eye-witness
information about an important site such as Mount Tabor. Presumably
these sites were pointed out to him by local guides. Eusebius' δείκνυται is usually used by him of important sites, but Jerome seems to
use *ostenditur* more widely. Jerome uses the word *ostenditur* (or its equivalent *demonstratur*, or *cernitur*) on 33 occasions as an addition to
Eusebius' description, where Eusebius only uses ἐστιν or something
similar. Most of these occasions refer to places where we know Jerome
actually went, from what he writes in *ep.* 108 and other works. Thus
in *ep.* 108 he writes that he and Paula were shown the site of Naim,
as already noted above, from the top of Mount Tabor, and in his
notice of the site in his version of the Onomasticon he changes
Eusebius' κώμη to *oppidum* and adds the word '*ostenditur*' (*On.* 141,4).
Other sites near Tabor but not mentioned in *ep.* 108 also have the
added note *ostenditur*, and we may presume he was shown them too
when they looked out over the surrounding countryside, (Sunem,
Seon) or journeyed nearby (Ullama).[238] Similarly, he writes in *ep.*
108, 11 that he and Paula were shown sites in the Dead Sea area
from the vantage point of Caphar Barucha, and in the *Onomasticon*
he notes *ostenditur* for the site of Segor (Bala, Zoara 153,15). Other
places where he notes '*ostenditur*' and we know he visited or was
shown, include Beeroth *sub colle Gabaon*, old Gaza, Theco [Tekoa],
Saron *a Caesaraea Palestinae ad oppidum Ioppe omnis terra quae cernitur*,
Thamna, and Faora which can be seen—*cernitur*—from Bethlehem.[239]
There are also a number of sites along the roads which he took on
his journey with Paula, where not only does he record they were
shown—*ostenditur*—but, as already noted in the case of Magdiel, he
changes Eusebius' κώμη μεγάλη to *paruus uicus*. That this is no accidental
change is clear from the fact that Eusebius never calls any site small.
Other sites on or near the roads Jerome would have passed on his
journey but did not mention by name in *ep.* 108 are Gelgel, between

---

[237] Cf. the discussion of Geth in his *Prol. in Ionam* above, on the Sapphoris/
Diocaesarea—Tiberias road: *haud grandis est uiculus, ubi et sepulchrum eius [sc. Jonah]
ostenditur.*

[238] Sunem: *On.* 159,11; Seon *iuxta Tabor. On.* 159,13; Ullama: *On.* 141,14.

[239] Beeroth: *On.* 49,8; Gaza *cernitur: On.* 63,16; Theco: *On.* 99,17; Saron *cernitur:
On.* 163,6; Thamna: *On.* 97,20; Faora *cernitur: On.* 169,19.

Antipatris and Neapolis, Dothaim between Sebaste and Legio/Megiddo, Zif between Hebron and Caphar Barucha, Thaanac south of Legio, Sior between Aelia and Eleutheropolis.[240] All these appear with *ostenditur* in his *Onomasticon* translation. He also notes Bethdagon as Capferdago *demonstratur* on the road between Diospolis [Lydda] and Iamnia.[241] In fact it is on the road between Diospolis and Ioppe, which he would have passed on his journey with Paula, but although he notes that it was pointed out, he does not correct Eusebius' mistake. This seems to be a rare example of a slip-up in Jerome's general accuracy.

3b. *Sites Jerome presumably saw: the vicinity of Bethlehem*
There are a number of sites on routes not mentioned in *ep.* 108 but which are not far from Bethlehem, and which Jerome would presumably have passed on other journeys, such as those on the roads to Lydda/Diospolis, where we know he went, or to Caesarea, or Emmaus/Nicopolis. Thus in the *Onomasticon* he notes that Geth was pointed out on the road from Eleutheropolis to Diospolis.[242] He notes three sites—Bethsames, Esthaol and Sorech *iuxta* Saraa—as being pointed out from the road between Eleutheropolis and Nicopolis.[243] No traces of this road have been found to date. It does not appear on the latest map of the *TIR*, which shows a road joining Eleutheropolis and Nicopolis east of these sites and there is a further problem in that Eusebius notes all the sites as being 10 miles from Eleutheropolis. It has been suggested that if there was a road from Eleutheropolis to Nicopolis it may have branched off from the Eleutheropolis-Aelia road 10 miles from Eleutheropolis, just after Socho.[244] Also in this area there are some sites where Jerome adds details to Eusebius but does not actually say they were pointed out to him: Rooboth is called a *vicus grandis*; Chebron, where there was an army unit is called an *oppidum*, as we saw for Legio above.[245] This may be due to some local knowledge.

---

[240] Gelgel: *On.* 69, 13; Dothaim: *On.* 77,18; Zif: *On.* 93,16; Thaanac: *On.* 99,10; Sior: *On.* 157,3.
[241] Capferdago: *On.* 51,15.
[242] Geth: *On.* 69,5.
[243] Bethsames: *On.* 55,12; Esthaol: *On.* 89,11: Sorech: *On.* 161,2.
[244] I owe this suggestion to Prof. I. Roll.
[245] Rooboth: *On.* 143,14; Carmel/Chebron *On.* 119,4.

3c. *Sites Jerome possibly saw*

There is no record that Jerome ever visited Scythopolis, although from the list of sites where he writes *ostenditur*, there may be indications that he was there. As there is no record of which way he returned from Galilee, it is quite possible that he even went there on this journey. As noted above, he says he was shown Iezrael, which he calls *pergrandis*, rather than Eusebius' ἐπισημοτάτη—very famous (*On.* 108,13 = 109,11). He may have seen this from the top of Mt. Tabor, but he could also have passed it if he took the Legio-Scythopolis road. He also notes that the site of Salumias is shown 8 miles from Scythopolis (*On.* 153,7). However there is a lacuna in our text of Eusebius here, and it is impossible to tell whether this was a translation of Eusebius' or an addition of Jerome's.[246] Finally, Jerome notes Salabim, which Eusebius calls a κώμη but Jerome up-grades to a *vicus grandis* in the territory of Sebaste (*On.* 159,22). If the identification is correct, this site is on the road between Scythopolis and Neapolis.

There remain problems with two other sites which Jerome notes were pointed out—*ostenditur*. When Jerome left Jericho, he seems to have gone on to Sichem/Neapolis via Vallis Achor and Bethel. There are, however, other ways up further north, via Phasaelis or Coreae. Taking one of these routes Jerome could have passed both Senna [Magdalsenna], which was pointed out 7 miles north of Jericho (*On.* 155,13), and Iano 12 miles from Neapolis (*On.* 109,11). It is just possible that he did this and passed Bethel and Silo on his way back from Galilee. This would have the advantage of passing rather nearer Bethel, which would otherwise have involved a backwards detour from the road from Vallis Achor. It is also possible, however, that Magdalsenna was pointed out to Jerome from Jericho, and Iano from Sichem/Neapolis. Alternatively, perhaps Jerome took more than one grand tour around the holy places, but as Wilkinson has pointed out, there is no evidence of this.[247]

---

[246] Jerome does seem to have further information about this site, connected to Melchisedec and visited by the pilgrim Egeria, but it is difficult to know whether it is from first-hand experience or a written source: cf. *ep.* 73, 7. In another case where Jerome says a site is shown *demonstrari*, of the sources of the Euphrates, he is quoting Sallust. (*On.* 83,9).

[247] J. Wilkinson 'L'apport de Saint Jérôme à la topographie' *RB* 81 (1974) 245f.

3d. *Sites Jerome did not see: Eusebius' use of* δείκνυται *compared with Jerome's use of ostenditur.*

There remain three sites, all east of the Jordan in the area of Esbus [Heshbon] and Philadelphia: Eleale (*On.* 85,10), Zeb/Zia (*On.* 95,3) and Mennith (*On.* 133,1), all of which Jerome notes as having been pointed out.[248] There is no evidence at all that Jerome ever went across the Jordan, and I think he is unlikely to have done this and not referred to it anywhere else in his writings. He would either have gone in order to see the holy sites with Paula, in which case he would have said so, or on some ecclesiastical-political business, in which case he is unlikely to have omitted it from his letters or polemics. It is, however, interesting to look at this together with Eusebius' use of δείκνυται.[249] Eusebius records that a site was pointed out—δείκνυται—(or similar) on 30 occasions, which Jerome translates with *ostenditur* or an equivalent. In two cases (Ararat and Ur) Eusebius is quoting Josephus.[250] If we look at the rest of the sites which Eusebius describes thus, we find that most of them refer to major holy sites:

Ager fullonis (*On.* 38,2 = 39,3);
Bethel (later the site of a church) (*On.* 4,28f. = 5,26f.);
Bethsur (*On.* 52,1 = 53,1);
Bunos or Galgala (later the site of a church) (*On.* 46,18 = 47,15);
Balanus (next to Joseph's Tomb in Shechem) (*On.* 54,23 = 55,24);
Bethsaida (the healing pools in Jerusalem) (*On.* 58,21 = 59,22);
Gabatha, Eccela, Ceila—all three mentioned in connection with the
    tomb of Habbakuk:
  Gabatha (*On.* 70,22 = 71,23);
  Eccela/Echela (*On.* 88,26 = 89,26,7);
  Ceila (*On.* 114,15 = 115,16);[251]

---

[248] In the case of Eleale (*On.* 85,10) Eusebius has σῴζεται εἰς ἔτι νῦν which Jerome could have translated as *usque hodie ostenditur* because he interpreted it as eye-witness evidence—at least one modern commentator is of the opinion that εἰς ἔτι νῦν (unlike ἔτι νῦν) is a 'contemporising formula': D.E. Groh 'The *Onomasticon* of Eusebius and the Rise of Christian Palestine' *Studia Patristica* 18, 1 (1983) pp. 23–31.
[249] On the spiritual significance of Eusebius' δείκνυται, see Hunt, 99f. and bibliography *ad loc.*
[250] Ararat: *On.* 2,23f. = 3,20f. (Josephus *AJ* i, 95); Ur Chaldeorum: *On.* 140,12 = 141,11 (Jos *AJ* i 150).
[251] Jerome may well have passed this site, for it is on the Eleutheropolis-Hebron road. However, only a road connecting these place to the south has been identified.

Gergesa (later site of a church) (*On.* 74,13 = 75,14);
Golgotha (*On.* 74,19 = 75,20);
Drys (Mambre) (*On.* 76,1 = 77,1);
Elthece/Thecua (Tomb of Amos) (*On.* 86,12 = 87,13);
Thamnathsara (Tomb of Joshua) (*On.* 100,1 = 101,1);
Iericho (*On.* 104,25 = 105,20);
Modeim (Tombs of Maccabees) (*On.* 132,16 = 133,17);
Sychem (Tomb of Joseph) (*On.* 150,1 = 151,1);
Puteus iuramenti (many sacred wells from the Bible in Gerar and
   around Ascalon) (*On.* 168,1 = 169,1).

The only minor site mentioned as being 'pointed out' west of the
Jordan is Chasbi next to Odollam, near Eleutheropolis (*On.* 172,6 =
173,9).[252]

The other sites mentioned as being 'pointed out' by Eusebius are
east of the Jordan, where they include both major holy sites as well
as more minor ones. Major sites include Abarim [Phasga, Nabau]
(*On.* 16,24 = 17,26; 136,6 = 137,5) the place where Moses died
(later the site of a church) and Beroth (where Aaron died) (*On.*
46,14 = 47,12). Aroer (*On.* 12,5 = 13,5) and Madiam (*On.* 124,8 =
125,6), cities of the Moabites and Midianites from the Bible are
identified and there is a graphic description of the gorge of the Arnon
which is 'pointed out' (*On.* 10,15 = 11,13). Minor sites include Iassa
'pointed out' between Medaba and Debus (*On.* 104,9 = 105,7), and
Nabo/Naboth south of Esbus/Heshbon (*On.* 136,9 = 137,8). It has
been noted that Eusebius has four major cities of reference—Eleutheropolis, Aelia/Jerusalem, Legio and Heshbon.[253] It is interesting

---

We note that Eusebius once says Eccela is 7 miles from Eleutheropolis, and once
that Ceila is 8 miles away, which Jerome modifies to *quasi in octavo miliario*. See on
this J. Rhenferd *Exercitatio philologica ad loca deperdita Eusebii et Hieronymi de situ et
nominibus locorum sacrorum* (1707) 7–8.
   [252] The *Onomasticon* notes more sites near Eleutheropolis than any other town:
C. Woolf 'Eusebius of Caesarea and the Onomasticon' *BA* 27, 3 (1964) 66f. esp.
78; 94; B. Isaac 'Eusebius and the geography of Roman provinces' in D. Kennedy
(ed.) *The Roman Army in the East* (Ann Arbor, 1996) 153–167 = *ib. The Near East
under Roman Rule: Selected Papers* (Leiden, 1998). Perhaps this points to some local
knowledge of Eusebius or his sources. For a very interesting discussion of the making of the *Onomasticon* and convincing deductions about Eusebius' sources, see E.Z.
Melamed 'Eusebius' Onomasticon' *Tarbiz* 3 (1932); 314–27; 393–409; 4 (1933)
78–96; 249–84 (in Hebrew).
   [253] C. Woolf *op. cit.* n. 252 above.

that all three minor sites over the Jordan where Jerome has *ostenditur* but Eusebius does not have δείκνυται are in the general area of Esbus/Heshbon, which is where Eusebius, contrary to his usual practice, uses δείκνυται for both major and minor sites. This issue remains unresolved.

Thus Eusebius uses the word δείκνυται (or an equivalent) to indicate that sites were 'pointed out' on 30 occasions. West of the Jordan, Eusebius uses this term only for major sites, but east of the Jordan he uses it for both major and minor sites. This may reflect a difference between Eusebius' sources. Jerome translates Eusebius' δείκνυται as *ostenditur.* He also uses the word *ostenditur* where there is no δείκνυται in Eusebius' text to indicate places which he, Jerome, has seen himself. This can be confirmed by comparing the list of sites thus described with those on the roads he actually travelled on as detailed in his *ep.* 108. Other sites noted as *ostenditur* can clearly be seen to be on routes he would have taken on other journeys he writes about, such as to Lydda or Caesarea. However, it is not always clear which route he took, and it is possible that his use of *ostenditur* can help decide this. In three cases, all of them minor sites east of the Jordan, his use of *ostenditur* is obscure.

Summary of 4.5. Jerome's revision of the Onomasticon

Jerome thus appears to have up-dated and corrected Eusebius' information about the sites he visited or saw himself. He adds details of new churches built since Eusebius' times and sometimes corrects details of the size of a site, which may have been incorrectly noted or may have changed in the intervening years. Such changes are to be found with regard to sites on routes we know he used, and are thus not likely to be the result of careless translation or inconsistency in nomenclature. Jerome does not, however, usually correct indications of distances or directions. This would seem a further indication that his corrections are those of an eye-witness. It is possible to see the size of a village while passing, but it is more difficult to ascertain directions or distances unless the traveller takes particular trouble to do so. Jerome is in fact remarkably consistent in his translations of terms used for sites, although he does follow the classical principle of stylistic variation where possible.

Summary of Chapter Four

Thus we have seen in this chapter how Jerome portrays his world centred on Jerusalem, surrounded by the continents. He is aware that this is a change from the Roman imperial concept, which saw the empire extending from Britain to Africa, from the Atlantic to India, centred on Rome. This schematic presentation may have been available to him in graphic form, painted on small tablets. His own regional concepts of the Holy Land seem to have been derived in the first place from Jewish sources, which saw the Promised Land extending from Cilicia via Palmyra to the Red Sea. Within this Jerome sited the much smaller actual Land of Israel, now appropriated for Christianity by being the site of the incarnation and crucifixion. Jerome has reasonably accurate measurements for this Land, but if he had a source it was likely to have been a sort of strip-map or a written itinerary, not a regional map. However, he had his own personal experience of fourth-century Palestine from the pilgrimage he took with Paula, which we can see that he used to update Eusebius' *Onomasticon* to provide contemporary information about the sites of interest to Christians. Using this material, it is possible to distinguish to a certain extent between rhetoric and *realia* in *ep.* 108, which includes the *iter* he wrote about his pilgrimage with Paula.

APPENDIX TO CHAPTER FOUR: THE PROBLEM OF EMATH

There appears to be a difference between Jerome and the *targum* when he identifies the entrance of Emath [Hamat] on the northern border with Syrian Epiphania, rather than with Antioch, like the *targum*. This would seem problematical, as the well-known town Epiphania/Hama is further south on the Orontes than Antioch, and as such could hardly be seen as the *northern* border, especially as Jerome returns to Antioch as the starting point for the eastern border. Jerome mentions the identification of this Epiphania '*iuxta Emesam*' with Hamat in his translation of the *Onomasticon* 91,11, (thus correcting Eusebius, who does not accept it). However, there was another Epiphania in Syria, which was, according to Strabo, part of the tetrapolis which made up Antioch, but separated by its own wall. This Epiphania is also mentioned later by Malalas, and both identify it, like Jerome, as founded by Antiochus Epiphanes. In Jerome's commentary on Amos vi, 1 he had identified two places called Emath: Epiphania, and Emath Magna, which he identifies with Antioch:

Emath magnam, quae nunc Antiochia nominatur. magnam autem uocat, ad distinctionem minoris Emath, quae appellatur Epiphania.

Midrash Leviticus Rabbah, a Palestinian *midrash* from around the fifth century, (5, 3) also identifies 'Hamat the Great' with 'Hamat of Antiochia.' It may be possible to understand Emath Magna in the commentary on Amos as the whole town of Antioch, which included the smaller Emath/Epiphania. Libanius writes that there was an *akra* on Mt Silpius in Antioch, which was called Emathia, because it was founded by Macedonians, and Strabo and Malalas also site Epiphania, the suburb of Antioch, on the mountain slopes.[254] Thus it is possible that Antiochian Epiphania was also identified locally with a place called Emathia/Emath. As noted above, Jerome sites the entrance to his Emath/Epiphania/Antioch on the coast. Ancient Antioch was not in fact on the coast, but it was on a navigable river, and Jerome actually relates that Paula sailed from Seleucia, which is on the coast, up the estuary of the Orontes, to Antioch.

We may conclude that both Jerome and the *targum* both identify Emath with Antioch, Epiphania being used by Jerome synonymously.

---

[254] Libanius *Or.* 11, 72–77; 87; 250; Strabo xvi, 4; Malalas viii. Cf. G. Downey *A History of Antioch in Syria from Seleucus to the Arab Conquest* (Princeton, 1961) 54–5.

CONCLUDING SUMMARY

In this book, I have looked at Jerome's hagiographical works, his saints' *Lives*, as evidence of his own world, both his conceptual world and the material world he lived in. The *Lives* present the world as he saw it, and as he would like it to be seen: they combine *realia* with rhetoric. In order to see how this is achieved, I have used detailed analysis of his writing and of parallel texts, as well as the archaeological evidence now available to us today.

The *Life of Paul* deals with a holy man in the desert. Jerome here was writing after the success of the Greek *Life of Antony* and creating Latin hagiography for the first time. He says that he is writing for the *simpliciores*, but had problems in lowering his style. However, it is clear that he is writing here extremely successfully on a number of levels, not only for simple people, but also for a more educated and sophisticated audience, with allusions to Virgil, for example. Jerome uses his own experience to create his work: his personal experience of the Syrian desert is used for Paul's Egyptian desert; paintings of Daniel in the lions' den he could have seen in the Roman catacombs may well be the source for his verbal picture of Paul and the lions.

There are a number of vivid parallels between this *Life* and the corpus of Jewish *aggadot* about the famous Jewish holy man and scholar, Rabbi Shim'on bar Yohai. Recent books by Boyarin and Schwartz have suggested that Jewish sources of the fourth century were sometimes written in reaction to Christian writings. However, close analysis of the *Life of Paul* in parallel with the *aggadot* on Rabbi Shim'on bar Yohai suggest that here, on the contrary, it is Jerome who is reacting to the Jewish *aggadot*. Indeed, he can even be seen to be conducting a hidden dialogue with Jewish *aggadah*, with Paul implicitly compared with the famous Jewish ascetic rabbi, showing the Christian ascetic surpassing his Jewish counterpart. If Jerome is indeed using aggadic material here, then it is material which has parallels in both the Palestinian Talmud and Midrashim, and in the later Babylonian Talmud. The implications of this would be that Jerome knew a version earlier than either which contained elements from both. This possibility has recently been suggested by Kraus for Jerome's *Commentary on Ecclesiastes*.

Analysis of structure and style of the *Life of Paul* shows a structure based on recurring and shifting groups of three, made up of two similar elements and one different, often transcendental—there are triads of Elijah, John the Baptist and Jesus; the persecuting emperors Valerius and Decius with Satan himself; a centaur, a satyr and a she-wolf. Previous scholars have discussed Antony and Paul as a pair, but in fact they form a triad where the third is Jerome: Jerome writes himself in as Paul's successor, the legendary ascetic saint of the desert.

The *Life of Hilarion* presents the christianisation of the Roman world, both the material world and, most important to Jerome, the world of literature. Here we have seen how Jerome christianises the most popular, and the most threatening, of pagan literature, the novel, specifically Apuleius' *Golden Ass*, to produce his *Life* of the saint. Scholars have often suggested that Jerome's saints' *Lives* were influenced by the Greek novel. But Jerome, who learned his Greek as an adult in order to read Christian literature, appears to have no direct knowledge of pagan literature in Greek. I have demonstrated here that he was indeed influenced by the Greek novel, but at second-hand, through the Latin novel of Apuleius. Jerome trims the pagan pornographic novel to his ascetic Christianity.

Dealing as it does with the christianisation of the whole Roman physical world, the *vita Hilarionis* is the longest of Jerome's saints' *Lives*, with the widest possible social and geographical scope: Jerome presents a large number of different classes of people and ranges over many different geographical settings all over the empire. All come under the influence of his Palestinian saint, Hilarion, who like Jerome himself, tries and fails to leave society for the desert. Jerome contrasts different types of authority figures—holy man and bishop, holy man and Roman *dux* and Jewish patriarch. A chariot race in the circus of Gaza forms the high point of the *Life*, with the Christians gaining a victory over their pagan rivals. However, the process of christianisation in Palestine is seen to be slow and incomplete. It is with people outside the traditional Roman establishment that Hilarion succeeds: the rural poor, the Saracens. Even his upper class contacts are with people outside the Roman nobility. Not all barbarians in the *Life of Hilarion*, however, are what they appear: 'semi-barbarian' Elusa is a reference to the mixture of languages there, rather than a comment on the cultural level of this town. Jerome engages in an overt polemic against paganism in Hilarion's confrontations with pagan cults: Marnas, god of Gaza, Venus at Elusa and Paphos, and a dragon in Illyria connected with the local cult of Cadmus.

In the *Life of Hilarion* Jerome is also seen to be creating a new Christian geography. Pagan cities had their own eponymous male heroes: now his holy woman Constantia functions as an eponymous female saint linking Gaza with Cyprus. Yet another aspect of Christian geography is expressed by the competition for the remains of Hilarion, which results in the theft of his body and its reburial in Palestine, although the spirit, Jerome says, remained in Cyprus. Thus whereas Palestine was the physical Holy Land, the spirit of Christianity is now spreading over the Roman world.

In the *Life of Malchus* Jerome presents aspects of the Christian ascetic appropriation of the human body: the *Life* deals with ownership and use of the body by the Christian holy man. With his Roman legal training, Jerome was aware of legal aspects of body-ownership. Thus he deliberately uses the Roman legal terminology of the *ius postliminii* about body-ownership, and converts it to a Christian metaphor. Virgil's story of Dido and Aeneas is used as an opposing context and countertext for the story. Malchus and his woman companion refuse to have sex in their cave and are thus victorious over their own bodies, in contrast to Virgil's heroes who succumb to their desires. Here too there are parallels to Jerome's own life and victory over his body, as well as his relations with his woman friend Paula. Jerome also uses biblical typology to underline his message in this *Life*, particularly the *typos* of the chaste Joseph. The background of the *Life* is found to have many features in common with Ammianus Marcellinus, who wrote about the same place, Mesopotamia, at the same time. Several features of the *Life* which appear real are shown to be biblical metaphors, while other apparent inventions are shown to have some basis in local reality—the much-debated *carnes semi-crudae* are shown to be a particular local food discussed in the Babylonian Talmud. The background against which Jerome's chaste hero is set, that of the over-sexed Saracens, is shown to be a commonly held fourth-century stereotype of these particular barbarians, present in both serious and satirical Roman sources, in pagan and Christian literature, and in the Babylonian Talmud, rather than a mere *topos* about barbarians in general.

Jerome's letter 108 was written as a *Life* of his friend, the saintly Paula. It is written using the literary conventions of Roman rhetoric, combining the genres of *consolatio*, *propempticon*, *encomium* and *epitaphium*.

Within it Jerome includes, as classical historians had included a geo-graphical *excursus* in their historical works, an *iter*—a travel account—of Paula's pilgrimage with him through the Holy Land. Analysis of Jerome's geographical concepts makes it clear that there are three elements in his geography—classical, Jewish and Christian. Jerome's classical geography is that of any educated Roman of his times. He may have had some access to maps, *breves tabellae*, but these are likely to have been the sort of strip-map familiar to us from the newly-found Artemidorus map or the Peutinger map. Jerome's geograph-ical concept of the wider bounds of the Land of Israel appears to be based on Jewish sources, probably the Targumim. But in *ep.* 108 he set himself to appropriate the Holy Land spiritually through his Christian rhetoric, particularly his satire: the genre of *iter* was tradi-tionally closely connected to satire. His use of satire and rhetoric make it difficult for us to take the evidence of the letter by itself as evidence of the *realia* of Palestine in the fourth century: for exam-ple, towns are placed as contrasting pairs to show the rise of Christianity and the decline of paganism and Judaism. Nonetheless, comparison of *ep.* 108 with his translation of Eusebius' *Onomasticon* shows clearly that he updated and corrected the latter more than has been recog-nised till now, consistently correcting details about places he saw on his pilgrimage through Palestine with Paula.

Thus in his four saints *Lives* Jerome views his world through the medium of his literary heritage—classical, Jewish and Christian. But he also had real, physical experience of the fourth-century Holy Land where he lived for so long, and he combines this experience with his literary sources to rewrite the biblical land as a new and Christian world for his readers. Moreover, Jerome uses his literary creations to construct a literary *persona* for himself. In writing the *Lives* of the saints Paul, Hilarion, Malchus and Paula he was also creating the *Life* of Saint Jerome.

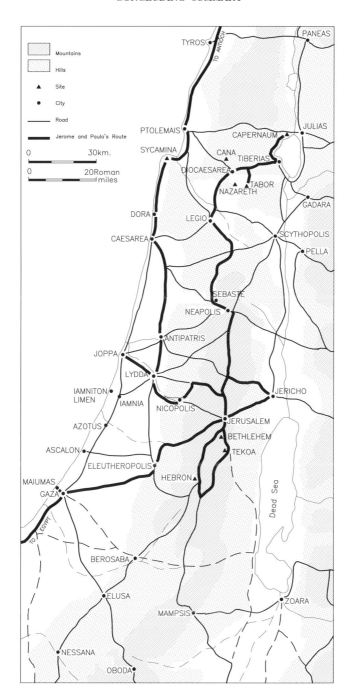

Map of Jerome and Paula's route in Palestine

BIBLIOGRAPHY

Books and Monographs

Abel, F.-M. *Géographie de la Palestine* vol. I (Paris, 1938)

Adams, C. & Laurence, R. (eds) *Travel and geography in the Roman Empire* (London/NY, 2001)

Aharoni, Y. *The Land of the Bible: A Historical Geography* (Philadelphia, 1967)

Alcock, S.E., Cherry, J.F., & Elsner, J. (eds) *Pausanias: travel and memory in Roman Greece* (Oxford, 2001)

Alexander, P.S. *The Toponymy of the Targumim with special reference to the Table of Nations and the Boundaries of the Land of Israel* (D.Phil. thesis, Oxford, 1974)

Alföldi, A. *The conversion of Constantine and pagan Rome* (Oxford, 1948, repr. 1969)

Antin, P. *Recueil sur saint Jérôme* (Bruxelles, 1968)

Anderson, G. *Sage, saint and sophist: Holy men and their associates in the Early Roman empire* (London/NY, 1994)

Auerbach, E. *Literary Language and its Public in Late Latin Antiquity and in the Middle Ages* (Eng. tr. Princeton, 1965)

Avi-Yonah, M. *The Madaba Mosaic map* (Jerusalem, 1954)

——. *Gazetteer of Roman Palestine* (Jerusalem, 1976)

Bagnall, R. *Egypt in Late Antiquity* (Princeton, 1993)

Baldwin, B. *Suetonius* (Amsterdam, 1983)

Bar, O. *Rabbi Simeon bar Yochai and his role in public affairs* (Ph.D., Tel Aviv, 2002, Hebrew with English summary)

Barnes, T.D. *Constantine and Eusebius* (Cambridge/London, 1981)

——. *Athanasius and Constantius* (Cambridge, Mass., 1993)

——. *Ammianus Marcellinus and the Representation of Reality* (Ithaca/London, 1998)

Bartelink, G.J.M. *Hieronymus: Liber de optimo genere interpretandi (epistula 57): Ein Kommentar* (Lugdunum Batavorum, 1980)

Bartelink, G.J.M., Hilhorst, A. & Kneepkens, C.N. (eds) *Eulogia: Mélanges offerts à Anton A.R. Bastiaensen à l'occasion de son soixante-cinquième anniversaire* (Instrumenta Patristica 24, Hague, 1991)

Baynes, N. *The Byzantine Empire* (London, 1925)

Becker, A.H. & Reed, A.Y. (eds) *The ways that never parted: Jews and Christians in late antiquity and the early middle ages* (Tübingen, 2003)

Binns, J. *Ascetics and Ambassadors of Christ: the monasteries of Palestine 314–651* (Oxford, 1994)

Bitan, A. & Rubin, S. *Climatic Atlas of Israel for Physical and Environmental Planning and Design* (Tel Aviv, 1992)

Bitton-Ashkelony, B. *Pilgrimage: Perceptions and reactions in the patristic and monastic literature of the fourth-sixth centuries* (Ph.D. thesis, Jerusalem, 1995, Hebrew with English summary)

Boardman, J. *Athenian Black Figure Vases* (London, 1974, repr. Singapore, 1980)

Bonamente, G. & Duval, N. (eds) *Historiae Augustae Colloquium Parisinum* (Macerata, 1991)

Bonamente, G. & Paci, G. (eds) *Historiae Augustae Colloquium Maceratense* (Bari, 1995)

Bosio, L. *La Tabula Peuteringiana: una descrizione pittorica del mondo antico* (Rimini, 1983)

Bowersock, G.W. *Roman Arabia* (Cambridge, Mass./London, 1983, repr. 1994)

——. *Fiction as History: Nero to Julian* (Berkeley, etc., 1994)

——. *Martyrdom and Rome* (Cambridge, 1995)

Bowman, A.K. & Thomas, J.D. *The Vindolanda Writing-Tablets (Tabulae Vindolandenses II)* (London, 1994)

Bowman, A.K. & Woolf, G. (eds) *Literacy and power in the ancient world* (Cambridge, 1994)

Boyarin, D. *Dying for God: Martyrdom and the making of Christianity and Judaism* (Stanford, 1999)

Brakke, D. *Athanasius and the politics of asceticism* (Oxford, 1995)

Braverman, J. *Jerome's Commentary on Daniel: A Study of comparative Jewish and Christian interpretations of the Hebrew Bible* (Washington, 1978)

Bremmer, J.N. (ed.) *The Apocryphal Acts of John* (Kampen, 1995)

Brent, A. *Hippolytus and the Roman Church in the Third Century: Communities in tension before the emergence of a Monarch-Bishop* (Leiden, 1995)

Brodersen, K. *Terra Cognita: Studien zur römischen Raumerfassung* (Hildesheim/Zurich/NY, 1995)

Brown, P. *The Cult of the Saints* (Chicago, 1981)
——. *The Body and Society* (New York, 1988)
——. *Authority and the Sacred: Aspects of the Christianisation of the Roman World* (Cambridge, 1995).
——. *Poverty and Leadership in Late Antiquity (Lectures in memory of Menachem Stern)* (Jerusalem, May 16–22, 2000)

Browning, I. *Petra* (London, 1989³)

Bunyan, J. *The Pilgrim's Progress from this World to that which is to come* (London, 1678, repr. Oxford, 1966)

Buora, M. & Plesnicar Gec, I.L. *Aquileia Emona: Archeologia fra due regioni dalla preistoria al medioevo* (Udine, 1989)

Buxton, R. *Imaginary Greece* (Cambridge, 1994).

Cameron, Alan *Porphyrius the Charioteer* (Oxford, 1973)
——. *Circus Factions* (Oxford, 1976)

Cameron, Averil (ed.) *History as Text: The writing of ancient history* (London, 1989)
——. *Christianity and the Rhetoric of Empire: The development of Christian discourse* (Berkeley, 1991)

Cameron, Averil & Hall, S.G. (eds and trs) *Eusebius: Life of Constantine* (Oxford, 1999)

Campbell, M.B. *The Witness and the other World: Exotic European Travel Writing 400–1600* (Ithaca, 1988)

Canivet, P. *Le monachisme syrien selon Théodoret de Cyr* (Paris, 1977)

Casson, L. *Ships and Seamanship in the Ancient World* (Princeton, 1971)
——. *Travel in the Ancient World* (Baltimore/London, 1994²)

Cavallera, F. *Saint Jérôme: sa vie et son oeuvre* (Louvain, 1922)

Chapot, V. *La Frontière de l'Euphrate de Pompée à la conquête arabe* (Paris, 1907)

Chitty, D.J. *The Desert a City: an introduction to the study of Egyptian and Palestinian monasticism under the Christian empire* (Oxford, 1966)

Christie, D. Burton *The Word in the Desert* (Oxford/NY, 1993)

Christou, D. *Kourion: Its monuments and local museum* (Nicosia, 1996)

Clark, E.A. *Jerome, Chrysostom and friends* (N.Y./Toronto, 1979)
——. *The Origenist Controversy: The cultural construction of an early Christian debate* (Princeton, 1992)

Cloke, G. *This Female Man of God: Women and spiritual power in the patristic age 350–450* (London, 1995)

Coffey, M. *Roman Satire* (Bristol, 1989²)

Cohen, J. (ed.) *From Witness to Witchcraft: Jews and Judaism in Medieval Christian Thought* (Wiesbaden, 1996)

Conder, C.W. & Kitchener, H.H. *Survey of Western Palestine* (London, 1881)

Courcelle, P. *Late Latin Writers and their Greek Sources* (Eng. tr., Cambridge, Mass., 1969)

Cox, P. *Biography in Late Antiquity: A Quest for the Holy Man* (Berkeley, 1983)
Curran, J.R. *Pagan city and Christian capital: Rome in the fourth century* (Oxford, 2000)
de Lange, N. *Origen and the Jews: Studies in Jewish-Christian relations in third-century Palestine* (Cambridge, 1976)
de Vogüé, A. *Histoire littéraire du mouvement monastique dans l'Antiquité: Première partie: Le monachisme latin*
   * *de la mort d'Antoine à la fin du séjour de Jérôme à Rome (356–385)* (Paris, 1991)
   ** *de l'itinéraire d'Égérie à l'éloge funèbre de Népotien (384–396)* (Paris, 1993)
   **** *Sulpice Sévère et Paulin de Nole (393–409); Jérôme, homéliste et traducteur des 'Pachomiana'* (Paris, 1997).
   ***** *de l'épitaphe de Sainte Paule à la consécration de Démétriade (404–414)* (Paris, 1998)
Demandt, A. *Die Spätantiken Römische Geschichte von Diocletian bis Justinian* (Munich, 1989)
Dilke, O.A.W. *Greek and Roman Maps* (London, 1985)
Donner, H. *Pilgerfahrt ins Heilige Land: Die ältesten Berichte christlicher Palästinapilger (4.–7. Jahrhundert)* (Stuttgart, 1979)
Donner, H. & Cüppers, H. *Die Mosaikkarte von Madaba* (Wiesbaden, 1977)
Downey, G. *A History of Antioch in Syria from Seleucus to the Arab Conquest* (Princeton, 1961)
Drijvers, J.W. *Helena Augusta: The Mother of Constantine the Great and the Legend of the Finding of the Cross* (Leiden etc., 1992)
Dunbabin, K.M.D. *The mosaics of Roman North Africa* (Oxford, 1978)
Dussaud, R. *Topographie historique de la Syrie antique et médiévale* (Paris, 1927)
Duval, Y.-M. *Jérôme: Commentaire sur Jonas* (*SC* 323, Paris, 1985)
———. (ed.) *Jérôme entre l'Occident et l'Orient* (Paris, 1988)
Eck, W., Galsterer, H. & Wolff, H. (eds) *Studien zur antiken Sozialgeschichte: Festschrift für F. Vittinghoff* (Köln, 1980)
Edwards, D. *Religion and Power: Pagans, Jews and Christians in the Greek East* (NY/ Oxford, 1996)
Edwards, M.J. & Swain, S. (eds) *Portraits: Biographical representation in the Greek and Latin literature of the Roman Empire* (Oxford, 1997)
Edwards, R.B. *Kadmos the Phoenician: A study in Greek legends and the Mycenaean age* (Amsterdam, 1979)
Elbogen, I. *Der Judische Gottesdienst in seiner geschichtlichen Entwicklung* (rev. and tr. Y. Amir, J. Heinemann *et al.* Tel Aviv, 1988, in Hebrew)
Elliot, A. Goddard *Roads to Paradise: Reading the Lives of the Early Saints* (Hanover and London, 1987)
Elm, S. *Virgins of God: The making of asceticism in Late Antiquity* (Oxford, 1994)
Elsner, J. *Art and the Roman viewer: the transformation of art from the pagan world to Christianity* (Cambridge, 1995)
Elsner, J. & Rubiés, J.-P. (eds) *Voyages and Visions: Towards a cultural history of travel* (London, 1999)
Eshel, Y. (ed.) *Judea and Samaria research studies: Proceedings of the 6th annual meeting— 1996* (Kedumim Ariel, 1997, in Hebrew)
Favez, C. *La consolation latine chrétienne* (Paris, 1937)
———. *Saint Jérôme peint par lui-même* (Bruxelles, 1958)
Festugière, A.J. *Antioche païenne et chrétienne: Libanios, Chrysostome et les moines de Syrie* (Paris, 1959)
Fine, S. *This Holy Place* (Notre Dame, 1997)
Fischer, M., Gichon, M. & Tal, O. *'En Boqeq: excavations in an oasis on the Dead Sea* II (Mainz, 2000)
Fischer, M., Isaac, B. & Roll, I. *Roman roads in Judaea* II: *The Jaffa—Jerusalem roads* (Oxford, 1996)

Fox, R. Lane *Pagans and Christians* (Harmondsworth, repr. 1988)

Frank, G. *The Memory of the Eyes: Pilgrims to Living Saints in Christian Late Antiquity* (Univ. of California, 2000)

Frankfurter, D. (ed.) *Pilgrimage and Holy Space in Late Antique Egypt* (Leiden etc., 1998)

Freeman, D.N. (ed.) *Anchor Bible Dictionary* (New York, 1992)

Freeman, P., Bennett, J., Fiema, Z.T. & Hoffman, B. (eds) *Limes XVIII. Proceedings of the XVIIIth International Congress of Roman Frontier Studies held in Amman, Jordan (September 2000)* (British Archaeological Reports 1084, Oxford, 2002)

Freeman-Grenville, G.S.P. (tr.), Taylor, J.E., Chapman, R.L. III, (eds), *The Onomasticon by Eusebius of Caesarea: Palestine in the Fourth Century AD* (Jerusalem, 2003)

Friedman, J.B., & Figg, K.M. (eds) *Trade, Travel and Exploration in the Middle Ages: An Encyclopedia* (New York, 2000)

Futrell, A. *Blood in the Arena* (Austin, 1997)

Gafni, I., Oppenheimer, A., Schwartz, D.R. (eds) *The Jews in the Hellenistic-Roman World: Studies in Memory of Menahem Stern* (Jerusalem, 1996)

Galinsky, K. *Augustan Culture: An interpretive introduction* (Princeton, 1996)

Geary, P. *Furta Sacra* (Princeton, 1990²)

Geerard, M. *Clavis Patrum Graecorum* (Turnhout, 1983)

Gibbon, E. *The History of the Decline and Fall of the Roman Empire* (ed. O. Smeaton, London/NY, 1913)

Gill, C. & Wiseman, T.P. (eds) *Lies and Fiction in the Ancient World* (Exeter, 1993)

Gill, D.W.J. & Gempf, C. (eds) *The Book of Acts in its First Century setting* II: *The Book of Acts in its Graeco-Roman setting* (Grand Rapids/Carlisle, 1991)

Gleason, M. *Making Men: Sophists and Self-Presentation in Ancient Rome* (Princeton, 1995)

Glucker, C.A.M. *The City of Gaza in the Roman and Byzantine Period* (Oxford, BAR, 1987)

Gould, G. *The Desert Fathers on Monastic Community* (Oxford, 1993)

Grabar, A. *Christian Iconography: A Study of its Origins* (Princeton, 1968)

Grimm, V. *From Feasting to Fasting: The History of a Sin: Attitudes to food in late antiquity* (London/N.Y., 1997)

Grützmacher, G. *Hieronymus: Eine biographische Studie* I–III (Berlin 1901, 1906, 1908, repr. Aalen, 1969)

Gutwein, K.C. *Third Palestine: A regional study in Byzantine urbanization* (Washington, 1981)

Hagendahl, H. *Latin Fathers and the Classics* (Göteborg, 1958)

Hägg, T. & Rousseau, P. (eds) *Greek Biography and Panegyric in Late Antiquity* (Berkeley etc., 2000)

Hall, E. *Inventing the Barbarian: Greek self-definition through tragedy* (Oxford, 1989)

Hall, L. Jones *Roman Berytus: Beirut in Late Antiquity* (London, 2004)

Hallet, J.P. & Skinner, M.B. (eds) *Roman sexualities* (Princeton, 1997)

Hamilton, R.W. *The Church of the Nativity in Bethlehem* (Great Britain, 1947², repr. Jerusalem, 1968)

Harpham, G.G. *The Ascetic Imperative in Culture and Criticism* (Chicago, 1987)

Harris, W.V. *Ancient Literacy* (Cambridge, Mass./London, 1989)

Hartog, F. *Le miroir d'Hérodote* (Paris, 1980)

Haxen, U. *et al.* (eds) *Jewish Studies in a New Europe* (Copenhagen, 1998)

Hayward, C.T.R. *Saint Jerome's Hebrew Questions on Genesis* (Oxford, 1995)

Herzog, R. *Restauration et Renouveau: La littérature latine de 284 à 374 après J-C* (Turnhout, 1993)

Heussi, K. *Die Ursprung des Mönchtums* (Tübingen, 1936)

Heuzé, P. *L'image du corps dans l'oeuvre de Virgile* (Rome, 1985)

Hickey, A.E. *Women of the Roman aristocracy as Christian monastics* (Ann Arbor, 1987)

Hildesheimer, N.H. *Beiträge zur geographie Palästinas* (no place, 1885) = *ib.* 'Geography of the Land of Israel' in H. Bar-Daroma (tr.) *The boundaries of the Land of Israel: research papers* (Jerusalem, 1965, in Hebrew)

Hinds, S. *Allusion and Intertext: dynamics of appropriation in Roman poetry* (Cambridge, 1998)

Hirschfeld, Y. *The Judean Desert Monasteries in the Byzantine Period* (New Haven/London, 1992)

Hofmann, H. (ed.) *Latin fiction: The Latin novel in context* (London/NY 1999)

Houtman, A., Poorthuis, M.J.H.M., Schwartz, J. (eds) *Sanctity of Time and Space in Tradition and Modernity* (Leiden/Boston/Köln, 1998)

Hritzu, J.N. *The Style of the Letters of St. Jerome* (Washington, 1939)

Humphrey, J. (ed.) *The Roman and Byzantine Near East 2: Some recent archaeological research* (Portsmouth, Rhode Island, 1999)

Hunt, E.D. *Holy Land Pilgrimage in the Later Roman Empire AD 312–460* (Oxford, 1982)

Ir-S[h]ai, O. *Jewish-Christian polemics around the Jerusalem church in the fourth century: historical perspectives (in the light of Patristic and Rabbinical literature)*: Ph.D. thesis (Jerusalem, 1993, in Hebrew)

Isaac, B. *Limits of Empire: The Roman Army in the East* (Oxford, 1990[1])

——. *The Near East under Roman Rule: Selected Papers* (Leiden etc., 1998)

——. *The Invention of Racism in Classical Antiquity* (Princeton, 2004)

Isaac, B. & Oppenheimer, A. (eds) *Studies on the Jewish Diaspora in the Hellenistic and Roman periods* (Tel Aviv, 1996)

Isaac, B. & Roll, I. *Roman roads in Judaea* I; *The Legio-Scythopolis road* (Oxford, B.A.R. 1982)

Jacobs, M. *Die Institution des jüdischen Patriarchen: eine quellen- und traditionskritische Studie zur Geschichte der Juden in der Spätantike* (Tübingen, 1995)

Jacoff, M. *The Horses of San Marco and the Quadriga of the Lord* (Princeton, 1993)

Jay, P. *L'exégèse de s. Jérôme d'après son commentaire sur Isaïe* (Paris, 1985)

Jones, A.H.M. *The Later Roman Empire 284–602* (Oxford, 1964, repr. 1990)

Jones, C., Wainwright, G., Yarnold, E., Bradshaw P. *The Study of Liturgy* (London/NY/Oxford, 1992[2])

Kamesar, A. *Jerome, Greek Scholarship and the Hebrew Bible: A Study of the Quaestiones Hebraicae in Genesim* (Oxford, 1993)

Kaster, R. *Guardians of Language: The Grammarian and Society in Late Antiquity* (Berkeley/L.A./London, 1988)

Kelly, J.N.D. *Jerome: his life, writings and controversies* (London, 1975)

——. *Golden Mouth: The story of John Chrysostom, ascetic, preacher, bishop* (London, 1995)

Kennedy, D. (ed.) *The Roman Army in the East* (Ann Arbor, 1996)

Kindler, A. & Stein, A. *A Bibliography of the City Coinage of Palestine from the 2nd Century BC to the 3rd Century AD* (BAR, Oxford, 1987)

Kingsley, S.A. *A Sixth-century AD Shipwreck off the Carmel coast, Israel: Dor D and the Holy Land Wine Trade* (Oxford, 2002)

Kleinberg, A. *Fra Ginepros Leg of Pork: Christian Saint's Stories and Their Cultural Role (sic)* (Tel Aviv, 2000, in Hebrew)

Kloner, A. & Tepper, Y. *The Hiding Complexes in the Judean Shephela* (Tel Aviv, 1987, in Hebrew)

Kofsky, A. & Stroumsa, G. (eds) *Sharing the Sacred: Religious Contacts and Conflicts in the Holy Land First-Fifteenth centuries CE* (Jerusalem, 1998)

Kollwitz, J. et al. (eds) *Lexikon der Christlichen Ikonographie* II (Rome etc., 1970)

Krumeich, C. *Hieronymus und die christlichen Feminae clarissimae* (Bonn,1993)

Kyle, D.G. *Spectacles of Death in Ancient Rome* (London/NY, 1998)

Lambert, B. *Bibliotheca Hieronymi manuscripta* (Steenbrugge, 1969–1972)

Laurence, P. *Jérôme et le nouveau modèle féminin* (Paris, 1997)

Lee, A.D. *Information and Frontiers: Roman foreign relations in Antiquity* (Cambridge, 1993)

Levi, A. & M. *Itineraria picta. Contributo allo studio della Tabula Peutingeriana* (Roma, 1967)

Levine, L.I. (ed.) *Jerusalem Cathedra* I (Jerusalem, 1981)

——. (ed.) *The Galilee in Late Antiquity* (NY/Jerusalem, 1992)

Lévi-Strauss, C. *The Raw and the Cooked: Introduction to a science of mythology* (Eng. tr. London, 1969)

Liebeschuetz, J.H.G.W. *Antioch: City and Imperial Administration in the Later Roman Empire* (Oxford, 1972)

Lieu, S.C.N. & Montserrat, D. (eds) *Constantine: History, historiography and legend* (London/NY, 1998)

Limor, O. *Holy Land Travels: Christian Pilgrims in Late Antiquity* (Jerusalem, 1998, in Hebrew)

Lübeck, A. *Hieronymus quos noverit scriptores et ex quibus hauserit* (Leipzig, 1872)

MacCormack, S. *The shadows of poetry: Virgil in the mind of Augustus* (Berkeley/LA/London, 1998)

Malamud, M.A. *A Poetics of Transformation: Prudentius and classical mythology* (Ithaca/London, 1989)

Malbon, E.S. *The sarcophagus of Junius Bassus* (Princeton, 1990)

Mango, C. *Art of the Byzantine Empire* (Toronto, 1986)

Maraval, P. *Lieux saints et pèlerinages d'Orient. Histoire et géographie. Des origines à la conquête arabe* (Paris, 1985)

Marcuzzi, L. & Zanette, M. *Aquileia* (Aquileia, 1993)

Marincola, J. *Authority and tradition in ancient historiography* (Cambridge, 1997)

Markus, R.A. *The End of Ancient Christianity* (Cambridge, 1990)

Marrou, H.I. *Histoire de l'éducation dans l'antiquité* (Paris, 1944)

Mathews, T.F. *The Clash of Gods: A reinterpretation of Early Christian Art* (Princeton, 1999²)

Mathisen, R.S. & Sivan, H.S. (eds) *Shifting frontiers in Late Antiquity* (Aldershot/Brookfield, 1995)

Matthews, J. *The Roman Empire of Ammianus* (London, 1989)

Maxfield, V.A. & Dobson, M.J. (eds) *Roman Frontier Studies 1989: Proceedings of the XVth International Congress of Roman Frontier Studies* (Exeter, 1991)

Mayerson, P. *Monks, Martyrs, Soldiers and Saracens: Papers on the Near East in Late Antiquity (1962–1993)* (Jerusalem, 1994)

McNamara, M. *Targum and Testament* (Shannon, 1972)

Meshorer, Y. *The City Coins of Eretz-Israel and the Decapolis in the Roman Period* (Jerusalem, 1984, in Hebrew)

Millar, F. *The Emperor in the Roman World* (London, 1977)

——. *The Roman Near East 31 BC–AD 337* (Cambridge, Mass./London, 1993)

Miller, K. *Mappaemundi: Die ältesten Weltkarten* III: *Die kleineren Weltkarten* (Stuttgart, 1865)

Momigliano, A. *Essays in ancient and modern historiography* (Oxford, 1947 repr. 1977)

——. (ed.) *The conflict between Paganism and Christianity in the fourth century* (Oxford, 1963)

——. *The development of Greek biography* (Cambridge Mass./London, 1971 repr. 1993)

——. *On Pagans, Jews and Christians* (Middleton, 1987)

Monserrat, D. (ed.) *Changing Bodies: Changing Meanings: Studies on the Human Body in Antiquity* (London/NY, 1998)

Montefiore, C.G. *Rabbinic Literature and Gospel Teachings* (1930, repr. NY, 1970)

Moxon, I.S., Smart, J.D., Woodman, A. (eds) *Past Perspectives: Studies in Greek and Roman historical writing* (Cambridge, 1986)

Müller, C. *Geographii Graeci Minores* I (Paris, 1861, repr. Hildesheim 1990)

Neusner, J. & Frerichs, E.S. *To See Ourselves as Others See Us: Christians, Jews, 'Others' in Late Antiquity* (Chico, 1985)

Newman, H. *Jerome and the Jews* (Ph.D., Jerusalem, 1997, Hebrew with English summary)

Netzer, E. & Weiss, Z. *Zippori* (Jerusalem, 1995)

Nicolet, C. *Space, geography and politics in the early Roman empire* (tr. H. Leclerc, Ann Arbor, 1991)

O'Donnell, J.J. *Augustine: Confessions* I: *Introduction and Text* (Oxford, 1992)

Oldfather, W.A. *et al.* *Studies in the Text Tradition of St. Jerome's 'Vitae Patrum'* (Urbana, Illinois, 1943)

O'Mahoney, A. *et al.* (eds) *The Christian Heritage in the Holy Land* (London, 1995)

Opelt, I. *Hieronymus' Streitschriften* (Heidelberg, 1973)

Oppenheimer, A. *Between Rome and Babylon: Jewish leadership and society* (Tübingen, 2005)

——. (ed.) *Jüdische Geschichte in hellenistisch-römischer Zeit: Wege der Forschung: Vom alten zum neuen Schürer* (Munich, 1999)

——. (with B. Isaac & M. Lecker) *Babylonia Judaica in the Talmudic Period* (Wiesbaden, 1983)

Ousterhout, R. (ed.) *The Blessings of Pilgrimage* (Urbana/Chicago, 1990)

Patrich, J. *The Formation of Nabatean Art* (Jerusalem, 1990)

——. *Sabas, leader of Palestinian monasticism: A comparative study in eastern monasticism, fourth-sixth centuries* (Washington, 1995)

Petit, P. *Libanius et la vie municipale à Antioche au IVe siècle après J.-C.* (Paris, 1955)

Piccirillo, M. *The Mosaics of Jordan* (Amman, 1993)

Piccirillo, M. & Alliata, E. (eds) *The Madeba Map Centenary 1897–1997: Travelling through the Byzantine Ummayad Period* (Jerusalem, 1999)

Pietri, C. *Roma Christiana* (Rome, 1976)

Poidebard, A. & Mouterde, P. *Le limes de Chalcis* (Paris, 1945)

Potter, D.S. & Mattingly, D.J. (eds) *Life, Death and Entertainment in the Roman World* (Ann Arbor, 1999)

Price, S.R.F. *Rituals and Power: The Roman Imperial Cult in Asia Minor* (Cambridge, 1984)

Raban, A. & Holum, K.G. (eds) *Caesarea Maritima: A Retrospective after Two Millenia* (Leiden, 1996)

Rapp, C. *The* vita *of Epiphanius of Salamis—an historical and literary study* (D.Phil., Oxford, 1991)

Rebenich, S. *Hieronymus und sein Kreis: Prosopographische und Sozialgeschichtliche Untersuchungen* (Stuttgart, 1992)

——. *Jerome* (London, 2002)

Reitzenstein, R. *Hellenistische Wundererzählungen* (Leipzig, 1906; repr. Darmstadt 1963)

Rhenferd, J. *Exercitatio philologica ad loca deperdita Eusebii et Hieronymi de situ et nominibus locorum sacrorum* (no place, 1707)

Rice, E.F. *Saint Jerome in the Renaissance* (Baltimore/London, 1985)

Rives, J.B. *Religion and Authority in Roman Carthage from Augustus to Constantine* (Oxford, 1995)

Robert, L. *Les Gladiateurs dans l'Orient grec* (Paris, 1940).

Roberts, M. *The Jeweled Style: Poetry and poetics in Late Antiquity* (Ithaca/London, 1986)

——. *Poetry and the Cult of the Martyrs: The Liber* Peristephanon *of Prudentius* (Ann Arbor, 1993)

Romm, J. *The Edges of the Earth in Ancient Thought: Geography, Exploration and Fiction* (Princeton, 1992)

Rousseau, P. *Ascetics, Authority and the Church in the Age of Jerome and Cassian* (Oxford, 1978)

Rousselle, A. (ed.) *Frontières terrestres, frontières célestes dans l'Antiquité* (Perpignan/Paris 1995)

Rubinstein, J.L. *Talmudic Stories: narrative art, composition and culture* (Baltimore, 1999)

Rubin, E. Habas *The Patriarch in the Roman-Byzantine era—the making of a dynasty* (Ph.D., Tel Aviv, 1991, Hebrew with English summary).

Salomonson, J.W. *Voluptatem spectandi non perdat sed mutet: Observations sur l'iconographie du martyre en Afrique Romaine* (Amsterdam/Oxford/NY, 1979)

Sanders, E.P. *et al.* (eds) *Jewish and Christian self-definition* I–III (Philadelphia, 1980–1982)

Sartre, M. *L'Orient romain: provinces et sociétées provinciales en Méditerranée orientale d'Auguste aux Sévères (31 avant J.-C.–235 après J.-C.)* (Paris, 1991)

Schäfer, P. (ed.) *The Talmud Yerushalmi and Graeco-Roman culture* I (Tübingen, 1998)
Schanz, M. *Geschichte der römischen Literatur bis zum Gesetzgebungswerk des Kaisers Justinian* IV, I: *Die römische Literatur von Constantin bis zum Gesetzgebungswerk Justinians: Die Literatur des vierten Jahrhunderts* (München, 1959)
Schiwietz, S. *Das morgenländische Mönchtum* (Mayence/Mödling, 1904–1938)
Schreckenberg, H. & Schubert, K. *Jewish Historiography and Iconography in Early and Medieval Christianity* (Assen/Minneapolis, 1992)
Schürer, E. *The History of the Jewish People in the age of Jesus Christ* I–III (rev. and ed. G. Vermes, F. Millar, M. Black, Edinburgh, 1979)
Schwartz, J. *Jewish settlement in Judaea after the Bar Kochba war until the Arab conquest 135 CE–640 CE* (Jerusalem, 1986, in Hebrew)
———. *Lod (Lydda), Israel: From its origins through the Byzantine Period, 5600 BCE–640 CE* (B.A.R., Oxford, 1991)
Schwartz, S. *Imperialism and Jewish Society, 200 BCE to 640 CE* (Princeton, 2001)
Scourfield, J.H.D. *Consoling Heliodorus, A commentary on Jerome, Letter 60* (Oxford, 1993)
Seeck, O. *Die Briefe des Libanius* (Leipzig, 1906; repr. Hildesheim, 1966)
Shahar, Y. *Josephus Geographicus* (Tübingen, 2004)
Shahîd, I. *Byzantium and the Arabs in the Fourth Century* (Washington, 1984)
Shinan, A. & Zakovitz, Y. *And Jacob came 'Shalem': Gen. 33:18–20 in the Bible, the old versions and the ancient Jewish literature* (Jerusalem, 1984, in Hebrew)
Simonetti, M. *Biblical Interpretation in the Early Church: An Historical Introduction to Patristic Exegesis* (tr. J.A. Hughes, Edinburgh, 1994)
Sivan, H. *Ausonius of Bordeaux: Genesis of a Gallic aristocracy* (London/NY, 1993)
Smith, G.A. *The Historical Geography of the Holy Land* (London/Glasgow, 1931,[25] repr. 1966)
Smythe, D.C. (ed.) *Strangers to Themselves: the Byzantine Outsider* (Aldershot etc., 2000)
Snodgrass, A. *An Archaeology of Greece* (Berkeley, 1987)
Sperber, D. *A Dictionary of Greek and Latin Legal Terms in Rabbinic Literature* (Ramat Gan, 1984)
Springer, A.R. *Prudentius, pilgrim and poet: The Catacombs as inspiration for the Liber Cathemerinon* (Ph.D. thesis, Wisconsin, 1984)
Stemberger, G. *Introduction to the Talmud and Midrash* (tr. M. Bockmuel, Edinburgh, 1996[2])
———. *Jews and Christians in the Holy Land: Palestine in the fourth century* (tr. R. Tuschling, Edinburgh, 2000)
Stern, E. *Dor, Ruler of the Seas* (Jerusalem, 1994)
———. *Excavations at Dor: Final Report* vols Ia–b. (Qedem Reports 2, Jerusalem, 1995)
Stern, M. *Greek and Latin authors on Jews and Judaism* I–II (Jerusalem, 1980)
Stevenson, J. *The Catacombs: Rediscovered monuments of early Christianity* (London, 1978)
Stewart, A. & Wilson, C.W. (eds and trs) *The Pilgrimage of the Holy Paula by St. Jerome* (PPTS, London, 1887)
Strack, H.L. & Billerbeck, P. *Das Evangelium nach Matthaus erlautert aus Talmud und Midrasch* (München, 1969[5])
Stummer, F. *Monumenta historiam et geographiam Terrae Sanctae illustrantia* (Bonn, 1935)
Sugano, K. *Das Rombild des Hieronymus* (Frankfurt am Main etc., 1983)
Syme, R. *Ammianus and the Historia Augusta* (Oxford, 1968)
———. *Emperors and Biography: Studies in the Historia Augusta* (Oxford, 1971)
———. *The Historia Augusta: A call of clarity* (Bonn, 1971)
Tardieu, M. *Les paysages reliques: routes et haltes syriennes d'Isidore à Simplicius* (Louvain/Paris, 1990)
Taylor, J.E. *Christians and the Holy Places: The Myth of Jewish-Christian Origins* (Oxford, 1993)
Taylor, M.C. *Critical Terms for Religious Studies* (Chicago, 1998)

Tillemont, S. Le Nain de *Mémoires pour servir à l'histoire ecclésiastique des six premiers siècles*, vol. XII (Paris, 1707)

Titchener, F.B. & Moorton, R.F., Jr. (eds) *The Eye Expanded: Life and the Arts in Greco-Roman Antiquity* (Berkeley etc., 1999)

Tomasch, S. & Gilles, S. (eds) *Text and Territory: geographical imagination in the European Middle Ages* (Philadelphia, 1998)

Trombley, F.R. *Hellenic Religion and Christianization, c. 370–529*, I (Leiden etc., 1993)

Tsafrir, Y., Di Segni, L., Green, J., with Roll, I. *Tabula Imperii Romani: Iudaea/Palaestina* (Jerusalem, 1994)

Turner, B.S. *The Body and Society* (London etc., 1996²)

Turner, V.W. & Turner, E. *Image and Pilgrimage in Christian Culture* (Oxford, 1978)

Urbainczyk, T. *Theodoret of Cyrrhus* (Ann Arbor, 2002)

Violardo, G. *Il pensiero giuridico di san Girolamo* (Milan, 1937)

von Albrecht, M. *A History of Roman Literature from Livius Andronicus to Boethius* vol. II (Leiden/N.Y./Köln, 1997, rev. G. Schmeling and the author)

von Hubert, H., Lichtenberger, H., Schäfer, P. (eds) *Geschichte—Tradition—Reflexion: Festschrift für Martin Hengel zum 70. Geburtstag* (Tübingen, 1996)

Voöbus, A. *A History of Asceticism in the Syrian Orient* I–II (Louvain, 1958–60)

Waddell, H. (ed. and tr.) *The Desert Fathers* (London, 1936 repr. 1987)

Walker, P.W.L. *Holy City, Holy Places?* (Oxford, 1990)

Wallace-Hadrill, A. *Suetonius: the Scholar and his Caesars* (London, 1983)

Ward, B. (ed.), Russell, N. (tr.) *Lives of the Desert Fathers* (Oxford/Kalamazoo, 1981)

Ward-Perkins, J.B. *Roman Imperial Architecture* (Harmondsworth, 1981² repr. 1983)

Watson, A. *The Law of Persons in the Later Roman Republic* (Oxford, 1967)

Weaver, D.J. *Matthew's Missionary Discourse* (Sheffield, 1990)

Wengst, K. *Pax Romana and the peace of Jesus Christ* (tr. J. Bowden, London, 1987).

White, C. *The correspondence (394–419) between Jerome and Augustine of Hippo* (Lampeter, etc., 1990)

Wiedemann, T. *Emperors and Gladiators* (London/N.Y., repr. 1995)

Wiesen, D. *St. Jerome as a Satirist* (Ithaca/NY, 1964)

Wightman, E.M. *Roman Trier and the Treveri* (London, 1970)

———. *Gallia Belgica* (London, 1985)

Wilken, R.L. *The Land Called Holy: Palestine in Christian History and Thought* (New Haven/London, 1992)

Wilkinson, J. *Jerusalem Pilgrims before the Crusades* (Jerusalem, 1977)

Wilson S. (ed.) *Saints and their Cults: Studies in Religion, Sociology, Folklore and History* (Cambridge, 1983, repr. 1987)

Wimbush, V.L. (ed.) *Ascetic Behavior in Greco-Roman Antiquity* (Minneapolis, 1990)

Wimbush, V.L., Valantasis, R. et al. (eds) *Asceticism* (NY/Oxford, 1995).

Winkler, J.J. *Auctor and Actor: a Narratological reading of Apuleius's The Golden Ass* (Berkeley/LA/Oxford, 1985 repr. 1991)

Wirth, G. et al. (eds) *Romanitas Christianitas: Untersuchungen zur Geschicht und Literatur der römischen Kaiserzeit: Johannes Straub zum 70. Geburtstag* (Berlin/NY, 1982)

Woodman, A.J. *Rhetoric in Classical Historiography: Four Studies* (London etc., 1988)

Articles and Papers

The titles of Hebrew papers have been translated; the titles of Hebrew journals have been transliterated.

Abel, F.-M. 'Bulletin: Palestine' *RB* 29 (1920) 157–9

Acworth, A. 'Where was St. Paul shipwrecked? A re-examination of the evidence' *JThS* n.s. 24 (1973) 190–3

Adamik, T. 'The influence of the Apocryphal Acts on Jerome's Lives of Saints' in *The Apocryphal Acts of John* (ed. J.N. Bremmer, Kampen, 1995) 171–182

Adkin, N. 'Tertullian's de praescriptione haereticorum and Jerome's Libellus de virginitate servanda (Epist. 22)' *Eirene* 30 (1994) 103–107

——. 'Jerome's use of Scripture before and after his dream' *Illinois Classical Studies* 20 (1995) 183–90

——. 'The *Historia Augusta* and Jerome again' *Klio* 79 (1997) 459–467

Alexander, P.S. 'Targum, Targumim' in *The Anchor Bible Dictionary* (ed. D.N. Freedman, NY, 1992) 320–331

Alliata, E. *et al.* 'The Legends of the Madeba Map' in *The Madeba Map Centenary 1897–1997: Travelling through the Byzantine Ummayad Period* (ed. M. Piccirillo, E. Alliata, Jerusalem, 1999) 47–101

Alt, A. 'Stationen der römischen Hauptstrasse von Ägypten nach Syrien' *ZDPV* 70 (1954) 154–166

Amélineau, E. 'Voyage d'un moine égyptien dans le désert' *Recueil de travaux relatifs à la philologie et à l'archéologie égyptiennes et assyriennes* 6 (1884) 166–194

Antin, P. 'La ville chez Saint Jérôme' *Latomus* 20 (1961) 298–311 = *Recueil sur Saint Jérôme* (Bruxelles, 1969) 375–389

Arjava, A. 'Jerome and women' *Arctos* 23 (1989) 5–18

Arnaud, P. 'Observations sur l'original du fragment du pseudo-bouclier de Doura-Europos' *Revue des Études Anciennes* 90 (1988) 151–6

Barnes, T.D. 'The composition of Eusebius' *Onomasticon*' *JThS* n.s. 26 (1975) 412–5

——. 'Jerome and the *Historia Augusta*' in *Historiae Augustae Colloquium Parisinum* (eds G. Bonamente, N. Duval, Macerata, 1991) 19–28

. Barouch, Y. 'Road stations in Judea during the Second Temple period' in *Judea and Samaria research studies: Proceedings of the 6th annual meeting—1996* (ed. Y. Eshel, Kedumim Ariel, 1997, in Hebrew) 125–35

Bastiaensen, A.A.R. 'Jérôme hagiographe' *CC Hagiographies: International History of the Latin and Vernacular Hagiographical Literature in the West from its origins to 1550*, vol. I (Turnhout, 1994) 97–123

Bauer, J.B. 'Novellistisches bei Hieronymus' *Wiener Studien* 74 (1961) 130f.

Ben Porat, Z. 'The Poetics of Literary Allusion' *PTL* 1 (1976) 105–128

Ben Shalom, Y. 'Rabbi Judah bar Ilai's attitude towards Rome' *Zion* 49 (1984, in Hebrew) 9–24

Benz, E. 'Die heilige Höhle in der alten Christenheit und in der östlich-orthodoxen Kirche' *Eranos Jahrbuch* 22 (1953) 365–432

Bertrand, A.C. 'Stumbling through Gaul: Maps, Intelligence and Caesar's *Bellum Gallicum*' *Ancient History Bulletin* 11 (1998) 107–122

Bickerman, E. 'Origines gentium' *Classical Philology* 47 (1952) 65–81

Bitton-Ashkelony, B. & Kofsky, A. 'The monasticism of Gaza in the Byzantine period' *Cathedra* 96 (2000, in Hebrew) 69f.

Bowersock, G.W. 'Mavia, Queen of the Saracens' *Studien zur antiken Sozialgeschichte: Festschrift für F. Vittinghoff* (eds W. Eck, H. Galsterer, H. Wolff, Köln, 1980)

——. 'Arabs and Saracens in the Historia Augusta' *Historia Augusta Colloquium, Bonn 1984/5* (Bonn, 1987) 71–80

——. 'Chalcis ad Belum and Anasartha in Byzantine Syria' in *Travaux et Mémoires: Mélanges Gilbert Dagron* 14 (2002) 47–55

Bowie, A. '*Exuvias effigiemque*: Dido, Aeneas and the body as a sign' in *Changing Bodies: Changing Meanings: Studies on the Human Body in Antiquity* (ed. D. Monserrat, London/NY, 1998) 57f.

Bowman, A.K. & Thomas, J.D. 'New texts from Vindolanda' *Britannia* 18 (1987) 125–142

Brakke, D. '"Outside the places, within the truth": Athanasius of Alexandria and the location of the holy' in *Pilgrimage and Holy Space in Late Antique Egypt* (ed. D. Frankfurter, Leiden etc., 1998) 445f.

Brock, S.P. 'Early Syrian Asceticism' *Numen* 20 (1973) 1–19

——. 'Greek and Syriac in Late Antique Syria' in *Literacy and power in the ancient world* (eds A.K. Bowman, G. Woolf, Cambridge, 1994) 149–160

Brodersen, K. 'The presentation of geographical knowledge for travel and transport in the Roman world: *itineraria non tantum adnotata sed etiam picta*' in *Travel and geography in the Roman empire* (eds C. Adams, R. Laurence, London/NY, 2001) 7–21

Brown, P. 'The Rise and Function of the Holy Man in Late Antiquity' *JRS* 61 (1971) 80–101

——. 'Asceticism: Pagan and Christian' *CAH* 13, 601

Burgess, R.W. 'Jerome and the *Kaisergeschichte*' *Historia* 44 (1995) 357f.

Burrus, V. 'The heretical woman as symbol in Alexander, Athanasius, Epiphanius and Jerome' *HTR* 84 (1991) 229–48

Burton, G.P. 'Proconsuls, Assizes and the Administration of Justice' *JRS* 65 (1975) 92–106.

Cadell, H. 'Les archives de Théophanes d'Hermoupolis: Documents pour l'histoire' in *Egitto e storia antica dall'ellenismo all'eta araba* (eds L. Criscuolo, G. Geraci, Bologna, 1989) 315–323

Cameron, Alan, 'Echoes of Vergil in St. Jerome's *Life of St. Hilarion*' *Classical Philology* 43 (1968) 55–6

——. Review of R. Syme *Ammianus and the Historia Augusta* (Oxford, 1968) *JRS* 61 (1971) 259

Cameron, Averil, 'Virginity as metaphor: Women and the rhetoric of early Christianity' in *History as Text: The writing of ancient history* (ed. A. Cameron, London, 1989) 184–205

Chauler, D.S. 'Saint Onuphre' *Les Cahiers Coptes* 5 (1954) 3–15

Chauvot, A. 'Remarques sur l'emploie de *semibarbarus*' in *Frontières terrestres, frontières célestes dans l'Antiquité* (ed. A. Rousselle, Perpignan/Paris, 1995) 255–271

Cohen, E. 'Pilgrimage centers: concentric and excentric' *Annals of Tourism Research* 19 (1992) 33–50

Coleiro, E. 'St. Jerome's Lives of the Hermits' *VChr* 11 (1957) 161–178

Coleman, K. 'Fatal Charades: Roman executions staged as mythological enactments' *JRS* 80 (1990) 44–73

Cook, J.G. 'The Sparrow's Fall in Mt. 10 29b' *Zeitschrift für die Neutestamentliche Wissenschaft und die Kunde der älteren Kirche* 79 (1988) 138f.

Cooper, K. 'A saint in exile: Thecla at Rome and Meriamlik' *Hagiographica* 2 (1995) 70f.

Cucchiarelli, A. '*Iter satyricum*: Le voyage à Brindes et le satire d'Horace' *Latomus* 61 (2002) 842–851

Dan, Y. 'On the ownership of the village of Thavatha in the Byzantine period' *SCI* 5 (1979/80) 258–62

Dauphin, C. 'Chronique archéologique: Dor 1979' *RB* 88 (1981) 591–592

——. 'Chronique archéologique: Dor: Église byzantine' *RB* 91 (1984) 256–258

——. 'Les "kômai" de Palestine' *Proche-orient chrétien* 36 (1987) 251–67

de Cavalieri, F. *Passio Sanctorum Mariani et Iacobi* Studi e testi (1900) 47f.

Degórski, B. 'Un Nuovo indizio per la Datazione della *Vita S. Pauli* di Girolamo?' *Studia Patristica* 33 (1997) 302f.

Delbanco, A. 'The decline and fall of literature' *The New York Review* (November 4th, 1999) 32–38

Delehaye, H. 'Saint Romain, martyr d'Antioche' *AB* 50 (1932) 241f.

——. '*Passio sancti Mammetis*' *AB* 58 (1940) 138f.

Devos, P. 'La date du voyage d'Égérie' *AB* 85 (1967) 165–194

de Vogüé, A. 'La "Vita Pauli" de saint Jérôme et sa datation; Examen d'un passage-clé (ch. 6)' in *Eulogia: Mélanges offerts à Anton A.R. Bastiaensen à l'occasion de son soixante-cinquième anniversaire* (eds G.J.M. Bartelink, A. Hilhorst, C.N. Kneepkens, Instrumenta Patristica 24, Hague, 1991) 395–406

di Segni, L. (tr.) 'The pre-Metaphrastic *Vita Charitonis*' in *Ascetic Behavior in Greco-Roman Antiquity* (ed. V.L. Wimbush, Minneapolis, 1990) 393–421
——. 'Εἷς θεός in Palestinian inscriptions' *SCI* (1994) 94–115
——. 'Metropolis and Provincia in Byzantine Palestine' in *Caesarea Maritima: A Retrospective after Two Millenia* (eds A. Raban, K.G. Holum, Leiden, 1996) 575–589
——. 'The "Onomasticon" of Eusebius and the Madeba Map' in *The Madeba Map Centenary 1897–1997: Travelling through the Byzantine Ummayad Period* (eds M. Piccirillo, E. Alliata, Jerusalem, 1999) 115–120
Dodge, H. 'Amusing the masses: Building for entertainment and leisure in the Roman world' in *Life, Death and Entertainment in the Roman World* (eds D.S. Potter, D.J. Mattingly, Ann Arbor, 1999) 205f.
Donceel-Voûte, P. 'La carte de Madaba: Cosmographie, anachronisme et propa-gande' *RB* 135 (1988) 519f.
Drexhage, H.-J. 'Die "Expositio totius mundi et gentium". Ein Handelsgeographie aus dem 4. Jahrhundert n. Chr. eingeleitet, übersetzt und mit einführender Literatur (Kap. xxii–lxvii) versehen' *Münstersche Beiträge z. antiken Handelsgeschichte* 2,1 (1983) 3–41
Duckworth, G.E. 'Classical echoes in St. Jerome's Life of Malchus' *The Classical Bulletin* 24 (1947/8) 29f.
Eade, J. 'Pilgrimage and tourism at Lourdes, France' *Annals of Tourism Research* 19 (1992) 18–32
Edwards, C. 'Unspeakable professions: public performance and prostitution in ancient Rome' in *Roman sexualities* (eds J.P. Hallet, M.B. Skinner, Princeton, 1997) 66–95
Elm, S. 'Perceptions of Jerusalem pilgrimage as reflected in two early sources on female pilgrimage (third and fourth centuries AD)' *Studia Patristica* 20 (1989) 219–223
Elsner, J. 'Hagiographic geography: Travel and allegory in the *Life of Apollonius of Tyana*' *Journal of Hellenic Studies* 117 (1997) 22–37
——. 'The *Itinerarium Burdigalense*: Politics and salvation in the geography of Constantine's empire' *Journal of Roman Studies* 90 (2000) 181–195.
Elsner, J. & Rubiés, J.-P. 'Introduction' in *Voyages and Visions: Towards a cultural his-tory of travel* (eds J. Elsner, J.-P. Rubiés, London, 1999) p. 1f.
Favez, C. 'Saint Jérôme peint par lui-même' *Latomus* 16 (1957) 655f.; *ib.* 17 (1958) 81–96; 303–316
Festugière, A.J. 'Lieux communs littéraires et thèmes de folk-lore dans l'hagiogra-phie primitive' *Wiener Studien* 73 (1960) 142–5
Fontaine, J. 'Unité et diversité du mélange des genres et des tons chez quelques écrivains latins de la fin du IVᵉ siècle: Ausone, Ambroise, Ammien' in *Christianisme et formes littéraires de l'antiquité tardive en occident* (Fondation Hardt: Entretiens sur l'antiquité classique 33, Vandoeuvres, 1976) 432–434
Foerster, G. 'Lohamei Haghétaot: Tombe Byzantine' *RB* 78 (1971) 586f.
Fraade, S.D. 'Rabbinic views on the practice of Targum and multi-lingualism in Jewish Galilee in the third-sixth centuries' in *The Galilee in Late Antiquity* (ed. L.I. Levine, NY/Jerusalem, 1992) 253–288
Frank, G. 'The *Historia Monachorum in Aegypto* and ancient travel writing' *Studia Patristica* 30 (1997) 191–195
——. 'Miracles, monks and monuments: the *Historia Monachorum in Aegypto* as pil-grims' tales' in *Pilgrimage and holy space in late antique Egypt* (ed. D. Frankfurter, Leiden etc., 1998) 487f.
Galazzi, C. & Kramer, B. 'Artemidor im Zeichensaal. Eine papyrusrolle mit Text, Landkarte und Skizzenbüchern aus späthellenistischer Zeit' *Archiv für Papyrusforschung* 44 (1998) 189f.
Gardner, P. 'Cities and countries in ancient art' *Journal of Hellenic Studies* 9 (1888) 47–81

Germer-Durand, R.P. 'Inscriptions romaines et byzantines de Palestine: Medaba' *RB* (1895) 588–589

Gilliam, J.F. 'Three passages in the *Historia Augusta*: Gord. 21,5 and 34,2–6; Tyr. Trig. 30,12' *Bonner Historia-Augusta-Colloquium 1968/9* (Bonn, 1970) 99–111

Ginzberg, L. 'Die Haggada bei den Kirchenvätern: V Der Kommentar des Hieronymus zu Kohelet' in *Abhandlung zur Erinnerung an Hirsch Perez Chajes* (Alexander Kohut Memorial Foundation, Wien, 1933) 22–50

Gleason, M.W. 'Festive satire: Julian's *Misopogon* and the new year at Antioch' *JRS* 76 (1986) 106f.

Goodman, M. 'Sacred Space in Diaspora Judaism' in *Studies on the Jewish Diaspora in the Hellenistic and Roman periods* (eds B. Isaac, A. Oppenheimer, Tel Aviv, 1996) 1f.

Gould, G. review of A. Goddard Elliot *Roads to Paradise: Reading the Lives of the Early Saints* (Hanover and London, 1987) *JThS* (1989) 627–31

Gowers, E. 'Horace, *Satires* 1.5: An inconsequential journey' *Proceedings of the Cambridge Philological Society* 39 (1993) 48–66

Graf, D., Isaac, B., Roll, I. 'Roman Roads' in *The Anchor Bible Dictionary* V (ed. D.N. Freedman, NY, 1992) 782–787

Granek, M. & Weingarten, M.A. 'The Third Party in General Practice Consultations' *Scandinavian Journal of Primary Health Care* 14 (1996) 66–70

Groh, D.E. 'The *Onomasticon* of Eusebius and the Rise of Christian Palestine' *Studia Patristica* 18, 1 (1983) 23–31

Harries, J.D. 'The shifting frontiers of *Romanitas*' in *Shifting frontiers in Late Antiquity* (eds R.W. Mathisen, H.S. Sivan, Aldershot/Brookfield, 1995) 31–44

Harvey, P.B., Jr, 'The Death of Mythology: The case of Joppa' *JECS* 2 (1994) 1–14

——. 'Saints and Satyrs: Jerome the scholar at work' *Athenaeum* 86 (1998) 35–56

Harvey, P.D.A. 'The twelfth-century Jerome maps of Asia and Palestine' (Paper given at the 17th International Conference on the History of Cartography, Lisbon, Thursday 10th July, 1997)

——. 'The cartographic context of the Madeba Map' in *The Madeba Map Centenary 1897–1997: Travelling through the Byzantine Ummayad Period* (eds M. Piccirillo, E. Alliata, Jerusalem, 1999) 103–107

Hayward, R. 'Saint Jerome and the Aramaic targums' *Journal of Semitic Studies* 32 (1987) 105–123

Hendrikx, E. 'Saint Jérôme en tant que hagiographe' *La Ciudad de Dios* 181 (1968) 661–7

Herbert-Brown, G. 'Jerome's dates for Gaius Lucilius, *satyrarum scriptor*' *CQ* 49 (1999) 535–543

Hermann, L. 'L'âne d'or et le christianisme' *Latomus* 12 (1953) 188f.

Higgins, I.M. 'Defining the Earth's center in a Medieval "Multi-Text": Jerusalem in *The Book of John Mandeville*: # Jerusalem as the Center of the Earth: From St. Jerome to Felix Fabri' in *Text and Territory: geographical imagination in the European Middle Ages* (eds S. Tomasch, S. Gilles, Philadelphia, 1998) 29–53

Hirschfeld, Y. 'The series of Byzantine forts along the eastern local road in the Hebron hill-country' *Qadmoniot* 46–47 (1980, in Hebrew) 78–84

——. '*Life of Chariton* in the light of archaeological research' in *Ascetic Behavior in Greco-Roman Antiquity* (ed. V.L. Wimbush, Minneapolis, 1990) 425–447

Horsfall, N. 'Apuleius, Apollonius of Tyana, Bibliomancy: some neglected dating criteria' in *Historiae Augustae Colloquium Maceratense* (eds G. Bonamente, G. Paci, Bari, 1995) 169–177.

Huber-Rebenich, G. 'Hagiographic fiction as entertainment' in *Latin fiction: The Latin novel in context* (ed. H. Hofmann, London/NY 1999) 187–212

Hunink, V. 'Apuleius, Pudentilla and Christianity' *VChr* 54 (2000) 80–94

Hunt, D. 'The Church as a Public Institution' *Cambridge Ancient History* 13 (1998) 238–276

Hunt, E.D. 'The date of the *Itinerarium Egeriae*' *Studia Patristica* 38 (2001) 410–416

Hunter, D.G. 'Vigilantius of Calagurris and Victricius of Rouen: Ascetics, Relics and Clerics in Late Antique Gaul' *JECS* 7 (1999) 401–430

Iliffe, J.H. 'A building inscription from the Syrian limes AD 334' *QDAP* 10 (1944) 62–64

Isaac, B. 'Bandits in Judaea and Arabia' *HSCP* 88 (1974) 171f. = *id. The Near East under Roman Rule* (Leiden, etc., 1998) 132–3

——. 'Milestones in Judaea, from Vespasian to Constantine' *PEQ* 110 (1978) 46–60

——. 'Eusebius and the geography of Roman provinces' in *The Roman Army in the East* (ed. D. Kennedy, Ann Arbor, 1996) 153–167 = B. Isaac *The Near East under Roman Rule: Selected Papers* (Leiden etc., 1998) 284–309

——. 'Orientals and Jews in the Historia Augusta: Fourth-Century Prejudice and Stereotypes' in *The Jews in the Hellenistic-Roman World: Studies in Memory of Menahem Stern* (eds I. Gafni, A. Oppenheimer, D.R. Schwartz, Jerusalem, 1996) pp. 101*–118* = B. Isaac *The Near East under Roman Rule: Selected Papers* (Leiden etc., 1998) 268–283

——. 'Roma Aeterna' *Historia* 2 (1998, in Hebrew) 19–31

——. 'Rome and Persia' in 'The Eastern Frontier' *Cambridge Ancient History* 13 (1998) 437f.

——. 'Between the old Schürer and the new: archaeology and geography' in A. Oppenheimer (ed.) *Jüdische Geschichte in hellenistisch-römischer Zeit: Wege der Forschung: Vom alten zum neuen Schürer* (Munich, 1999) 181–91

James, M.R. 'On the History and Antiquities of Paphos' *JHS* 9 (1888) 175–89

Jameson, H.C. 'The Greek Version of Jerome's *Life of Malchus*' *TAPA* 69 (1938)

Kamesar, A. 'The evaluation of narrative aggadah in Greek and Latin patristic literature' *JThS* 45 (1994) 37–71

Kaster, R.A. 'The Shame of the Romans' *TAPA* 127 (1997) 1f.

Kirschner, R. 'The Vocation of Holiness in Late Antiquity' *VChr* 38 (1984) 105–124

Kobak, A. 'From Belsen to Butlins' *Times Literary Supplement* 5054 (Feb. 11th 2000) 31f.

Konowitz, E. 'The program of the Carrand Diptych' *Art Bulletin* 66 (1984) 484–488

Kraus, M. 'Jews, Pagans and Christians in dialogue: Jerome on Ecclesiastes 12:1–7' *HUCA* 70/71 (1999–2000) 183–231

Krauss, S. 'The Jews in the works of the Church Fathers, vi: Jerome' *Jewish Quarterly Review* (1894) 225f.

Krueger, D. 'Typological Figuration in Theodoret of Cyrrhus' *Religious History* and the Art of Postbiblical Narrative' *JECS* 5 (1997) 393–419

Kyle, D.G. 'Rethinking the Roman arena: Gladiators, sorrows and games' *Ancient History Bulletin* 11 (1997) 94–7

LaFleur, W.R. 'The Body' in *Critical Terms for Religious Studies* (ed. M.C. Taylor, Chicago, 1998) 36f.

Laird, A. 'Fiction, bewitchment and story worlds: The implications of claims to truth in Apuleius' in *Lies and Fiction in the Ancient World* (eds C. Gill, T.P. Wiseman, Exeter, 1993) 147f.

Laurence, P. 'Les pèlerinages des romaines sous le regard de Saint Jérôme' *REL* 76 (1996) 226–240

——. 'Rome et Jérôme: des amours contrariées' *Révue Bénédictine* 107 (1997) 227–249

Lawrence, M. 'Columnar sarcophagi in the Latin West' *Art Bulletin* 14 (1932) 175f.

Leclerc, P. 'Antoine et Paul: métamorphose d'un héros' in *Jérôme entre l'Occident et l'Orient* (ed. Y.-M. Duval, Paris, 1988) 257–265

Levine, L.I. 'R. Shim'on bar Yohai and the Purification of Tiberias: History and Tradition' *HUCA* 49 (1978) 143–85

Levine, L.I. 'The status of the patriarch in the third and fourth centuries: sources and methodology' *JJS* 47 (1996) 1–32

Leyerle, B. 'Landscape as cartography in early Christian pilgrimage narratives' *Journal of the American Academy of Religion* 64 (1996) 119–143

Limor, O. 'Christian Sacred Space and the Jew' in *From Witness to Witchcraft: Jews and Judaism in Medieval Christian Thought* (ed. J. Cohen, Wiesbaden, 1996)

Lössl, J. 'Satire, fiction and reference to reality in Jerome's *epistula* 117' *VChr* 52 (1998) 172–192

MacEachren, A.M. 'A linear view of the world: Strip maps as a unique form of cartographic representation' *The American Cartographer* 13 (1986) 7–25

MacEachren, A.M. & Johnson, G.B. 'The evolution, application and implications of strip format travel maps' *The Cartographic Journal* 24 (1987) 147–158

Mackowski, R., S.J. 'Scholars' Qanah' *Biblische Zeitschrift* 23, 2 (1979) 278f.

Magness, J. 'Redating the forts at Ein Boqeq, Upper Zohar, and other sites in SE Judaea, and the implications for the nature of the *Limes* Palaestinae' in *The Roman and Byzantine Near East* 2: *Some recent archaeological research* (ed. J.H. Humphrey, Portsmouth, Rhode Island, 1999) 189–206

Maguire, H. 'Adam and the animals: Allegory and literal sense in Early Christian Art' *Dumbarton Oaks Papers* 41 (1987) 363–373

Maier, F.G. 'Der Tempel der paphischen Aphrodite in der Kaiserzeit' in *Romanitas Christianitas: Untersuchungen zur Geschicht und Literatur der römischen Kaiserzeit: Johannes Straub zum 70. Geburtstag* (ed. G. Wirth *et al.*, Berlin/NY, 1982) 768f.

Maisler, B. 'Reqem and Hagar' *Tarbiz* 20 (1949, in Hebrew) 316–319

Marshall, A.J. 'Governors in the Roman World' *Phoenix* 20 (1966) 231–246

Mayer, W. 'What does it mean to say that John Chrysostom was a monk?' Paper presented at the Fourteenth International Conference on Patristic Studies, Oxford, August 2003

Mayerson, P. 'Mauia, Queen of the Saracens—A cautionary note' *IEJ* 30 (1980) 123–131 = *id. Monks, martyrs, soldiers and Saracens: Papers on the near East in Late Antiquity (1962–1993)* (Jerusalem, 1994) 164f.

——. 'The City of Elusa in the Literary sources of the Fourth-Sixth Centuries' *IEJ* 33 (1983) 247–253 = *id. Monks, Martyrs, Soldiers and Saracens: Papers on the Near East in Late Antiquity (1962–1993)* (Jerusalem, 1994) 197–203

——. 'The Wine and Vineyards of Gaza in the Byzantine Period' *BASOR* 257 (1986) 75–80 = *id. Monks, Martyrs, Soldiers and Saracens: Papers on the Near East in Late Antiquity (1962–1993)* (NY/Jerusalem, 1994) 250f.

——. 'The Saracens and the *limes*' *Bulletin of the American Schools of Oriental Research* 262 (1986) 35–47 = *id. Monks, Martyrs, Soldiers and Saracens: Papers on the Near East in Late Antiquity (1962–1993)* (NY/Jerusalem, 1994) 271–283

——. 'Saracens and Romans: Micro-Macro Relationships' *BASOR* 274 (1989) 71–79 = *id. Monks, Martyrs, Soldiers and Saracens: Papers on the Near East in Late Antiquity (1962–1993)* (NY/Jerusalem, 1994) 313f.

——. 'The use of the term *phylarchos* in the Roman-Byzantine east' *Zeitschrift für Papyrologie und Epigraphik* 88 (1991) 291–295 = *id. Monks, Martyrs, Soldiers and Saracens: Papers on the Near East in Late Antiquity (1962–1993)* (NY/Jerusalem, 1994) 342–346

Megaw, A.H.J. 'Byzantine architecture and decoration in Cyprus: metropolitan or provincial?' *DOP* 28 (1974) 59f.

Meinardus, O.F.A. 'Melita Illyrica or Africana? An examination of the site of St. Paul's shipwreck' *Ostkirchliche Studien* 23 (1974) 21–36

——. 'St. Paul shipwrecked in Dalmatia' *BA* 39 (1976) 145–7

Me'ir, O. 'The story of Rabbi Shim'on ben Yohai in the cave' *'Alei Siah* 26 (1989, in Hebrew) 145–60

Melamed, E.Z. 'Eusebius' Onomasticon' *Tarbiz* 3 (1932, in Hebrew) 314–27; 393–409; *ib.* 4 (1933) 78–96; 249–84

Merkelbach, R. 'Der griechische Wortschatz und die Christen' *ZPE* 18 (1975) 101–48

Merrills, A.H. 'Monks, monsters and barbarians: re-defining the African periphery in late antiquity' *JECS* 12 (2004) 217–244

Millar, F. 'Paul of Samosata, Zenobia and Aurelian: the Church, local culture and political allegiance in third-century Syria' *JRS* 61 (1971) 5–8.

——. 'The World of the *Golden Ass*' *JRS* 71 (1981) 63–75

——. 'Hagar, Ishmael, Josephus and the origins of Islam' *JJS* 44 (1993) 23–45

——. 'Ethnic identity in the Roman Near East, 325–450: Language, religion and culture' *Mediterranean Archaeology* 11 (1998) 159–176

Miller, P. Cox, 'The Blazing Body: Desire and Language in Jerome's Letter to Eustochium' *JECS* 1 (1993) 21–45

——. 'Jerome's Centaur: A Hyper-icon of the Desert' *JECS* 4 (1996) 209–233

——. 'Strategies of representation in collective biography: constructing the subject as holy' in *Greek Biography and Panegyric in Late Antiquity* (eds T. Hägg, P. Rousseau, Berkeley etc., 2000) 209–254

Mitford, T. Bruce 'The Cults of Roman Cyprus' *ANRW* 18.3, 2178f.

Momigliano, A. 'Pagan and Christian historiography in the fourth century AD' in *id. Essays in ancient and modern historiography* (Oxford, 1947, repr. 1977) 107f. = *id.* (ed.) The conflict between Paganism and Christianity in the fourth century (Oxford, 1963) 79–99

——. 'Ancient biography and the study of religion in the Roman Empire' *Annali della scuola normale superiore di Pisa* 16 (1986) 25f. = A. Momigliano *On Pagans, Jews and Christians* (Middleton, 1987) 159f.

Moscadi, A. 'Le lettere dell'archivio di Teofane' *Aegyptus* 50 (1970) 90–154

Mussies, G. 'Marnas god of Gaza' *ANRW* 18.4 (1972) 2312f.

Nautin, P. 'Le premier échange épistolaire entre Jérôme et Damase: Lettres réelles ou fictives?' *Freiburger Zeitschrift für Philosophie und Theologie* 30 (1983) 331–444

——. 'Hieronymus' *TRE* 15 (1986) 304–315

Negev, A. 'Survey and trial excavations at Haluza (Elusa), 1973' *IEJ* 26 (1976) 92–93

Newman, H.I. 'Between Jerusalem and Bethlehem: Jerome and the Holy Places of Palestine' in *Sanctity of Time and Space in Tradition and Modernity* (eds A. Houtman, M.J.H.M. Poorthuis, J. Schwartz, Leiden/Boston/Köln, 1998) 215–227

Noth, M. 'Die topographischen Angaben im Onomastikon des Eusebius' *ZDPV* 6 (1943) 41f.

O'Donnell, J.J. review of R. Herzog *Restauration et Renouveau: La littérature latine de 284 à 374 après J-C* (Turnhout, 1993) in *Bryn Mawr Classical Review* 5,5 (1994) 415–426

Opelt, I. 'Griechische und lateinische Bezeichnungen der Nichtchristen: ein terminologischer Versuch' *VChr* 19 (1965) 1–22

——. 'Des Hieronymus Heiligenbiographien als Quellen der historischen Topographie des östlichen Mittelmeerraumes' *Römische Quartalschrift für christliche Altertumskunde und Kirchengeschichte* 74 (1979) 151f.

——. 'San Girolamo e suoi maestri ebrei' *Augustinianum* 28 (1988) 327–338

Oppenheimer, A. 'Jewish Lydda in the Roman period' *HUCA* 59 (1988) 115–136

——. 'Rabban Gamaliel of Yavneh and his tours of Palestine' *Perlman Festschrift* (Tel Aviv, 1988, Hebrew) 1–8 = *id.* 'Rabban Gamaliel of Yavneh and his circuits of Eretz Israel' in *id. Between Rome and Babylon: Jewish leadership and society* (Tübingen, 2005)

——. 'The attitude of the sages towards the Arabs' in *Jewish Studies in a New Europe* (ed. U. Haxen *et al.*, Copenhagen, 1998) 572–9

Ovadiah, A. & Mucznik, S. 'Orpheus from Jerusalem—Pagan or Christian image?' *Jerusalem Cathedra* I (ed. L.I. Levine, Jerusalem, 1981) 152–166

Patlagean, E. 'Ancient Byzantine hagiography and social history' in *Saints and their*

Cults: Studies in Religion, Sociology, Folklore and History (ed. S. Wilson, Cambridge, 1983, repr. 1987) 101–119

Paschoud, F. 'A quel genre littéraire le poème de Rutilius Namatianus appartient-il?' *Revue des Études Latines* (1979) 315–322

Peeters, P., review of F.M.E. Pereia *Vida de santo Abunafre* in *AB* 25 (1906) 203–4

Perrone, L. 'The mystery of Judaea; [Jerome *ep.* 46] The holy city of Jerusalem between history and symbol in early Christian thought'. Paper given at conference on *Jerusalem: its sanctity and centrality in Judaism, Christianity and Islam* (Jerusalem, June 1996)

Pillinger, R. 'Neue Entdeckungen in der sogenannten Paulusgrotte von Ephesos' *Mitteilungen zur Christlichen Archäologie* 6 (2000) 16–29.

Poidebard, A. 'Coupes de la chassée romaine Antioche-Chalcis' *Syria* 10 (1929) 22–29

Potter, D.S. 'Entertainers in the Roman Empire' in *Life, Death and Entertainment in the Roman World* (eds D.S. Potter, D.J. Mattingly, Ann Arbor, 1999) 256–325

Prawer, J. 'Jerusalem in the Christian and Jewish perspectives of the early middle ages' *Settimane di studio del centro italiano di studi sull'alto medioevo* 26 (1980) 739f.

Purcell, N. 'Maps, Lists, Money and Power' *JRS* 80 (1990) 178–82

Raban, A. 'The Inner Harbor Basin of Caesarea: Archaeological Evidence for its Gradual Demise' in *Caesarea Maritima: A Retrospective after Two Millenia* (eds A. Raban, K.G. Holum, Leiden, 1996) 628–666

Radke, G. 'Topographische Betrachtungen zum Iter Brundisinum des Horaz' *Rheinisches Museum* 132 (1989) 54–72

Rapske, B. 'Acts, travel and shipwreck' in *The Book of Acts in its First Century setting II: The Book of Acts in its Graeco-Roman setting* (eds D.W.J. Gill, C. Gempf, Grand Rapids/Carlisle, 1991) p. 1f.

Rebenich, S. '*Insania circi*. Eine Tertulliansreminiszenz bei Hieronymus und Augustin' *Latomus* 53 (1994) 153–158

——. 'Asceticism, Orthodoxy and Patronage: Jerome in Constantinople' *SP* 33 (1997) 358f.

Reed, N. 'Pattern and purpose in the Antonine Itinerary' *AJPh* 99 (1978) 228–254

Rees, B.R. 'Theophanes of Hermopolis Magna' *BullJRylLib* 51 (1968) 164–183

Reifenberg, A. 'Caesarea, a study in the decline of a town' *IEJ* 1 (1950–1) 20–32

Rivet, A.L.F. 'The British section of the Antonine Itinerary' *Britannia* 1 (1950) 34–39

Roll, I. 'Survey of Roman roads in Lower Galilee' *Excavations and Surveys in Israel* 14 (1994) 38–40

——. 'Roads and transportation in the Holy Land in the early Christian and Byzantine times' *Akten des xii. internationalen Kongress für christliche Archäologie* teil II (Jahrbuch für Antike und Christentum Ergänzungband, 20,2, Münster, 1995) 1166–70

——. 'Roman Roads to Caesarea' in *Caesarea Maritima: A Retrospective after Two Millenia* (eds A. Raban, K.G. Holum, Leiden, 1996) 549–558

Rosenfeld, B.-Z. 'R. Simeon b. Yohai: wonder worker and magician: scholar, *saddiq* and *hasid*' *REJ* 158 (1999) 349–384

Rubenson, S. 'The Egyptian relations of early Palestinian monasticism' in *The Christian Heritage in the Holy Land* (ed. A. O'Mahoney *et al.*, London, 1995) 35–46

——. 'Philosophy and Simplicity: the problem of classical education in early Christian biography' in *Greek Biography and Panegyric in Late Antiquity* (eds T. Hägg, P. Rousseau, Berkeley etc., 2000) 110–139

Rubin, Z. 'Jerome's *Vita Hilarionis* and the conflict of religions in Palestine in late antiquity' (Paper given at conference of the Israel Society for the Promotion of Classical Studies, Ramat Gan, 1996)

——. 'Porphyrius of Gaza and the conflict between Christianity and paganism in southern Palestine' in *Sharing the Sacred: Religious Contacts and Conflicts in the Holy Land First-Fifteenth centuries CE* (eds A. Kofsky, G. Stroumsa, Jerusalem, 1998) 31–66

Ruggini, L. Cracco & Cracco, G. 'Changing fortunes of the Italian city from Late Antiquity to Early Middle Ages' *Rivista di Filologia e di Istruzione Classica* 105 (1977) 448–475

Rutherford, I. 'Tourism and the sacred: Pausanias and the traditions of Greek pilgrimage' in *Pausanias: travel and memory in Roman Greece* (eds S.E. Alcock, J.F. Cherry, J. Elsner, Oxford, 2001) 40–52

Salway, B. 'Travel, *itinararia* and *tabellaria*' in *Travel and geography in the Roman empire* (eds C. Adams, R. Laurence, London/NY, 2001) 22–66

Schwabe, M. 'Libanius' letters to the Patriarch in the Land of Israel' *Tarbiz* I/II (1930, Hebrew) 85–110

——. 'Documents of a Journey through Palestine in the Years 317–323 CE' *Eretz Israel* 3 (1954, Hebrew) 181–185

Scourfield, J.H.D. 'Jerome, Antioch and the Desert: a Note on Chronology' *JThS* 37 (1986) 117f.

Ševčenko, N. 'The Hermit as Stranger in the Desert' in *Strangers to Themselves: the Byzantine Outsider* (ed. D.C. Smythe, Aldershot etc., 2000) 75–86

Shanzer, D. '*Asino vectore virgo regia fugiens captivitatem*: Apuleius and the Tradition of the Protoevangelium Jacobi' *ZPE* 84 (1990) 221–229

Shaw, B. 'Eaters of Flesh, Drinkers of Milk' *Ancient Society* 13/14 (1982/3) 5–31

Shelton, K. 'Roman aristocrats, Christian commissions: The Carrand Diptych' *JACh* 29 (1986) 166–180

Sivan, H. 'Pilgrimage, monasticism and the emergence of Christian Palestine in the 4th century' in *The Blessings of Pilgrimage* (ed. R. Ousterhout, Urbana/Chicago, 1990) 54–65

Smith, C. Delano 'Geography or Christianity? Maps of the Holy Land before AD 1000' *JThS* 42 (1991) 147–148

Starowieski, M. 'Les commentaires bibliques patristiques dans le *Des viris illustribus* de S. Jérôme' *Studia Patristica* 34 (2001) 459–469

Stempinski, Y. 'Horvat Maskana: Roman road' *Hadashot Arkheologiot* 108 (1998, Hebrew) 175

Stroumsa, G. 'Philosophy of the Barbarians: On Early Christian Ethnological Representations' in *Geschichte—Tradition—Reflexion: Festschrift für Martin Hengel zum 70. Geburtstag* (eds H. von Hubert, H. Lichtenberger, P. Schäfer, Tübingen, 1996) 339–368

Summers, R.G. 'Roman Justice and Apuleius' Metamorphoses,' *TAPA* 101 (1970), 511–31

Syme, R. 'Ipse ille patriarcha' in *id. Emperors and biography: Studies in the Historia Augusta* (Oxford, 1971) 17–29

Talbert, R.J.A. 'Rome's empire and beyond: the spatial aspect' in *Gouvernants et gouvernés dans l'imperium Romanum (IIIe av. J.-C.–Ier ap. J.-C.), Cahiers des études anciennes* 26 (1989) 215f.

Thomas, R.F. 'Virgil's *Georgics* and the Art of Reference' *HSCP* 90 (1986) 171–198

Thomsen, P. 'Palästina nach dem Onomasticon des Eusebius' *ZDPV* 26 (1903, repr. 1970) 97f.

Titchener, F.B. 'Autobiography and the Hellenistic Age' in *The Eye Expanded: Life and the Arts in Greco-Roman Antiquity* (eds F.B. Titchener, R.F. Moorton, Jr., Berkeley etc., 1999) 155–163

Tkacz, C. Brown, '*Labor tam utilis*: the creation of the Vulgate' *VChr* 50 (1996) 42–72

Tomlin, R. 'Christianity and the Late Roman Army' in *Constantine: History, historiography and legend* (eds S.C.N. Lieu, D. Montserrat, London/NY, 1998) 21–51

Toynbee, J.M.C. 'Roma and Constantinopolis in Late Antique Art from 312–365.' *JRS* 37 (1947) 135f.

Tropper, A.D. 'Tractate 'Avot' and the early Christian succession lists' in *The ways that never parted: Jews and Christians in late antiquity and the early middle ages* (eds A.H. Becker, A.Y. Reed, Tübingen, 2003) 178f.

Tupet, A.M. 'Didon magicienne' *REL* 48 (1970) 229f.

Turner, C.H. 'Fragment of an unknown Latin version of the Apostolic Constitutions' *JThS (OS)* 13 (1911) 492f.

———. 'A primitive edition of the Apostolic Constitutions and Canons' *JThS (OS)* 15 (1913) 53f.

———. 'Notes on the Apostolic Constitutions: the compiler an Arian' *JThS (OS)* 16 (1914) 54f.

———. 'Notes on the Apostolic Constitutions: the text of Cod. Val. 1506' *JThS (OS)* 21 (1919) 160f.

———. 'Notes on the Apostolic Constitutions: the text of the eighth book' *JThS (OS)* 31 (1929) 128f.

Turner, V.W. 'The Center Out There: Pilgrim's Goal' *History of Religions* 12 (1973) 191–230

Ullman, L. & Galili, E. 'A Greek Inscription mentioning ΣΥΚΑΜΙΝΩΝ discovered off the Carmel coast' *SCI* 13 (1994) 116f.

Underwood, P.A. 'The Fountain of Life' *DOP* 5 (1950) 43f.

Urbach, E.E. 'The rabbinical laws of idolatry in the second and third centuries in the light of archaeological and historical facts' *IEJ* 9 (1959) 149–165; *ib.* 229–245

van Berchem, D. 'L'itinéraire Antonin et le voyage en orient de Caracalla 214–5' *CRAI* (1973) 123–126

Varon, P. '*Ius postliminii* and the soldier' in *Roman Frontier Studies 1989: Proceedings of the XVth International Congress of Roman Frontier Studies* (eds V.A. Maxfield, M.J. Dobson, Exeter, 1991) 407–409

Vessey, M. 'Jerome's Origen: The Making of a Christian Literary *Persona*' *Studia Patristica* 28 (1993) 135f.

Vincent, H. 'Une mosaïque byzantine à Jérusalem' *RB* 10 (1901) 436–444

———. 'La mosaïque d'Orphée' *RB* 11 (1902) 100–103

Vincent, H. & Avi-Yonah, M. 'Mosaic pavements in Palestine' *QDAP* 2 (1933) 172–3

Ward-Perkins, B. 'Continuists, catastrophists, and the towns of post-Roman northern Italy' *PBSR* 45 (1997) 157f.

Wasink J.H. 'Hieronymus' *RAC* (Stuttgart 1991) 118–139

Vauchez, A. 'Iconographie et histoire de la spiritualité: À propos d'un ouvrage récent (D. Russo *Saint Jérôme en Italie*)' *Le Moyen Age* 95 (1989) 142–144

Weber, E. 'The Tabula Peutingeriana and the Madeba Map' in E. Alliata *et al.* 'The Legends of the Madeba Map' in *The Madeba Map Centenary 1897–1997: Travelling through the Byzantine Ummayad Period* (eds M. Piccirillo, E. Alliata, Jerusalem, 1999) 41–46

Weingarten, S. '*Postliminium* in Jerome: A Roman legal term as Christian metaphor' *Scripta Classica Israelica* 14 (1995) 143–150

———. 'Jerome and the *Golden Ass*' *Studia Patristica* 33 (1997) 383f.

———. 'Was the pilgrim from Bordeaux a woman? A reply to Laurie Douglass' *JECS* 7 (1999) 291–297

———. 'Road use in late antique Palestine' *Limes XVIII. Proceedings of the XVIIIth International Congress of Roman Frontier Studies held in Amman, Jordan (September 2000)* (Edited by P. Freeman, J. Bennett, Z.T. Fiema & B. Hoffman. British Archaeological Reports 1084. Oxford, 2002) 243–257

———. review of G.S.P. Freeman-Grenville (tr.), J.E. Taylor, R.L. Chapman III, (eds) *The Onomasticon by Eusebius of Caesarea: Palestine in the Fourth Century AD* (Jerusalem, 2003) *Scripta Classica Israelica* 23 (2004) 312–314

Weiss, Z. 'Adopting a novelty: the Jews and the Roman games in Palestine' in *The Roman and Byzantine Near East 2: Some recent archaeological research* (ed. J. Humphrey, Portsmouth, Rhode Island, 1999) 23–49

Welten, P. 'Bethlehem und die Klage um Adonis' *ZDPV* 99 (1983) 189–203

Whittow, M. 'Ruling the Late Roman and Early Byzantine City: A Continuous History' *Past and Present* 129 (1990) 3f.

Wiedemann, T.E.J. 'Between man and beasts. Barbarians in Ammianus Marcellinus' in *Past Perspectives: Studies in Greek and Roman historical writing* (eds I.S. Moxon, J.D. Smart, A. Woodman, Cambridge, 1986) 189–211

Wilkinson, J. 'L'apport de Saint Jérôme à la topographie' *RB* 81 (1974) 245f.

Will, E. 'Antioche sur l'Oronte, métropole de l'Asie' *Syria* 74 (1997) 99–113

Winter, P. 'Der literarische Charakter der Vita beati Hilarionis des Hieronymus' in *Programm zur Gedächtnisfeier für den Senator Philipp Ferdinand Adolf Just* (Zittau, 1904) 3f.

Wisnieski, R. '*Bestiae Christum loquuntur* ou des habitants du désert et de la ville dans la *Vita Pauli* de saint Jérôme' *Augustinianum* 40 (2000) 105–144

Wittkower, R. 'Marvels of the East: A Study in the History of Monsters' *Journal of the Warburg and Courtauld Institutes*, 5 (1942) 159f.

Woolf, C. 'Eusebius of Caesarea and the Onomasticon' *BA* 27, 3 (1964) 66f.

Woods, D. 'The Emperor Julian and the Passion of Sergius and Bacchus' *JECS* 5 (1997) 345– 367

Wuilleumier, G. 'Cirque et astrologie' *MEFRA* (1927) 184–209

Texts and Editions

1. Jerome's Works

Jerome's works were first seriously edited by Erasmus of Rotterdam, and published in 1516 in Basle by Amerbach-Froben.[1] Erasmus also wrote the first *Life of Jerome* that was no mere hagiography.[2] His edition was followed by Vittori (Rome, 1565, *non vidi*), Martinay (Paris, 1693–1706, *non vidi*) and Vallarsi (Verona, 1734–42, *non vidi*).[3] Vallarsi's second edition, published in Venice (1766–72) is the text to be found in Migne's *Patrologia Latina* [*PL*] vols 22–30, Supplement vols. 1 & 2. It is usually sufficient to cite the *PL* by volume and column number only, without the date, but in the case of Jerome's works, fire destroyed Migne's press and type-sets in 1868 and the column numbering differs for volumes produced before and after this date. Many errors were introduced into the second printing, so I have cited from the better, earlier text, and append a list of the volumes I have used and their respective dates.

Edition used of Jerome in the Patrologia Latina
PL   22 (1854)
PL   23 (1845)
PL   24 (1845)
PL   25 (1865)
PL   26 (1845)
PL   27 (1866)
PL   28 (1865)
PL   29 (1865)
PL   30 *Opera suposititia* (no date)

---

[1] Erasmus worked on the letters and treatises; the Amerbachs and their associates concentrated on the biblical commentaries. See E.F. Rice *Saint Jerome in the Renaissance* (Baltimore/London, 1985) 116–122 with bibliography *ad loc.*

[2] *Eximii doctoris Hieronymi Stridonenesis vita ex ipsius potissimum litteris contexta per Desiderium Erasmum Roterodamum* (Basel, 1516, *non vidi*). Rice *op. cit.* 130–2, who notes (131) that 'Erasmus silently suppressed the lion.'

[3] Rice *op. cit.* 122.

Volume 30 of the *PL* contains works erroneously attributed to Jerome. The commentary on Job in *PL* 26 is no longer thought to be a genuine work by Jerome. For some of Jerome's works there are still no critical editions or texts better than Vallarsi. This is the case with the text of the *Quaestiones hebraicae in Genesim (QHG)* where the *Corpus Christianorum Series Latina (CCSL)* uses the text edited by Lagarde, which is full of errors. Modern scholars[4] thus prefer the Vallarsi text in *PL* 23. However, in general the texts in the *CCSL* or *CSEL* editions are to be preferred over the *PL*. The new edition by R. Gryson, P.A. Deproost *et al.* of the Commentary on Isaiah, *Commentaire de Jérôme sur le prophète Isaïe* I–IV, V–VII (Freiburg, 1993–4) now supersedes the *CCSL* edition by Adriaen.

Ninety-six of Jerome's homilies on the psalms delivered to his monks at Bethlehem scattered among other works were identified as Jerome's by Dom G. Morin at the end of the nineteenth century and have been republished in the Supplement to the *PL* and in *CCSL* 78.

CCSL *72–80*

72	(ed. P. Antin, 1959)	*Quaestiones hebraicae in Genesim*
		Com. in Psalmos
		Com. in Ecclesiasten
73–73a	(ed. M. Adriaen, 1958)	*Com. in Esaiam*
74	(ed. S. Reiter, 1960)	*Com. in Hieremiam*
75–75a	(ed. F. Glorie, 1964)	*Com. in Hiezchielem*
		Com. in Danielem
76–76a	(ed. M. Adriaen, 1959)	*Com. in Prophetas Minores*
77	(ed. D. Hurst, M. Adriaen, 1959)	*Com. in Matheum*
78	(ed. D.G. Morin, 1958)	*Tractatus in Psalmos*
		Com. in Marci Evangelium
		Varia
79	(ed. P. Lardet, 1982)	*Contra Rufinum*
79a	(ed. J.-L. Feiertag, 1999)	*Contra Iohannem*
79b	(ed. A. Canellis, 2000)	*Altercatio Luciferiani et Orthodoxi*
80	(ed. C. Moreschini, 1990)	*Dialogus adversus Pelagianos*

Electronic resources
The text of the *CCSL* edition of Jerome is available on CD-ROM in the Cetedoc library of Christian Latin texts. I have used the version CLCLT-2 (Turnhout, 1994).

The text of the *PL* first edition of Jerome is available as the *Patrologia Latina Database* published by Chadwyck-Healey. I have used the version on-line at Tel-Aviv University which is regularly up-dated.

Lives of Paul, Hilarion and Malchus
In the case of Jerome's saints' *Lives*, the text published by H. Hurter in the *Acta Sanctorum* was the basis for Oldfather and his colleagues who published *Studies in the Text tradition of St. Jerome's 'Vitae Patrum'* (Urbana, Illinois, 1943).[5] The *vita Pauli* has

---

[4] See on this C.T.R. Hayward *Saint Jerome's* Hebrew Questions on Genesis (Oxford, 1995) p. 27.

[5] A new critical text of all Jerome's saints' *Lives* is now promised by Paul B. Harvey Jr. I have not seen the Italian translation with notes by B. Degórski *Vite degli eremiti Paolo, Ilarione e Malco. Girolamo* (Collana di testi patristici 126, Roma, 1996).

now been published in a critical text by R.[= B.] Degórski *Edizione critica della 'Vita Sancti Pauli primi eremitae' di Girolamo* (Roma, 1987), using 92 of the 142 manuscripts, the oldest of which, the Veronensis xxxviii (36), is dated to 517. I have not seen the bowdlerised version published by Kozik: I. Kozik *The First Desert Hero: St Jerome's Vita Pauli, with Introduction, Notes and Vocabulary*. The *vita Hilarionis* with some corrections, a commentary and Italian translation has been published by A. Bastiaensen, *Vita di Ilarione*, in *Vite dei Santi* 4 (Rome, 1975). C.C. Mierow published the *vita Malchi* with an English translation, basing himself on the 35 Vatican manuscripts, 'Sancti Eusebii Hieronymi Vita Malchi monachi captivi', in *Classical Essays presented to J.A. Kleist* (St. Louis, 1946) pp. 31–45, and there is now a Spanish critical edition: P. Edgardo, M. Morales *Edición crítica de 'de Monacho captivo' (vita Malchi) de San Jerónimo* (Roma, 1991).

English translations include: W.H. Fremantle *Saint Jerome's Lives of Paul, Malchus and Hilarion*, (Nicene and Post-Nicene Fathers, London, 1892); M.L. Ewald *St Jerome's Life of St Paul the First Hermit, of Hilarion, of Malchus* in R.J. Defarrari (ed.) *Early Christian Biographies* (Fathers of the Church, Washington, 1952); *Life of Paul*: Helen Waddell *The Desert Fathers* (London, 1936 repr. 1987); Paul B. Harvey Jr *Jerome Life of Paul the First Hermit: Introduction and Translation* in V.L. Wimbush (ed.) *Ascetic Behavior in Greco-Roman Antiquity: A Sourcebook* (Minneapolis, 1990) p. 357f. Of these translations, Waddell's *Life of Paul* is by far the most beautiful, but incomplete and accurate to the spirit, rather than the letter; Fremantle is antiquated, Ewald sometimes problematic and Harvey the most serviceable. Details of translations into other modern languages are to be found in *CCSL* 72, pp. xv–xvi (P. Antin). There is now a Hebrew translation of the *vita Pauli* in A. Kleinberg *Fra Ginepros Leg of Pork: Christian Saint's Stories and Their Cultural Role (sic)* (Tel Aviv, 2000). In addition to the notes on the *Lives* of Paul, Hilarion, and Malchus by Vallarsi to be found in *PL* 23, further notes and commentary by H. Rosweyde are to be found in *PL* 73, 101–116 (*vPauli*); 193–206 (*vHilarionis*); 205–210 (*vMalchi*).

Letters
Jerome's letters have been published in several editions. I. Hilberg published a critical edition in 1910 in the *CSEL* (54–56), and this has now been reprinted with the addition of indices, further bibliography and a list of corrections to the text by M. Kamptner (*CSEL* 54–56, Vienna, 1996²). There is an annotated edition with French translation published by J. Labourt, *Jérôme: Lettres* vols. i–viii (Paris, 1949–1963) but the annotations run out by the end. There are three editions of English translations of the letters, none of them complete: the Loeb classical library has a translation of a selection of eighteen letters: *Jerome: Select letters* (ed. and tr. F.A. Wright, Cambridge, Mass/London, 1933 repr. 1991); the Nicene and Post-Nicene Fathers series has a translation by W.H. Fremantle *The principal works of St. Jerome* (London 1892) which includes most of the letters, but misses out letters that are mainly biblical commentary, such as *ep.* 78, which deals with the camping places of the Children of Israel in the wilderness. The Ancient Christian Writers series has a translation of the first twenty-two letters: *The letters of St. Jerome*, vol. I, tr. C.C. Mierow, intr. and ann. T.C. Lawler (Westminster, MD, 1963, *non vidi*).

Individual letters have been published as monographs: *ep.* 57 by G.J.M. Bartelink *Hieronymus: Liber de optime genere interpretandi (epistula 57): ein Kommentar* (Leiden, 1981); *ep.* 60 by J.H.D. Scourfield *Consoling Heliodorus: A Commentary on Jerome, Letter 60* (Oxford, 1993) with translations and full commentaries. F. Stummer *Monumenta historiam et geographiam Terrae Sanctae illustrantia* (Bonn, 1935) contains commentary in Latin on *epp.* 46 and 108. Many articles by N. Adkin deal with letter 22, both contents and text and he has now published *Jerome on Virginity: a commentary on the* Libellus de viginitate servanda *(letter 22)* (Cambridge, 2003).

Ep. *108, the* Life of Paula

Ep. 108, the *Life of Paula,* has been edited by A. Bastiaensen and C. Mohrmann as *In memoria di Paola,* in *Vite dei Santi* 4 (Rome, 1975, in Italian). The Latin commentary on the geographical parts of *ep.* 108 by F. Stummer *Monumenta historiam et geographiam Terrae Sanctae illustrantia* (Bonn, 1935) has already been noted. Other translations of, and commentaries on the geographical section include A. Stewart, C.W. Wilson (ed. and tr.) *The Pilgrimage of the Holy Paula by St. Jerome* (PPTS, London, 1887, in English); J. Wilkinson *Jerusalem Pilgrims before the Crusades* (London, 1977, in English) pp. 47–52; H. Donner *Pilgerfahrt ins Heilige Land: Die ältesten Berichte christlicher Palästinapilger (4.–7. Jahrhundert)* (Stuttgart, 1979, in German) pp. 138–170; O. Limor *Holy Land Travels: Christian Pilgrims in Late Antiquity* (Jerusalem, 1998, in Hebrew) pp. 133–154.

De viris illustribus

Jerome's *de viris illustribus,* his brief biographies of famous men, has been edited with commentary and Italian translation by A. Ceresa-Gastaldo *Gerolamo: Gli Uomini Illustri* (Firenze, 1988). There is an English translation by E.C. Richardson *Jerome: Lives of Illustrious Men* (Nicene and post-Nicene Fathers III, 2nd series (1892, repr. NY, 1995).

Polemics

Some of Jerome's polemic writings, *Contra Rufinum, Contra Iohannem, Altercatio Luciferiani et Orthodox* and *Dialogus adversus Pelagianos* have been edited, as noted above, in the *CCSL* series: 79, 79a, 79b, and 80. P. Lardet has also produced a substantial commentary on the *Contra Rufinum: L'apologie de Jérôme contre Rufin: un commentaire* (Leiden, etc. 1993), published separately.

Onomasticon

Jerome's translation of and additions to Eusebius' *Onomasticon* has been published side by side with Eusebius' Greek text by E. Klostermann *Eusebius Werke III, I: Das Onomastikon der biblischen Ortsnamen* (*GCS* 11,1, Leipzig, 1904). The new English edition and translation by J.E. Taylor, G. Freeman-Grenville and R.L. Chapman *The Onomasticon by Eusebius of Caesarea* (Jerusalem, 2003) is sadly not totally reliable.[6]

Chronicon

Jerome's translation of and additions to Eusebius' *Chronicon* have been edited by R. Helm (rev. V. Beshevliev, U. Treu) *Eusebius Werke: Die Chronik des Hieronymus* (*GCS* 47, Leipzig, 1984) and much work was done on his sources by A. Schoene *Die Weltchronik des Eusebius in ihrer Bearbeitung durch Hieronymus* (Berlin, 1900).

Vulgate

R. Weber's edition of the Vulgate: *Biblia Sacra Vulgata* (Stuttgart, 1969, repr. 1983) includes Jerome's translations of many of the books of the Hebrew Bible from Hebrew and Aramaic, his translations from the Apocrypha, his two translations of the Psalms from Greek and from Hebrew, and his translation of the Gospels from the Greek. This edition also includes a critical text of Jerome's prefaces to his translations of some of the Biblical books.[7]

---

[6] See my review of this translation in *Scripta Classica Israelica* 23 (2004) pp. 312–314.

[7] Jerome's preface to his translation of the book of Chronicles from the Septuagint, *Praef. in lib. Paralipomenon juxta LXX* is, however, only to be found in *PL* 29, 423–4.

For a convenient summary of the complex situation about the Vulgate, see Catherine Brown Tkacz '*Labor tam utilis*: the creation of the Vulgate' *VChr* 50 (1996) 42–72.

Commentaries
Apart from the *CCSL* editions above, there have been various editions of Jerome's commentaries on biblical books, including especially Y.-M. Duval *Commentaire sur Jonas* (*SC* 323, Paris, 1985) with useful commentary and E. Bernard (ed.) *S. Jérôme: Commentaire sur S. Matthieu* I–II (*SC* 242; 259, Paris, 1977–9). Other books on his commentaries include J. Braverman *Jerome's Commentary on Daniel: A Study of comparative Jewish and Christian interpretations of the Hebrew Bible* (Washington, 1978); P. Jay. *L'exégèse de s. Jérôme d'après son commentaire sur Isaïe* (Paris, 1985, *non vidi*).

Quaestiones hebraicae in Genesim
This has been translated with commentary by C.T.R. Hayward *op. cit.* n. 4 above. There is also a complementary study by A. Kamesar *Jerome, Greek Scholarship and the Hebrew Bible: A Study of the* Quaestiones Hebraicae in Genesim (Oxford, 1993).

2. *Other ancient texts*

For editions of talmudic sources: G. Stemberger (tr. M. Bockmuehl) *Introduction to the Talmud and the Midrash* (Edinburgh, 1996²).

AMBROSE
Beyenka, M. M. (ed. and tr.) *St Ambrose: Letters* (Fathers of the Church 26, Washington, 1954)
PL 16

AMMIANUS
Clark, C.U. (ed.) *Ammiani Marcellini Rerum gestarum Libri qui supersunt* (Berlin, 1910)

APOLLODORUS
Frazer, J.G. (ed. and tr.) *Apollodorus: The Library* (Cambridge/London 1976)

APOSTOLIC CONSTITUTIONS
Dix, G. (rev. H. Chadwick) *The treatise on the Apostolic Tradition of St. Hippolytus of Rome* (London, 1968).
Funk, F.X. *Didascalia et Constitutiones Apostolorum* (Paderborn, 1905)
Metzger, M. (ed. and tr.) *Les Constitutions Apostoliques* i–iii (*SC* 320, 329, 336, Paris, 1985–7)

APPIAN
Viereck, P. & Roos, A.G. (eds), Gabba, E. (rev.) *Appiani Historia Romana* (Leipzig, 1961)

APULEIUS
Helm, R. *Apuleius Metamorphoseon Libri XI* (Leipzig, 1931)

ATHANASIUS
Bartelink, G.J.M. *Athanase d'Alexandrie: Vie d'Antoine* (*SC* 400, Paris, 1994)

AUGUSTINE
O'Donnell, J.J. *Augustine: Confessions* I: *Introduction and Text* (Oxford, 1992)

AUSONIUS
Weis, B.K. (ed.) Ausonius: *Mosella* (Darmstadt, 1989)

CHAUCER
Robinson, F.N. (ed.) *The works of Geoffrey Chaucer* (Oxford, 1957²)

CHORICIUS
Foerster, R. & Richsteig, E. *Choricius: Dialectis* (Leipzig, 1929, repr. Stuttgardt, 1972)

CODEX THEODOSIANUS
Mommsen, T., Meyer, M. (eds) *Theodosiani Libri XVI cum Constitutionibus Sirmondianis* (Berlin, 1962²)
Parr, C. (ed. and tr.) *The Theodosian Code and Novels and the Sirmondian Constitutions* (Princeton, 1952)

EGERIA
Franceschini, A. & Weber (eds) *Itinerarium Egeriae* (*CCSL* 175, Turnholt, 1965) 37–103
Maraval, P. (ed. and tr.) *Égérie: Journal de voyage (Itinéraire)* (*SC* 296, Paris, 1972)
Wilkinson, J. *Egeria's Travels* (Warminster, 1999³)

EPIPHANIUS
Dummer, J. *Epiphanius* II: *Panarion* (*GCS*, Berlin, 1980)

EUSEBIUS
Bardy, G. (ed. and tr.) *Eusèbe de Césarée: Histoire Ecclésiastique* (*SC* 31, 41, 55, 73; Paris, 1952–67)
Cameron, Averil & Hall, S.G. (ed. and tr.) *Eusebius: Life of Constantine* (Oxford, 1999)
Helm R. (ed.), Besevliev, V., Treu, U. (revs) *Eusebius: Werke 7: Die Chronik des Hieronymus* (*GCSEL* 47, Berlin, 1984)
Klostermann, E. *Eusebius Werke III, I: Das Onomastikon der biblischen Ortsnamen* (*GCS* 11,1, Leipzig, 1904)
Schoene, A. (ed.) *Eusebi Chronicorum Canonum* (Zurich, 1866 repr. Dublin, 1967)

EXPOSITIO TOTIUS MUNDI ET GENTIUM
Rougé, J. (ed. and tr.) *Expositio totius mundi et gentium: Introduction, texte critique, traduction, notes et commentaire* (*SC* 124, Paris, 1966)

GEOGRAPHERS
Müller, C. *Geographii Graeci Minores* I (Paris, 1861, repr. Hildesheim 1990)

HORACE
Morris, E.P. (ed.) *Satires and Epistles* (Oklahoma, 1968)
Rudd, N. (tr.) *The Satires of Horace and Persius* (Harmondsworth, 1973)

ITINERARIA *et alia geographica*
Geyer, P. (ed.) '*Antonini Placentini Itinerarium*' (*CCSL* 175, Turnholt, 1965) 129–174
——. (ed.) *Theodosii: De situ terrae sanctae* (*CCSL* 175, Turnholt, 1965) 115–125
Geyer, P., Cuntz, O. (eds) *Itinerarium Burdigalense* (*CCSL* 175, Turnholt, 1965) 1–34
Fraipont, I. (ed.) *Eucherii quae fertur de situ Hierusolimae epistula ad Faustum presbyterum* (*CCSL* 175, Turnholt, 1965) 237–243

ITINERARIUM ANTONINI
Cuntz, O. (ed.) Wirth, G. (rev.) *Itineraria Romana* I: *Itineraria Antonini Augusti* (Stuttgardt, 1990)

LIBANIUS
Foerster, R. *Libanii Opera* I–XI (Leipzig, 1903–1922)

LUCILIUS
Charpin, F. (ed.) *Lucilius: Satires* livres i–viii (Paris, 1978)

MARCUS DIACONUS
Grégoire, H. & Kugener, M.-A. *Marc le Diacre: Vie de Porphyre, évêque de Gaza* (Paris, 1930)

MASADA DOCUMENTS
Cotton, H.M. & Geiger, J. *Masada II: The Yigal Yadin Excavations 1963–1965: Final Reports: The Latin and Greek Documents* (Jerusalem, 1989)

ONUPHRIUS
Vivian, T. (ed. and tr.) *Histories of the Monks of Upper Egypt and the Life of Onnophrius* (Kalamazoo, 1993)

PROCOPIUS
Chauvot, A. *Panégyriques de l'empereur Anastase Ier: Procope de Gaza, Priscien de Césarée* (Bern, 1986)

THEOPHANES ARCHIVE
Roberts, C.H. & Turner E.G., *Catalogue of the Greek and Latin Papyri in the John Rylands Library Manchester* vol. IV (Manchester, 1952)

PASSIONS
Delehaye, H. 'Passio Sancti Mammetis' *AB* 58 (1940) 138f.
de Cavalieri, F. (ed.) 'Passio Sanctorum Mariani et Iacobi' *Studi e testi* (1900) 47f.

PELAGIUS
Rees, B.R. *Pelagius: Life and Letters* (Woodbridge/Rochester, 1998)

RUTILIUS NAMATIANUS
Doblhofer, E. (ed.) *Rutilius Namatianus: De reditu suo sive Iter Gallicum* (Heidelberg, 1972)

SOZOMENUS
Sabbah, G. (ed.) *Sozomène: Histoire Ecclésiastique* I–II (*SC* 306, Paris, 1983)

TARGUM NEOPHYTI
Macho, A. Diez, (ed.), McNamara, M. (Eng. tr.) *Neophyti 1: Targum palestinense ms. de la biblioteca Vaticana*, IV (Madrid, 1974)

TESTAMENTUM PORCELLI
Testamentum Suis (Testamentum Porcelli): http://www.th-augsburg.de/~harsch/tst_porc.html

THEODORET
Canivet, P. & Leroy-Molinghen, A. (eds) *Theodoret de Cyr: Histoire des moines de Syrie* I (Paris, 1977, *Sources Chrétiennes* 234)
Price, R.M. (ed. and tr.) *Theodoret of Cyrrhus: A History of the Monks of Syria* (Kalamazoo, 1985)

VINDOLANDA TABLETS
Bowman, A.K. & Thomas, J.D. 'New texts from Vindolanda' *Britannia* 18 (1987) 125–142
———. *The Vindolanda Writing-Tablets (Tabulae Vindolandenses II)* (London, 1994)

VITA CHARITONIS (PRE-METAPHRASTIC)
Di Segni, L. (ed. and tr.) *Vita Charitonis* in V.L. Wimbush (ed.) *Ascetic Behavior in Greco-Roman Antiquity* (Minneapolis 1990) 393–421

GENERAL INDEX

GEOGRAPHICAL INDEX

Ancient Judaism
and Early Christianity

(Arbeiten zur Geschichte des Antiken Judentums
und des Urchristentums)

———

MARTIN HENGEL *Tübingen*
PIETER W. VAN DER HORST *Utrecht*·MARTIN GOODMAN *Oxford*
DANIEL R. SCHWARTZ *Jerusalem* ·CILLIERS BREYTENBACH *Berlin*
FRIEDRICH AVEMARIE *Marburg* ·SETH SCHWARTZ *New York*

———

27 E. Juhl Christiansen. *The Covenant in Judaism and Paul.* A Study of Ritual Boundaries as Identity Markers. 1995. ISBN 90 04 10333 3

28 B. Kinman. *Jesus' Entry into Jerusalem.* In the Context of Lukan Theology and the Politics of His Day. 1995. ISBN 90 04 10330 9

29 J.R. Levison. *The Spirit in First Century Judaism.* 1997. ISBN 90 04 10739 8

30 L.H. Feldman. *Studies in Hellenistic Judaism.* 1996. ISBN 90 04 10418 6

31 H. Jacobson. *A Commentary on Pseudo-Philo's* Liber Antiquitatum Biblicarum. With Latin Text and English Translation. Two vols. 1996.
ISBN 90 04 10553 0 (Vol.1); ISBN 90 04 10554 9 (Vol.2);
ISBN 90 04 10360 0 (Set)

32 W.H. Harris III. *The Descent of Christ.* Ephesians 4:7-11 and Traditional Hebrew Imagery. 1996. ISBN 90 04 10310 4

33 R.T. Beckwith. *Calendar and Chronology, Jewish and Christian.* Biblical, Intertestamental and Patristic Studies. 1996. ISBN 90 04 10586 7

34 L.H. Feldman & J.R. Levison (eds.). *Josephus'* Contra Apionem. Studies in its Character and Context with a Latin Concordance to the Portion Missing in Greek. 1996. ISBN 90 04 10325 2

35 G. Harvey. *The True Israel.* Uses of the Names Jew, Hebrew and Israel in Ancient Jewish and Early Christian Literature. 1996. ISBN 90 04 10617 0

36 R.K. Gnuse. *Dreams and Dream Reports in the Writings of Josephus.* A Traditio-Historical Analysis. 1996. ISBN 90 04 10616 2

37 J.A. Draper. *The* Didache *in Modern Research.* 1996. ISBN 90 04 10375 9

38 C. Breytenbach. *Paulus und Barnabas in der Provinz Galatien.* Studien zu Apostelgeschichte 13f.; 16,6; 18,23 und den Adressaten des Galaterbriefes. 1996. ISBN 90 04 10693 6

39 B.D. Chilton & C.A. Evans. *Jesus in Context.* Temple, Purity, and Restoration. 1997. ISBN 90 04 10746 0

40 C. Gerber. *Ein Bild des Judentums für Nichtjuden von Flavius Josephus.* Untersuchungen zu seiner Schrift *Contra Apionem.* 1997. ISBN 90 04 10753 3

41 T. Ilan. *Mine and Yours are Hers.* Retrieving Women's History from Rabbinic Literature. 1997. ISBN 90 04 10860 2

42 C.A. Gieschen. *Angelomorphic Christology.* Antecedents and Early Evidence. 1998. ISBN 90 04 10840 8

43 W.J. van Bekkum. *Hebrew Poetry from Late Antiquity.* Liturgical Poems of Yehudah. Critical Edition with Introduction and Commentary. 1998. ISBN 90 04 11216 2

44 M. Becker & W. Fenske (Hrsg.). *Das Ende der Tage und die Gegenwart des Heils.* Begegnungen mit dem Neuen Testament und seiner Umwelt. Festschrift für Prof. Heinz-Wolfgang Kuhn zum 65. Geburtstag. 1999. ISBN 90 04 11135 2

45 S. von Stemm. *Der betende Sünder vor Gott.* Studien zu Vergebungsvorstellungen in urchristlichen und frühjüdischen Texten. 1999. ISBN 90 04 11283 9

46 H. Leeming & K. Leeming (eds.). *Josephus' Jewish War and its Slavonic Version*. A Synoptic Comparison of the English Translation by H.St.J. Thackeray with the Critical Edition by N.A. Mescerskij of the Slavonic Version in the Vilna Manuscript translated into English by H. Leeming and L. Osinkina. ISBN 90 04 11438 6

47 M. Daly-Denton. *David in the Fourth Gospel*. The Johannine Reception of the Psalms. 1999. ISBN 90 04 11448 3

48 T. Rajak. *The Jewish Dialogue with Greece and Rome*. Studies in Cultural and Social Interaction 2000. ISBN 90 04 11285 5

49 H.H.D. Williams, III. *The Wisdom of the Wise*. The Presence and Function of Scripture within 1 Cor. 1:18-3:23. 2000. ISBN 90 04 11974 4

50 R.D. Rowe. *God's Kingdom and God's Son*. The Background to Mark's Christology from Concepts of Kingship in the Psalms. 2002. ISBN 90 04 11888 8

51 E. Condra. *Salvation for the Righteous Revealed*. Jesus amid Covenantal and Messianic Expectations in Second Temple Judaism. 2002. ISBN 90 04 12617 1

52 Ch. Ritter. *Rachels Klage im antiken Judentum und frühen Christentum*. Eine auslegungsgeschichtliche Studie. 2002. ISBN 90 04 12509 4

53 C. Breytenbach & L.L. Welborn (eds.). *Encounters with Hellenism*. Studies on the First Letter of Clement. 2003. ISBN 90 04 12526 4

54 W. Schmithals & C. Breytenbach (ed.). *Paulus, die Evangelien und das Urchristentum*. Beiträge von und zu Walter Schmithals zu seinem 80. Geburtstag. 2003. ISBN 90 04 12983 9

55 K.P. Sullivan. *Wrestling with Angels*. A Study of the Relationship between Angels and Humans in Ancient Jewish Literature and the New Testament. 2004. ISBN 90 04 13224 4

56 L. Triebel. *Jenseitshoffnung in Wort und Stein*. Nefesch und pyramidales Grabmal als Phänomene antiken jüdischen Bestattungswesens im Kontext der Nachbarkulturen. 2004. ISBN 90 04 12924 3

57 C. Breytenbach & J. Schröter, *Die Apostelgeschichte und die hellenistische Geschichtsschreibung*. Festschrift für Eckhard Plümacher zu seinem 65. Geburtstag. 2004. ISBN 90 04 13892 7

58 S. Weingarten. *The Saint's Saints*. Hagiography and Geography in Jerome. 2005. ISBN 90 04 14387 4

59 A. Hilhorst & G.H. van Kooten (eds.). *The Wisdom of Egypt*. Jewish, Early Christian, and Gnostic Essays in Honour of Gerard P. Luttikhuizen. 2005. ISBN 90 04 14425 0

60 S. Chepey. *Nazirites in Late Second Temple Judaism*. A Survey of Ancient Jewish Writings, the New Testament, Archaedogical Evidence, and Other Writings from Late Antiquity. 2005. ISBN 90 04 14465 X

61 R.T. Beckwith. *Calendar, Chronology and Worship*. 2005. ISBN 90 04 14603 2 (in preparation)

DATE DUE

HIGHSMITH #45230   Printed in USA

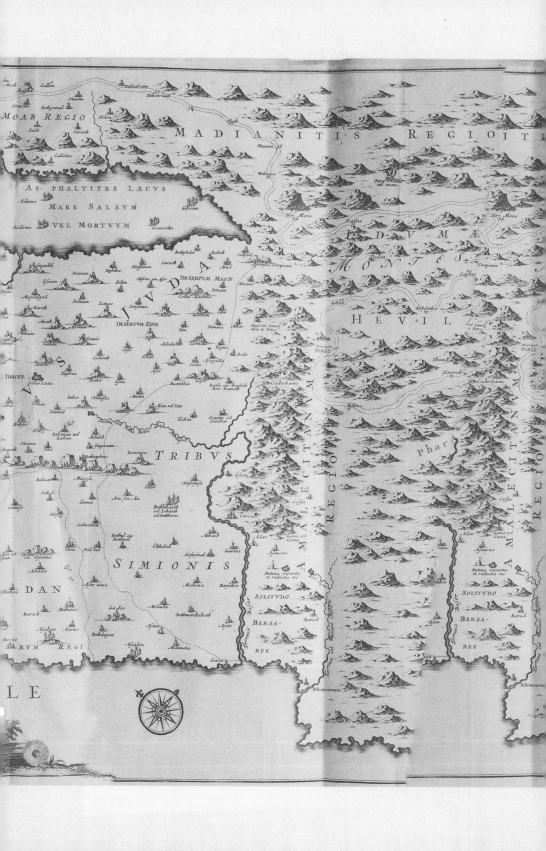